CULTURE AND THE CROWD

Also by Deric Regin

JOB, THE MAN OF THE RUBBLE
FREEDOM AND DIGNITY

Chilton Book Company
Philadelphia / New York / London

Deric Regin

CULTURE

and the Crowd

A Cultural History of the Proletarian Era

In Memoriam
Kathleen Ferrier and A. Marja

Long, too long America,
Traveling roads all even and peaceful you learn'd from
  joys and prosperity only,
But now, ah now, to learn from crises of anguish,
  advancing, grappling with direst fate and recoil-
  ing not,
And now to conceive and show to the world what your
  children en-masse really are. . . .

             Walt Whitman

Foreword

In presenting a survey of the widest possible range of cultural achievements during the last two centuries, I have obviously committed a crime against intellectual modesty. With due apologies for my inordinate appetite, however, I should not like to be held responsible for worse. My venture into the rich field of contemporary culture is not driven by gargantuan gluttony, but carefully charted, and as meticulously planned as if it were a history of statistics.

Readers wishing to know what the following pages are

about might perhaps be best instructed first on what not to expect. This work is not a cultural hisory of the last two centuries as such. That would require five or six more volumes. Though its scope is wide, its objective is narrow. It merely investigates our culture inasmuch as it relates to the trend of proletarianization.

It is therefore clearly not a survey of all that has happened in the fields of philosophy, religion, art, literature, education, and so on, everything arranged according to the scale of importance. It is not an accumulation of great names and great works.

It definitely does not try to distribute pluses and minuses. It is not in the first place intended to deal out marks of approval or quality ratings. Examples are chosen to demonstrate historical change, not intrinsic merit. Though not dogmatically afraid of value judgments, it prefers to avoid private opinions on the better or worse of the modern situation.

This book does not claim to be the last word on the various problems with which it deals. It is a tentative approach to a development still incomplete.

Finally, this study has no axes to grind. The author believes that the proletarian society is neither a blessing nor a curse, but simply an historical reality to be met with common sense.

Acknowledgments

This book has been in preparation for some time, and before acknowledging my debt to the scholarly colleagues who in one way or another have given me a helping hand, I wish to express my gratitude to those of my friends who, otherwise committed to contemporary culture by talent and profession, have contributed to my understanding of its problems.

They are painters, poets, musicians, actors, and architects of varying age and nationality, with whom I have studied, worked, traveled, hoped, and planned; who, through often emotional and explosive conversations, have opened my mind to the scope and limitations of our age.

If I cannot possibly name them all, I should like to single out two of them who are no longer among us and to whose memory this work is dedicated—A. Marja, remembered for his rebellious temper in any gathering, his devastating polemics, his socially committed verse, and especially for the many hours of friendship in his attic at Groningen; and Kathleen Ferrier, for the musical purity of her recitals, her wit at after-concert parties, but above all for the great simplicity and warmth at her home in Hampstead.

I am indebted to my students, who have gone through many of the arguments elaborated in the following pages and whose challenge, doubt, or shock at my conclusions have often caused me to reformulate and widen my thoughts.

I wish to thank those friends in Europe, Communists, who through sometimes heated and trembling, but never inimical, debates have given their side of the story. Although I fundamentally disagree with their view and methods of proletarianization, I appreciate their criticism no less than their friendship. I have learned from them.

Finally, a good number of scholars have been exposed to my ideas, which they have met with professional reserve, doubt, or utter rejection—but sometimes with enthusiasm. I want to mention Benjamin Hunningher of Amsterdam University, who has helped me on various occasions, and Johan Hollak, of the same institution, who has corrected many of my faulty judgments in matters of philosophy.

Eva Keuls of Emory, Henry Shapiro of the University of California at Riverside, and William Mathes of Seton Hall have read parts of the work, for which service I am deeply obliged. I should like to thank my friend Herbert Flaig, who with critical doubt has withstood the assault of the ideas which I tried out on him, and has read some chapters. I am especially indebted to Elizabeth Vermey of Bryn Mawr, who has read the entire manuscript with acute criticism. Nancy Farrand Regin, as always, has been my editor with unflinching patience and endurance.

None of these should be blamed for the flaws and shortcomings of this work. They are mine alone. I am also responsible for the translation of materials quoted from French, German, Italian, and Dutch sources, poetry as well as prose.

Permission to quote from the following is gratefully acknowledged:

The House of Intellect by Jacques Barzun. New York: Harper & Row, 1959.

America and the Image of Europe by Daniel J. Boorstin. Cleveland: World (Meridian), 1961.

The American Commonwealth by James Bryce. 2 vols. New York: Putnam (Capricorn), 1959.

The American Mind by Henry Steele Commager. New Haven, Conn.: Yale University Press, 1950.

Poems: 1923–1954 by e e cummings. New York: Harcourt, Brace & World, 1954.

Four Quartets by T. S. Eliot. New York: Harcourt, Brace & World, 1943.

An Introduction to Metaphysics by Martin Heidegger, trans. by Ralph Manheim. New Haven, Conn.: Yale University Press, 1959.

Education for Modern Man by Sidney Hook. New York: Alfred A. Knopf, 1963.

"The Report of the President's Commission on Higher Education" by R. M. Hutchins. *Educational Record,* XXIX (April, 1948).

Roan Stallion by Robinson Jeffers. New York: Random House, 1935.

Selected Poetry by Robinson Jeffers. New York: Random House, 1938.

"Die Zeit Fährt Auto" from Erich Kästner, *Gesammelte Schriften.* Reprinted by permission of Atrium Verlag A. G., Zurich, Switzerland,

Literature, Popular Culture, and Society by Leo Lowenthal. Palo Alto, Calif.: Pacific Books, 1967. Reprinted by permission of the author.

The Collected Poems of Louis MacNeice, edited by E. R. Dodds. Copyright © The Estate of Louis MacNeice 1966. Reprinted by permission of Oxford University Press, Inc.

The Bedbug by Vladimir Mayakovsky. Cleveland: World (Meridian), 1960.

The Mencken Chrestomathy by H. L. Mencken. New York: Alfred A. Knopf, 1949.

Plupart du Temps by Pierre Reverdy. Paris: © Editions Gallimard, 1945.

Sämtliche Werke by Rainer Maria Rilke. Frankfurt, Germany: Insel Verlag.

Und Auf Einmal Steht Es Neben Dir by Joachim Ringelnatz. Berlin, Germany: Karl H. Henssel Verlag, 1966.

The Higher Learning in America by Thorstein Veblen. Reprinted by permission of The Viking Press.

The Organization Man by William H. Whyte. New York: Simon & Schuster, 1956. Reprinted by permission of Simon & Schuster.

Contents

Part
ONE

We call culture the total sum of those spiritual developments which occur spontaneously.

JaKob Burckhardt

1

The Average Way of Living

Doomists and illusionists

The writer of cultural history commits himself to an ambitious venture and seems to act in defiance of that wisdom which today produces carefully narrowed fields, called areas of specialization. The nature of cultural history requires synthesis, and this inevitably implies broadly organizing themes. To many of today's specialists, absorbed in the technicalities of small but workable truths, synthesis has almost come to mean contemptible speculation. Much as respectable scholars ought to avoid wild guesswork and generalities, on the other hand it is equally important that some of them specialize in the difficult discipline of putting the strands of history together. Beneficial as is the detailed knowledge of the digestive tract, the nervous system, the blood circulation, there comes a time when one needs to contemplate the whole body. Cultural history is interested in the body. Thus, however modest a cultural historian may be, the nature of his very terrain and techniques is invariably bound to make him look arrogant to the more sectarian specialist, whose detailed monographs he nevertheless gratefully uses.

Culture is not society. Culture is the expression of a society in forms of art, literature, or thought. It is the bequest of a historical community. Not all bequests, however, are of equal importance. Some societies, like impoverished families, leave little worth preserving, and consequently their record in history will be meager. Cultural history in this sense is an account of an inheritance, of an imprint, an impact—not a report on society itself, not, in the first place, of the actual events and acts of society. The problems involved in this discipline appear baffling at times. They are compounded, however, when the subject matter deals with the contemporary scene. For the appreciation of the arts and philosophies of the last two hundred years is naturally influenced and hampered by human partiality, which at best makes the historical statement tentative.

There are two attitudes which utterly preclude a helpful understanding of our age. The first represents a belief in an imminent doom which is soon to afflict the world with calamities, thereby bringing to an end the civilized way of living as we know it. The doomists seem the more misleading since they are usually sincere and reflect thoughtfully on world events. And although their apocalyptic visions may well be products of a neurotic despair, their emotionalism does not express itself without the support of pertinent facts. They are always well prepared for the intellectual argument.

Nor is doomism a novelty in modern times. It frequently appears when changes of a social and political nature perplex the human mind and threaten to take away a supposed historical security. At such a time, figures like Savonarola arrive. Significantly, Savonarola was not merely a religious demagogue exciting the credulous masses. He had some outstanding intellectuals on his side as well, notably Michelangelo and Pico della Mirandola. They had, like their contemporary Machiavelli, reasons to doubt the future glory of Renaissance Florence, as history was soon to confirm. But this did not mean that the city was destined for a catastrophic end. Although catastrophes are frequent features of history, the idea of doom is an unhistorical notion.

The second uncooperative attitude, while it often reveals itself as cheap optimism, is, in actuality, a product of fear. It is characteristic of those who lack the courage to look the realities of their own age in the face, and prefer to steep themselves in protective illusions. The illusionist is usually anxious not to appear "romantic," by which he means nostalgic for past glory and past greatness. Unlike the doomist he desperately wants to look ahead, and thus creates a mirage of wish-dreams. This satisfies him the more since it makes him feel truly progressive. The future is his. And a great future at that!

The illusionist is not uncommon among those teachers who, substituting opinion for knowledge, are forever committed to an education of sloganeering. Consequently, what might have been the art of teaching, degenerates into a routine of indoctrination. In this mechanical system, it is imperative that the illusionist, since he lacks true optimism, push a regime of deliberate optimism. Doubt and questioning are fatal sins to him. Failure and decline are anathema. Thus history must always show progress, by which he means the expansion of goods, spiritual as well as material. It also means that while we have achieved high living standards, decent laws, great material comfort, and a booming economic production, we are inevitably going to top these off with the glamor of a brilliant culture.

Those who feel the need either to moan or to swoon

will not find satisfaction in an attempt to *understand*. An analysis, aiming at evaluating twentieth-century achievements within historical proportions, sets rational limitations, which the man of doom as well as the man of wish-dreams must fear as undermining his emotional bastions. Man in one way or another is understandably partial to his own age. It is precisely this, however, which requires the extra effort of contemplating the process of change. A man, looking in his mirror, is naturally inclined to flatter himself, and see the changes that make him look more mature—not those that show him old. Similarly, modern man by nature is ill equipped to give a true account of his own time. But he can be served by the aid of a rationale, guiding him in the discipline of change—history.

One of the most decisive changes that have troubled this century is the gradual transformation of a democratic into a proletarian order. This process, since it is not yet completed, is naturally a very much debated and debatable phenomenon, and the popular consensus under the weight of inertia is hardly aware of its existence at all. Some of us perhaps would rather not be made aware of this transformation, because for us it carries the stigma of degradation. This is an assumption as unfortunate as it is erroneous, stemming from an unhistorical conception of the idea of proletariat. For in this conception the proletariat is vaguely related to rude manners and dirty fingernails, and although it would be unfair to say that we have transcended this level altogether, we believe passionately in civilized sophistication as a desirable goal. Thus the proletarian, the unwashed but noble poor, must be elevated and educated to this sophistication. To accept that something so perfect as American democracy is changing into a proletarian system is to many almost tantamount to treason.

Attributes of the proletarian order

The proletariat is not what many old-fashioned socialists try to make it out to be. The proletarian is not the

factory laborer, the slum-dweller of the capitalistic industrial city, the man destined by an abstract formula of history to generate the violent overthrow of the middle-class
production system. He is by no means a newcomer in the
development of world history, emerging with the industrial expansionism of the nineteenth century. The proletarian may belong to the peasantry as well as to the city
masses. He roams with the Gypsy bands of Middle Europe, he hides as a Waldensian in the Italian Alps, or he
fights the Pope with the Albigenses in Languedoc. He
may trade in the souks of Aleppo or in the ghetto of
Prague. Whether he is classed among national or racial
minorities or belongs to the monolithic masses of wage-
earners, the proletarian is chiefly marked by his disaffili-
ation from the vital organs of his own society. Income is
hardly decisive. He can be as wealthy as a Rothschild
and the *Jew Süss,* or enjoy as a Negro a millionaire status
in an affluent world—still he dwells outside the center,
the political and cultural initiative of his society.

The proletariat is the aggregate of outsiders, fringe-
dwellers of the basic community, and therefore not included in the central and spontaneous organization of its
historical form. Watching and waiting at the periphery,
the classical proletariat subsisted off the crumbs from the
feast of the elite, which ruled inside the established walls
of the social headquarters. It had no part in the inner
workings of a society, it could not contribute to the formulation of a national or civic unity. Although one must
assume that the representative artists, poets, philosophers, theologians, or musicians were somehow the
spokesmen for a specific community as a whole, the proletariat in classical times was merely a passive element in the cultural achievements. At best it was being
reflected—it could not reflect itself.

The so-called elite, directing the political and cultural
shape of civilization, was determined by birth as well as
talent. The stress was on both, but in some fields conspicuously on the latter. Badly informed educators, branding
European instruction as elitist, mean to imply a class
prejudice. Nothing could be more erroneous. Continental

education in general has tended to be elitist only by its severe rejection of the undisciplined mind and the nursing of high-grade intellect. Traditionally, since the Middle Ages and the Schools of the Brethren of the Common Life, it has attracted and encouraged talented students from the lower middle classes and below. Consequently, most of the great scholars of Western civilization, from Erasmus on, have come from a social stratum not remarkable for inherited privileges.

Nor can it be said that the outstanding composers, artists, or poets of the past have been aided by birth. In general, it seems fair to say that elitism is chiefly characterized by severe demands for quality. In contrast, the proletarian order depends heavily on the thrust of quantity. Once this distinction is firmly made one can, and must, of course, add the necessary modifications. Classical society did frequently fail in the qualitative respect through certain class biases, whereas the modern world cannot with any measure of justice be accused of trying to exclude the gifted. The contrary is perhaps true. The problem here, however, deals mainly with priorities. While classical society occupied itself in the first place with the rigorous exploitation of the most talented, the proletarian system seems to aim by preference at the greatest number of the most solid and most average.

The proletariat then represents the alien element of the classical society, and the cultural history of the last two centuries reflects the self-consciousness of this extraneous position. Any understanding of modern cultural development requires the acceptance of a few basic premises, without which one is easily misled into emotional confusions.

First of all, proletarianism is characterized by mass movement in contrast to class dynamics. It is therefore not very enlightening in this respect to attach much value to the old-fashioned slogan of class-struggle. Regardless of its use for political agitation, as a historical tool this notion, with the help of more than a hundred years of social change, has proved to be most unreliably speculative. As outlined above, it is clear that the proletariat, once awakened, was not in the first place class-conscious. Peat peasants, mine workers, Jewish traders, religious fringe sects, or factory laborers, all of whom belonged to the historical proletariat, had no common cohesion. Consequently, they had no reason to identify themselves with a common class. The basic guideline for a rational evaluation of the modern cultural outlook is given in the rule that the proletariat, far from being class-conscious, on the contrary, is mass-conscious. Any historical survey like this one would miss its point if it were not focused on the only decisive underlying cultural struggle of our age: the unmitigated battle between the principle of individual and that of collective, of authenticity and conformity, of originality and public opinion, of elite and of average.

Secondly, there is no denying that this mass-consciousness is spreading. The increase is not merely a matter of a greater awakening of the crowd and of a firmer confidence in its quantitative power, it is also reflected in the minds of the intelligentsia who, by the same token, are proportionately losing their traditional intellectual confidence. A survey of the last two hundred years of cultural alienation must report that the force of mass-consciousness is winning over that of self-consciousness, with the inevitable result that Western civilization is undergoing a transformation, which expresses itself culturally as a process of general leveling. The leveling of values in social relations and ethics, in terms of arts and letters, means partly a standardization by which the novel, the theater piece, the work of scholarship, or the Christian message can be spread more widely as a general commodity. Against this flood tide of saleable quantity, individual poetic and dramatic expressions, the profound scholarly discovery, and religious intensity must seem to many to be losing propositions.

In the third place, it would be an inadmissible error to infer that this trend is necessarily detrimental to the viability of our society. The contrary may well be true. Naturally, we all dislike the idea of leveling and standardization. Not infrequently we try to deny that these phenomena exist to any significant degree at all. Numerous writings about the meaning of mass-education and mass-culture have appeared, most of them written from an emotional and partisan point of view, one way or the other. In the cultural analysis offered here, the possible beneficial or detrimental aspects of proletarianism will hardly be a contributing factor. The alternative "good" or "bad" in historical evaluations is usually irrelevant and rarely conducive to mature judgment. The historical meaning of Alexander the Great, Luther, the Industrial Revolution, or the First World War is not determined by moral values, but by its relevance to change. Accordingly, our primary interest here must be those achievements which represent the change from a harmonious classical to a restless proletarian culture.

Next, it is imperative to understand that this change affects us all. We all are members of a proletarian order, regardless of income and social status. Our aims, tastes, aspirations, and opinions are proletarian, inasmuch as they reflect common needs and group fulfillments. They express the average concern. We are the streamlined average asserting ourselves in the weight and numbers of consensus. Therefore, there is no reason to scoff haughtily at the other man's status, for culturally we belong to the same order. It is precisely our proletarian equality which obviates any supposed significance of class-struggle. For better or worse, the nature of modern culture is decided by consensus needs, by the prevalence of the classless multitudes of average people (which we all are) over the spontaneous energy of self-reliance.

Finally, the conception of our cultural situation will always remain blurred if what is, and should be, understood as proletariat is not recognized as the expression of cultural estrangement. Inasmuch as we are the prevailing proletarians, we are the historical strangers of our own civilization. This has nothing to do with the current cult of alienation, about which many sociological commentaries have been written in recent years. Our problem here is not the sentimental, self-pitying attitudes which are merely *symptoms*, but the underlying universal awareness of alienation itself as it has developed during the past two hundred years. Proletarian culture is the self-expression of the modern mass-consciousness, which identifies itself with those who in former times were at the margins of the classical society, having no part in the shaping of its historical configurations.

Proletarianism, thus, not being a matter of industrial labor, it follows that its cultural insignia are neither dirty hands, low wages, dismal dwellings, nor class-struggle. As the predominance of mass dynamics, it is typified by its extraneous position in respect to an established cultural elite, and this is what is symbolized in its art and letters.

Therefore, dealing with the last two centuries of cultural history, one can find reflected in the various fields of artistic and intellectual expression extraneous elements breaking up the cohesion of the classical forms of harmony. This will be elaborated in the appropriate following chapters, but by way of introducing the general theme a few examples may be allowed here. In the plastic arts, the classical ideal of *composition* disappeared and was replaced by a new technique of distortion. In the portrayal of the human being, man from the victorious image of the Renaissance conqueror, the grandiose titan as Michelangelo saw him, or the profoundly existential sufferer of Rembrandt's vision, was transformed into a fragmented pointillist mosaic, then into the twisted and contorted shapes of Van Gogh's non-heroes, until twentieth-century avant-gardism, from Picasso to De Kooning, leaves nothing of human dignity save disconnected components and strident pink streaks.

In music, the technique of distortion and disfiguring translates into that of dissonance. Basically, dissonance is almost as old as musical harmony itself. But initially it represented merely a playful element of ornamentation. At the height of the classical expression of music, Bach, from his early chorale adaptations to the *Art of the Fugue,* delighted in coloring his contrapuntal logic with subtle and sometimes not-so-subtle dissonance. Mozart and Beethoven followed him and frequently startled their contemporaries with unconventional sound combinations. From then on, the history of gradually developing disharmony was a fact, until in the twentieth century with multitonal, atonal, and serial techniques the established tonic system has been destroyed. An originally alien element, first used merely as ornamentation, now comes to be welcomed as the essential foundation of music.

Similar trends, as will be demonstrated later, are discernible in poetry, for instance, when the "beautiful" sonorous syntax is undermined and fragmented; or in the novel, when what originally constituted its composition (plot or the fabric of characterization) disintegrated and, from *Finnegan's Wake* to *The Sound and the Fury,* was replaced by a kaleidoscopic whirl of glittering and disconnected details. Whereas in classical drama, from Aeschylus to Ibsen, the demand for action was honored in a strongly centralized protagonist, modern drama has replaced him by the pathetic figure of the anti-hero committed to non-action.

The ex-centric forces of the collective, having, after two centuries of political and social developments, negotiated their dominant sway over the inner elite, must now inevitably be accounted for in the contemporary history of culture. In this sense, modern cultural history can only be a report on the process of universal estrangement. At the risk of being tedious, I reiterate that involved here is not the *cult* of alienation, but an exposition of a historically grown consciousness, presented without the emotional overtones that usually accompany the former. This also implies that the multifarious aspects of alienation will be neglected for a more unifying treatment, viewing this phenomenon chiefly as the cultural theme of the conflict between mass-consciousness and self-consciousness. Nevertheless, these varieties do exist and may here at least be summarized in a brief survey.

Theoretical minds like to distinguish between the particular brands of self-alienation, for instance. It must be clear, however, that in our context all forms of alienation indicate a separation of a part of the subjective self or cause the self to feel separated from its environment. Similarly, some French philosophers distinguish a special form of *extraneation* as differing from that alienation which to them has a definite dialectic structure. In Hegel's conception, which is basic for the theory of alienation, the term implies an objectification of the self (for instance in work and in language), which as a dialectic expression can be suspended and restored to the self in the philosophical Idea. When this moment of the return to the absolute self does not take place, the notion of extraneation would be applicable. This may well be a subtle philosophical distinction. For the understanding of the historical and cultural changes in our time, however, this is not overly helpful.

Cultural estrangement sometimes reveals itself in the turning of established values inside out, so to speak, whereby externals become essentials. This sort of externalization is evident everywhere in a society in which the wrapping of the product becomes of primary importance, not infrequently at the expense of the contents. It is then that in education "skills and techniques" are stressed above subject matter. It is then that the organization of the "public image" also emerges and that, instead of their personal selves, artists or politicians try to promote expedient projections, streamlined and tailored for public use.

Here, we are clearly verging on that modern proclivity of exchanging means for ends. It may well be one of the most characteristic aspects of modern society. The masses originally served the individualistic ends of the established elite. Much as we may reject this as undemocratic selfishness, it makes us also understand why classical culture was the fruition of the minds of a few who spoke for the entire community. With the gradual shift of the point of gravity to the masses, what originally were merely

means now claim to be legitimate ends. Cultural achievement in the classical society was an autonomous product
which might or might not be sold. In the new order, with
the opening of the mass market for the "culture consumers," art, literature, and scholarship inevitably tend to become commodities. More and more the official standards
are set by dealers and literary agents, or otherwise by the
vast demands of "college reading."

Related to this is that kind of cultural alienation which
shows man, or modern man's work, as merely a fragment
of a whole. Schiller, in the sixth letter of his *On the Aesthetic Education of Man* (1795), was already concerned
about man's enslavement to a mechanical routine in
which he is merely a cog without any personal gratification of labor. What Schiller feared, in our technocratic
age has become accepted practice. To be sure, students
do riot against the assembly-line production of the multi-
university, but they invariably learn to adjust to the conformist streamlining of the academic market.

Much has been said about the symptoms of *anomia*,
the social or political apathy especially of young people
who feel disaffiliated from their own environment. In this
the element of dehumanization plays a large part. In a
technologically dominated world, it is inevitable that
man has come to identify himself and his security with
abstract formulas. When the immediacy of the sounds of
horse and hoof are gone, and man counts his advantages
by the quantity of mechanical horsepower, it is not surprising that he also slowly learns to abstract his own existence. It is then that instead of enjoying a house to live
in, he has, as Le Corbusier teaches him, a "machine to
live in." It is then that Russian constructivism and the
neoplasticism of the *Stijl* group draws the ultimate conclusion of abstract art and reduces man's experience to
pure squares and blocks. It is then that academic philosophy, far from probing the centuries-old problems of man
and life, specializes in the equations of algebraic types of
logic.

These and other forms of cultural estrangement rarely

appear as separate entities; they are more likely to be intermingled and entangled in various combinations. Consequently, it serves no great purpose to worry about their theoretical classifications. They all ultimately derive from the one basic conflict that is haunting and disturbing the modern human consciousness: the combat between allegiance to the individual and to the collective.

As long as man is plagued by this alternative, he is bound to search restlessly for anchorage. His history during the last two centuries is one of incessant escape. Coeval with the physical dynamics of the Western frontier and the surge of economic indices, his mind has meandered away from the secure positions which originally constituted the idea of "home" for him. This expressed in poetry becomes the nostalgia for the *Heimat*, representing the homeless stranger in time and space. But also, and perhaps foremost, this suggests the eternal Wanderer: Faust, Brand, Peer Gynt, and Melville's Ishmael as the modern man. Is he not Shelley's Alastor, in search of a spiritual identity? Man, while wondering what it may mean that "we have killed God," joins Nietzsche no less fervently in his yearning for "deep eternity." Having conquered virtually all the freedoms on his expansionist drive into abundance, it slowly dawns on him that he may have irrevocably lost the freedom of being at home.

Thus the history of contemporary man is beset with baffling questions. An account of the culture of restlessness and escape can hardly be expected to provide solid answers. The science of relativity has taken away from man his fixing points in time and space. What then is to be the new order? Is there a universe that he can still claim as his own? Similarly, a philosophy of relativity teaches him that reason and existence fail in the fourth dimension of the absolute absurd. Einstein's discovery confirms the existentialist plight of what Jaspers calls our "floating being." Man has toppled the arrogant trinities of truth from Aquinas to Hegel. How continue? Escape into formulas of symbolic logic, or the behavior statistics of rats and mice? How can he now translate human experience into forms of art, having repealed the laws of style and syntax, having suspended the rules of perspective and tonic structure?

Modern man has successfully deflated what he thinks to be the illusions of the classical elite. The bastions of authority are dismantled. The categories of time and space have failed. He counts his freedoms. The old gods are held captive in museums. That is his freedom, so he is told. Coherence and composition, rhyme and meter—he has annulled all constrictions. The ancient certainties are bogies. He is free, so he is told. The creeds of reason or redemption, grace or progress—they are but soap bubbles in the sky. But he keeps his dream of culture. Culture there must be at all cost. Culture without certainties? He has one certainty left. He clings and swears allegiance to his last security. He is one of the group. He has one certainty left—the standard of the average.

Individuality is the aim of political liberty.
                                    James Fenimore Cooper

Liberty is the power of the collective.
                                            Pierre Proudhon

2

The Rebellious Way of Living

The ancient order and the new

The old-fashioned way of teaching the great events
which mark the difference between the classical and the
modern age is characterized by an exclusive stress on the
French Revolution, followed by an account of Napoleon's
spectacular victories and defeats. In this treatment the
year 1815 is a convenient device to give history a breath-
er, label the new epoch reactionary, and catch up with

such major trends as the Industrial and Romantic revolutions, as if they were mere afterthoughts. This distortion of the true emergence of modern history is still lingering on in some textbooks, probably owing to professional as well as commercial inertia. In recent years, however, historians more and more have awakened to the idea that the French Revolution, though perhaps a most spectacular event, is by no means an isolated one. At the end of the eighteenth century, in virtually all the countries of Europe as well as in North America, cracks appeared in the crust of the old society and began their destructive work.

These coinciding upheavals, to be sure, often originated from different sources and the revolutionary tendencies were dissimilar from nation to nation. The decisive events in the United States clearly focused on secession rather than on revolution. The American colonists aimed at commercial independence and a political liberty based on the Glorious Revolution of 1688. Hence their adoption of John Locke, the theoretical spokesman for William III, as their guide. In Geneva, the disturbance of 1768 was a provincial affair brightened up by the rivalry of Rousseau and Voltaire, the first being on the side of the bourgeois, the latter on that of the aristocrats. In Holland, the revolutionary structure was unique inasmuch as the Oranges were the only ruling dynasty supported by the populace. There the rebelling Patriots represented a minority of oligarchic regents and Amsterdam merchants. In Austria, the revolution came from above, strangely conducted by the enlightened but unbalanced Joseph II. As for France, there were essentially four revolutions brewing simultaneously: the peasants, nobles, bourgeoisie, and the city workers all had their own set of objectives and ways to achieve them. National differences aside, though, these revolutions bore a unifying mark. They represented the gradual, sometimes not so gradual, transition from an old to a new order.

This however holds equally true for the Romantic and the Industrial revolutions. It is a trifle absurd for history

books to begin considering their development at a point
when their initial phase was positively passed. Both
movements in their earliest rumblings predated the
French Revolution. As broad cultural thrusts, they were
clearly coeval with the political disturbances of the era.
Nothing could be more helpful than to consider the industrial, artistic, and political revolts as three aspects
of one and the same profound cultural transformation.
This does not mean that we can very easily detect their
direct relationships. There are good reasons, of course,
why they have traditionally not been taught as coinciding events. These are practical reasons. Besides being
most diverse in nature, the three revolutions are in each
instance extremely complex. A parallel detailed treatment
of these massive movements would tax even the most
powerful scholar and might well frighten the beginner
away in confusion. With due consideration of the pedagogic realities, the romantic, political, and industrial upheavals must nevertheless be understood as the cooperating components of a gigantic cultural revolution, which,
in its unifying scope, has made modern man.

Taking a brief look at the political situation first, we
should neither think frivolously about generalizing the
various revolutions nor be unduly struck by their complexities. Aided by two centuries of hindsight and countless reams of printed commentary, we can with some care
and restraint try to answer the difficult question: What
are these political shocks at the end of the eighteenth
century in essence about?

We ought not, however, to make the mistake for simplicity's sake of streamlining intricate historical structures into crude and misleading patterns. To say that
the democratic revolutions are about the bourgeoisie and
their emergence as a new power is indeed to make the
story simple. But it is also erroneous. To begin with, as
early as the seventeenth century the Dutch Republic had
already established a fairly homogeneous burgher society, reflected spontaneously in its cultural expressions.
But besides this, the eighteenth-century revolts were by no

means so predominantly focused on the third estate as is often assumed. In France, for instance, one could legitimately contend that the nobility set off the explosions. The middle classes at the meetings of the Constituent Assembly in Versailles, of course, played a glamorous role. It is significant, however, that the French Revolution is traditionally celebrated on the anniversary of the storming of the Bastille, an event not connected with the bourgeoisie but with the city mobs. Finally, it ought to be stressed that the real and first truly spectacular gains of 1789 fell to the peasants. On the crucial August 4th, the political structure of France changed literally overnight.

The victory of the peasants was the result of their terrorist threats, creating the "great fear," and the looting and burning of castles or manor houses. Mob violence for the first time paid off. The peasants not only were the first to win, they also won permanently. The advantages gained by the middle classes, as expressed in the Constitution of 1791, were considerable but limited, and by no means lasting. To pretend then that the French Revolution was about the bourgeoisie makes little sense, under the circumstances. Soon it was up to Napoleon Bonaparte to establish his own version of the revolution. Admittedly, the Code Napoléon was, in a sense, a codification of many of the ideas that emerged in the Assembly of 1789. But the new constitutions of the Consulate and the Empire took away most of the political power that the bourgeoisie had obtained in the early years of the revolution. Napoleon's function and importance, at least in the domestic respect, were revealed in his overriding preoccupation with the establishment of order in France's chaos.

It was precisely the bourgeoisie that had created the chaos: that bourgeoisie proclaimed by Abbé Sieyès, in his pamphlet *What Is the Third Estate?*, as the new national order. Sieyès, however, was a priest and a count at that. Understanding little of the forms and varieties of the third estate first-hand, his untrained idealism presented it as a unified block of willpower. Soon he was inevitably to learn that there were many middle classes, and that they regarded each other with more envy and rivalry than they ever felt for the nobility. Anyone intimately familiar with European class structures knows that a bourgeois class solidarity does not exist. Never in history have they, as an autonomous unit, fought either the first or the second estate, much less the lower classes. Historically and socially, they were an aggregation of separate classes, each with its own specific interests and prejudices. The Terror regime during the National Convention was a direct result of the inherent distrust and disunity of the middle classes, and in a spectacular manner denied Sieyès' claim of their national unity and cohesion.

The political revolutions of the eighteenth century then were not about the bourgeoisie but about a varied number of often conflicting issues which defy any attempt at simplification when considered in their contemporary context. It is only when aided by the knowledge of their subsequent development that one can detect some historical perspective in the rebellious movements. In the first place, they were not about groups, people, or individuals. They reflected a new universal awakening, new concepts of freedom, and new concepts of property.

Clearly at stake was the problem of equality, which was a matter of authority. However, this was no novelty. The eighteenth century democratic revolutions merely proceeded with the struggle initiated in the time of the Renaissance. Elsewhere, we shall trace the unfolding of the consciousness of equality from the era of the Reformation. It was then that the new distribution of authority became a leading motif in the intellectual history of Western society. The revolutions of the seventeenth and eighteenth centuries (and we may as well add those of the nineteenth and twentieth centuries, too) brought the problem of political authority to a vehement crisis. Reduced to the simplest formula, the question was: Does the sovereignty of a nation lie with an elite agency, the monarch and his council, for instance, or with the people as a collective?

The eighteenth-century revolutions merely pushed with greater violence the problem of the people's sovereignty. This inevitably entailed the full thrust of the collective, that is, crowd action. The French Revolution preeminently demonstrated not a new program but the new technique of collective violence. The success of the "great fear," the peasants' fury, the women's march to Versailles, the storming of Bastille and Tuileries, the Terror of 1793 and 1794, and finally the escalating wars, launched to spread the gospel of equality to other nations, were signs of new ways and means in reaching objectives.

Whereas the issue of equality in the eighteenth century revealed only a change in procedure, the notion of property presented a basic new outlook on life. Property, as John Locke could still explain it on behalf of the classical world, is a mental as well as a material quality. For the French revolutionaries, however, property was exclusively physical property. Moreover, their celebrated *Declaration of the Rights of Man* stressed that property was sacred. Thus we have entered the age of forthright materialism. We are in the century of La Mettrie's *Man a Machine*, Holbach's *The System of Nature* and Helvetius' *Treatise on Man,* all professedly materialist expressions.

Of course, there have been materialists at all times. With the ascent of the middle classes in Western society, the enjoyment of "goods," always attractive to all stages of life, became a new way of existence. A quick glance at the burgher life of the Dutch Republic and its seventeenth-century culture suffices to reveal it as thoroughly materialistic, staunchly loyal to the panoramas of food displayed in some of their pictures. But the early phase of bourgeois life was not aware of materialism, since it was still harmoniously interwoven with the warp of religious and spiritual needs. In the eighteenth century, materialism became separated from man's mind—the beginning of the two cultures which worry twentieth-century man. Nothing could be more exemplary for the experience of cultural estrangement of those days. To call material property sacred is its most ironical expression. Classical society knew materialism and enjoyed it, but it could not conceive of it as sacred. Only the modern mind is able to force such an unhallowed notion as physical matter into the hallowed sphere of the untouchable taboo.

Leaving the political strands loose for a while in order to focus on the Romanticist mind, we ought again to distinguish essentials from by-products. The Romantic movement saw as its task the fighting of an ancient regime as much as any political Jacobin. If this is kept in mind, much wandering off into side issues can be avoided. The most unproductive way of finding out the aims and lasting importance of the Romantic revolt is to use the antiquated clichés about alleged emotionality, sentimentality, excessiveness, unbalanced display, and rhetoric. To be sure, some Romanticists tended to indulge in eccentricities and cheap tears, especially in the later phases of the movement. But one ought not to condemn a style for its excesses. We do not condemn the harmonious forms of classical literature because eighteenth-century pedants and dogmatists wrote their poems and plays in fanatic accord with the rules of prosody. No more should one judge Romanticism by its worst representatives.

The Romantic movement did not aim at replacing reason with emotion. On the contrary, its earliest poets, such as Blake or the Schlegels, not infrequently extolled the power of reason. They simply wanted to place reason in conjunction with spontaneous feelings in order to create a generating conflict and to galvanize the imagination. It was the time of the emergence of electricity. This was the thing that the Romanticists understood. They had a deep sense of polarity. It was, significantly, also the time of the birth of dialectic reasoning in philosophy. By allowing reason and emotion to coexist in a kind of polar order, whereby they mutually negated yet also affirmed each other, the artist was to benefit by a heightened, intensified imagination. And imagination, as Wordsworth confirmed, is "reason in her most exalted mood." It

> Is but another name for absolute power
> And clearest insight, amplitude of mind.

The Romanticist found this amplitude of mind wholly lacking in the eighteenth-century classicists, whose polished veneer seemed to him merely a substitute for insight as well as imagination. He revolted against the tyranny of formalism and extolled in Shakespeare precisely what Voltaire had despised as barbarous: the flight of conception and fantasy, defying all preset formulas and prosody. The Romanticist fought the ancient diction of Pope's satires, Boileau's literary recipes, or Wieland's rococo lyrics. Instead of a detached stylized polish, he wanted immediate conveyance of the subjective experience. This immediacy, this sans-culottism of the arts, destroyed the majestic formality of classical expressions. It could be rendered in the speech and style of the humble people, as Wordsworth, Victor Hugo, or the painter Millet saw them, or in the simple tonality of the folk-song lyricism reappearing with the ballads of Scott, Eichendorff, or Heine.

Immediacy showed up in the direct appeal to nature as teacher and example, without the medium of academic rules. The painters of Barbizon were men of the "open air," as much as was the poet Lenau when going through his somber reed-lands. Immediacy also revealed itself in the willing surrender of the privacy of grief. Thus the Romantic age began the cultivation of melancholy as echoed in Schubert's *Winterreise,* de Vigny's misanthropy, Eichendorff's nostalgia for the *Heimat,* or the tedium of the Italian poet Leopardi.

While the Renaissance man, individualist though he might be, still conveyed his personality through the formal media of style, the Romanticist placed his personality in the foreground. The cult of the individual emerged.

The artist henceforth was under pressure to be original, that is, to turn himself inside out, so to speak, to publicize his inner self. It was the inner self-experience which now set the rules, the dogmas, the laws—not the establishment, the Academy, the tradition.

Whereas the political and artistic revolutions were clearly generated by minds agitating deliberately against an old order, this cannot be said of the Industrial Revolution. The inventors, entrepreneurs, and manufacturers who, each in their own way, helped to shape the new industrial world were not consciously combating an old society. In fact, the actual rebels here were the counter-revolutionaries, the machine wreckers. Yet the Industrial Revolution destroyed the classical cohesion as much as did its political and artistic counterparts. The England of 1740 was still the world of small, limited, private needs and supplies. By 1815 its outlook was entirely changed.

We cannot enter into the many reasons why England in this development played such a predominant part. It is only worth noting that while virtually all other major or minor nations at that time were involved in and impeded by political upheavals, England could forge ahead with its industrial and economic experiments. It had its own revolution a century ahead of other countries. There were a few minor political riots around the turn of the eighteenth century, such as that involving Sir Francis Burnett and his fight against an alleged infringement of the freedom of press in 1810. But on the whole, the overriding social clash in England at that time was concerned with economic changes.

The simplest definition of the Industrial Revolution tells us that it represented a change from hand to machine tools. It is helpful but it explains the story only partly. If one asks oneself how the Industrial Revolution fitted into the total cultural framework of the age, this formula cannot provide the answer, of course. Although any conscious rebellion against an old order may seem absent, it is highly significant that an overwhelming majority of the men who were responsible for the new industrial dispensation belonged to dissenter groups. The Quakers were among the first to excel in the fields of such disparate trades as brewing and banking. They were also instrumental in the new development of the iron and steel industry. Among the inventors, James Watt was a Presbyterian, Thomas Newcomen a Baptist, and Samuel Crompton a Swedenborgian. The Scots, Highlanders as well as Lowlanders, always the fiercest fighters and rebels, were the greatest single group to influence and shape the revolution.

There were a number of reasons why the Nonconformists took the leading parts on the new industrial scene. These were to be traced to their living and working habits and their superior education on all levels. Beyond this, there was the obvious though obscure terrain of psychological motivations which, though we cannot here even begin to disentangle them, are clearly not to be overlooked. The Nonconformist sectarians were, after all, revolutionaries. We must at some point or another admit that behind the indices and statistics of their economy there fermented an unconscious force geared to destroy the old establishment.

The Industrial Revolution destroyed the old structure which provided, at the same time, both a balance and stagnation. All the familiar changes in production, marketing, communication, the new methods of mining, spinning, weaving, or farming point to new basic conceptions of life in general. Whereas, previously, economic production was led by private demands, now the thrust of mass demands and mass supplies was set in motion. Whereas under the monarchic system the economy was focused but limited, by 1800 the commoner had taken command and the economy became free, unlimited but chaotically pluralistic.

How did these changes affect mankind as a whole? We know their immediate psychological impact. We are familiar with the disturbances of the workers, especially between 1811 and 1815, when Luddites and other desperate groups broke up frames and attacked gig mills and corn dealers. Since the laborers were eventually also to benefit in industrial society because of the new jobs created by mechanized power, these riots, important as they were, may be considered as only of transitory value. A more lasting impact, and one of a more universal order, was registered in the mind of man questioning the destiny of human freedom in the developing mechanized system. It began with a few outstanding thinkers and then spread until the human problem became a collective worry in the twentieth century. The question must be asked: Why did otherwise forward-looking intellectuals consider industrialization a growing evil? Why, from the beginning, in spite of all their romantic attraction, was there a resistance movement against the railroads? Why did the authorities of Eton and Oxford, for instance, refuse to cooperate in the establishment of local stations? Part of this may well have to be explained as inherent human inertia and conservatism. Part of it must also be seen as the fear of possible cultural extinction. No matter whether one agrees or disagrees with Kierkegaard's entry in his *Journals*, which condemned the railroad mania as the end, "the final spurt," of a period of culture, the historical fact remains that the first intellectual resistance arose on behalf of mankind, on behalf of the integrity of the human being.

There are many factors at work in the process of total industrialization that explain this resistance. Two of them are of particular significance here inasmuch as they bear on the universal cultural situation. They are the elements of fragmentation and combination. Fragmentation usually appears under the heading of the system of interchangeable parts. Through the preset formulas of mechanics, the machine is basically a pattern of components, each of which can be replaced at will. The economic advantages in this are so obvious that further discussion seems unnecessary. The point here is that it gradually dawned on man that, in the expansion of machinery, he himself had become an interchangeable part, a thought driven home to him with monotonous emphasis by the system of assembly-line production. Division of labor had existed before the industrialized society of modern times. Now, however, man became conscious of its meaning and its alienating effect. Hegel, the first thinker to include the category of work in a broad philosophic system, as early as his Jena lectures of 1803–04 probed the dehumanizing nature of specialization and deplored the debasing and blunting of the worker's mind by mechanical routines. Man now recognized himself as only a fragment. He lost contact with the totality of the product. This trend of fragmentation was felt not only in connection with industrial labor. As we shall have further occasion to observe, it was to be one of the most characteristic phenomena in all fields of contemporary civilization.

The second aspect, that of combination, applied equally to the laborers and to the manufacturers. Labor unions, still disguised as innocent-looking clubs, were active throughout the eighteenth century. With the growth of mechanization, their cause became more urgent, their protest more strident. The Combination Acts of 1799 and 1800 declared organized action for higher wages to be illegal—the beginning of a long struggle for the control of human labor. Combination was no less important for the employers. They huddled in social clubs and scientific associations, not so much to fraternize as to control and keep up prices. Especially in the mining and metal industries, this incipient trust movement operated very efficiently. The coal proprietors of the Tyne, the smelters of Bristol, and the ironmasters of the Midlands banded together in monopolizing power-blocks. It must be understood that the legislation against combination applied both to the workers and the industrialists, although enforcement upon the latter was slack.

We see here the emergence of the group as the nucleus of power. What is understood by the ugly word "massification" was a historical development that marked the new Western society as a whole. It was also visible in the process of urbanization, which students of the Industrial

Revolution have called the "integrative tendency." Early manufacturing was scattered in rural areas. With the rise of mechanized power and the factory system, industries gradually concentrated near deposits of coal and iron or at important transport routes. The shift was away from the country and into the towns, which soon became places of teeming, congested life with all the social combustion that, for better or worse, was to produce the modern metropolitan brand of culture. Combination on the cultural level predicated mass action, mass opinion, mass taste.

Man and multitude

Although the three revolutions may not seem to have approached each other any more closely, with these loose ends in our hands, we are at least able to make a few general statements about the consciousness of modern man, inasmuch as he is involved in these upheavals. Just as Renaissance times show coevally a number of revolutions in practically all fields of culture, so the period around 1800 demonstrates parallel revolutions in the arts, literature, education, religion, economic thought, and philosophy. Just as it is dangerous and yet apparently inevitable to speak of *the* Renaissance man appearing over the horizon of the fifteenth and sixteenth centuries, so it is hazardous, and yet inevitably necessary, to speak of *the* modern man, mass man, the proletarian. He is a highly disputable being, hiding himself in the confusing tendencies which distinguish our age, and one should not pretend, certainly not at this early point in his history, to be able to understand and describe him fully.

He is at least old and mature enough however to be compared with the man of the Renaissance who, emerging from his revolutions with a mind full of confidence and poised for discovery and conquest, be it of territory, science, or arts, was above all distinguished by the consciousness of individuality. By contrast, the modern mind is self-conscious about individuality. In classical times, action merely occurred. After 1800, man began to talk about action, to insist on action. Why this difference? Because the man of the Renaissance had a wide space to travel, his destination was indeed manifest. The American frontiersman was the last descendant of this breed. When his task was fulfilled at the end of the nineteenth century, modern man had no place to go. In his frustration, he became the go-go man, self-conscious about action but without destination. This is reflected in his entire preoccupation with culture, which he wants to consider as terra incognita yet experiences as a domain of fulfillment, in which he tries in vain to open up new roads of exploration—in essence the theme of this work. This inhibition has caused him to become a security seeker. He needs the group. His action becomes group action, group protest, group philanthropy.

It is in the light of this self-consciousness about the function of the individual that one must consider the revolutions at the end of the eighteenth century. For, from the analysis above, it would appear that whatever the issues at stake, in the complicated revolutionary situation there was invariably in the background the consciousness of the single in the tide of the group, the individual in the rise of the collective, the nonconformist in the crush of conformity, man's authenticity in the age of equality. Difficult though it is to trace the mutual relations between the three revolutions, in the totality of the cultural experience their ideas and motivations all converge in the awareness of a split between Person and Public.

It would be a happy coincidence if we could conveniently sort out these revolutions by partisanship and class them on the side of either the individual or the collective. History, however, is rarely so obliging. More often than not it presents us with an anarchy of trends and issues that tend to cross party lines. Political revolutions on the surface seemed to favor the masses. This was what Schiller assumed when he turned against the French

Revolution, which he, granting its beneficial value for society as a whole, nevertheless attacked for its detrimental effect on the position of the individual. The general line of thought seems reasonable enough, but looking closely at the events one can, without strain, make a case for the Constitution of 1791 as a document issued to protect the rights of the individual, in spite of the fact that the implications of equality inevitably favor the masses. The same ambiguity is inherent in the American Constitution, which, by the wording of the Preamble, is for the "common defense" and the "general welfare" and other such pluralities, but nevertheless, in the fifth to eighth amendments, shields the individual to an almost paradoxical extent. It is ostensibly for the people, whom Hamilton despised as the "great beast." But his worry was unfounded, if we are to believe James Fenimore Cooper, who in *The American Democrat* explained that the Constitution was not at all the work of the people but rather of the states. And later Charles Beard was to interpret it as a document representing economic group interests in the first place.

The Romanticist not infrequently is depicted as the arch-individualist, forever busy escaping society. Undoubtedly he preferred to place the emphasis on the authentic personal experience and as such he was plainly on the side of the individual. It would be an error, however, to assert that he was therefore against society. His sense of antithesis and polarity rather led him to bring individual and community into confrontation with each other. To be sure, he was preeminently a wanderer. He did escape, but often simply to reflect on the separation from his environment. If the Romanticists were primarily individualistic, many of them were remarkably gregarious and inclined to the formation of circles. The Romantic movement in Germany alone established within the period of one decade four successive schools: at Jena, Heidelberg, Württemberg, and Berlin. Many of the Romantic writers were profoundly involved in the social events of their time. Some of them, Victor Hugo, Lamartine, Shelley, Byron, Heinrich Heine, Ludwig Uhland, excelled in political activities. Turning to the American Transcendentalists, who after all represent some of the best qualities of Romanticism, we see that virtually all of them were concerned with the betterment of society. It is not only evidenced by that by-product, the Brook Farm experiment, but far more by the specific writings of Whitman, Melville, Thoreau, Brownson, and Theodore Parker—all of whom questioned the relationship between democracy and individualism. Emerson's fundamental theme throughout his life was that of the polarity between society and solitude, which his compromising mind tried to conciliate in the "diagonal line."

A similar equivocal condition is manifest in the development of industrialization. Naturally, the *laissez-faire* arrogance of the manufacturers easily leads to the conclusion that they represented the utmost in egotistic behavior, with heartless disregard for the collective. The ensuing trend of social Darwinism, based on a dubious principle and often executed with ruthless elbows, seems a true concomitant of the Industrial Revolution. It is undeniable that the process of industrialization caused hardships, pauperism, and squalor. It should not be overlooked, however, that in the long run the masses were to benefit in various ways from the new order. It provided them with new jobs and cheaper, longer-lasting woolen and cotton clothing. It further made available popular newspapers in large editions and stimulated popular education. The Industrial Revolution indeed awakened the worker to the importance of mass solidarity, which actualized itself not merely in the ascendance of labor unions, but eventually also in matters of taste, design, manners. In short, what is known as the modern mass society could not have grown without the thrust of industrialization.

If there is no sound reason to classify any of the revolutions by party preference, there can be no doubt, as I hope the discussion above has elucidated, that they all, culturally speaking, were concerned with the split in man's awareness of himself. Whereas, in classical times, the separation between individual and group was rarely envisaged since one seemed to be securely embedded in the other, by 1800 man as an entity appeared to drift away from his environment, and, at least in the minds of those who cared to think about it, the two threatened to become incompatible. This divorce within the human consciousness was probably neither product nor cause of the eighteenth-century revolts. It was merely vividly illustrated by the events of that time. The deliberate or entailing break-up of the old order, kept together by the centralized and centralizing source of elite power, was the common aspect of the political, artistic, and industrial revolutions. Although hardly any of their contemporaries realized it, their common cultural problem was the historic alternative of the few and the many.

How much of a cultural problem this was, indeed, found its expression in the thoughts of a group of radicals who, relatively obscure as they were at that time, nonetheless threw the spotlight on an essential aspect of the revolutionary era. The Babouvists, followers of Gracchus Babeuf, were the first recognizable socialists, and prematurely foreshadowed much of what was to happen in the history of mass dynamics. Their famous *Manifesto of the Equals* of 1796 was extremely important in that, more than half a century before the *Communist Manifesto,* it explained in far more precise, though less elaborate, terms than those of Engels and Marx the meaning for the future of total equality. The group of the Equals recognized that the French Revolution, as far as equality was concerned, had failed, and that it had merely replaced one power block with another. The true revolution was still to come, they predicted. It would be one infinitely greater and more radical. It would establish total equality. The Babouvists wanted nothing less than this absolute equality, which makes no distinction between human beings except in sex and age. As there is one sun and the same air for everyone, so there should be one education and one standard of life. They would consent to anything for the cause of equality. They would make a clean sweep to achieve it. "All the arts may perish as long as we have true equality."

It is significant that the group had its hesitations about the last statement and that for this reason it replaced the manifesto with a milder document. The first appearance of a political mass movement signaled the apprehension that its efforts might well result in the extinction of culture. To what extent, if at all, this fear was justified is not under discussion here. The fact remains that early socialism recognized a firm connection between the arts and the old elitist society. A warning here seems not out of order. One should not draw hasty inferences from the foregoing. To conclude, for instance, that the *Manifesto of the Equals* suggests the incompatability of socialism and culture would be erroneous. Most forms of socialism during the last two centuries have had open eyes for the need to spread appreciation and knowledge of the arts among the workers. They have been ardently committed to organizing educational agencies for this purpose. They have had dreams, so far unfulfilled, of a new brand of art issuing from and typifying the worker. One certainly need not elaborate the point that many contemporary artists and writers have been professed and active socialists.

The issue of socialism or socialization is not at stake here, but rather the question of total equality. Since the totally equalitarian state, toward which we gradually seem to be heading, has not yet been established, there is no point in speculating whether or not total equality necessarily excludes the thriving of cultural achievements. We know that the totalitarian leveling of the regimes of Stalin and Hitler eradicated the arts, literature, and thought. But these abnormal developments seem scarcely fair tests for our point.

It is, however, wholly understandable why many leading thinkers in the nineteenth century began to worry about the possible fading away of Western civilization. No matter whether or not we agree with their arguments, we cannot simply overlook the historical fact that such towering figures as Burckhardt, Nietzsche, Kierkegaard, Melville, and Flaubert, to name only a few, forecast a gradual return to barbarism. They based their somber appraisal on the newly emerging role of violence. While we cannot here anticipate their pronouncements about the relationship between individual and crowd, person and public, the notion of violence belonged unmistakably to the era of eighteenth-century revolutions.

Violence of all types, including mob violence, is no stranger to any age in history. But during the revolutionary era, being discussed here, a new kind of mob violence arose: the kind that succeeded. Since it is extremely difficult to compare in all their complexities superficially similar events at different junctures of history, it is not rewarding to ask why the peasants in the Germany of 1524 were defeated and those of France in August 1789 victorious. Mob violence now apparently paid off for the peasants as well as the city workers. But we will be wrong if we exaggerate the importance of the terror of crowds. Even though time and again during the nineteenth and twentieth centuries the agitation of the masses was to influence events, there is no reason to overlook the many occasions when it was suppressed.

The masses undeniably do play a part as agencies of violence, but their effect is obscured by the emotional atmosphere that surrounds them. It is perhaps more instructive to consider the changes in the structure of society in more exact terms. What is to count, and to count more and more, is the arrangement and management of industrial society by numbers. The organization of numbers explains the success of unionization, of the rise of popular parties and coalition blocks, of vote-getting techniques, of bulk, of advertising, of mass media, of the cult of statistics and that of record-breaking. The proletarian order, by the very nature of its success, is founded on the philosophy of quantity.

The quantitative nature of the modern mind is demonstrated by the new methods of the technological world order. That characteristic principle of our days, built-in

obsolescence, is not a sinister conspiracy of greedy corporations but the logical conclusion of an arithmetic of
mass production. Under the auspices of the machine,
man's life is inevitably controlled and guided by numbers. The machine represents quantity. Since it knows
neither option nor exception, it is outside the jurisdiction
of quality. It can only adjust to greater or smaller numbers. The good etchers print their plates manually to
allow for the accidental, the casual, and the exception
which lie in the realm of quality. The others merely
produce bulk, stereotypes.

The machine is the patron of the mass mind. Inasmuch
as it stands for numbers, it represents violence. For how
else can one evaluate the nature of violence save by
recognizing it as an action to achieve goals through bulk,
when the instruments of choice, selection, and freedom
have failed? This type of action may at times be necessary, and even beneficial. The merits of violence cannot
be discussed in general terms. But to understand the
meaning of wars, for instance, one must consider them as
the terror of numbers. Whereas in classical times, however, the employment of force, because it is the exploitation of quantity, was assessed as abnormal, brutal, or despotic, in modern times the violence of numbers is elevated to legitimacy in the controlled efficiency of the
technological system.

The masses not only benefit from technology, in a
sense they also initiated it—the latter obviously not by
conscious, deliberate design, but rather under the pressure of mass needs and popular satisfaction. The new
nineteenth-century printing methods could not have been
successful without the need for a popular press, while
Ford's assembly line could not have been established
without the need for mass mobility. The regime of quantitative preferences under which we are living has made
force attractive and the abnormal comfortable. Under
these circumstances, it is not surprising that in the nineteenth century some intellectuals, who may well be considered the last of the old tradition of humanist scholars,

regarded the sovereignty of science with alarm. Kierkegaard in his *Journals* cried out: "In the end all corruption
will come from the natural sciences." With our greater
experience of technocratic conditions and our greater adjustment to their conforming tendency, we may disagree
with such statements. The point here is merely that with
the triumphant spread of mechanization the individual
feels his world and the values of quality for which he
stands beleaguered by the tide of quantities.

How does the individual react to this? In the first
place, he can withdraw into seclusion, ignore the social
turbulence around him, and concentrate serenely on his
work. The nineteenth century was the age of the ivory
tower. Many of the most brilliant of its representatives,
unable to face the transition to a mass society, chose a
hermit's existence or kept themselves at a cool distance
from the social events. Goethe, Kierkegaard, Nietzsche,
Burckhardt, Wordsworth, Thoreau, and Emerson in one
way or another separated themselves from the crowd. To
us, in our frantic stress on commitment, this seems almost
a betrayal of life itself. For the nineteenth-century individualist, however, the hermitage was the last bastion of
civilized life against the flood tide of the masses. Gustave
Flaubert in a letter of April 24, 1852, asserted that since
mankind had rejected the individual, he must live for his
vocation and huddle with his dreams in an ivory tower.
This seclusion in the twentieth century is no longer possible. The ivory tower is razed.

In the second place, the individualist can respond with
a particular violence all his own. Frustrated and alarmed
by the coercion of the multitude, the modern nonconformist mind fosters the peculiar attitude of negation. It
is an intellectual type of nonaction, although often
enough producing a defeatist social sabotage. Originally,
however, the concept of negation was by no means destructive. It emerged in the Romanticist mind as part and
parcel of the idea of polarity, in which a mutual negation
stimulates the energy of the extremes, and from which, it
was hoped, a third transcending power would arise. We

are clearly in the age of dialectics, a logical kind of reasoning indeed, developing alongside the Romanticist esthetics.

For many a Romantic writer, however, the mutuality between opposite poles was soon forgotten. Originally only a means, intended as a technical device, negation soon became an end in itself. Negation, then, from creative stimulus turned into the intellectual nihilism that was to play one of the commanding roles on the contemporary cultural stage. It began playfully enough with the notion of a lightfooted irony, cultivated especially by the German Romanticists. Appearing under the name of the *Sataniske*, it gave a glimpse of the cult of the devil, culminating in Goethe's *Faust*. But Mephistopheles' "ever denying mind" was perfectly balanced, and eventually in this work the destructive spirit loses out. The misgivings which such men as Goethe and Hegel have about the Romantic negation were rooted in the fear that it undermined the mutuality of dialectics, and thus the cohesion of totality. Unfortunately, they generalized and took the aberration for typical. It is true, nonetheless, that it was within the Romantic movement that the idea of the destructive first became a factor in cultural history.

Kierkegaard, in his dissertation on the notion of irony, again with some one-sidedness, pointed to the nihilistic aspects of Romantic irony. He approached the problem from the Hegelian angle but appealed above all to the Socratic sense of irony. Thus he found fault with the ironic techniques of Ludwig Tieck and Friedrich Schlegel because they seemed to him to violate reality with extreme subjectivism. In the appropriate place we shall develop this further and trace destructivism as a technique of modern art and literature to its historic origins. Here it may be sufficient to stress that the irony of the absurd, by many claimed as a mark of twentieth-century expression, was in fact initiated by the inordinate projection of subjectivity in the works of some of the Romanticists.

As a final remark on the decisive effects of the three

revolutions, it seems judicious to conclude that the new brand of violence which they released should not, as has been done, be blamed on the masses as such. We all, as modern men, belong to the multitude and we share its power. But we belong no less to the dismayed breed of nonconformists confronted with the erosion of man's individual autonomy. The inherent energy of terror propelling the course of our culture was not indeed brought about by the rising masses, but by the polarization of man and multitude, that is, that element of cultural estrangement concomitantly appearing with the political, economic, industrial, educational, religious, artistic, and literary revolts that mark the onset of the modern era.

*Two souls, alas, reside within my breast
And seek to separate one from the other.*

Goethe

3

The Violent Way of Living

The self-contradicting century

Viewed as a whole, contemporary culture seems to be fed
by the dynamic forces that were unleashed and became
dominant in the eighteenth-century revolutions. On this
conviction is based the treatment of the various fields discussed in this work. It is, more specifically, through the
separation of individual and multitude in the consciousness of modern man that the peculiar characteristics of
our expressions in the arts, literature, and thought will be
explained. But before we take up this task, we ought to
have a clear conception of the relationship between the

outlines of the general historical development and the cultural aspects of the nineteenth and twentieth centuries. The two, of course, do belong together (even if one does not always see how), and knowledge of one supports that of the other.

The era of revolutions, whatever else it brought about, forced to full realization, as we have noted, the split of two cultural principles, that of the few and that of the many. The role of this split consciousness was to be reflected in the formation of the "two cultures," about which so much has been said recently. It is also manifested in the remarkable fact of the nineteenth century being one of self-contradicting tendencies. In analyzing these, we should constantly bear in mind that the contemporary historical and cultural events were directed by the issues of the political, industrial, and artistic revolutions of the eighteenth century. It would be more elucidative to say that the three revolutions were continuous, though in distinct waves of intensity, throughout the last two centuries. The political revolutions did not stop with Napoleon's dashing entrance on the stage or with the Congress of Vienna. The question of equality, as the Babouvists predicted, was to be raised again, and the problem of accumulation and distribution of property arose with equal frequency. The dates 1830, 1848, 1871, 1905, and 1917 represent only a few eruptions of a large volcanic field.

Similarly, the Industrial Revolution was not a unique event, but fundamentally a series of breakthroughs, all indicating the same pressure of material expansion. Some historians speak of a second Industrial Revolution, allegedly occurring in the middle of the nineteenth century when new economic arrangements were prompted, for instance, by the Bessemer process of steel making, the invention of the dynamo, the internal combustion engine, and Liebig's agricultural chemistry. Such a classification, however, is confusing in that, by accentuating a period marked by intensive renewals, it obscures the fact of continuity.

Finally, it is highly inadequate to present the Romantic movement as petering out by about 1830. By that time the Romanticist style of painting was just beginning to develop. Romanticist music, excluding such preliminaries as can be found in Beethoven's subjectivism, did not come into its true characteristic own until the middle of the century. What is labeled as Victorian literature demonstrates many of the Romantic traits, especially the weaker ones, more pronouncedly than, say, Shelley's or Byron's verse. Nor is it extremely accurate to speak, as the Germans do, of late Romanticism, vaguely coinciding with the Victorians, since it suggests an end-phase.* The Romantic revolution never ended. Time and again, as we shall discuss further, the rebellion on behalf of free unlimited expression of the subjective experience against classical formalism reappears in different avant-garde programs.

Behind the Jekyll-and-Hyde appearance of the nineteenth century throbbed the internal necessity of pushing trends to reckless booms, building pressures to the brink of explosion, not only of a revolutionary nature, but forcing any experience to the breaking point. The psychological urge toward accumulation may perhaps explain in part why this century presented itself, outwardly at least, in the antinomies of extremes.

The period following the Congress of Vienna is traditionally, though rather superficially, labeled as reactionary. The justification for this is obvious. The regimes dividing the spoil after the Napoleonic catastrophe turned the calendar back by half a century and on the basis of "legitimacy" forced the restoration of superannuated systems of government. However, the fact that they were successful and maintained a peace that endured an unprecedented number of years indicates that their reactionary attitude was more complicated than the label admits. The Metternich mentality is representative of the search for order necessitated by the chaos ensuing from Napoleon's downfall. Metternich in fact was the vicar of

* The German equivalent *Nach-Romantik* is even more final.

that power system which, under the name of Holy Roman Empire, had been replaced by Napoleon's own surrogate, the Continental system.

For Metternich and the other engineers of the Vienna peace settlement—Castlereagh, Frederick William III, Alexander I, and Talleyrand—regarded the so-called Concert of Europe as a legitimate successor to the defunct Holy Roman Empire. Unrealistically, their sense of order led them to underestimate the vitality of the political revolutions they suppressed. Soon they were to learn how vigorously the counter currents of revolt were eroding the foundation of their establishment. The age was clearly one of a call for order. Equally clearly, it was an age of disorder. Few centuries have challenged conservative peace of mind so persistently and on such a wide scale. Street riots, machine breaking, student demonstrations, assassinations, and full-fledged revolts combined to give it a disposition of unrest, seemingly belying what has been said about the quest for order.

Linked with this inclination toward unrest was the deliberate advocacy of revolution as a tool for progress. Revolution, as planned violence, seems an almost natural fulfillment of the *Manifesto of the Equals,* except, of course, that it did not fulfill. The revolutionary thirst remains unsatisfied up to the present day. Utopias, however nobly conceived, cannot be established through terror. By polarizing the world unrealistically (and unhistorically) in two hostile camps of workers and bourgeois, the *Communist Manifesto* of 1848 proclaimed that the goal of total equality "can be attained only by the forcible overthrow of all existing social conditions." The following year, Richard Wagner published his essay on *Art and Revolution,* a political as well as an esthetic manifesto directed against the capitalist system and the Philistine, whom elsewhere he called "the most ruthless and craven product of our civilization." The passion of revolution was preached in an age that both Kierkegaard and Emerson accused of being without real passion. In *Statism and Anarchism,* published in 1873, the anarchist Bakunin cried out: "There can be no revolution without a sweeping and passionate destruction, a salutary and fruitful destruction."

A revolutionary century then? Undoubtedly. But also one preeminently standing for evolution. The Hegelian principle of struggle, not indeed by revolutionary leaps, but by evolutionary logic appeared to guide the contemporary mind, consciously and unconsciously. Darwin's age was, culturally speaking, Hegel's age. Although one does not have to agree with Nietzsche's remark that Darwin learned everything from Hegel, it is perfectly correct to view *Origin of Species* as the most vivid illustration, in biological terms, of Hegel's all-embracing philosophy. Evolution was not merely the basis of a theory. It was also behind a method of handling economic, political, and social problems, the style of negotiation and bargaining at which the Anglo-Americans especially excelled. The great gains during the last century in the social conditions of the developed Western nations were not products of revolution; they were obtained by the gradual dialectics of evolution.

The nineteenth century was unmistakably marked by a new excitation of democratic awareness. It was the time of emancipation. Negroes, Catholics, Jews, and other minority groups benefited by a new awakening of tolerance. Suffrage, through successive acts of legislation, was extended in most countries; women were gradually cast in more and more independent roles. This was a period of progress, the social and human progress that, beginning in the Renaissance, had been given a popular boost by the Enlightenment.

This very age, however, is no less noted for its loss of faith in progress. Besides the sophisticated ridicule with which men such as Kierkegaard, Burckhardt, and Nietzsche treated the doctrine of enlightened progress, there was visible a creeping doubt in the efficacy of the democratic process. The diverse personalities of Alexander Hamilton, Thoreau, Cooper, Whitman, or de Tocqueville, though filled with good-will toward new ways and opportunities, refused to close their eyes to what they considered imminent dangers. They were justified. On the heels of popular uprisings, the first modern despots followed. Napoleon Bonaparte, whether we like the thought or not, was the true product of the French Revolution. As the last, though obviously perverted, champion of its cause, when no one else could master the revolutionary chaos, he was ready to perform with dictatorial powers. Napoleon III, although with considerably less talent, adopted the emperor's cloak, but revolutionary experience had taught him to cater ostensibly to "the people." His Caesarism, though mitigated and eventually bungled, was no less real than that of his uncle.

Proceeding with the clash of trends, one could further consider the issue of nationalism. Some historians have made a cult of nationalism as a determinant of modern society. It has a long history, however, beginning with the rise of monarchies in the Middle Ages, and surging to new prominence with the commercial competition of the sixteenth and seventeenth centuries. Undeniably, though, the emotional potential of nationalism reached its threatening fullness with the new imperialism after 1870. It was also powerfully at work in the unifications of Germany and Italy. At its most strident pitch, it manifested itself in the jingoism that now became popular in all Western countries, not excluding the United States.

On the other hand, there is the equally convincing account of movements crossing the borderlines of nationality. Clearly they were less idealistic than the eighteenth-century cosmopolitanism, for instance, of Herder. On the whole they were practically inclined. The International Red Cross, established in 1864 at the first Geneva Conference, combined efficient organization with broad-based humanitarianism. Internationalism can also be religious or political. The former is found in the rise of ultramontanism, an effort carried on chiefly by German and French intellectuals to concentrate the Roman Catholic church more firmly under the regime of the Pope. The latter may be seen in the Organization of Workingmen, the Socialist International of 1864, 1889, and 1919. International cooperation, vaguely and ineffectually suggested at the Congress of Vienna under the rather suspicious name of Holy Alliance, acquired at least a glimmer of reality in 1899 at the first Hague Peace Conference.

Earlier we noted that the revolutionary era had brought about the separation of the individual and his environment, the conscious self and the collective—an estrangement to prevail throughout the next centuries, which constitutes one of the *leitmotifs* of this work. In this context, no more can be said about this type of polarization than that individual and collective each adopted their own champions. There were, as will be elaborated, various schools of art and literature that based their esthetics on hyper-individualization. There soon was a popular psychology boring into the depth of the ego, and there was, after 1841, the eventually influential philosophy of Existence, postulating the authenticity of the self. Counter to this ran the tide of collectivism promoted by the many socialist groupings, the humanitarian, scientific, revisionist, Christian, anarchist, syndicalist, and lately National Socialists, who, motley collection though they be, all aimed at rescuing Western civilization from the decadence of individualistic, elite domination.

Confusingly, both the manifestations of individualism and collectivism divided again along conflicting lines. Forceful and determined individualism there was, indeed, in the building of solitary refuges and the withdrawal into ivory towers. But on the opposite side, there was the no less typical nineteenth-century "rugged individualist" of the American frontier, the managerial despots typified by Carnegie, Mellon, and Rockefeller, and the cutthroat competitive spirit which has been called, not too felicitously, social-Darwinism. Similarly, collectivism split into antithetic movements. There was humanitarianism and there was ruthless utopianism. On the one hand we have the noble though sadly failing undertakings of Owen's New Harmony, Fourier's *phalanstères*, and George Ripley's Brook Farm, and on the other the autocratic violence of Marx's, Bukanin's, or Lenin's routes to the perfect society.

The paradoxical quality of the age should make us shrink from the generalities by which students so often have sought to capture the whole nineteenth century. Consider the problems of religion. On the surface it may seem an age of a secular, antireligious persuasion. It began with the Biblical criticism of Strauss, Feuerbach, and Renan as a radical extension of Hegel's *Philosophy of Religion,* which would have filled the master's mind with astonishment. It continued with Marx's materialist and Stirner's nihilist rejections of Christianity and culminated in Nietzsche's guilt-laden confession that we have killed God. Kierkegaard, the most religious of thinkers, launched his stunning attack on Christianity in 1854. Modern atheism, incipient as early as Hobbes and increasing through such eighteenth-century authors as La Mettrie and Holbach, soared to its greatest successes in the nineteenth century, finding organizational media for the spread of its gospel.

Yet when all is said, a legitimate case can also be made for the century as a religious era. It reveals a sensational expansion of Christianity throughout the world. The Roman Catholic church managed a resounding comeback, partly through the tolerant attitude of the Protestants, partly by her own realistic adjustment to a new social order. This was also the great age of the missions, including that known as the Inner Mission, operating in the deprived areas of the industrial cities. It was the great age of the Bible society and of evangelism, both in Europe and at the western frontier of the United States.

Parallel to the religious development ran that of the antinomy of materialism and spiritualism. Like the previous one, this trend indicated a shift from a human need for worship to the need for enjoyment. The early volumes of the English periodical *The Nineteenth Century,* a journal of public opinion first published in 1877, reflected this change in continuous contributions for or against such new trends as materialism, science, agnosti-

cism. One author, in the June issue of 1884, put it suc-
cinctly: "If human life is in the course of being fully described by science, I do not see what materials there are
for any religion. . . . We can get on very well without
one, for though the view of life which science is opening
to us gives us nothing to worship, it gives us an infinite
number of things to enjoy." Here is a quiet confession of
that materialism prepared by some of the writers of the
Enlightenment and in the nineteenth century powerfully
presented in Friedrich Büchner's famous *Force and Matter*.

Besides this type of enjoyment, however, there was in
the same period a strongly developing tendency toward
spiritualism. Apart from orthodox Christian revivalism,
there arose new sects devoted to the cause of spiritual
experience. In New York in 1875, Madame Blavatsky
founded the Theosophical Society. It urged the control
and purification of the soul and the discipline of annihi-
lating the intrusion of matter into the "astral body." In
the same year, Mary Baker Eddy's *Science and Health*
appeared, to serve as the handbook of Christian Science,
which could be considered as a late reincarnation, so to
speak, of neoplatonic doctrines. These and other testimonies of extra-physical powers were illustrated by similar anti-materialist techniques in art and literature. The
strangely ethereal beings in Maeterlinck's plays, or the
féerique tonal moods of Debussy's dances convey the
same vague yearnings for transcendence. In painting, a
connection may be detected in the evasive symbolist style
of the Pre-Raphaelite Burne-Jones and the Yellow Book
illustrator Aubrey Beardsley; in Switzerland it is represented by Böcklin and Hodler, and in Holland by the
monumentalist school of Konijnenburg and Toorop. In
the arts, however, a far more significant conflict of opposites would be met in the dual reign of Romanticism and
Realism.

Is the nineteenth century the unassailable epoch of optimism? Superficially it seems so. The unprecedented expansion of trade, building, transportation, and land ex-

ploitation, the entirely new appearance of the human environment owing to the Industrial Revolution fills the mind with awe and pride. The gradually growing participation of ordinary people in governmental and managerial procedures, as well as in the accumulation of property of all kinds, generated confidence and feelings of plenitude, width, and scope, accentuated further by the American experience of abundance. This confidence in the righteousness of man's self-developing progress lies at the roots of the optimistic temper which seemed to distinguish the age. From Adam Smith's *The Wealth of Nations* to Andrew Carnegie's *Gospel of Wealth* one can trace a faith, growing in self-assurance, in man as the maker of a more glorious future, a faith also demonstrated in such arrogantly ugly erections as the Eiffel Tower, the Crystal Palace, and the Sacré-Coeur.

A pressing question now arises: Why was the age, for all its patent, sometimes blatant, optimism, also the era of emerging pessimism? The answer must be sought in the fact that the optimism applied almost exclusively to scientific, commercial, and economic developments, whereas the pessimism was chiefly apparent in the works of poets, novelists, thinkers, and musicians. In other words, the conspicuous optimism of the nineteenth century was part of the materialist disposition of modern man, whereas his pessimism stemmed from his belief in the values of that "metaphysical consolation" which Schopenhauer ascribed to music. Although it would be impossible to prove, it may well be that nineteenth-century pessimism grew precisely from the awareness that the easy confidence of that very time found its source predominantly in material values.

This is not the place to elaborate on the details of nineteenth-century cultural pessimism. Its importance is sketched by the line of thought running from Schopenhauer, through Nietzsche and Eduard von Hartmann. For the first time in history, musicians became consistently melancholy. The idioms of pining and yearning pervaded thematic textures, from the tenderest poetic

Schumann to the most ostentatious Tchaikovsky. It was in this period also that for the first time the prophecy of the cultural decline and fall of Western civilization was heard. Hegel in his quiet, apodictic way, already declared that the arts were exhausted, that everything had been fully said (*ausgesagt*). From the middle of the century on, scholars from various countries worked out theories to support the inevitability of the end of classical culture. The German Karl Vollgraff, the Russian Danilevsky, the Frenchman Gustave Le Bon, the Englishmen Petrie and Toynbee, the Dutchman Huizinga, and the Americans Brooks Adams and Henry Adams, on the strength of biological and other principles, produced their apocalyptic speculations. With the tremendous impact of Spengler's *The Decline of the West,* a magistral though not always convincingly reasoned book, the idea of living in an end-phase of culture took a firm hold on the modern mind. Without having to agree with these forecasts, one must simply take note of them as expressions of cultural pessimism. As a historical trend, it arose as a countermovement to the confidence of the progressives. It confirmed once again how the age was locked and caught in a paradox of contrasting forces, a paradox typifying the century and not surprisingly becoming a new philosophical category in Kierkegaard's thought.

It remains remarkable that nineteenth-century society, for all its eruptions, kept itself comparatively balanced in otherwise such schizophrenic conditions. It was not until the closing decade that the general confidence began to totter. While Bismarck had epitomized the age in its confidence and balance, after his dismissal, the Wilhelmine period was truly symbolized by the shaky and immature emperor Wilhelm II. The true measure of Bismarck's virtuosity, though conspicuous enough in the conduct of the three short wars that led to Germany's unification, lies in the manner by which he kept the peace after 1871. Like Frederick the Great, and unlike Napoleon, Bismarck knew when to stop fighting. When he was gone, after 1890, the picture in Europe changed.

Political adventures, launched with more bluff than courage, betrayed weakness rather than wisdom. This loss of equilibrium was reflected in the decadent satire of Wilde and in Jarry's *Ubu* plays, as well as in the languid elegance of the curvilinear techniques of *Jugendstil* and *Art Nouveau*.

The same decade marked what has been called the watershed in American history. In the 1890's, the United States completed the transformation from a chiefly agricultural to an industrial society, and with this the country seemed to outgrow its original, not altogether unattractive, limiting provincialism. With the westward expansion reaching fulfillment, there seemed to come the time of reflection and stock-taking. This resulted in a self-conscious hesitancy, replacing the untrammeled determination that had shaped the course of events up to that time. The American began to think about himself, especially about himself and his relationship to the European homeland, a contemplation superbly analyzed in many of Henry James' novels, from *The American* (1877) to *The Ambassadors* (1903). It was at this point that American isolationism became a theme, not in the sense of a determined rejection of political involvement, but in the consciousness that the American experience in the broadest meaning, though unmistakably unique, was yet undetachable from European history. The growing awareness of this cultural unity was frustrating for those who had been led to believe in the absolute autonomy of the United States. It expressed itself either in an unjustified resentment against Europe, or in the equally unjustified flight of the expatriate in that decade.

The violent century

Turning to our own age, we find that the message of violence preached in the previous century now becomes actualized. The periods that obviously divide the twentieth century in distinct phases are manifestations of terror: wars, revolutions, totalitarian brutality. The history of the nineteenth century can be divided in various ways, but somehow one always seems to come up with the milestones marking peace, unification, prosperity, emancipation, and, in England, legislative bills providing enlarged suffrage. The present century shows the unquestionable extension of democratic progress; it is, after all, the era of the New Freedom, of new deals and fair deals. In most Western countries, frustrated minorities are tolerantly being incorporated into the national unity. Yet what stands out is the dread produced by the Russian Revolution, the Great Depression, the two World Wars, and the despotism of Stalin and Hitler. With this behind us, it is small wonder that the modern mind is neurotically occupied with a possible third global war, a projected conflagration exceeding all the horrors of recent history. Unwarranted and weak in faith as this attitude may seem, we must resign ourselves to the fact that the age of anxiety, as anticipated by Kierkegaard, has come to fruition as inexorably as the violence endorsed by the thinking of Babeuf, Marx, Sorel, Bakunin, and Nietzsche.

The year 1905 marked a crucial juncture, in which occurrences of a diverse nature jointly and individually revealed something of the loss of balance and the loss of faith in the general disposition at that time. The clash between Russia and Japan, with the humiliating defeat of the former, could be considered a minor war if it had not been for the significant events it entailed, and its distinction of producing the first decisive victory of a non-Western over a European power. It signaled the beginning of the global spread of power away from the European scene, a development soon to be underscored by the deployment of American might in the coming wars.

An immediate result of the Russian debacle was the reorientation of her foreign affairs toward the European theater in order to recover some of her lost prestige. This shift, so clearly prompted by weakness, naturally invited further catastophe when, in the end, it contributed to the outbreak of the First World War. The basic fragility of the Czarist order was tested in the revolution of that year, "the first breach in the absolutist system," as Trotsky called it. It must be understood, however, that the petition of the workers, which set off the explosion of Red Sunday, January 22, was a rather reasonable request for basic rights, such as individual liberty, freedom of press, speech, and meeting, universal compulsory education, and eight-hour workdays. Yet the revolution of 1905 preluded the more radical fury to come twelve years later.

The incidents of 1905 were flashing warning signals, which few attempted to read. Understandably, contemporaries, without the perspective of hindsight, could see little meaning in the disconnected events springing up around their daily rut. Nevertheless, it remains puzzling that the ominous cracks appearing in the Western cohesion at this time caused so little worry. Beginning with the first Morocco crisis of 1905, a series of diplomatic breakdowns occurred, which, through minor Balkan wars, led straight to the World War. The bluff and mutual distrust accompanying these crises betrayed the general instability of the minds that created them. The blame for this fell on the particular statesmen and diplomats involved. They represented, however, a society which as a whole gradually seemed to lose its bearings.

The restlessness and instability of this world were vividly illustrated by the successive avant-garde art forms which now began to demand attention. Expressionism was officially founded in 1905 with the exhibition of the *Brücke* group in Dresden. Significantly, in this age when musical tonality, perspective, dramatic plot, and other technical securities fell away, man's conception of the universe also lost the classical certainties of the categories of space and time. Space and time had fixed man comfortably and almost serenely in Newton's cosmic arrangement. The special theory of relativity, launched by Einstein in 1905, was a difficult and complex explanation of the physical structure of the universe, only to be set forth in the tokens of a specialized code. But the technicalities do not concern us here. The implications of the theory have had their impact on the modern mind, which found itself deprived of its time-honored physical securities and left with the mathematical abstraction of a fourth dimension.

The causes and the course of events which shaped the two world wars are too well known to have to be related in this context. What distinguished them from previous wars was their global impact. Never before had wars had such psychological effects on men, regardless of their proximity to the battlefields, as these disasters. This is particularly true of the First World War. There are probably many reasons to account for this. The chief reason, however, may well lie in the shrinking of the world due to faster communications. The news from the fronts was spread so rapidly by the improved technique of reporters and the mass circulation of newspapers that the horrors, photographed unashamedly, could be distributed to a vast public in raw immediacy. World War I was the first major disaster in which man, regardless of national or personal involvement, experienced destruction collectively. It was this that made it and its successor truly global and total wars.

In addition, their destructive character was amplified in the mind by the technological nature of modern warfare. This, extended to the emerging gigantic war industry, changed the concept of the martial from a heroic exploit in which man could express himself personally with his whole, be it bestial or intelligent, being to a mechanized organization of lethal fire in which more and more the decisive actions of victory were relegated to hardware. Modern warfare thus became massified. Classical military skill was based on the principle of man against man, spear against spear, blunderbuss against blunderbuss. In contrast, our scientific weaponry is designed for mass destruction. Planes, tanks, automatic rifles, bombs of varying sophistication, all aim at maximum killing with minimum personal involvement. This alienated form of the concept of "fight" is emphasized by the advanced technique of killing by remote control. The next total war may well be conducted by generals playing on the push buttons of a grand computerized destruction organ.

Whatever else the world wars represent, for the collective consciousness they signify the terror of bulk, quantity, machines, hardware—in short, all that is extraneous to the human experience. The literature that issued from these nightmares trembles with the helpless protest against the industrial organizers of massive wars. Poets and novelists, though always sensitive to human suffering, had never condemned warfare in either general or specific terms. Now, for the first time, they filled their volumes with descriptions and presentations of the military as a peril to humanity.

The two world wars are irrevocably linked to the rise of totalitarian regimes. Their political meaning and repercussions belong in another chapter. In this introductory survey, it suffices to note that their effect was devastating for the arts and other cultural forms, and that in spite of the disappearance of Mussolini, Hitler, and Stalin the impact of totalitarianism is by no means undone. Inasmuch as totalitarian rule thrives on the energy of the masses, it can teach us, though not as yet with conclusive evidence, something about the violence of numbers and its relationship to culture. We must then ask what we can learn from those elements of terror in our world which linger on despite the abandoning of ultra-totalitarian systems.

The years following the Second World War may be characterized by the prevalence of stalemate, exemplified by the division of the competing forces of "East and West." In the latter, the historical stagnancy is painfully demonstrated by the unproductive Eisenhower and Kennedy administrations. Culturally, one recognizes a similar era of deadlock which, while never lacking in bustling vitality, has not yet produced anything really new—anything that cannot be understood as an emulation of the avant-garde of the 1920's and 1930's. Within and outside the arts man is worried and undecided about the dead-lock of conformity and nonconformity. He is fearful of the process of leveling, which is sponsored under the ascendance of the collective. He condemns it in Hitler's ruthless *Gleichschaltung*, yet he allows it to spread grad-ually in the standardizing of his own suburban dwellings, of his own stereotyped education, of his own taste, man-ners, artistic preferences.

Modern man protests against conformity, which seems to make him an interchangeable part of a streamlined mechanism. He is, however, unable to resist the lifelong career of "fitting-in," which, from his earliest training to his retirement, determines the measure of his success. He is rightfully appalled by the technocratic and bureau-cratic organization of human beings, which the totali-tarian regimes impose for the glory of the state. But he is not unhappily engaged in large-scale public organization of what in other times had been intimate and private experiences. The notion of "goodness" plays a fundamen-tal part in his social awareness. But whereas the gospel of Matthew hands down to the Christians the warning "when thou doest alms, let not thy left hand know what thy right hand doeth," today's Christian society has transmuted the privacy of charity into mass giving con-trolled by institutions operating with the efficiency and organization of large business corporations. Man's love is organized in marches, sit-ins, teach-ins, public fasts on the campus. Whereas the good Samaritan was the epitome of compassion because he recognized suffering when he happened to see it, modern man organizes groups on weekends to travel hundreds of miles to do good in a pre-selected area.

These aspects, though they ought to make us sincerely apprehensive, are not necessarily fatal symptoms. The process of standardization admittedly seems an unrelent-ing infringement on human dignity, but in this crowded world it has obvious practical advantages, without which modern living might be well-nigh impossible. The sys-tem of fitting man into bureaucratic slots naturally raises the specter of a robot existence, but the emergence of the average team man has undeniably solidified the workings of the corporate and managerial structure that holds our economy together. And, although it is easy to have and to proliferate doubts about the leviathan of organized charity, it would be shortsighted to overlook the benefits that, through its apparatus, have fallen on needy individuals and institutions.

Such a generous appraisal, however, can definitely not be extended to one phenomenon of modern life, which, though rarely questioned, constitutes a conspicuous aspect of mass society. There is no case to be made for the rise of mass hysteria save a negative one. Hysteria as a personal form of behavior is baffling enough to define and analyze with anything resembling clinical correctness. Collective hysteria is even more difficult to fathom. But we can clearly recognize the alarming symptoms. One may only vaguely guess at such possible causes as failure, defeat, incompetence, or impotence, but the acts of uncontrolled and violent behavior are unmistakable. Hysteria shows itself in reactions of intensity out of all proportion to the immediately relevant cause. It comes from an inflated mental condition.

The cheap psychology of Hitler's *Mein Kampf* is hardly a contribution to our knowledge, but it does provide us with a key to our understanding of his success in whipping up crowds into frenzy. He candidly banked on the assumption that the great revolutions of history were not realized by scientific knowledge of the masses, but rather by "fanaticism and often by an ondriving hysteria." It would be soothing, indeed, if we could believe that mass hysteria is simply a product of totalitarianism. Unfortunately, the same symptoms appear in our own allegedly democratic world. They appear, for instance, in any newspaper on any given day. Fifty years ago, the daily news was still offered with full respect for the reason and the discriminating power of the reading public. If the great event occured, headlines naturally stressed and accompanied it. Today the great event is *made*, daily, hourly, by inflating the emotional reverberations of a selected incident out of all proportion to reality. Sensation, as substitute for understanding, is the true measure of hysteria. It appears in the shapes and gestures of distortion and disproportion. One can hear it in the frantic go-go techniques of the disc-jockeys, in the aggressiveness of the commercials, and see it in the savagery that goes under the name of football or boxing.

With the demise of the hero, man has turned to the cult of the idol. They have worship in common, but idolization is marked by the replacement of an image for the real thing. The great performers of the classical epoch, political, religious, artistic, or otherwise, have rarely been met with crowd hysteria. Without underestimating the talents of Rudolph Valentino, in the gallery of outstanding stars—Roscius, Burbage, Garrick, Iffland, Devrient, Talma, Bernhardt, Duse—he is a negligible figure. Yet it is he who was distinguished in death by the sensational spectacle of weeping women swooning before his bier. None of the phenomenal singers such as Jenny Lind, Melba, Chaliapin, Caruso, or Ruffo ever received even a shadow of the adulation that has been piled on our own Elvis Presley. And without decrying the charm of the minstreling Beatles, we can only state that in the history of performing music the ovations earned by such masters as Joachim, Nikisch, Toscanini, or Paderewski are tepid compared with the maniacal fury that surrounds the rock 'n' roll idols. Mass hysteria preys on the weak, on the nonhero. In the history of the United States, the attractive and well-meaning John Kennedy will probably not be remembered for the achievements one connects with great Presidents. It is precisely his nonachievement that has possibly caused the sentimentality about his death, a sentimentality aggravated when the image worshipping becomes a prey for the sensational exploitation by the book and newspaper trade.

Little can be gained, however, by condemning mass hysteria without attempting to understand it. It is the product of the insecure mind, knocked out of balance by the traumatic shocks of world wars, depressions, totalitarian cruelties, and nursed in an environment of fleeting joys without the framework of central principles. Mass hysteria is the only negative aspect of the contemporary world that cannot turn itself into a positive asset of mass society. Condemning this cultural menace will not mitigate its effects, but for our own education we must register it thoughtfully.

Part
TWO

The public, collectively considered, is a good and generous master.

Oliver Goldsmith

The artist merely clarifies and fulfills the will of the people.

Franz Marc

4

The Ornamental Way of Living

Social, socialist, satirical

The fact that during the nineteenth century the common man more than ever before became the subject matter of painting does not in itself necessarily indicate a major change in cultural expression. Although quantity may well be decisive at times, questions about the quality of a particular change clearly must first be investigated. Displaying the life and daily concerns of simple workers on canvas, for instance, may be motivated by an esthetic pleasure in the artist's mind, totally lacking that necessary feeling of identification which suggests the possible proletarian nature of art. The interest of Valázquez in dwarfs and buffoons, and of Rembrandt in the heads of Negroes must, in all likelihood, be explained as merely pictorial curiosity.

Yet it is difficult to draw exact borderlines between artistic curiosity and social concern. It is significant that with the establishment of the early bourgeois society in the seventeenth-century Netherlands, the first signs of popular realism in art also appeared. The happy characters of Frans Hals, the tavern scenes of Brouwer and Adriaen van Ostade, or the domestic slice-of-life pictures by Jan Steen obviously did not emerge unrelated to the social changes of the time. No one, however, would evaluate these works as anything but the products of an elitist understanding of art. A more immediate social identification with the masses is not found until the nineteenth century, and even then the picture was by no means unequivocal. Millet, concentrating consistently on the simple occupations of rural workers, received from hostile critics the epithet "socialist"—around 1860 still a very dirty word, and one from which Millet found it necessary to cleanse himself. But can one really say that the clean lines and mild colors of his peasant scenes represent the essential rural proletariat? Or do they rather convey a "back to nature" movement with the almost inevitable by-product of idealized primitive life?

Most likely one is faced here with the self-conflicting quality which marks the entire history of the nineteenth century. Gustave Courbet is traditionally, with a great deal of justification, seen as a revolutionary figure. He is depicted as fighting on the side of socialism, and it is believed that he helped to tumble the column in the Place Vendôme from its pedestal during the days of the Commune. His picture *The Stone-Breakers* has been called a socialist manifesto, and he himself explained that it was inspired by the dismal lot of some workers he had observed. A revolutionary mind clearly lay behind those works of Courbet which caused such shocks at the Salons of 1849 and 1853. But was it one in real sympathy with the struggle of the collective? Should one not, from the evidence of Courbet's style and method, rather conclude that his was a hyperpersonalized temper, ardently asserting the supreme prerogatives of the individual over the masses?

When, in 1861, Courbet was approached by art students who wanted to take instruction from him, he made it abundantly clear where he stood. In an open letter of reply, he told them: "I deny that art can be taught, or in other words, I believe that art is completely individual, and that the talent of each artist is but the result of his own inspiration." The statement was typical of nineteenth-century culture, in that it revealed the "rugged individual," but the other characteristic aspect of the age, the commitment to society as a collective, was ignored and denied by Courbet's proclamation. This ambivalent attitude is, in reverse sense, however, also evident in the case of Dostoevski. His work, with the prevailing theme of compassion for human suffering, was in a vague, yet incontestable way "social." As such, it was accepted and admired by Van Gogh as well as Tolstoy. But Dostoevski's political view was plainly conservative. Whereas Courbet was actively on the side of the Commune, Dostoevski, in a letter to Strachow of May 18, 1871, regarded the events of that year with abhorrence. He declared himself against socialism and against those who saw in this "fury" beauty instead of monstrosity.

The ambiguity of the commitment to the social collective is again revealed when one considers the Victorian brand of socialism, which, though not without its own sincere convictions, dealt with the social problem in a rather infuriatingly condescending manner. John Ruskin's preoccupation with art throughout his life did not represent an interest in pure esthetics, but an attempt to identify art with morality. Carlyle called Ruskin's *Stones of Venice* a "sermon in stones," and his *Seven Lamps of*

Architecture offered such chapters as "The Lamp of Obedience" or "The Lamp of Sacrifice." In a lecture on *Art and Morals*, delivered at Oxford in 1870, Ruskin declared to his students that "the fact of either literature or painting being truly fine of their kind, whatever their mistaken aim or partial error, is proof of their noble origin."

For the Victorian such as Ruskin, socialism consisted in elevating the underprivileged masses to the level of his own exalted culture. Thus, in *The Political Economy of Art*, he advised the collecting of pictures "as a means of refining the habits and touching the hearts of the masses of the nation in their domestic life." His reaction to the Commune of 1871 was a series of monthly letters to "the workers and the labourers of Great Britain." Instead of publishing them under a title with an immediate appeal to the common man, he came up with the learned *Fors clavigera*, a name giving him the opportunity of devoting long pages to patronizing etymological explanations.

A similar course, aimed at steering between the brutalities of anarchism and communism, on the one hand, and the forces of bourgeois noninterference on the other, was charted by the remarkable British painter Ford Madox Brown. Looking at his major painting *Work*, one is intrigued by a group of workers and navvy excavators elegantly arranged in a neat composition, rendered in the clean, precise lines of the Pre-Raphaelite style. One is also struck by two well-dressed gentlemen on the right, whom one may presume from their appearance to be the archetypal industrialists of the time, watching their enslaved workers. Fortunately the artist has left us an explanation of his intentions, which serves to correct our judgment. Thus we are instructed that the figures are Thomas Carlyle, the celebrated writer who had just launched a protest against the social system in England, and the Rev. F. D. Maurice, the early leader of Christian Socialism for whose Workingmen's College (also appearing in the picture) Brown gave popular art classes. There is nothing in *Work*, despite its subject, that can qualify it as a product of mass-culture. It originated in a feeling of sympathy, perhaps empathy, but in no sense from that need of total identification, which, though not representing the whole phenomenon of proletarian art, is at least its minimal prerequisite.

The split-consciousness, or self-consciousness, about collectivist art easily creates utopian vistas such as one meets in the writings of William Morris. In one pamphlet after the other published for the Socialist League, Morris staged his quixotic crusades against the Machine, without ever considering whether machine and collective might not form a necessary mutual symbiosis, whereby each gains momentum from the other in their historical rise to power. Instead, he fostered his self-proclaimed "optimistic socialism" to promise the masses a new, proletarian art. According to his brochure of 1887, *The Aims of Art,* this ought to develop as follows: The state of the Middle Ages with its love of craftsmanship and personal labor cannot, of course, be restored. The rule of machinery, being firmly established, must be obeyed. But its very nature, its labor-saving quality, will have a self-destroying effect. For the more labor saved, the more leisure acquired, and this process will ultimately reach the point where the workman will learn to rediscover personal labor. Then he will know again "that the true secret of happiness lies in the taking of genuine interest in all the details of daily life," and in elevating these by art rather than by the "unregarded drudges," the machines.

Throughout the nineteenth century there was a widespread feeling that an old superannuated art must be replaced by a new one representing "the people." The people, naturally, was a vague concept, and hence the theories basing a future art on it were invariably of a woolly nature. Horatio Greenough may not have been the most astonishingly great sculptor, but his ideas about a new popular art were significant in that they represented the American viewpoint. In the United States, no less than elsewhere, the mood was ripe for a "new" culture, divested of the classical formulas and techniques. Greenough, in his 1852 lectures on art, fulminated against the stagnant academies just as vigorously as his fellow Romanticists in Europe. He was also against those who believed that American institutions were not favorable to the development of the arts. On the contrary, he asserted, these institutions were far more beneficial than the "hotbed" culture to be found elsewhere. "The monuments, the pictures, the statues of the republic will represent what the people love and wish for."

Greenough, though he had lived and studied in Europe, made the mistake of following the national isolationism, thereby overlooking the fact that the same search for popular art forms was going on even more intensively in Europe. His statement is nonetheless instructive, because it came from the American continent where the individualistic frontier temper could never come to terms with the demands of the collective. One finds this conflict most acutely expressed in Whitman's *Democratic Vistas*, where the hopes for a democratic culture clash with the doubts about American conformist inclinations. The gains for the collective were merely of a materialist nature. "I say that our New World democracy, however great a success in uplifting the masses out of their sloughs . . . is, so far, an almost complete failure in its social aspects, and in really grand religious, moral, literary, and esthetic results." Whitman, looking forward to a unique, popular American culture, set his hopes entirely on the "soul," the self—precisely the archenemy of the collective. Whitman's was a true American dilemma, in that, while striving for a popular mass culture, he could not sacrifice the old elitist idea of individualism as the chief source of creativity.

The two nineteenth-century figures who came nearest to a possible identification with the masses were, of course, Tolstoy and Vincent van Gogh. Tolstoy in his *What Is Art?* tried to redefine art along the religious and social lines of his thinking late in life. Art to him, according to the uncensored edition of 1898, was not the manifestation of a mysterious idea of beauty, not the expression of man's emotions by external signs, nor the production of pleasing objects. Art "is a means of union among men, joining them together in the same feelings, and indispensable for the life and progress toward well-being of individuals and of humanity." Deploring the decline in the art of his day, he accused the upper classes of having made it inaccessible to the masses. Art in the future, Tolstoy believed, would convey only universal feelings. "Only those productions will be considered art which transmit feelings drawing men together in brotherly union."

Here was a clear program of proletarian esthetics. The very intimate and private feelings put into esoteric language by the symbolists Valéry, Mallarmé, and Verhaeren made for a perverted literature. A healthy work of art, in contrast, "will have to satisfy the demands not of a few people living in identical and often unnatural conditions, but it will have to satisfy the demands of all those great masses of people who are situated in the natural condition of laborious life." If one asks what are the universal feelings that can satisfy the popular demands, Tolstoy answers that in our time the really "fresh feelings" can only be religious, that is, Christian emotions, a conception that separated him categorically from the large socialist movement, which in that period had its own artistic claims.

It is significant that Tolstoy, when pointing to the examples of what he meant by an art for the people, mentioned the names of such literary figures as Dickens, Hugo, Dostoevski, and the painters Millet, Jules Breton, and Lhermitte. Significant, because these are precisely the names of those whom van Gogh, at various times in his letters, singled out as his favorite artists. He could not possibly have known Tolstoy's essay, nor was Tolstoy familiar with van Gogh's work. Thus we must assume a deeply seated common ideal binding the two together. They, moreover, resembled each other in the experience of defying their social environment to live "among the people," and in the quality of their missionary zeal which equated social with religious commitments.

Van Gogh's deepest involvement in what may be conceived of as a true mass-experience of life occurred during his earlier period. To be sure, the pictures from the south of France, with their childlike arrangement of colors, are more "attractive" for broad popular consumption. But to get a glimpse of the real fusion of the artist's mind and the common man's perception, which after all should be the basis of a possible proletarian art, one must study the life and work of the van Gogh of North Brabant and Drente. Especially illuminating is a letter he wrote to his brother on April 31, 1885, concerning the *Potato-Eaters*. Explaining the problem of depicting the essentials of rural workers, he wrote: "The painting of peasants' life is something serious . . . you must paint peasants as if you were one of them yourself, as if you felt and thought as they themselves do."

The secret of van Gogh's immediacy lies in the equation of love and work. This is probably true, too, of John Ruskin. Both he and van Gogh had the tough puritanical reverence for labor; but whereas the former merely taught, the latter practiced it also. The two words occurring most frequently in van Gogh's letters are work and duty. "Duty is absolute" to him. This was not a rigid regime alone, but a total life experience. It was on this basis that work could be done as an act of love. Nowhere can one find a better statement of his artistic (and religious) credo than in the letter of November 21, 1881, to his friend van Rappard. "Which doctrine do I proclaim? Let us surrender our soul in our affairs and let us work with the heart, and love that which we love." This Tolstoy could have said with equal conviction. But there is one essential difference between the two that makes one understand why van Gogh came closer to achieving his aim than did Tolstoy. The latter never faltered in his paternalistic sympathy with the world of the common man, but the former shared it indeed with the openmindedness of a child.

The awkward appearance of van Gogh's technique may mistakenly lead to the conclusion that he was an industrious, though extraordinarily gifted, dilettante. The contrary is true. His temper was purely artistic, to such an unlimited extent that it even stunted his technical development. For all his perplexing and often sophisticated insights, he never lost the naïvely creative rudiments of childhood. He simply cultivated a part of the primitive child's vision, probably unwittingly, but nevertheless in straight countermovement to his intellectual development. It was also perfectly obvious in many of his letters. He could be the most brilliant and urbane correspondent in his letters to van Rappard; his wit then was fast, his psychology adult, and expressed in superb phrases switching from Dutch to English to French. Yet in many of his letters to Theo he appeared just as natural in a rather chatty, disconnected reporting of his daily life. His language here is seemingly that of the uneducated, with deficient vocabulary in often incomplete and shaky sentences (difficult to render in a translation), but essentially that of a child whose thoughts and utterances ramble along.

It was van Gogh's childlike vision that we have recorded in the sowers, the diggers, the cornfields, the flowering almond trees, or the shabby interiors. It was this childlike vision that joined the artist to the proletarian world and made him, and makes us, participate in it. It was this childlike vision, finally, which redeemed van Gogh's inordinate and blind individualism, an individualism fundamentally isolating him from the masses whom he still sought to represent. For, no more than Courbet, had he the faintest understanding of collective life and collective participation. The single theme of his biography is fear of the group. He could not perform in the context of an art class, or in the missionary community at the Borinage. He drove his friends from his daily existence, even those few who, like van Rappard and Gaugin, were sympathetic toward his mind and work. Thus, for all its popular themes and attractions, van Gogh's oeuvre is curiously impregnated with the self-indulgence in forms and colors of autonomous beauty that results from the pleasures of art for art's sake.

In the twentieth century, the childlike vision was never again to be so pure and guileless. But it reappears no less disarmingly in the unabashed use of prime colors of some of the expressionists and non-representative painters, in the happy fantasies of Joan Miró, in the juxtaposed mannikins of Jean Dubuffet, in the playful dream fragments of Paul Klee, or in Morgenstern's nonsense poems, without, however, seeming to contribute conspicuously to an art of the masses. On the whole, the artist of this century appears to be less deliberately concerned with the creating of an authentic proletarian style. There have been more professedly socialist and communist writers and artists than in the previous century, but there are few who attempt to square their work intentionally with their political convictions. If Picasso's paintings can be called representative of the proletarian era, it is not because they show a sympathetic concern for the masses. Communist poets, such as the Frenchman Aragon or the Chilean Pablo Neruda, put highly personal experiences into sophisticated poetical idioms.

There are, however, exceptions. The political battle for the masses was expressed in partisan poems by Mayakovsky, endorsing Stalin's Five Year Plan, or in some of the verses by futurist Italian poets. More effectively, there was a strong satirical movement, which, combining social critique with artistic presentation, had its own traditional justification. In modern times, it may be traced back to the epic art of Hogarth, Goya's etchings on the horrors of war, and the *Charivari* cartoons by Daumier. In this century, when able to avoid the sentimentality and rhetoric of, say, Käthe Kollwitz, it castigated the ills of society in the journalistic wit of Georg Grosz and the mordant cut of Frans Masereel's prints, or reflected them more dispassionately in the pictures by Kirchner and Beckmann. The expressionist satire came to full strength in the German cabaret climate during the Weimar Republic and in the related political lyrics, such as those by Brecht, Kästner, and others.

Something of this social and socialist satire was also to

be found in the American periodical *The Masses,* which functioned in New York from 1911 to 1917. It was, as it called itself, "a monthly magazine directed to the interests of the working people," and it was able to attract some of the sharpest minds and most articulate writers of the time. Its radical left-wing persuasion spread over a wide cultural field. It was for wholesale revolution. In an editorial statement of January 1913, one read that *The Masses* was "a revolutionary and not a reform magazine . . . a magazine directed against rigidity and dogma." On the whole, it appeared to be an attempt of intellectuals to communicate with the less educated people in a common way about social mistreatment, politics, war. Not surprisingly, it never became popular. Thumbing through the brittle pages of the successive volumes, one is constantly aware of the artificiality in the relationship between intellectual and worker, as it is reflected in the presentation. There is an unmistakably abstract quality about the various contributions. The layout, the cartoons, and the small poems all convey a wooden and almost mechanical stiffness. The result is not dissimilar to the two-dimensional didactic deliberateness of most of Brecht's characters, who also have never caught the imagination of large audiences.

The determined, self-conscious efforts to create a socialist art style have, it seems, unavoidably resulted in mechanical representations defeating the very goals that the champions of the collective had set themselves. This original objective was the melioration of the masses, who were humbly estranged by the industrialist system. Unfortunately, however, the sincere but intellectual endeavor to construct a popular style of artistic communication has, in many cases, produced the embarrassing results of a world-picture that is mechanically abstract and depersonalized. One sees it in the illustrations of *The Masses* and in the epic parables of Brecht. One finds it no less emphatically revealed in the murals of the Mexican artist Diego Rivera. In his essay of 1929, *The Revolution in Painting*, Rivera explained the communist attempt to give

art to the masses. Art, according to him, must play a political role. What was needed was an "art with revolution
as its subject." This revolutionary subject matter was to
the proletarian painter what the rails are to the locomotive.

This is interesting and fair enough. But when we consider what this meant in the language of his art, we discover that the political role of art served more the en-
hancement of technology than man's struggle to emancipate himself from its enslaving grip. In *Making a Motor*
at the Detroit Institute of Arts, for instance, the workers
seem to have become incorporated in the assembly system. While ostensibly glorifying human labor, they have
become witnesses of the dehumanizing process that makes
them part of the machinery.

Collecting, recollecting, distributing

The intellectual attempt to construct a proletarian art or
the artist's efforts to identify himself with the masses by
making them his subject matter has thus, on the whole,
contributed little to a convincing manifestation of a
"new" culture. Nevertheless there is such a thing as popular art. There are "pop" concerts and crowded art galleries. There is a popular movie industry, there are comic
strips and television shows. There is, after all, a mass-
culture the possible detrimental or beneficial aspects of
which have been debated on various levels by scholars
and journalists alike. These popular arts again point to
the remarkable presence of modern man's split awareness
of his own society. During the last two centuries, two di-
verging lines of culture have begun to develop, that of
popular and that of rather esoteric forms of artistic enjoyment. At the present time there seems to be a vast gap
between those who like to be guided by the best-sellers'
report and the in-group who consider themselves the
guardians of "high" literature. Radio stations have definite ideas about what should be programmed, and the

British Broadcasting Corporation, besides offering the pedestrian Light program and the urbane Third program, caters to the latitudinarian with its Home service.

In a sense, one can say that the classical society showed a similar split-service in the field of music, especially in connection with dance music. While the court danced the elegant minuet, the country folk tripped the *ländler*. The difference here, however, was not based on a particular preference, but on class, environment, and habit. In the nineteenth century the minuet as a viable dance and musical form died out. Significantly it was replaced by the waltz, a dance that, far from being confined to a class, became truly popular and international.

The development of the waltz as a cultural expression strikingly illustrates the early process of proletarianization. There are a number of theories about its origin, but leaving the confusion of musicology aside, the picture in its simplest outlines shows a transformation from the heavier *ländler* to the more suave *walzer*. The waltz emerged sometime between 1770 and 1780, to become popular when it was included in Soler's opera *Una cosa rara,* performed in Vienna in 1786. Whereas the *ländler* was a country dance, hopped and stamped in boots and heavy shoes, the waltz adapted itself to indoor performances. The wild hopping and kicking was replaced by elegant sliding, the *staccato* rhythm of the *ländler* changed into the *portamento* of the waltz.

The waltz thus not only replaced the *ländler,* but also the minuet. Compared to the latter, it represented the new democratic spirit of the nineteenth century. The waltz became the dance of the people, regardless of class. Its democratic nature was further borne out by the close position of the partners, an intimacy never allowed by the aristocratic minuet. Its swinging and whirling motion soon became the generating power for a new popular type of entertainment, the Viennese operetta.

The importance of this sort of musical development lies in the manner in which regional folk elements have grown into globally spread popular expressions. The positive, creative aspect of this fact is offset, however, by the negative effect of the operetta form being relegated to a second-rate status of culture. We are willing to enjoy it and praise it publicly, but we will not tolerate excerpts from *The Merry Widow* in the symphonic repertory of the concert hall, as we do those from, say Wagner's *Tristan und Isolde.* Thus we emphasize the cleft between magnificent popular music and magnificent music for the connoisseur.

The name of Wagner is relevant, because he had something to say about the popular roots of art. His *Art and Revolution,* published in 1849, is a remarkable piece of rebellious writing, almost coinciding with the *Communist Manifesto.* Whereas Marx and Engels concentrated their attack on the bourgeois, Wagner had his own scapegoat. In his vision of the future, the Philistine was the cultural variant of the bourgeois, just as the artist took the revolutionary place of the Marxist proletarian. It is no use taking this analogy too dogmatically, of course. Wagner's political fire, moreover, was soon extinguished. But he remained an artistic rebel throughout his life, a fact most conspicuously demonstrated in his scores. In his later essay on *The Future Work of Art,* he proclaimed the people as the real source of great art. The music drama which Wagner envisaged must issue forth from spontaneous folk life. The idea later would be repeated by the expressionist painter Franz Marc in his *Aphorisms* of 1911. Distinguishing between the people and the masses, he believed that the first gave art its essential style. If they failed and did not know what they wanted or wanted nothing, the artist could not fulfill and clarify their will. He remained isolated.

The concept of the people was, of course, vague and misleading at all times. Wagner made no attempt to define it helpfully; instead he seemed to be satisfied with the notion of a mysterious force, reminiscent of the romantic Folk Spirit, which supposedly was the cohesive organic energy carrying the seeds and continuity of a culture. If one looks for the results of this revolutionary appeal to the people in the actual music dramas, one finds little or nothing that is developed from original folk elements. No folk songs or folk dances are incorporated into Wagner's operas, as they were soon to be into those of Slavic, Hungarian, and Spanish composers, and had been in some of Bach's works. Thus there appears an embarrassing gap between the composer's revolutionary creed and the realized form of his music dramas.

It is unlikely, however, that Bayreuth would ever have become a rallying point for mass culture had Wagner, indeed, mixed ingredients of folk art into his compositions. Bartók's preoccupation with traditional Hungarian tunes has not made his music more accessible to a large audience. Nor is Stravinsky's *Les Noces* a striking example of proletarian art. On the contrary, though the story deals with primitive rural life and marriage customs culled from popular Russian sources, the musical nature of the score is beyond the reach of the untrained listener. In order to find the real field of broad, popular enjoyment, rooted in revived folklore, one has to go to such new cultural manifestations as jazz.

Clearly, whichever way one turns, one is bound to end up at the embarrassing bifurcation dividing our world into a "high" and a "low" culture. We recognize the self-defeating implication behind this discriminating split, which seems to deny the real victory to the proletarian potential of modern civilization. Yet we cannot avoid recognizing the fact that whenever a truly imaginative form of art, music, or literature, representative of the collective, emerges, it is inexorably classed separately from the classical tradition as a "low" specimen of culture. The inference thus is that "high" culture results from an elitist, individual-ruled society, with the "low" culture a mere product of the collective mind—a prejudice as unfair as it is indestructible.

However, when it comes to the distribution of "high" culture, the contemporary picture fits in perfectly with the general trend of proletarianization. The vague notion of mass-culture, when practically narrowed down by its attackers and defenders alike, is more often to be understood not in a creative, but rather in an administrative sense. Rightly so. For it is in the administration and distribution of the arts for the enjoyment of a large public that the modern collectivist society has been able to operate most beneficially. The change from a classical to a postclassical epoch, in terms of artistic appreciation and command, represented the change from private to public enjoyment. For that reason, the new era established the institutions of public concert halls, libraries, museums, and festivals. They all emerged, at least conspicuously, during the nineteenth century, and in our own age they have become the common property of the masses.

The library, originally the property of monasteries, feudal palaces, or professional scholars, under the pressure of popular, adult, and mass education, adapted itself to the new purposes and became a public institution. Libraries were founded at the time when the novel began to flourish. In fact, the first English circulating library was established in 1740, the very year in which Richardson's *Pamela* was published. It was, however, not until the next century that the free public library developed. In our time the library has become the guardian of the accumulated knowledge of Western civilization, which in an egalitarian world must not be the domain of a few select, initiated, intellectual leaders, but the common possession of all. What is valid for the historical treasure of scholarship can be no less valid for that of the arts. This makes it understandable that along with the rise of the public library there was the emergence of the museum, the popular display place of the arts of the historical society. What at one time was almost exclusively appreciated by prelates, princes, and wealthy bourgeois patrons, from the nineteenth century on came to be appropriated for the enjoyment of the masses.

The institution of the international festival is one of the most telling examples of the contemporary trend toward organized, administrated culture. Originally, the festival was a spontaneous manifestation developed from popular religious cults into artistic, dramatic representations, in which the liturgical elements gradually lost out to secular entertainment. The modern art and music festival is, of course, entirely severed from religious and popular foundations. Its only claim to popularity lies in the massiveness of its worldwide appeal. Perhaps one may see a trace of popular origin in the establishment of what must be the oldest of the modern music festivals, that of Birmingham, which dates back as far as 1768, when the town was still a sleepy place of no more than 35,000 inhabitants. Its hospital being in need of funds, local authorities decided to raise money by a series of concerts, which resulted in a successful 800-pound profit. From then on, the festival became a tradition with a growing international reputation, in which Mendelssohn, for instance, was to play a prominent role.

The local, unassuming nature of its origin, however, marks an exception. The history of the international festival on the whole is characterized by the power and the glory of culture-craving industrialists, artistic parasites and snobs, or aggressive chambers of commerce. As a result of the rapidly expanding tourist trade after the Second World War, festival attractions are now packaged with those of ravishing sites, feudal castles, regional costumes, and superior wines or cheeses. Through the pressure of competition, the festivals have been under obligation to attract the best artists, and they have served the musical world seriously by seeking to offer the unusual or the "never before performed" work side by side with the obvious pieces of the classical repertory.

It would be impossible to deny importance to the trend of bringing works of scholarship, art, and music into the public domain. For all its commercial and snob appeal, organized mass culture represents a movement of large-scale enlightenment. Our endorsement, however, should not preclude an unbiased historical look at the meaning of this development. One must, for instance, pause and dwell on the remarkable phenomenon of collecting, which appears to be behind the mind creating museums and libraries. This is equally true of the popularization furthered by the better radio programs and record companies, which have combined to bring to light, classify, distribute, and annotate large quantities of works by forgotten minor composers. The "collector's item" is a term invented by the commercial mind that understands mass guidance. Collecting in the classical society was accidental, rare, and the activity of the few. Popular collecting started with the bourgeois, the man of property who measured life's enjoyment by the module of acquisition. Here, as elsewhere, the burgher society represented the mere prelude to the mass society. The principle of accumulation, select and restrained at first, became a large, unrestrained mass activity. University libraries now hoard vast quantities of volumes, frequently without clear prospect of usefulness. Libraries and museums tend to lose their typical distinctness. The Yale library, for the benefit of its rare book collection, erected a building whose immediate, attractive feature appears to be the public display facilities.

Why are we so frantically engaged in the almost compulsive activity of collecting? Superficially, it may seem to be tied up with improved popular education, improved international communications, and perhaps the general affluence that enables us to build and expand the machinery essential for this occupation. These answers, however, merely explain the success of methods. There must also be a psychological energy behind them to account for the initiation, continuity, and expansion of the trend. But this factor, of course, is by its very nature a deeply hidden source, not easily identifiable.

We may wonder if there were similar situations at different periods in history. If it strikes us that ancient Alexandria created a splendor of museums and libraries, did the same historical trends prevail then as now? The Alexandrian civilization, like ours, did indeed follow a great classical era, whose achievements it industriously preserved, studied, and annotated. But there was no real proletarian or egalitarian expansion to be compared to ours, and thus the analogy can hardly be conclusive. In general one must acknowledge that then, as now, there apparently was a consistent need of historical guidance.

Collecting is recollecting. The preoccupation with gathering and preserving the tokens of the past is done by the historical mind, looking backward and inclined to reflection rather than action, to preservation rather than formation. These contrasts should, of course, not be taken in any absolute sense, as if they necessarily exclude each other. But, as every one knows, the modern temper, for all its insistence on being "new," is naturally inclined to dwell in the past. Especially in the United States is there a strong binding to the foundations of its institutions, hence the substantial popular interest in historical works. In no other country is the notion of heritage so obsessively stressed and the search for "antiques" so expensively pursued. The collecting of "Americana" is a national pastime, occupying all levels of income and status. It is remarkable to learn that what is gradually unfolding as a proletarian world order reveals a collective mentality disposed to the conservation and distribution of past achievements rather than to creating new forms and styles that truly represent its own character.

Proletarian man, in spite of his destructive, rebellious stance against the classical order, in spite of the political and artistic revolutions against the old regimes of elite prerogatives, still nostalgically adopts and treasures the objects of classical culture. It may well be that this irreconcilable antinomy between destructive rebellion and nostalgic conservation prevents him from producing his own epochal configurations. Proletarian man, notwithstanding multifarious proclamations and avant-garde claims, is unable to represent himself in his own authentic style. The average man of the twentieth century has made "gracious living" his ideal home—an existence that is indeed a third-rate copy of the image he has made of the life in the ducal castles visited during hasty tourist jaunts. Proletarian man, far from being a renewer, is an emulator, and a deficient one to boot. His emulation is not rooted in real understanding and admiration, but comes perversely, in spite of his convictions and his denunciation of the classical order. Thus he constantly betrays himself. He blindly betrays and denies what, after all, does develop as his own cultural style. For he *has,* of course, his own cultural style. One can find it spread over the pages of the Sears, Roebuck catalogue. There is the unabashed, unself-conscious promotion of his proletarian design for living, classified, specified, and priced. Instead of acknowledging this self-revelation and identifying himself unrestrictedly with his own morphology, he borrows limitlessly the ornaments of the bygone elitist tastes, which he nevertheless claims to despise so much.

The disturbing aspect of what must, ultimately, be called the proletarian "style" is the absence of that element most characteristic of historical style in general: ornament. Culturally, the Dorian, Ionian, Babylonian, Byzantine, Saracenic, Romanesque, Gothic, Renaissance, baroque, or rococo expressions in the manuals of art history are distinguished and classed according to the development of the ornamental particulars. From the Romantic movement on, however, the arts and architecture of the Western world are conspicuously without unifying ornamental order. There was no Romantic style. There were a number of Romanticist convictions, theories, and expressions, but there was no such thing as Romantic ornament. What might be called Romantic architecture was basically an indulgence in eclecticism, a playing with Neo-Gothic, Neo-Greek, Neo-Colonial elements.

It is enlightening to note what happens when, at the end of the nineteenth century, the realist revolt against architectural eclecticism set in. One of the pioneers of "functional building" on the European continent, H. P. Berlage, deploring the chaos in nineteenth-century architectural design, declared that epochal style was not superimposed decoration but a necessary product of usefulness. His own architecture was, gradually at first, stripped of unfunctional details. What we saw developing during the successive decades of the early twentieth century in the efforts of Wright, Le Corbusier, the Bauhaus group and their followers was a streamlined efficiency, which, as true machine culture, is almost bare of ornament. Without judging the values of beauty in contemporary architecture (an elusive matter of personal preference at all times), one must draw the historical conclusion that it is marked by a self-willed lack of that cultural element which determines style.

Moreover, twentieth-century architecture has, in another way, allowed eclecticism to reassert itself. To be sure, it has cleared up the chaotic bewilderment of the ornamental pluralism that excited previous generations. But the pluralism is revived in another sense, namely in the arbitrariness of types, of ideas, of private motivations behind the new forms. Thus ours is an architecture that may derive from such diverse sources as the Japanese teahouse, the Bauhaus block, the *Art Nouveau* curves and curls, the stilt dwelling, and it may show, side by side, churches whose engendering concept has been the barn, the fish, the wigwam, the open book, or even (in Amsterdam) the coal scuttle.

What is true for architecture is no less conspicuous in the contemporary forms of music, not because, as Camille Saint-Saëns said, it is "an architecture of sound," but because the same absence of unifying cohesion marks the world of musical composition today. Musicologists of coming centuries will have to account for the coexistence of the disparate musical varieties of the twentieth century. They will find, for instance, the techniques of impressionist Ravel, expressionist Hindemith, atonal Bartók, twelve-tonal Schönberg, neoclassical Stravinsky, neoprimitive Stravinsky, semitraditional Puccini, Neo-Wagnerian Strauss, not to speak of the many brands of jazz and folk-music—or electronic music. It would not be difficult to produce a similar array for the numerous styles of painting or ways of writing poetry that go under the same label of modernity. Although the conclusion is hard to substantiate, we may suspect that the modern trend of eclecticism and pluralism is a product of the collector's mind, thriving on the forces of accumulation.

Stylistic ornament was originally a spontaneous flower

of a growing civilization, but when man can no longer understand its organic necessity, he tends to conceive of ornament as an extraneous, superimposed object to adorn his dreary existence. Thus modern man is inclined to the belief that because he has supplied himself with material abundance and general affluence, with decent laws and solid social institutions, and has acquired the most efficient management control and administrative prowess, he is by a mysterious kind of logic also entitled to what he considers "high" culture. This is nothing but the logic of illusion. Nor does it follow that a society preeminently competent in scientific and technological skills should necessarily excel in profound works of art and philosophy as well. Behind this dubious thinking, there is an obvious misinterpretation of the function of culture. The concept of culture as the fulfilling result of whatever grows naturally from the historical stem of a society, is replaced by the notion that culture is the indispensable and finishing touch of prosperous life, a collective status symbol that is to be had at all costs. This deliberate forcing of culture upon society has resulted in the boom of the cultural center, which in reality is a complex of architecture curiously devoid of native, authentic, home-grown achievements of the first order. The modern cultural centers represent more truthfully large development projects, not dissimilar to the shopping centers that preceded them and set the example.

This historical development could not have succeeded if it had not been for the genius of the commerical mind, which adroitly makes use of the mass market to transmute cultural manifestations into the terms of consumption. The economic preponderance in the distribution of art in a mass structure hardly needs to be elaborated. Any issue of the *Saturday Review* or of *Variety* will illustrate to what extent literature and the theater arts have become primarily book-trade and show-business. The dealer and the impresario are the real taste-makers of mass-culture. The agent has become the indisputable patron of the art for the masses.

While this is obviously regrettable, it should by no means be presented as despicable. The need for large-scale administration and distribution, which undeniably helps and enriches the modern expansionist world, makes it inevitable that the principle of economics and commerce be made central. Today it would be naïve to conceive of any private, governmental, or institutional acquisition of art without the aid of expert middlemen, whose occupation is trade. There is an obvious price tag on the processing, handling, and packaging of the objects of sophistication. The orchids growing in the forest are the work of spontaneous nature and cost nothing, but those cultivated for the decoration of an alien environment ought not to be scorned, though they be the visible signs of expenditure, commerce, and luxury.

5

The Artistic Way of Living

Programs, explanations, contours

The previous chapter is chiefly concerned with the new relationships between artist and audience in the modern mass structure. It touches only indirectly on the change in technical-esthetic methods. As these are the immediate reflection of the artistic idea in general, they require special scrutiny. The artist of the classical era had virtually nothing but his work to speak for him. The portrait, the fugue, the sonnet incorporated the entire volume of craft, esthetics, vision, life-experience, insofar as the painter, composer, or poet could and wanted to express them. In contrast, the history of contemporary art since the Romantic movement is characterized by the significant development of the artistic manifesto. Apparently the new social order in the Western world caused a need for deliberate programming of the meaning of art, which previously had been assumed to be self-evident.

Since nothing in history is entirely without precedent, one can predictably find early forerunners of this self-defensive artistic proclamation. In order to anticipate hostile critics, the Roman dramatist Plautus offered humble apologies in the spoken prologue of some of his comedies. From Aristotle and Horace to Boileau, there have been treatises on the fundamentals of "poetic art." Lope de Vega, Corneille, and Lessing, Donatus, Heinsius, and Vossius concentrated on the technique of the drama. Among the many theories of painting, it suffices to mention the *Book of the Art*, by Giotto's pupil Cennino Cennini, the *Treatise on Painting*, which Leon Battista Alberti wrote in 1436, the *Notebooks* by Leonardo da Vinci, the *Autobiography* and separate essays by Benvenuto Cellini, the *Idea of the Painters, Sculptors, Architects* by Federigo Zuccaro (1607), the *Conference on Expression* by Charles Le Brun, and the *Grand Style of Painting* (1759) by Sir Joshua Reynolds.

All these declarations had in common the pedagogic aim of setting the rules and limits of what the authors thought was the true, perennial art. They did not in the first place attempt to be "new." It was only with the Romantic movement that artists apparently felt the need to be revolutionary and to denounce and destroy previous esthetic beliefs. The modern artistic manifesto was a declaration of war. The public had to be informed that the classical standards were superannuated. What was valid for the past no longer had value and had to be replaced by modern principles. Once this idea of revolution was established, however, it became a pattern to be repeated by successive generations. New art styles follow each other with increasingly rapid frequency. Whereas Gothic or Renaissance had a life span of several centuries, the contemporary schools of art tend to become as ephemeral as the seasons of *haute couture.*

The manifesto was the concomitant program of that new institution the art school, the group, the circle, the *ism*, often promoted by its own organ, the art and literary magazine, which served to repeat the particular message issue after issue. Even within the spread of a movement independent and varying creeds might be launched. The Romantic revolution thus was explained in the *Athenaeum* of the Schlegels (starting in 1798), in Wordsworth's preface to the second edition of the *Lyrical Ballads* (1800), and in Victor Hugo's preface to *Cromwell* (1827). Each of these presented a different aspect of Romanticism, though they were on common ground in their zeal to undo the time-honored principles of classical literature.

The accent in these proclamations was on originality, the entirely new, an urge that had never bothered the classical artist. All the expressions of classical culture were "original," and one can recognize it without the auxiliary manifesto. "Styles" in the history of modern art arose in the self-conscious pursuit of something "extra," or one could say extraneous, in relation to the original aim of spontaneous artistic probing. When Friedrich Schlegel, in the third volume of the *Athenaeum*, remarks that "individuality is the original and eternal in man," when Victor Hugo, in his preface to *Cromwell*, stresses the importance of original genius, or when Walt Whitman, in the introduction to *Leaves of Grass*, says that the greatest poet is a seer, an individual complete in himself, then we hear nothing that the artist of classical times could not also have endorsed. The proclamations of these three authors, however, presented the notions of the individual and originality, not as the normal, but as the abnormal state. Artistic style thus had to be eccentric, that is, drawn away from the center of society. Consequently, from Romanticism on, the *cult* of the individual and originality developed, extending through the avant-garde groups of the twentieth century.

The numerous manifestos appearing between 1798 and 1940 had little in common, except that they were invariably, either by implication or by deliberate phrasing, an expression of self-asserting individualism. This was so even when, as in the case of the Bauhaus program, a definite social message was included. This at times almost fevered individualism essentially reflects the prime contemporary conflict of the self with the objective world—the theme of this book. The objective world is a nebulous notion, of course, for man's consciousness is by nature mostly nebulous. But when it has to express itself, the forms that this fear of the objective, the "other," take on are slightly more articulate. In various creeds of the new artistic schools it takes the form of the idea of nature. Clearly, nature is not too crisp a notion either. But it provides at least the first communicative link between the inner consciousness, always inclined to hide and mystify, and the outer world.

Although the concept of nature was not always entirely the same for contemporaries around 1800, e.g. Wordsworth and Goethe, its centrality in the thought of both indicated how disturbing was the split at that time between man and nature. Goethe is usually not referred to as a Romanticist. Neither is it expedient to call his periodical the *Propyläen* an organ for the promotion of Romantic art. Its three years of existence, however, coincided exactly with those of the *Athenaeum,* and some of the leading Romanticists, notably August W. Schlegel, welcomed Goethe's magazine with approval. Goethe, like the Romanticists, deplored the moral and cultural state of the eighteenth century. In agreement with his friend Schiller, he believed that the ancient Greek society pointed the way to a possible restoration. His contributions to the *Propyläen* were consistently inspired by Greek art. He specifically singled out the celebrated piece of sculpture the *Laocoön,* which, however, is a specimen of late Hellenistic art, not at all representative of Greece at its highest and most harmonious. It is significant that Goethe should see his esthetic ideal in this work, with its

virtuoso but tortured pathos and the unrepressed conveyance of feeling. Romantic or not, Goethe was certainly
no neoclassicist, and his introduction to the *Propyläen*
confirms this. Recognizing that the crucial problem of his
age lay in the polarity of man and nature, he saw in the
artist the one who can best bridge the gap between the
two. Although not even the greatest genius can hope to
overcome the chasm between art and nature, the artist
must try, and hence, "instead of giving work that is
merely superficially effective, emulate nature itself, and
create a spiritual and organic totality."

The absence of any destructive attitude toward the
classical forms resulted from Goethe's inherent antipathy
to revolutionary disturbance. As such he did not belong
to the ranks of the Romanticists. Yet his insistence on the
identification of the artist with nature fitted in strikingly
with the views of the Romantic movement. It fitted in
with Wordsworth's pantheistic involvement in nature and
with Blake's resistance to the neoclassicist artist Joshua
Reynolds, who asserted that rules can be extracted from
nature—rules that must be obeyed in order to prevent
the art work from falling into deformity. It certainly fitted in with the attack of Constable on the French eighteenth-century painter Boucher. Boucher struck the Eng-
lishman as the "climax of absurdity," because his style led
art away from nature by adhering to fashion. Constable,
sharing Goethe's view of the decline of the eighteenth
century, also confirmed the fear of the alienation of art
from nature.

The revolutionary element in Romanticism agitated
against the "unnatural," which was fundamentally the objective environment estranged from human experiences.
Constable ridiculed eighteenth-century painting for its imitation of previous forms rather than of nature; hence
painters such as Boucher presented landscapes that were
in fact stage sets. Boucher's pastoral scenes presented
"the pastoral of the opera house." This reminds one of
Schumann's criticism of the composer Rossini, another
eighteenth-century figure, who was typified as a butterfly

(compared to Beethoven's eagle image). Rossini, Schumann wrote in his *Aphorisms,* "is the most striking stage painter," who left one nothing when artificial light and theatrical illusion were taken away from him.

To the Romanticist, the identification of the artist with nature occurred through the agency of the eye. But the German painter Caspar David Friedrich, in his Romanticist views of landscape painting, warned: "Close your physical eye, so that your mental eye first sees your own image." The painter should not merely reproduce what he sees before him, but also what he sees within himself. Apparently, there is, according to him, a sort of mystical unity between inner and outer eye. This conception was worked out in what may be called the Romanticist manifesto of art, the *Letters on Landscape Painting* (1815–1824) by Carl Gustav Carus. Nature, Carus contended, is written in a language that man has to learn through the medium of the artist. The artist has the necessary trained eye, and eye was all-important to Carus. It should, however, not observe nature as if it were something "arbitrary, indefinite and senseless, but as determined by a divine primal life."

Clearly, careful study and observation is not an artistic method introduced by realist and impressionist painters. Romanticists are frequently depicted as woolly escapists, unwilling or unable to face the objective facts of their environment. Although this may be true for some of them, it represents a misconception when it is applied in general terms. The Romanticists on the whole wanted to come to grips with the world, but not so much the world as an aggregate of individual objects as a unity in which they themselves participated. This points to the chief difference between the Romanticists and the realists who appeared later in the century. What became fundamental for them was the eye, not indeed as vision, but as scientific instrument. What has been said of Monet . . . "nothing but an eye, but such an eye!" . . . to the romanticist seemed to refer to sight estranged from the self and becoming a laboratory tool.

Whereas Corot, expressing his objectives as a landscape painter, believed that feeling should be the guiding principle, because "beauty in art is the truth, steeped in the impression we have received," naturalistic impressionism was truth seen "through a temperament." This distinction between feeling and temperament as guiding agencies of art may be illustrated by the works of Corot and Monet. Though Corot's landscapes convey a poetic subjectivity, unknown in the classical renderings of van Ruysdael, van Goyen, Hobbema, or Lorrain, the scene as total setting is intact, the common landscape is still preserved. In contrast, Monet's *Water Lilies,* a large canvas covering an entire wall of the Museum of Modern Art in New York, is a hyper-individualistic experiment with color fragments, light, and atmosphere, estranged from the world as the common eye knows it. The widening distance between man and nature, exacerbated by the scientific manner of observation, is nowhere better accounted for than in Zola's *The Experimental Novel,* an essay of 1880. Although not aware of this split, let alone promoting it, Zola advocated the introduction of laboratory techniques in writing. "We have experimental chemistry and medicine, so we shall have an experimental physiology, and after that an experimental novel." Since the novelist is equally an observer and an experimentalist, he ought to go the entire way of the scientist and acquire a knowledge of the "machinery" of man's intellectual and sensate manifestations.

Zola's essay was a sort of manifesto of realist art in its most comprehensive sense. Zola was just as interested in the mutual relationship of man and environment (for him society rather than nature) as was the romanticist. But his different method caused the observation of the objective phenomena to become divorced from the inner, the subjective vision.

In this century the chasm between man and nature has become irrevocable, not necessarily because of an even more intensified scientification of nature, but foremost because the idea of man as an autonomous entity loses its force in the sway of a consensus society. It is in our century then that Dada arose as a cry of despair, as a statement of futility on behalf of humanity. Dada is nothing. It is, as a dadaist manifesto of 1919 declared, "the last sigh of a dying society." Thus it represents a movement utterly destructive of all current values. Francis Picabia, the painter who joined it late in life, cried out: "Dada is nothing, nothing, nothing. Like your hopes it is nothing. Like your idols, nothing."

The destruction of forms, so defiantly pursued by dadaism, is no less characteristic of surrealism, but with an entirely different motivation behind it. Surrealism did not, as the prefix *sur* might suggest, try to transcend the phenomena and objects of nature, but rather to penetrate them for their underlying latent meaning. It was out to destroy the conventional meanings of the objects of reality or of the words in the language. The pictures of Max Ernst or Salvador Dali distort the common experience of human reality, to replace it by a hidden (sometimes allegedly subconscious) primitive value. Although the effect is quite dissimilar, the disfigurations in the cubist rendering of bottles, fish, guitars, newspapers, and match boxes by Braque and Picasso point to the same need of dehumanizing landscape and still life, an inclination no less devastatingly demonstrated in the contemporary portrait.

The ultimate step in the process of depersonalizing the image of man and his world was taken by Mondriaan and van Doesburg in their neoplasticism. Dissatisfied with cubism, because it was not developing abstraction toward its final goal, Mondriaan turned to the radical technique, which he explained in his manifesto on *Plastic Art and Pure Plastic Art*. It was a declaration of war against all "limiting forms." Plasticism was "the reduction of the natural form and color to a more or less neutral state." This neutrality required the annihilation of the conventional knowledge and experience of nature. In practice, it ended with vertical and horizontal lines dividing squares in the primary colors—red, blue, and yellow. Abstract plasticism was the last phase of the Romantic revolution, which itself began with the undermining of the stale formulations of the eighteenth century. In the twentieth century, however, all forms of human experience and nature are being destroyed and reduced to a mere abstract formula.

Why is it that the artist of the postclassical era is in need of such an extraneous form of communication as the manifesto? Why should the artistic mind, after having traditionally been directed toward practice only, in modern times turn to a self-conscious self-evaluation, commenting on its own product? Why is it symptomatically inclined to declare war against the previous generation? Why must it now explain, under separate cover, what originally was inherent in the work of art itself? Why, for instance, did the simple cube style of the Bauhaus require Gropius' extensive and intelligent expositions, while the complicated Gothic was built without annotations save the beauties of naves, columns, triforia, fleurons, vaults, and cornices?

If there were easy answers to these questions, cultural history would probably be superfluous. History in general may well exist precisely because so little that is of profound importance in the change of societies can be proved scientifically. It seems reasonable, however, to suggest that the growing aggressiveness of the manifesto over the years indicates a stiffening self-defensiveness. No person or thing, however, has been attacked! Except for Shelley's *Defense of Poetry*, a response to Thomas Love Peacock's doubt about the future of literature, the manifestos have aimed at targets without their authors themselves being under fire. More often than not, the artistic creed is primarily directed against society, and the proclaimed renewal is comprehensive and social, rather than narrowly esthetic.

The self-appointed prophet role of the artist wanting to manifest requires a special, extraordinary voice, the voice of the trumpet perhaps. This may account for the rhapsodic style in which some of the more militant manifestos have been presented. In any case, with the need for the "movement" there follows the need for ostentatious exclamation, for a kind of headline emphasis. Naturally, in the age of self-advertisement this makes sense. The trend runs remarkably parallel with the significant development in the arts of the *contour*. The classical painters, even those, from Botticelli to Ingres, who were fascinated by the purity of line, established the forms of their composition through the play of relative color values. Graphic outline was excluded from the classical technique of painting. The change came, gradually however, with the need for demonstrating programs, social or esthetic.

The contour arrived with the strands of caricature and satire in Daumier's prints and was carried over to his expressive paintings. With the impressionist painters the brusqueness of the coloring may result in the delineation of contours, as in Manet's *Woman in Evening Dress* or *Arriving at the Masked Ball*. Contour helped Cézanne to construct his geometric patterns in still lifes and bathing figures. It is, above all, firmly established in van Gogh's stubbornly struggling brush work. Twentieth-century fauvists and expressionists followed him. Rouault combined contour technique with impressions of stained glass mosaics, while Kokoschka seems to use it to strike his landscapes and portraits with the lash of terror. Picasso exploits it heavily for his feasts of brutality. Fernand Léger and Rivera employ it for the polished precision of their motor art. The expressionist strokes and stripes of Emil Nolde, Ernst Ludwig Kirchner, Max Beckmann, Otto Müller, and Erich Heckel demonstrate psycho-social conflicts. When nonrepresentative art entered history, the contour attained its most independent function, whether in Kandinski's improvisations, in Mondriaan's grids, or in André Masson's surrealist doodles.

The same urge of ostentatious demonstration predictably developed in contemporary music and is especially noticeable in the way melodic lines are presented. Melody and harmony originally were organically interwoven. In Bach's composition the integrated unity of counterpoint, harmony, tune development and rhythmic variety found its unequaled peak. If this harmonious integration has sometimes been called the purest of absolute music, it is because after Bach extraneous, superemotional, and literary values mixed with the purely musical expressions. Gradually, melody gained a more independent role. The "lovely" tune emerged, still carefully profiled by Mozart, Haydn, and Beethoven, then inflated with mood by the Romanticists.

Thanks to the orchestral innovations of Weber, Wagner, Berlioz, and others after them, the melodic line was reinforced with brass sound. The Wagner of *The Ring* or *Tristan* subdued *leitmotif* and tune with his lush modulation and chromaticism. Brahms' classical restraint managed to blend the melodic contours in and out of the compositional structure. The orchestration of César Franck's symphony pushed the tension of melody and harmonic variation to the breaking point. With such composers as Liszt and Tchaikovsky, however, the emotional outbursts of tune complexes destroyed the last vestiges of classical equilibrium in music. The reaction to this in the twentieth century reveals itself in the nonmelody of atonal or polytonal compositions. But the ferocity of percussion and trombone effects absorbed in jarring rhythmic unrest has produced a new accentuated profile. The jagged statements of some sections of Hindemith's *Mathis der Maler,* the obsessive *ostinato* beat of Stravinsky's *L'Histoire du Soldat,* and the savage shrieks of Milhaud's *Le Boeuf sur le Toit* are only a few representative examples of a new idiom which thrives on contour without the benefit of tune.

The situation in literature is complicated by the fact that in this field there are various modes with different historical developments. The novel is a latecomer and practically the product of the process of proletarianization. Although one can hardly say for certain, it may well be that for this reason the art of the novel, from the beginning, showed a line of untrammeled storytelling side by side with another line, which used the narrative for extraneous purposes, thus supplying it with a deliberate contour. While the first kind stretches continually from Fielding, Scott, and Twain through Hemingway, the second is represented by Voltaire's *Candide* or by Goethe's *Wilhelm Meister* and similar forms of the *Bildungsroman*. Later, in the works of Zola, Dreiser, and German novelists of the 1920's and 1930's, the social message provided its own contour.

Classical lyricism presented a harmonious balance between subjective content and objective formulation, perfectly demonstrated in the sonnets of Dante, du Bellay, Shakespeare, and Milton, or in the rondels of Christine de Pisan, Charles d'Orléans, and Clément Marot. In the eighteenth century, as the poetic sensitivity declined, the cult of formulation took on a tyrannical function. Thus the nineteenth century demanded new dictions and idioms to stress the subjective voice. Contour then was applied at worst in self-pitying overemphasis, or in more genuine cases, in using epic delineations to suggest personal grief—a technique predominently used by the German Romanticists with their ballad-like lyrics. Heine employed the ballad technique with a specific ironical touch, laying the groundwork for the political cabaret lyrics of the Weimar Republic.

Perhaps literary contour shows its most incisive thrust in the modern drama, which, ignoring the classical interlocking play of characterization and plot, throws both out of balance by the primacy of thought and thesis. Here Goethe's *Faust* is the prototype of the modern expressionistic drama. Though changing in direction and style, it demonstrates a continuing line from Ibsen's *Peer Gynt* and *Brand* through Strindberg's mystery plays and their German, French, and American descendants. Under the influence of the French thesis play and the early social preoccupations of Ibsen, Shaw developed his own style of pamphleteer drama, in which the political message usurps the fundamental rights of character and structure.

It would appear that the deliberate molding of "message" or other extra-artistic accentuations helps the modern artist to establish closer contact with the public. In this added link of communication there is a strong suggestion of the element of immediacy, which has more and more come to characterize modern culture. Immediacy is necessitated by the faster pace of life and communication. Above all, the factor of immediacy is vital in the organization of mass demands, mass media, and mass production. It has something to do with what has been called the "graphic revolution," basically the change from written information to pictorial image, a move that the advertising agencies exploit with eroding effect. It produces and sustains the billboard landscape and the comic strip mentality; it makes the masses ready for movies and for television. Pictorial supremacy clearly has made the plastic arts the most popular branch of contemporary culture, immediately distributable among the crowd. In the theater it introduces a spectacular visual lavishness unknown since the Roman stage. In a more complicated way perhaps, it accounts for the piling up of disconnected images in symbolist and surrealist poems, such as those of Mallarmé, Dylan Thomas, Breton or Éluard. The urge for immediacy has made a photogenic face the greatest asset for political office, wrapping superior to contents, and the cover girl the guardian angel of popular journalism.

Dots, fragments, cogs

To establish a unified order, classical cosmology needed an intellectual focusing point, a center of origin, tautly holding together the diverse details of its system of experience. Whether God or man, sun or earth took up this central position was relatively unimportant, for a hierarchy of values remained decisive, even though the names of the values might change. It was the need for hierarchy that made the Renaissance artist develop a system of perspective by which space was arranged according to stages of distance, and determined by the regulating concept of the horizon. At the same time, in the early fifteenth century, the Flemish masters began to apply new oil techniques in order to establish a greater spatial reality by a new distribution of values in three successive planes. The man of the Renaissance, whether Copernicus or Kepler, Marco Polo or Barentz, Jan van Eyck or Masaccio, wanted to conquer space, and in order to do so he needed a central position, conceptional and visionary, from which to operate.

Just as the classical painter arranged the details of his composition by the formula of perspective, so the classical composer, at the time when a wide field of variations and modulations was opening up, restricted himself through the limitations of major and minor scales. In this scale system the major and minor triads and their inversions dominated the proceedings. Robert Schumann compared the triad with the trinity of past, present, and future, pointing to the third as being as pivotal as the present. Indeed, even without this analogy, it is clear for anyone with a basic knowledge of musical harmony how central is the third in determining the unity of the tonic system. The third is as much a unifying fixing point in music as is the vanishing point in the pictorial composition. When in the twentieth century the security of the classical triad is sacrificed, and the centrality of the strong and determined third is replaced with the weak and empty fourth, the whole character of the musical composition reflects a loss of unity just as much as do modern paintings without perspective. The parallel may be extended to the structure of the contemporary novel or play, which, without acutely focused plot, protagonist, or character, tend to convey a quality of disconnectedness.

The classical painter was not so much interested in space itself as he was in the relationship between the objects distributed in space. He used effects of lighting chiefly to enhance the spatial or psychological interest, as did such *tenebrists* as Caravaggio, Rembrandt, or Georges de La Tour. The Dutch landscape artists, though at times fascinated by the washed light-fall of their native country, more often than not preferred to Italianize their scenes. The play of light and atmosphere as an independent phenomenon did not become prominent until the nineteenth century when artists began to concentrate on it. Corot filled his canvases with a lyrical mood, while Caspar David Friedrich sometimes steeped them in an atmosphere of almost lugubrious magic. In Turner's *Rain, Steam and Speed,* the order of space is whipped up to an effervescent turmoil. The browns, olive-greens, and messy whites of his *Music Party* build a composition of misty impressions which, detached from concrete objects, destroy the feeling of physical reality.

With the impressionists, indeed, light was no longer studied and observed as the object-constructing medium it used to be for the classical painter but for its own scientific sake. It was handled and taken apart into its components. Gradually, the spatial forms were determined by prismatic color distributions. The play with refracted light causes the composition to loosen and crumble, and eventually the neoimpressionists and pointillists put their landscapes in multicolored atomistic structures of dots. This dotting method, to be sure, provided a new technical unity, but it was a unity separated from the order of cosmic space. The pointillist painter resembled a scientist of the laboratory who tends to study fragments of physical phenomena separated from the universal order of nature.

The process of fragmentation in the arts could not have happened without the aid of a curious proclivity toward abstraction. Whether this trend was related to the general instrusion of science into the arts and the humanities is a question that defies conclusive answers. There was, however, a definite search for fixed formulas and for geometrical and decorative patterns. Cézanne's strong sense of structure neglected the old compositional means of carefully organized values and instead concentrated on triangles, trapezes, and other planimetric definitions to shape his landscapes, portraits, and still lifes. What grew almost surreptitiously with Cézanne, the carving up of space into flats, became an ostentatious display with the cubists. Around 1910, Braque and Picasso began to disassemble the three dimensions of reality and distance, take them out of their natural order, and juxtapose them so as to release the hidden meanings of the pictured objects.

Besides fragmenting the triple order of space, the cubist similarly dissolved the structure of time. For this he employed the device of synchronization. Observing a given number of aspects characterizing an object requires the element of time. However, by presenting the dimensional aspects simultaneously, the cubist artist destroyed the unifying function of continuity, and thus Juan Gris in his *Still Life with Lamp,* for instance, and Kurt Schwitters in his paper and board collages, such as *Victory,* give snippets and slices of objects, which release these objects from the laws of time and space. The subject-object unity, on which classical art is based, is reduced to a graphic abstraction. Simultaneity produces like effects of fragmentation when futurist painters set out to capture the phenomenon of movement. In his *Nude Descending a Staircase,* Marcel Duchamp, in order to present the continuousness of action, simply juxtaposed slices and fragments of the human figure, so that what we see, far from representing a nude, is a descending movement of repeated patterns. The futurist sense of motion and the cubist play of patterns sometimes combine compatibly, as in Giacomo Balla's *Spring,* for example.

The juxtaposition of form and color components, which replaces the hierarchy of values, is responsible for the flattening process in the arts and the related characteristically decorative style of our age. Juxtaposition is by no means confined to painting alone. When in the twentieth century the tonal system dissolved, composers such as Schönberg, Webern, Alban Berg, and Egon Wellesz abandoned the old logic of harmonic progressions. The melodic flow seems, to the ear, arbitrary, and harmonies and individual notes seem disconnected. Wagner, who anticipated the atonal freedom by challenging the security of key in continuous modulations, still managed to retain a firm musical cohesion. Shostakovich, in his opera

Katarina Ismailova, sometimes employed a sort of brutalized Wagnerism, but the texture falls apart in fragmented bursts of sound. Similarly fractioned, though more subdued, is the music of Berg's *Wozzeck.* One of the characteristic impressions of contemporary compositions, regardless of schools, is this display of incoherence, supported by the infinite opportunities of modern orchestration or serial techniques. In literature, surrealists such as Apollinaire and Breton juxtaposed their images, thereby destroying the conventional syntax to avoid transmitting conventional meanings. So did e e cummings when he wrote:

> love is less always than to win
> less never than alive
> less bigger than the least begin
> less littler than forgive

What is called "stream of consciousness" is actually not a stream at all, but a montage of fragmented thought; Virginia Woolf and James Joyce sometimes applied means in line with Sergei Eisenstein's definition of cinematography: a combining of "shots that are depictive, single in meaning, neutral in content . . . into intellectual contexts and series."

The question can be, and has been, raised whether the complete destruction of the fundamental rules of composition, language, and grammar is compatible with artistry. The question is theoretical. With our slowly acquired freedoms and tolerance we like to think that the artists set their own rules, by inspiration, as it is popularly said. Yet in a proletarian society there is validity in the popular questions: Is an art that seemingly does not demand intensive training and craftsmanship still art? Does a poem or a prose work that destroys the common grammar of language, and thus appears incomprehensible and unable to convey common thought, still belong to literature? These questions can only be answered conclusively by the judgment of later centuries. We can merely react with likings, preferences, or doubts, all clearly of a tentative nature. The question whether twelve-tone compositions, which with their cerebral and abstract formulations strike no chords with a larger public than that of a musical in-group, really belong to the sphere of music is again wholly academic. Paul Hindemith, while teaching at Yale, dismissed serial music because he claimed it was not singable. One could indeed adopt the principle that all sound formations that are neither singable nor danceable fall outside the domain of music. These could then be classed as mere organized sound, as for instance such experiments as Pratella's *Musica futurista*, the *Intonarumore* of Russelo (*ca.* 1914), the "concrete" music of the 1950's, or the electronic music of the 1960's. But this is an obviously arbitrary and theoretical act. The question whether or not a certain compositional expression can be labeled music is comparatively irrelevant. More important is the cultural relevance of a musical or artistic manifestation that is entirely dependent on the approval of a narrow circle of insiders in a society otherwise directed by popular consensus.

Fragmentation shows a conception of art that is historically alienated from the classical vision. Although the methods of modern painters and sculptors are developed gradually from the traditional techniques, the artist of the twentieth century has finally arrived at a state that isolates him from his own culture. The gradual development of this historical process may prevent us from seeing the essential change. Historical observers five hundred years from now, however, judging without our biased attachments, will undoubtedly compare Renaissance art with futurism, baroque with dada—an act probably as unfair as it is inevitable. It would be pointless to speculate on where their preference will fall. But it is not impossible now to understand why they, inescapably taking the classical art forms as the norm, regardless of any commitment to intrinsic quality, must view our present manifestations as the abnormal and estranged expressions of the earlier era.

This culturally isolated state, inasmuch as it presents

the quality of fragmentation, is related to the pluralistic character of the mass society. On the surface it seems rather far-fetched to connect the equalitarian structure of society with the esthetic convictions which produce fragmentation in pointillist, cubist, or dadaist forms. Though the link may be tenuous, it cannot be denied that, in both, the loss of a sense of hierarchy causes the cultural anatomy to fall apart. Just as the values of class-taste, class-manners, class-habits disappear in this self-equalizing world, so must the carefully distributed color values and spatial proportions be leveled in an esthetic without authoritative forms. In the classical music scales the tones function according to a preset arrangement and the chords built on them relate to each other in a fixed proportion of importance, the entire complex of harmony being controlled by the triad of the root tone, the third, and the fifth. In twelve-tone compositions, however, all the twelve tones of the scale are democratically equalized, without the guidance of a harmonic source of authority.

Since the Romantic movement, the whole conception of artistic authority has gradually been transferred to the individual's likings—a revolution to have no less drastic ramifications than the rebellions against traditional government. In other words, authority in the arts, like that in government administration, from a centrally located focusing point has been distributed and scattered. With the individual opportunities infinitely increased, the concentration of style and conception relaxes proportionately, resulting in the pluralistic and fragmented world picture as we know it today.

The looming threat of imminent disintegration has, of course, not gone unnoticed. Society has its own self-protective energy. Thus, for example, socialization is nothing but a legislative emergency device to reconstruct the lost cohesion by mechanical means, at a time when too much free play of individualism jeopardizes the total security of the commonweal. In similar fashion one can see a natural countertrend entering contemporary esthetics. It is nowhere more urgently expressed than in Gropius' manifesto of the Bauhaus with his exhortation to architects, painters, and sculptors to join forces and work for the composite unity of building. Art is not a profession but a craft. And it is through craftsmanship that the totality of the creative arts must be reachieved.

If there is an echo of William Morris audible here, it is only a faint one, for Morris would have condemned the professed championing of the machine, which marked the activity of the Bauhaus movement. This ironical recourse to machinery points to an inherent self-contradictory attitude. The Bauhaus was unconditionally committed to the individual, yet it embraced the principle of technology. Herbert Read, in the introduction to a work about the Bauhaus, describes its doctrines without apparently realizing their contradictory nature. Pointing aptly to the fact that this group wanted to overcome alienation in the technological world through "training in creative cooperation," he continues with the statement that in the Bauhaus program the individual once more was to take command over his destiny. This in the modern situation "means taking command of the machine and using it for creative purposes."

The obvious conflict here lies in the opposing forces of mechanics and creative conception, which, reduced to more general terms, is the clash between the collective and the individual. There is no reason, of course, to preclude all hopes for a cooperative pact between artist and machine. The Bauhaus effort, moreover, is not the only testimony to this aspiration. While the artist of the nineteenth century was still defiantly negative toward the machine, in the twentieth century, unable to lick the industrial trend, he has, though not in all instances, of course, decided to get on the technological bandwagon.

This trend of the mechanization of the arts is revealed in the motorized efficiency of Léger's *The City* and Max Ernst's mechanized *Elephant Celebes*. It can be seen in the polished forms of the constructivists Pevsner and Malevich and, in general, in any of the streamlined arrangements of purely abstract or semiabstract patterns of van Doesburg, Vasarely, Braque, Klee, and many others. In sculpture it can take the shape of the robotized figures of Duchamp-Villon, Boccioni or Zadkine, be reduced to the slickly levigated objects of Brancusi, Arp, and Barbara Hepworth, or structured into real machinery by Calder and Naum Gabo. The futurists, of course, make a real cult of technology, eulogizing cars, planes, and other speeding crafts. Their poets in general follow the free verse patterns of Walt Whitman, the earliest apostle of the machine. Marinetti, in his *Poupées électriques* of 1907, gave a futurist manifesto with an exclamatory touch: "We shall sing . . . factories suspended from the clouds by the strings of their smoke . . . adventurous ocean steamers . . . locomotives with big breastplates." The beat of the machine, finally, is imitated by the obstinate rhythms and the hissing and grinding sounds of the early Stravinsky compositions or those of Milhaud and Honegger (*Pacific 231*).

Whereas these expressions of art, conspicuous though they be, represent merely symptomatic exceptions, contemporary building, becoming more and more exclusively a form of engineering, is producing giant-size machine structures. The Bauhaus appeal to functionality is representative for virtually all of today's architecture. The modern dwelling, in Le Corbusier's phrase, has become a *"machine à vivre."* The tall office and apartment tower is a huge apparatus for efficient movement, communication, and other services. The cultural centers distributed in the populous areas are erected as stark industrial contraptions without organic ornamentation, forbidding in appearance and rising outside the scale of humanity. The sometimes grimy but always warmly human family store is replaced by the dehumanized hygiene of that retail factory, the shopping center. While accepting the gains of service and comfort, we should not be blind to the fact that instead of using technology for artistic purposes, we have gradually surrendered personal and personalized experience to mechanical expedience—a shift perfectly legitimate as long as we acknowledge it candidly.

The machine, being an arrangement of interchangeable parts, represents mechanical organization in contrast to individuality, spontaneity, option. As such it can hardly be conceived of as a decisive aid to the artist, and the fact that Gropius, Le Corbusier, and others nevertheless set their hopes on technology as an artistic source arises from misconception and perhaps panic. In a mass society technique must prevail at all costs. Hitler's regime closed the Bauhaus at Dessau. As the demon of mass consensus he understood that it represented the last vestiges of an elitist vision of craftsmanship, incompatible with the technological principle of leveling. Friedrich Georg Jünger, who in his *Failure of Technology* studied this phenomenon as intensively as anyone—albeit one-sidedly—argued that "technological thinking is plainly collectivistic. Such collectivistic thinking, however, pre-supposes an individual freed and cleansed from all con-flicting considerations, an individual who is willing to abandon himself unreservedly to the collective." This view is obviously based on the experiences of the Third Reich, which Jünger opposed. He must have seen the es-tablishment of the *Kulturkammer,* as indeed we all should, as the ultimate submission of personal experi-ences to the masses. Joseph Goebbels, the Nazi minister of culture and propoganda, said as much, in fact, in a speech of November 1933, claiming to have "replaced the individual by the people and the human being by the community."

The result of this "new order," as everyone knows, was the end of all art and creative culture within the borders of the National Socialist realm. It came by arbitrary brutal force. But the principle, the conflict of mass tech-nology and art, remains and, with Hitler out of the way, one may hope that its solutions will be negotiated more tolerantly. It would be foolish, however, with almost two hundred years of historical evidence against us, to be-lieve that technology is going to allow an honorable com-promise with the artist. One cannot argue with hopes, of course. But those of the Bauhaus leaders, at least have been shattered. The elements of their program, resuscitated after the war, are not those of the composite unity of art and architecture of a medieval type of craftmanship. They are merely the principles of hard functionality in block and box arrangements. But while it is clear that today the engineer has decisively taken over from the artist, one should not make the mistake of interpreting this change as a depressing prospect. In the pluralist, fragmented world of the masses, technology has become the agency to prevent the social texture from disintegrating, and one ought therefore to welcome it.

Once this is done, one can with genuine gratitude recognize the great advantages of what may be called the good common taste, which is giving the technological age its own pleasant grace. It can be found in the emergence of the industrial park, in the way apartment blocks are spaced around grassy areas, in the artistic promotion materials of Olivetti and other corporations, in the design of airport accommodations, in the interiors of new banks and public service buildings, or in the elegance of the parkways. But just as common sense cannot substitute for Platonic philosophy or dialectic logic, so common taste cannot replace the *B-minor Mass*. However, it can provide the proletarian way of living with its own modest dignity.

Savage, sadist, fascist

Goya, producing his series of etchings, the *Disasters of War*, introduced an element of sadism combined with a touch of sexuality, which, though not entirely new, marked the beginning of a trend in the history of art and literature that adopts violence as one of the fundamental tenets of its esthetics. Violence and the portraying of cruelty, of course, have never been foreign to any period in history. Medieval and Renaissance painters alike, while glorifying their saints, have left us scenes of unabashed indulgence in torture, but these are incidental expressions, not representative of an epochal style. It is significant, moreover, that the neurotic mind of Hieronymus Bosch was really not discovered until our age. And while the terrors of war and ferocious battles had always been favorite topics, (the etchings of the seventeenth-century Jacques Callot, the *Miseries of War*, made in the service of the Duke of Lorraine, thematically anticipated Goya's work), the classical painter—and this still holds true for Goya's contemporary Antoine Jean Gros with his Napoleonic battles—viewed the military through the esthetics of heroism.

This began to change with Goya. The picturesque violence that he learned from some of the seventeenth-century Dutch and Flemish masters was combined with social criticism, and thus the violence was no longer jolly and *"boertig,"* but had adopted a shade of the sinister. Comparing Goya's etchings to a drawing by Antonio Pollaiuolo called *Fighting Nudes* (*ca.* 1460), one recognizes the difference between the classical and the romantic. The Florentine gave the obvious content of violence in a clean, detached, nonviolent rendering; Goya, in contrast, by committing himself, initiated a new style, rebelliously subjective (Romanticist), and the edge of social critique provided a slightly sadistic cut, which was to develop into real savagery in the twentieth century.

The modern *Zeitkritik,* emerging for the first time in the same period, may well have been inwardly related to the masochistic passivity of spleen, so characteristically a touch of the Romantic spirit. What is still vague and psychologically unfathomable, however, in the time-critique of Schiller, Fichte, Hegel, Goethe, Heine, Thoreau, Melville, Whitman, Burckhardt, Kierkegaard, Nietzsche, Flaubert, or Dostoevski, for instance, was graphically displayed in the growing trend toward satirical art. While Hogarth's pictures are still merely narrative, Daumier's treatment a hundred years later lifted the social anecdote out of the picturesque reportage and exposed its most crude and wicked angles to the searchlight of his criticism. Like Wordsworth, he was the artist of the common man, but without any admixture of rural bliss. His scene is set in the livid grey atmosphere of the city, his figures,

whose coarse features are aggravated by a brutal contour, are harshly arranged. With Toulouse-Lautrec, the
contour can be no less coarse, but the touch is more sophisticated. The cynicism in the casualness of *Woman
Pulling Up Her Stocking* is heightened by the Mephistophelian figure standing at her side, just as the mask
smirking over the nude ugliness of *Fat Mary* accentuates
the vulgar display of womanhood. In Beardsley's curvilinear finesse the individual involvement has disappeared
altogether to be replaced by sadistically deformative urbanity.

It was by no means in the satirical critique alone that
the new barbarism showed up. A strange proclivity for
horror may represent another strand in the history of
sadistic fantasy. The Gothic novels of Horace Walpole
and Mrs. Ann Radcliffe began a Romanticist trend perhaps most convincingly presented by the later tales of
E. T. A. Hoffmann and Edgar Allan Poe. In 1796, Matthew Gregory Lewis published the novel *Ambrosio, or
the Monk,* a story that startlingly combines torture,
supernatural horror, sadism, and sexual indecency. But it
was above all in a new, provocative attitude toward the
public that the element of sadism found its most widespread application. It was the nineteenth-century artist
who discovered the value of scandal.

The psychology of scandal is rooted in the Romanticist
revolt against patrician formalism. It is, for instance, styl-
istically apparent in the play of Romantic irony, a not
always successful device, yet one colorfully indicative of
the rebellious spirit of the time. Kierkegaard analyzed it
critically in his dissertation, dismissing the irony of Schlegel, Tieck, and the theorist Solcher as not living up to the
real "infinite negativity" of Socrates' irony. Tieck's theatrical irony, nevertheless, was an historical event, creating
a theater of the absurd, which was to have a long exciting record of its own. Whatever the intrinsic qualities of
Tieck's literary irony, it was a manifestation against the
existing polished, civilized forms. Romantic irony aimed
at (mildly) scandalizing the neat harmonious world con-

ception by destroying the objective, accepted forms through the irrational impulses of the subjective ego. Far more poetically equipped than both Schlegel and Tieck, Heine created a truly ironical style, whereby a lyrical tension was built on the polarity between the conventional ballad pattern and the negating intrusion of first person singular. With Friedrich Schlegel's *Lucinde,* which tried to demolish the entire traditional conception of wedlock and love, the attempt to embarrass the bourgeois moved outside the realm of playful irony and became a deliberate dismantling of conventions.

The young Richard Wagner assumed wholeheartedly the posture of one determined to scandalize the established order. Taking his place in the ranks of the rioters of 1848, he went into exile after their defeat, deciding to continue the revolution, which failed in politics, through the medium of art. His enemy was clearly always the same bourgeois Philistine. The Philistine, evil incarnate, promoting a system based on unrelenting materialism, still claimed the sponsorship of culture. It is, of course, justifiable to be amused by the irony that the Wagnerian cult, which was soon to rise, was in great part sustained by those very Philistines whom he affected to despise, a development he himself was never zealous to discourage. But neither cult nor debunking serves as a clear evaluation of Wagner's genius. Camille Saint-Saëns struck the balance when he declared that while "Wagneromania is an excusable absurdity, Wagnerophobia is a disease." Behind Wagner's humbug and histrionic postures there was a sincere core of revolutionary vision evidenced in his music. The message of *The Ring,* clothed in a gigantic, cumbersome manifestation of mythology and fanfare, is messianically directed against a world order founded on the economy of greed. The charlatan often hid the prophet. At the decisive turns of the nineteenth century Wagner, along with Kierkegaard, Nietzsche, and Darwin, belonged to the great historic scandalizers of the age.

Of a somewhat different order were the scandals that disrupted the artistic *Salons* in France. That these excitements should have taken place in France especially cannot be attributed to the quality of the artists alone, for Turner's impressionism of the 1830's, provoking no anger at all, was relatively far more revolutionary than that of the 1860's in France. The fact that, with the exception of the minor incidents surrounding Whistler and, on an entirely different plane, the morality scandal involving Oscar Wilde, England was less susceptible to this kind of upheaval may perhaps be explained by the greater social stability there, which prevents such political revolutions as those on the Continent. In any case, the French seem to have a particular bent for cultivating their form of *épater le bourgeois*. By arranging two nude women among elegantly dressed gentlemen in a wooded setting and calling this composition *Luncheon on the Grass,* Édouard Manet delighted in the casual touch of absurdity that seemed to plague the no-nonsense bourgeois immensely. In his *Olympia* the accentuated contour of the woman's body adds an element of vulgarity wholly acceptable to present-day taste but shocking to the refinement of nineteenth-century esthetics.

The work causing public shock is not always of the greatest artistic merit. Its importance, more often than not, lies in a propaganda value, a symbolic quality of revolt. So Victor Hugo's *Hernani* is a worthless drama, lacking anything that is not already new in Shakespeare's work, and one that at its first appearance in 1830 represented the "new" merely in its negative flouting of all neo-classicist rules. It served its propagandist purpose, however, for, owing to the ensuing furor, Romanticism in France was established. The provocation of the classical establishment by *Hernani* was only mild compared to that with which the public was challenged in 1896 by the performance of Alfred Jarry's *Ubu Roi.* As an expression of devastating contempt for the classical order in general it actually belongs more to the temper of the early twentieth century, especially because of the typical avant-garde quality it initiated. From then on the Romantic revolt, originally directed to particular cultural formalisms, became total. It aimed at the destruction of the whole hierarchy of values. Yeats, who happened to attend the premiere, commented pointedly by wondering what more was possible after Mallarmé, Verlaine, and his own verse. "After us the Savage God," was his answer.

The Savage God is not the only concept represented by Ubu. Ubu is also the proto- and archetype of the proletarian revenge on the elitist order. He is the jester usurping the throne of the old king. Jarry's vision is the primitive state of anarchy which was to prevail during the first decades of the twentieth century. This primitivism revealed itself in the influence of Negro sculptures, dances, and rhythms on the modern artist. It showed up in the futurist glorification of noise and warfare, in the Vortex manifesto of June 1914, with Ezra Pound's proclamation of the "Vortex of Fear," and in the dadaist obsession with seeing the sense of chaos in all things. The general disposition of the artist at that time seems to have been guided by an almost unconscious scandal complex with its anarchistic sadism coming to a climax during the First World War. The historic scandal-raising performance, in 1917, of Satie's *Parade* by the Diaghilev Ballet Russe with the cooperation of Picasso and Cocteau is representative of a whole era that seems to have been primarily aiming at the replacement of Renaissance man by the Neanderthal.

While the savage of the Romanticist was still "noble," the hero of the avant-garde is the rampaging beast of destruction. The playing with the polarity of Beauty and Beast in Victor Hugo's manifesto of Romanticism merely resulted in the promotion of the grotesque, which is ornamental in scope, the gargoyle type of bestiality decorating Gothic cathedrals. The Satanist cult of the Romanticists culminated in the "ever negating" figure of Mephistopheles, but he still loses out against the redeeming forces that save Faust. In the twentieth century, however, the bestial prevails. The norms of dignity are annulled. Beauty is superstition. The ferocious element is no longer an ornamental touch, playfully challenging the purity of line and classical proportions, but has become the thing itself. The conception of violence is not merely conveyed through the selection of the topic; it has permeated the technical resources of the contemporary artist.

It is in the uncompromising brush work of van Gogh at Saint-Rémy, in the color dynamics of the *fauves,* in the tormented landscapes of de Vlaminck, and the cruel deformity of Permeke's peasants' heads. It is in Kirchner's psychology of *Angst* hanging over his street scenes, in the cutting bite of Beckmann's triptychs, in the naked thrust of George Bellows' fighting bodies. It is wherever the artist finds it necessary to disfigure the human image, as in Francis Bacon's ghostly decomposing figures, in Portinari's fragmented natives of Brazil, in the depersonalized puppets of Dubuffet. Sculptors have not lagged behind in demolishing man's heroic image of himself. Barlach's panic-stricken bodies seem to lose their humanity in the heavy material from which they are built, Henry Moore hollows them out into empty cadavers, Giacometti stretches and twists them into necromantic horror.

Why is it that the twentieth-century artist seems so feverishly committed to the deformation of the human species? What esthetic principle tells him to destroy and disfigure what for centuries of classical norm had been viewed with pride and pleasure as a source of beauty? Why does the modern public masochistically delight in going to picture galleries to see the human being in his most degraded state, assaulted by savagery, reduced to fragments of hallucination and dread? Why does it adopt Picasso as its favored master? The classical mind would have judged his work a display of vulgarity and barbarism. Yet today's average observer, isolated from the origin of Western civilization, gapes at the coarse contours that rend the cohesion of the natural order into cubistic bits and pieces, as if an atomic blast had satanically challenged Newton's perfect universe.

Why, to vary the theme, has contemporary music developed into a state of anarchistic disjunction in which the dissonant rules with unchecked terror? Dissonance developed as gradually in history as did the technique of pictorial distortion. Arnold Schönberg, defending contemporary music in his *Harmonielehre,* stressed that dissonance is by no means a novelty in musical history. Physically speaking, this is clearly correct. The dissonant was recognized immediately when sixteenth-century harmony established the modern modality. The monk Giovanni Maria Artusi, a musical theorist, in his *On the Imperfection of Modern Music* (1600–1603), complained about the "rumbling of harmonies, intolerable to the ear." From its beginnings the history of music has seen the development of greater and harsher intrusions of alien chords. Through the times of Bach, Mozart, and Beethoven, each being no less classical for all his bold use of disturbing harmonic combinations, the process finally reached the breaking-point with Wagner's curiously shifting modal textures. The resulting polytonality and atonality are produced fundamentally by the liberty of distributing alien chords at will, whereby the entire harmonic field, as it were, becomes alienated.

The gradualism of this democratic process here, as elsewhere, is plainly evident. But Schönberg, concentrating solely on the physical logic, misleadingly ignored the metaphysical dimensions of the problem. A quantitative increase, which the growth of the modern dissonant reveals, after all, sometimes rises to the saturation-point whereby a recognizable change in quality takes place. Originally, the dissonant was merely ornamental. But just as the bestiality of the grotesque in art eventually changed from accidental ornamentation into an overriding agent of terror, so the dissonant changed from a colorful harmonic touch into a deliberate regime of barbarity. What Picasso means in a pictorial sense, Stravinsky means in terms of music appreciation.

It would be a grave mistake to infer from what has been said about the predominance of brutality that the modern arts, for that reason, ought to be evaluated as an inferior expression of culture. Modern painting and litera-

ture on the whole have been accepted with restrained enthusiasm, and as long as people greet their contemporary
art with as much acclaim as previous generations did
theirs, the question of ultimate quality historically remains open. More significant than either scorn or praise
is the effort to understand why it is that we have adopted
as our esthetics the absolute absence of esthetics and filled
the vacuum with the bravado of destruction and fragmentation.

One might have expected that after the Second World
War an upsurge of creative reconstruction in the arts
would have announced itself. One might have expected
that, after Communism and National Socialism killed the
last remnants of cultural life in Europe, the liberated Old
and the unscathed New World would have reacted with
a spontaneous constructive esthetic of new forms. Instead, the quarter of a century after the truce has presented itself as an era of stalemate, of chaos, and this in
spite of the exuberance and throbbing vitality that has
kept the cultural world in a hectic state, at least in a
quantitative sense. It seems, however, that new forms of
poetry, painting, or music are painfully absent. Perhaps
one must hope that they will be discovered in later decades, but at this moment the total field of today's culture seems one of frantic disorder. Under the circumstances it would be premature to evaluate the arts of the
last two or three decades according to their intrinsic
merits. It would be preferable to give the inconclusive
cultural situation at least the benefit of the doubt.

One thing, however, stands out with disquieting certainty. The general trend after 1945 points to a persistent
emulation of eccentric avant-garde ritual, without at the
same time moving foreward, producing "movement," as
the word avant-garde implies. This means a retrograde
avant-garde, that is, no avant-garde at all. Yet the word is
promoted and spread around as a magic formula for success. Unfortunately and misleadingly, what is offered as a
new style, op-art or pop-art for instance, appears to be
merely variations of dadaist, futurist, cubist, and sur-

realist experiments, domesticated and made palatable for commercial use. Op-art seems a clever scientific variation of neoplasticism, while pop-art appears as a popularization of the *Neue Sachlichkeit*. The commercial character of these and other allegedly new forms in itself presents no problem, and one could welcome it as an expedient way to distribute art to the larger public. It is merely the imitative quality of the external scandal-cult that raises suspicion.

During the early phase of the proletarian era, that is, roughly prior to the First World War, man could still be scandalized. Thus dadaism, and futurism, in their sensation-seeking exploits, were undoubtedly successful. Since 1945, however, now that everything is permitted, no one is really scandalized. And so the playing with old avant-garde shock-treatments becomes a mere gesture. Avant-garde has reached the status of establishment. It can be sold to the general market. It has become an institution —the very thing it sought to fight. Sadism and savagery in art have become an institution.

The only radically new extension to the scandal-syndrome of the 1910's and 1920's may be seen in the emergence of the Happening, an expression of Bohemian resistance that appears in varying forms. It is international in scope. In September 1966, the "First International Destruction in Art Symposium" was held, a festival of five rich days of Happenings. In its more brutal mood the Happening can be a sort of public wrecking party, while for the milder temper it may mean a genteel togetherness, sharing poetry, conversation, narcotics, or, preferably, Nothingness. In virtually all cases, however, the Happening suggests total equality of being, leveled participation. The "new Bohemia" of New York's lower East Side wants the "combine," the total equality, not excluding that of sex. The radicalness of their Happenings is apparent when they stage their dramatics, which, spontaneous and improvised, require the participation of all. Thus, there is neither public nor actor. The separation between stage and auditorium, which after all implies the acceptance of an elite artist, is abandoned. The cultural leveling is complete. The Happening is the ultimate in immediacy and destroys the traditional communication between artist and society through an absolute equality of experience.

The Happening is, of course, only an isolated symptom of a complicated trend. On the whole, what is offered as Underground art still retains some of the elitist quality inherent in the early twentieth-century avant-garde. Its strongest manifestation, its film, revives the clashing montage experiments of Hans Richter and Eisenstein, applied, however, to an unbridled obsession with sexuality, persistently perverse. In this field the greatest historic achievement may well be Kenneth Anger's *Scorpio Rising,* which combines the themes of narcotics, homosexuality, motorcycle cult, sadism, and fascism in a frantic narrative of destructiveness, ending in holocaust and the image of a leather belt on which is studded the legend: The End. This movie is a true product of our cultural consciousness, which seems furiously preoccupied with the techniques of devastation.

The expressions of a particular cultural era are plainly not unrelated. Collectively they point to a historical meaning that perhaps might not be extracted from each individually. Much as we dislike it, the question must be raised to what extent the brutality of Naziism, Marxism in the Soviet Union and in China, and the indulgence of the savage in the arts are all symptoms of the same underlying collective urge. It would not be very subtle to lump together all these phenomena of cruelty as if they were of the same order. But they ought to make us think. They should make us wonder if the gradual dissolution of the concept of authority and the commensurate rise of mass power have released latent energies of violence, which in previous times could be substantially contained.

Bluntly sweeping conclusions will not help here. Ever since Gustave Le Bon published *The Crowd: A Study of the Popular Mind* in 1895 and stated that the multitude in history effects the downfall of civilizations, there has been a seemingly endless echo of confirming voices. He himself, in a later work, *The Actual Evolution of the World*, was convinced that in coming decades the violence of the masses would produce the new Caesars. This was written in 1927. But surely the crowd is not exclusively corrupt! When André Malraux, in *The Voices of Silence*, said that the masses "rarely transcend a taste for brutality," he actually presented a half-truth. For the crowd can also join in devotion (religious worship), in enthrallment (the theater), or in harmless gaiety (the beach). The trouble begins only when the collective aims are exclusively materialistic. It is then that the thrust of greed and the dynamics of economic expansionism produce a creed of quantity, bulk, and force. It is then that we must expect the collective mentality to show signs that restraint on the latent violence residing in every mass formation is disappearing.

Positioned, as we are, in the yet uncompleted process of proletarianization, we should be careful not to anticipate ultimate conclusions. But with the signals flashing around us, it would be irresponsible to ignore the symptoms of a collective irrationality that threatens to flood the last resources of human freedom. It is permeating the actions and oratory of the leaders of labor unions, minority movements, student malcontents, faculty groups, and protesting clergy. The volcanism of unreason is general and epochal. To seek scapegoats here would merely foster deceit. When, according to a popular magazine, a leader of the French Underground artists, claiming that his Happenings are directed against the old classical art, calls this art fascist, he seems to mislead himself historically. For it is the Happening, or any such manifestation of non-art, non-theater, or non-poetry which, with exhibitionist abandon, exercises the newly gained freedom of violence. The crucial historical question is, do not Hitler, Lenin, Stalin, and Mao epitomize the rising power of savagery, which the arts, since the beginning of this century, have displayed in increasingly popular configurations of barbarism?

A poet in our time is a semi-barbarian in a civilized community. He lives in the days that are past.
                                        Thomas Love Peacock

6

The Poetic Way of Living

Commoners all?

The Romantic revolution did not arrive unheralded. The appearance of the *Lyrical Ballads* and the *Athenaeum* in 1798 were only two of the more conspicuous signs of revolt. There had been ominous rumblings before. The tempestuous works of the Sturm und Drang writers and many of Blake's publications preceded them. In general it is safe to say that the new movement represented a series of explosions, occurring in various countries and causing a chain reaction of repetitive blasts, which were to demolish the classical order of art and literature. While concentrating on the significance of this development, it is imperative to distinguish between outer forms and historical purpose. The complex and multifarious aspects of the Romantic movement have caused many a critic to select specific, if isolated, phenomena to support a one-sided theory. The first thing to recognize, however, is that Romanticism's major characteristic was its self-contradicting ambiguity, a feature narcissistically cultivated moreover by some of its adherents.

It would appear then that with due recognition of the many-faceted effects, the actual generating energy of the movement was concerned with the destruction of the classicist-form cults. The core of the revolt lay in the rejection of a regime of esthetic rules, authorized from above by the standard-bearers of an antiquated tradition. One specific area in which the battle was fought concerned the change in literary *diction*. This was formulated in the most explicit way by Wordsworth in the 1800 preface of *Lyrical Ballads*. Defending his verse against hostile critics, he claimed to have taken pains to avoid "what is usually called poetic diction." This, he continued, "has necessarily cut me off from a large portion of phrases and figures of speech which from father to son have long been regarded as the common inheritance of poets." Instead of this exalted poetic diction, Wordsworth preferred a "language really used by men," a language inspired by ordinary things and that "low and rustic life," where the people are "less under restraint and speak a plainer and more emphatic language."

Clearly the age of the common man in literature had begun. It is in many cases hard to tell to what extent the interest was of a social or of an esthetic nature, or perhaps a vague mixture of both. Sometimes one must suspect the plea for a common diction to have been made without any thoughts of common people in mind. William Hazlitt's agitation against eighteenth-century classicism rested on his dislike for a pompous style, which "uses a word twice as big as the thing you want to express." While Wordsworth concentrated on poetic diction, Hazlitt twenty years later, in one of his essays in *Table Talk,* concerned himself chiefly with the "familiar style" in prose. He objected to Dr. Johnson's style because it lacked discrimination, selection, and variety and because he used none but "tall, opaque words." In contrast, he demanded an unvarnished medium, able to convey ideas by its sheer simplicity. "I hate anything that occupies more space than it is worth. I hate to see a load of band-boxes go along the street, and I hate to see a parcel of big words without anything in them." To those who believed that his "familiar style" led to vulgarity, he replied, on the contrary, "there is nothing that requires more precision, and, if I may so say, purity of expressions."

Hazlitt's plea was for lucidity at a period when heroic values were being deflated and the pomp of ancient grandeur stripped from society in general. With wigs and culottes abolished, it was only fair that the flourish of words should disappear from written and spoken communications. With monarchs in the process of being retired into exile or of being reduced to mere servants of a parliamentary system, the regal tone had lost its impressive ring. This was vividly illustrated by one of the issues connected with the premiere of Hugo's *Hernani* in 1830. Théophile Gautier, who, with his fellow poet Gérard de Nerval organized the riots, reported in his *History of Romanticism* that for three days a battle raged about supposedly trivial lines such as the following, uttered by the King of Spain:

Is it midnight?—Midnight soon?

The conventional public in 1830 found it an unbearable thought that royal dignitaries should formulate their questions in such pedestrian terms. To Hugo, the common diction apparently must apply to the speech of all classes, and if the life of royalty was still worthy of the theater, then it had to be democratized for stage use. The elevated diction thus disappeared, as it did also in the developing new opera. At least one must wonder whether

Wagner, with his dream of an art rooted in the people, was not consistent in creating a revolutionary sing-speech. In spite of the rhetorical verse libretto, it bears the mark of a leveled, common diction, shared by gods, giants, dwarfs, and humans and setting the example for the modern music drama.

At that time, of course, the family drama in prose already had a history of about a hundred years of groping and perfecting, and even before the efforts of Lessing and Diderot at dramatizing simple middle-class problems, familiar speech was by no means unknown. Shakespeare used it for workmen's scenes, especially when he needed comic relief. Breero, the seventeenth-century Dutch poet, put common characters on the stage and provided them with a vividly realistic, racy prose dialogue. In the nineteenth century, however, the spectacular rise of the middle-class drama gave a tremendous boost to the acceptance of daily-life speech in literature in general.

Common diction is a sure sign of the rising order of the proletariat, not in the narrow political sense, but primarily in its broadly cultural scope. For common diction, far from revealing class consciousness, cuts across classes with the usual universal leveling characteristic of the process of proletarianization. In this development of Romanticist equalitarianism the United States has played its historic role. William Cullen Bryant's tone was still hesitant and full of Wordsworthian echoes:

> O fairest of the rural maids!
> Thy birth was in the forest shades;
> Green boughs, and glimpses of the sky,
> Were all that met thine infant eye.

But soon Walt Whitman was to lend his vigorous impetus to the movement. His verse was equalitarian in its encompassing breadth and pioneer spirit.

> All the hands of comrades clasping, all the
> Southern, all the Northern,
> Pioneers! O pioneers!

Whitman represented the Jacobin radicality in the revolt against classicism. His poetry no more abides by prosodic rules than does the chant of a thrush. Its message pours liberally over all; it sings for coon hunters, flatboatmen, spinning girls, farm hands, duck shooters, mechanics, and woodcutters and in general identifies itself with all that is wide, open, throbbing, and universal.

Not all the common man's poetry was of course, as universal and blithely proletarian as Whitman's. Some of it was outright political in the limiting sense. When, in 1819, the British government crushed a meeting of the Reform movement, causing the "Manchester massacre," Shelley responded with a simple allegory "The Mask of Anarchy." Its verse is simple and in tone almost the opposite of the more usually Platonic Shelley. It is pitched to the workers' level and it ends with a rousing exhortation, which shows that, three decades before the *Communist Manifesto,* the socialist movement, intellectually at least, was fully established.

> Rise like Lions after slumber
> In unvanquishable number—
> Shake your chains to earth like dew
> Which in sleep had fallen on you—
> Ye are many—they are few.

Shelley also planned a series of poems to support the workingmen and their social struggle, an unfinished project of which only a little was completed, most notably the "Song to the Men of England":

> Men of England, wherefore plough
> For the lords who lay ye low?
> Wherefore weave with toil and care,
> The rich robes your tyrants wear?

This kind of lyricism may not represent the most subtle verse, but it is historically important in that it initiated a mode of political poetry that integrally belongs to modern literature. To be sure, in England it was not a genre to which the most eminent men of letters dedicated themselves. If they did, as in Shelley's case, they hardly excelled. William Morris' battle songs for the Socialist League are rather silly affairs. D. H. Lawrence was wittier at least. When the London police confiscated his pictures for alleged obscenity, the author, in "Innocent England," replied with a humorous touch that his paintings must be destroyed so the English artists may learn to use a *cache-sexe,* a fig-leaf, or a wreath of mist.

The French political lyric is represented by Aragon's "Ballad of the Twenty-Seven Condemned of Nadiejdinsk," for instance, depicting a scene of the Russian Civil War. Vladimir Mayakovsky's communist verse sounds echoes of Whitman's chant, presenting them in futurist typography:

> The working-class
> speaks
> through my mouth,
> and we,
> proletarians,
> are drivers of the pen.

Walter Hasenclever, the German expressionist writer, in *The Political Poet,* gave a serious account of what seemed to him the decline of political influence in the modern world and urged the poet to take over and lead the people through justice instead of through warfare and weapons.

The political verse belongs to a far wider type of poetry, which emerged as a characteristic by-product of the new society. It shows varying aspects, but collectively it could perhaps best be called journalistic lyricism. This needs to be qualified, for today's journalism to many of us does not evoke the most elevated thoughts. Journalistic poetry, however, carries no necessarily pejorative overtones. Good journalism is the serious art of distributing, analyzing, and interpreting actuality. In the eighteenth and nineteenth centuries it brought the newspaper of the old gazettes and corantos type up to date by serving the new popular demand for information. It also produced an encyclopedic mentality in literature. Thus the authors of the French Enlightenment popularized much of the available scientific thinking, especially that with a particular bearing on social stagnation and intolerance —an activity of first-rate journalistic order.

In Germany this kind of topical literature flourished around 1830 with the *Young Germany* group, which followed along the lines of the French *philosophes* but with a more radically political thrust. Heine was, independently, related to this movement, and some of his verse presents in simple metrical form social and political critiques along with that popular touch which gives this genre the character of poetic journalism. Heine's prominent contribution to democratized poetry is the more remarkable, since in specific statements he shows himself to be convinced that "in the world of poets the Third Estate is not useful, but only obnoxious." In separate aphorisms he declared that democracy leads to the end of literature because of the "freedom and equality of style." The democrats would be against love and roses and would instead demand hymns to the potato. "The Parnassus is going to be leveled and asphalted."

While defining journalistic lyricism, one must clearly distinguish it from the traditional forms of satire. The classical satire, that of Archilochus, Juvenal, Martial, Dryden, or Pope, ordinarily comes in highly sophisticated formal diction and shuns the colloquial. Dante, Milton, and Vondel were not above putting their political grievances into lyrical lines, but these never bear a recognizable journalistic mark. Heine's verse does, at least when dealing with topical events. For instance, the poems entitled *Zeitgedichte*, which are simple lyrics, usually in quatrains, comment mostly sarcastically on the failures and foibles of Germany at that time.

Heine introduced no novelty. Goethe and Schiller before him cooperated in the epigrams of 1796, called the *Xenien*, using this form to ridicule contemporary figures and situations in a light colloquial language. Neither of the two, however, was equipped to provide the popular touch to bring off this genre effectively. More important was the Mephistophelian wit that Goethe brought to his *Faust* and that was to become the foundation of the later cynical brands of poetry. One of the earliest specimens of the modern poem of social commitment is Adalbert von Chamisso's "The Old Laundry Women." In "The Beggar and His Dog," the final word (*verreckt*) introduces the colloquial dissonance, not inappropriately in the context of the Romanticist concern for the common man. There were also, of course, influences from remoter times at work here. As a good Romanticist, Heine could not escape the magic of the medieval ballad. While his fellow poets were chiefly inclined to adopt the serious, innocent tone, Heine, in addition, employed a romantic form of irony that had its roots in a late medieval mentality. Of this, the goliardic songs and François Villon's ballads are probably the most obvious examples.

One of the crucial aspects of this modern genre-poetry lies in the topical *anecdote*, the vivid illustration lending immediate conveyance to information and, as such, an essential device for the art of journalism, which thrives on the immediate and incidental. The jounalistic lyricism cultivated by Heine uses the anecdote not merely for social and political purposes, but, more remarkably, it turns the intimate subjective experience into an anecdote. Thus, in Heine's love lyrics, his emotional feelings related in ballad form acquire the air of casual reportage. In *Lyrisches Intermezzo,* one of his best-known volumes, his erotic vicissitudes are conveyed in anecdotic stories about a lotus flower, the Dom in Cologne, a fig tree, a royal prince, a tea party, a falling star, or a gigantic coffin. The lyrical and epic modes become curiously intermixed, and the resulting clash brings out another facet of the newly discovered romantic irony.

The modern genre-verse—political, social, journalistic, anecdotic—besides being indebted to Heine's contributions, was no less vigorously generated by Byron's *Don*

Juan. This satire, written as a colloquial report of contemporary events in the light of the poet's ridicule, unlike
the smooth satire of Pope (whom Byron admired, incidentally), is a clear representative of the new order. The
casual wit, the negation of classical technique, the deliberately impure rhymes, the comical enjambments, the destruction of the old polished alexandrine, the Mephistophelean absurdities, the resentment against the established dispensation—all combine to make it a grand
manifestation of the romantic revolution. In the twentieth century, Byron as well as Heine are the sources of a
new journalistic lyricism, which, without necessarily being popular with the masses, still reflects the contemporary equalized world. Thus in Erich Kästner's "The Age
Drives a Car," the disturbing and disturbed period between the world wars is described in a crisp, matter-of-
fact style, which is typical for the *Neue Sachlichkeit* of
the time and which, by its prosaic understatement, acquires an accent of cynical realism.

> The cities grow. And stocks go up in price.
> If one has money, one has credit too.
> The bank book speaks. The balance sheet is silent.
> The people lock each other out. They strike.
> The globe revolves and we revolve along.
>
> The merchants bargain. And the traders deal.
> The money circulates as if by duty.
> Factories grow. And factories collapse.
> What yesterday existed now is gone.
> The globe revolves. But we don't notice it.

Other influences besides that of romantic irony were at
work in the development of popular genre-poetry. There
was the simple fact of the rise of the daily newspaper and
its stress on local reporting. There was the ascent of
prose literature at the expense of poetry. There was the
impact of Whitman's verse on the expressionist lyricists
of the 1920's, with its unrestricted interest in the objects
of human environment, no matter what. Alongside the
strand of romantic irony there was the later playful ab-

surdity that has made attractive and modern the poems of Edward Lear, Lewis Carroll, Wilhelm Busch, and Christian Morgenstern. Finally, one must not underestimate the contributing effects of the new genre of the *thing-poem*. One of its earliest examples is Mörike's intimate "On a Lamp," which began a trend culminating in Rilke's middle period. Such poems as "The Panther," "The Gazelle," "The Swan," "Blue Hortensia," or "Last Evening," all Rilke's *New Poems*, seem to penetrate phenomenologically the essence of things. They belong in no sense, of course, to the light modern reportage poetry, but Rilke's technique of isolating thing and incident could easily be utilized by those poets whose lines were more attuned to the immediacy of a superb cabaret climate. The song-like lyrics of Kästner, Klabund, and Brecht reveal this. Joachim Ringelnatz often wrote a Rilkean verse, simplified and cabaretized by tender understatements, as in "The Way Home at Night":

> A lamp swings through the night.
> Clap clap—
> I will remember,
> That my mother is still awake
> And will wave my hat to her.
>
> We are not what we ought to be,
> We are merely fond of each other,
> But my mother is old and far.
> And my heart is so full today.

The anecdotic genre-poem has been most common in Germany, mid-Europe, and Holland where the work of Goethe, Heine, and Rilke is almost common knowledge. Yet the Anglo-American countries, delving into their own common sense and utilizing the common diction introduced by Wordsworth and Byron, have produced their own poetic reportage. In "Nineteen Hundred and Nineteen," Yeats, in a post-war mood, meditated on bygone heroic days and urged his readers to mock the great who were so busy leaving monuments behind. Louis Mac-Neice in "Autumn Journal" described the change from a world of essentials and universal concepts to one of individual daily bothersome objects:

> So blow the bugles over the metaphysicians.
> Let the pure mind return to the Pure Mind;
> I must be content to remain in the world of Appearance
> and sit on the mere appearance of a behind.

With this we are in the generation of "clinical" poetry, which in technique and tone actually represents a counterpart to the German *Neue Sachlichkeit*. Its utilitarian character makes this mode of poetry well-suited to the American taste. Sometimes the versification has an old-fashioned, even epigonic, ring, as that of Frost, for instance, who seemed an anachronism in the age of Rilke, Eliot, Apollinaire, cummings, and Pound. Though lacking in vibrant originality, the popular appeal of his work has pointed to an apparent need for a new conventionality at a time when the furies of avant-garde schools are exhausted, and the large new public wants its art, theater as well as poetry, comprehensible. In a less traditional vein, William Carlos Williams, Ezra Pound, e e cummings, and Archibald MacLeish have explored the poetic borderlines of colloquial diction. Marianne Moore in "Poetry" appropriately adopted the proletarian suspicion of poetic values in general and solved the problem with sound common sense. She, too, dislikes poetry, but says that reading it with complete contempt one discovers in verse things that are "useful."

The common diction of poetry—political, rustic, journalistic, anecdotic, cynical, or otherwise—has in great measure adjusted literature to the level and needs of modern society. While it may be more rewarding to stress the change from an elite to a utilitarian poetry as an illustration of the proletarianizing trends, one can hardly ignore the art of prose. For the novel, after all, is the product of mass need, and its two centuries' history must inevitably reflect the increased role of the common man in a cultural respect. The novel is customarily seen as a bourgeois expression of literature, a view obviously correct, but one not without a misleading superficiality. The middle classes rose with the cities in the late Middle Ages. Perhaps the *fabliaux,* the rough, realistic tales of that time, signaled their awakening consciousness. Their real cultural fruition, however, did not occur until the time of the early Dutch Republic, notably in painting, but to a minor extent also in realistic prose. It took a few more centuries to develop a fully confident novel technique, one with a recognizable broad, popular appeal.

The middle classes, culturally speaking, were proto-proletarian. They belonged to the masses, and while they hesitated to choose between elite and collective, invariably in the arts and literature their tastes ran contrary to the classical sense of order. Above all, they were naturally proletarian-minded in their leveling of the heroic. The rise of the novel in the eighteenth century coincided with the early bourgeois drama, both representing the negation of the sublime classical hero. With the hero's glamor diminishing, the heroic diction also disappeared. Prose dialogue is the common man's communication. To be sure, there is a marked difference between Tom Jones and George Babbitt, but both belong to the same world of mass awareness and leveling tendencies.

The novel indeed, in the most general terms, is one of the strongest expressions of mass-consciousness. As soon as its popularity began to manifest itself, apprehensive, though not necessarily hostile, voices were heard. Oliver Goldsmith, for example, though fearing the potential change from quality to quantity, was not unwilling to see the advantages of an author being dependent on the public rather than on the patron. This problem, incipient and vaguely realized in the eighteenth century, became acute when in the nineteenth century serialization of novels appeared more and more successful. It was then that the novelist reached his largest audience and that Alexandre Dumas and Eugène Sue ran their novel factories. It was then also that commentators such as Hazlitt warned that popular taste lowers the standards of literature, that the novelist Flaubert complained that the time for beauty was over and that the modern novelist lacked a sound basis. Behind the critique of mass circulation and mass-taste there was the obvious fear of mass-terror in social and political matters. Thus James Fenimore Cooper in his *Home as Found* did not speak as a literary observer, but as a social critic when he declared that he knew of "no nation in which the expression of opinion is so certain to attract persecution and hostility as our own, though it may be, and is, in one sense free."

In the twentieth century the circulation of popular novels, of course, is still increasing, but this is chiefly under the market pressure of best-seller lists and college course reading material. The avid novel-reading audience is a rapidly disappearing community. The mass media offer a more immediately gratifying entertainment. Flaubert's early awareness that the bond between writer and crowd was breaking up becomes more evident today with the widening split between the novel for the connoisseur and the novel for the book club. Disregarding the forced reading in college courses, poetry has virtually become a cult of the initiates of highbrow in-groups—a dubious phenomenon in an age of collectivism. What is considered to be the genuine representative of the twentieth-century novel is usually not at all intellectually accessible to the large public. In the unfortunate, but inevitable, classification of "high" and "low" culture these works then are relegated to a super-class and adopted and commented upon by an intellectual consensus group, estranged from the popular consciousness. While Hugo, Balzac, Dickens, Dostoevski, or Tolstoy belonged to all classes, the "cultural" novel of the twentieth century is the domain of professorial research and exegesis.

Considering the well-advanced stage of the mass-society, there is obviously a sterile element in this situation. In addition, a curious new genre has emerged, which, abandoning the classical objective narrative, dilutes the plot with private experience. In Thomas Mann's *Buddenbrooks* or *Tonio Kröger* the autobiographical material was still translated into a firmly developed "story." With the novels of Proust and Joyce, however, the narcissistic lingering on the subjective self and the minute analysis of personal case histories began to prevail. This solipsism by no means becomes universal, of course. But since it appears frequently in the modern novel, one is bound to wonder about its symptomatic nature. Most of Gide's characters, for example, reveal the author's own psychological problems, put in moral (*The Counterfeiters*) or religious (*Strait Is the Gate*) perspective. Self-devotion of this kind corresponds with the cult of the ego, which has made psychoanalysis so unabashedly fashionable, and with the self-pitying pose of lost generations, angry young men, and beatniks. Never before have so many detailed autobiographies and memoirs appeared; in no age have so many relatively insignificant people sold their life stories to the public. Although solipsism in the art of prose writing may be symptomatic, this does not, of course, imply any negative reflection on quality. The sterility of Narcissus has its own beauty, but he can hardly represent the archetype of a mass society. He may well be the last symbol of a dying elite.

In competition with the livelier and more immediately rewarding entertainment of television, the films, show business, and mass sports, the novel must inevitably be a declining proposition as a proletarian form of literature. The question has been raised, and not merely by outsiders and defeatist prophets of doom, whether the art of literature in general is in an atrophic state. Clearly the question is dangerously speculative. But if it arises in the very heart of the professionals, one can hardly ignore it. On the occasion of the thirty-fourth International P.E.N. Congress in New York, its president wrote an article expressing great doubt about the future of literature. "Poets began literature, we're liable to finish it." The reason—the predominance of science. Heine, as we have noted, blamed the alliance between democratization and poetry. Hegel merely assumed that all had been said. Whatever the truth in these judgments, it cannot be asserted that

writers since Hegel have not tried hard enough to rejuvenate the ancient forms of literature. Those who for
that purpose choose to apply the common man's speech
are historically justified, for this is in keeping with the irrevocable rule of common opinion, common sense, common taste.

Wanderers all?

The Romanticists have often been accused of escapism,
a nebulous term, especially considering the fact that this
reproach not infrequently comes from critics who profess
to be scientifically realistic. There are numerous methods of escape, and in our drugged society, which promotes addiction of any kind—liquor, narcotics, television—it will not do to throw stones at others. There is no
good reason to believe that science and laboratory research is not motivated by intellectual escape. Confident
boasts of social "realism" in many cases turn out to be expressions of a utopian creed. Moreover, the Romanticists
themselves often participated in political realism—Uhland, Heine, Hugo, Lamartine, Shelley, Byron being the
most conspicuous examples. Nor were they antipathetic
to science. Many of them were absorbed in scientific phenomena and experiments, sometimes in an amateurish
way, not infrequently in a perfectly professional manner.
Let us admit that man has a fundamental need to escape
and that this need in modern society, for one reason or
another, has become more evident. Among the many escape routes there are those that evade the problems of industrial society, those that shun the problems of metaphysics, those that flee the facts of materialism, and those
that run away from the heights of idealism. The modern
mind is almost inexorably forced to choose some existence of flight.

There are many kinds of Romanticists, and their ways
of escape differ according to the world from which they
desire to escape. One of the most conspicuous configura-

tions in literature since the Romantic movement is the Wanderer. In classical poetry, of course, there was no lack of journeying and moving about. But there was rarely the Wanderer in the modern sense, as we associate him with Faust, for instance, who leaves a secure, secluded home base for the search of a vague absolute. Homer's Ulysses is, after all, on his way home, but Joyce's Leopold Bloom meanders aimlessly in his native city. There lies the difference. Bunyan's Pilgrim is the archetype of classical man, Everyman indeed, who, though tempted and attracted by terrestrial joys, is constantly reminded of the celestial realm which he claims as his religious fatherland.

With Romanticism, poetry and prose began to cultivate a new voyager who, without real sense of practical direction or of home-coming, rather deliberately drifts away from his own community. The new German novel was fond of depicting him. Wilhelm Meister is his prototype. Wilhelm must be educated to the reality of his own society, but when he grasps it, he still keeps wandering, brooding, with no other impetus but philosophical reflection. Following Goethe, Ludwig Tieck wrote his *Sternbalds Wanderungen,* while Novalis published his *Heinrich von Ofterdingen,* whose protagonist is in search of the Blue Flower, symbol of the pure infinite. In the ballad-like lyrics of the German poets, the Wanderer is often the self-exiled dreamer, who seems to seek an outside position to foster nostalgia. There is nostalgia in Hölderlin for ancient Greece, in Tieck, Novalis, and Uhland for the Middle Ages. There is nostalgia in Eichendorff's longing for the ancestral castle in Silesia, and in Chamisso for *Schloss Boncourt* in France.

The pattern of the Wanderer persisted throughout the nineteenth century and deep into the twentieth. The archetype of Faust, the man estranged from his original location, reappeared time and again in numerous varieties. Peer Gynt's life is a vain struggle for self-assertion: Ibsen's other restless hero, Brand, journeys in the rugged Scandinavian mountains, neglecting simple social duties in

order to find the essence of absolute being and love.
Strindberg, at the end of his life, turned to the Faustian
theme in the mystical search of *To Damascus* and *The
Great Highway.*

The dislocated seeker of truth in English literature is
revealed as the mild meditative poet—in fact, Wordsworth himself in "The Prelude," where he gently gropes
for the relationships between man and nature, man and
society. He appears more adventurously Faustian in
Byron's *Childe Harold's Pilgrimage* and *Don Juan* and
more mystically idealistic in Shelley's *Alastor.* In all
these instances, however, there is the same prevailing
mood of detachment from the community of origin. In
many cases this results in a pining boredom, the suffering
of a *mal du siècle,* an intellectual defeatist frustration
which makes Werther commit suicide. It is the impotent
languishing which drives Chateaubriand's René to the
United States, precisely to a country where he does not
belong and is to suffer as an alien outsider.

But what about the Americans themselves? Are they
not in their historical role of restless immigrants the preeminent Wanderers? Undoubtedly. The dynamics of the
vast tide of immigration indicate an underlying psychology of escape. The trek to the West, the frontier-penetra-
tion, is the story of fugitives. Ironically, however, the
great American literature does not deal with the heroism
of the frontier. No great literary epic has been written
about this historic movement. And with the exception of
Twain and Whitman, most authors of the golden age of
American literature were extremely negative about the
typical American achievement of the nineteenth century.
Edger Allan Poe's pure esthetic judgment was absolutely
foreign to the pragmatic drive of the expansionist society.
James Fenimore Cooper condemned it. His stories are
persistently about Wanderers. But they are not frontiers-
men, for these the author viewed as destructive agents of
greed. His heroes rather go into the wild woods (*The
Leatherstocking Tales*) or roam the seas (*The Pilot*).
According to Parrington, Cooper "found himself nowhere

at home . . . and sought a haven of refuge in vicarious existence, at times in the wilderness beyond the soil and smutch of the Jacksonian frontier, at times in the Utopian world of *The Crater* where an honest man could find free play for his creative energy."

The transcendentalists, though in many ways different from both Poe and Cooper, represented the same alien enclave in a world of increasing materialism. Thoreau's life was a flight from a society of industrial greed to the Concord and Merrimac rivers, to the Maine woods, or to the autonomous existence of Walden Pond, where he could thoughtfully see "the nervous, bustling, trivial nineteenth century" go by. Emerson may seem less eccentric, but he, too, lecturing from place to place, was a voice in the wilderness. And who but Melville, fleeing to the whales of the South Seas and the cannibals of the Marquesas Islands, could complete more convincingly the picture of a cultural age of Wanderers?

The restless temper of this nation of immigrants revealed itself in many kinds of fugitive tendencies. The irony in the works of Cooper and the transcendentalists, which, while thoroughly native, still defied the very American expansionist spirit, was repeated later when the waves of expatriates began to manifest themselves. Dissatisfied in rather vague and general terms with the cultural state of America, important literary figures such as Henry James, Sinclair Lewis, T.S. Eliot, Ezra Pound, William Faulkner, F. Scott Fitzgerald, and Ernest Hemingway, to name a few, sought to find a more congenial setting in Europe. Henry Adams, who himself could never find rest in his homeland, understanding the nature of this estrangement, pointed out that the expatriate remained a true American and was no more satisfied abroad than at home. Indeed, with the exception of Eliot and Pound, the expatriate merely represents the modern type of Wanderer, who, though a cultural outsider, cannot detach himself completely from his original community.

The Faustian seeker, dislocated from spatial security,

was a more conspicuous figure in the nineteenth century then today. But he has a counterpart, who, though emerging in the same Romantic environment, has become more ubiquitous in the twentieth century. He is the Wanderer in time. He is dislocated in the chronology of human existence. Becoming self-conscious about historical order, he lives in fears of historical age and suffers from an intensified sense of time. Ugo Foscolo, the early Italian Romanticist in nocturnal mood, found that the evening made him rove in meditations,

> . . . on the trails
> which lead to a perennial Nothingness, and meanwhile this evil time escapes.

Human existentialism, facing the void of Nothingness, experiences time as evil. This was to be confirmed by the *poètes maudits,* the poets who felt themselves condemned by a Philistine pragmatic society. One of their most prominent representatives, Charles Baudelaire, in *Spleen et Idéal,* spoke of time as eating our lives, while "the dark enemy that sucks our heart, on the blood that we lose grows strong." This dark enemy was the new realization of boredom, the *ennui,* in German the *Weltschmerz,* which is fundamentally a being ill at ease with his own epochal time. The tedium, rooted in the feeling of futility, makes apparent the frustration of the poet unable to be a constructive link in the modern order of materialist expediency. He is not merely condemned by the Philistine but also by the whole historical disposition of the age. The realization of time then is like that of a dragging disease, as Rilke described it in his "Requiem to a Friend":

> and time is long
> and time goes by and time grows out and time
> is like a long recurring illness.

The outsider in the order of time is the man for whom practical action remains a futile way of living. The sterility he cultivates represents one more negating element in the unheroic trend of the period. Flaubert's *Sentimental Education* is one of the early novels of the non-hero. Frédéric, its protagonist, is the modern futilist who cannot make sense out of his enterprises and lingers fruitlessly over wasted years. The classification "historical," which Zola gave to this novel, is justified, but for better reasons than the fact that the story is set against the background of the 1830 revolution, for Frédéric is hardly involved in the uprising. The main point is the expression of the doubt in Frédéric (and Flaubert) about the efficacy of action as such and in the context of the time. The nineteenth-century sufferer from tedium was unable to locate himself in the evolving order of time and felt derailed from the historical track.

Man gone astray in the order of real time is depicted in virtually all of Kafka's tales. His characters live in an environment that seems convincingly "real" yet is without relevance to daily experience as we know it. Similarly the sanatorium patients in Thomas Mann's *The Magic Mountain* lead an existence that seems lifted out of historical time, so that they maintain a fool's paradise in which the real issues of life (their tuberculosis, for instance) become irrelevant. In contrast, in the nineteenth century it was still possible to adopt a faith in destiny, either in the "manifest" version of the American frontier, or by the unperturbed optimism of the progressivist, or else in Nietzsche's enraptured embrace of an *amor fati*. The infatuation with destiny in Spengler's world view was cooled down to a Spartan loyalty to fate. But after him, the term destiny loses its meaning for the twentieth-century mind. Destiny implies a sense of history, that is, sense of time and ripeness, and these are attributes obviously frustrated in a century of technological imperialism, of devasting wars, and of the cruelties of Hitler, Stalin, and Mao. Sense of time requires security in the contemporary setting and unflinching trust in the future. Both seem such vague and relative conceptions to us that we can hardly understand how previous centuries, at least in their cultural manifestations, revealed them so confidently.

Sense of time also requires the feeling of cohesion. Discussing the trend of fragmentation in the fine arts, we analyzed some of the contributing factors. To these may be added the neuroses resulting from the shattering of the bonds in modern family life, the wars in Europe, and the migrating restlessness in the United States. Finally, what has been described as the loss of temporal security completes the picture. It is reflected in the broken coherence of thought, plot, and syntax of much of today's literature. Faulkner's novels, especially *The Sound and the Fury,* are frequently kaleidoscopic renderings of disconnected action and thought. The plotless play in our century has become as characteristic as the plotless novel. Thus the figures in Beckett's *Waiting for Godot* and *Endgame* hover and drift aimlessly without relationship to environment or time continuum. They express the feeling of namelessness, which Robert Musil, the Austrian novelist, described decades earlier as "that dissolution through immense numbers which makes the difference between this and all other times. The loneliness and anonymity of the individual in the ever–growing masses which implies a new spiritual outlook whose consequences cannot as yet be discerned."

In poetry the Romanticist on the whole retained a firmly integrated verse. Wordsworth, though prolix at times, never failed in distributing values of meaning and modality in the classical way. With Whitman things began to change. His sentences pile up indiscriminately, so that the structure of the poem loosens, and the parts are continuously on the brink of detaching themselves from the whole. The surrealists, in their efforts to disrupt the conventional meaning of words and images, might also attempt to neutralize the time sequence. Thus Pierre Reverdy in "Departure" disconnected the individual elements of information, sentences and images, so that the relations, temporal as well as spatial, between man, woman, and train are, if not anulled, at least broken.

The horizon curves
    The days are longer
    Journey
A heart leaps in a cage
    A bird sings
    It is dying
Another door is to open
    At the end of the hall
      Where a star
      Begins to glow
A dark woman
      The lantern of the leaving train

The futurists, who learned a great deal from Whitman, took the ultimate step. In one of his manifestoes of 1912, Marinetti, the leader of the movement, declared that his aim was the destruction of the traditional sentence, the abolition of adjective, adverb, and all punctuation, in order to create the full liberty of movement. To illustrate his intentions he added a prose poem, "The Battle," which was to convey the immediacy of warfare. It begins as follows:

mid-day 3/4 flutes groans dog-days tumbtumb
alarms Gargaresch to-tear-one-self-away
cracklings march Tintinnio knapsacks rifles
sandals spikes cannons manes wheels coffins
Jews pancakes bread-with-margarine ditties
food-stalls abuses eye-sore stench

and so on for five more pages. But surely in this montage technique the dynamics of movement have become an abstraction. Time is frozen to a standstill.

Abnormals all?

Besides the Wanderer in space and the Wanderer in time, there are other strangers whom contemporary literature treats with specific care. There is the underdog for example. The little man falls outside the classical conception of the heroic. Being thus useless for the tragic experience, he can merely function for comic relief. As such, Shakespeare, Goldoni, Molière, and Holberg incorporated him into their plays, where he appeared under the mask of slave, clown, servant, soldier, porter, and other menial characters.

The underdog, as we have already noted, appears in Chamisso's anecdotic lyrics, "The Laundry Woman" and "The Beggar and His Dog," in which he is treated with the light touch of genre-painting. Wordsworth made him an integral part of Romanticist philosophy. He is the rural man who teaches the poet the modern common diction. He is the leech-gatherer in "Resolution and Independence," who reminds the roving individualist of the simple daily links and relations with society. In "The Old Cumberland Beggar," the solitary tramp is nature's friend who, in contrast to those captive in that "House, misnamed Industry," is blessed. Wordsworth made a passionate plea for the beggar in his noble uselessness:

> But deem not this man useless,—Statesmen! ye
> Who are so restless in your wisdom, ye
> Who have a broom still ready in your hands
> To rid the world of nuisances; ye proud,
> Heart-swoln, while in your pride ye contemplate
> Your talents, power, or wisdom, deem him not
> A burden on the earth!

The underdog in modern literature is a rewarding variation on the theme of the non-hero, which has become one of the archetypes of modern myth. He had already emerged before the rise of socialism, as the interest of Wordsworth and Chamisso proves, but there is no denying that he was an inevitable concomitant of the awareness of mass society. The man in the crowd, who heretofore knew nothing about himself save that he was an insignificant link at best and a nuisance at worst in the organization of society, was now selected to play a leading role in literary plots. This cultural changeover did not occur without its sacrifices. But there he is. The central-ity of the non-hero is a portentous phenomenon in mod-ern history because he explains, more than anything else, the alien and abnormal character of our cultural world.

The underdogs may be recruited from the community of miners, as in Zola's *Germinal*, of laundry-workers, as in *The Dram-Shop*, of peasants, as in *Earth*. They can be presented in the solidarity of rebelling weavers, as in Gerhart Hauptmann's *The Weavers*, or of that of the fish-ermen in Herman Heyerman's *The Good Hope*. They can be the slum drifters of Gorky's *The Lower Depths* or the bums of O'Neill's *The Iceman Cometh*, and they can be put in the American rural scene of Frank Norris's *Octo-pus* or the city environment of Upton Sinclair's slaughter-house men in *The Jungle*. The rewarding aspect in the presentation of the underdog and the analysis of his psy-chology lies in the interest that the lower classes will ob-viously have in the concentration on their own plight, while the intellectuals on the other hand stand easily ready with their sympathy vote.

Above all there is the revolutionary's reward of aban-doning the ancient esthetics of the beautiful for a new creed of the ugly. The underdog has his own social land-scape, and in the accurate description of squalor, grime, disease, and deprivation the modern author can prove his talents in the esthetics of the ugly. The ugly of course is the standard of the abnormal. It is discovered in classical art, but only on rare occasions. Leonardo, Michelangelo, Rembrandt, and Franz Hals were not timid about por-traying ugly faces. Nor was Rabelais hesitant about the publicizing of private natural acts. But the ugly remained the exceptional state and was a challenge to a new beauty. Thus Hogarth still belonged to the classical school, for as Friedrich Schlegel said in the *Athenaeum*, "Hogarth has painted the ugly, while expressing the beautiful." Naturalistic literature, however, does not try to transcend the hideous; on the contrary, it is deliber-ately concerned with keeping the quality of the dismal intact.

The history of literature, and, in fact, all history, is chiefly concerned with the acts of outstanding characters. but with the rise of the new mass society the question suggested itself whether the crowd should not be given the old protagonist's role that traditionally had fallen to the individual. It was thus that in the nineteenth century the French historian Michelet based his description of the French Revolution on the idea that the real hero of the event was the people. Michelet's conception was attractive, but it has been little emulated. Nor was Thomas Carlyle's unique effort to present this revolution in its immediacy an example of sound historiography. But in its own fictional treatment it did evoke the emotionality of the crowd. There were also a few literary attempts to bring the masses into the foreground. Schiller's *Wilhelm Tell* made the Swiss people its protagonist, but at the dubious price of weakening the psychology of the individual personages. Georg Büchner in *Danton's Death* brought the Parisian population on the stage, Gerhart Hauptmann in *The Weavers* made a group of workingmen the center of dramatization for the first time in history, while Ernst Toller did the same in *Man and the Masses* and *The Machine-Wreckers*. That these efforts were rare must probably be explained by the fact that focusing on crowds inevitably entails the weakening of characterization. For that reason, the scenes in Toller's plays become allegorical and schematic. One of the best renderings of mass-power and mass-emotion is to be found in Melville's *Benito Cereno,* which does not do injustice to the characterization of the Spanish and American captains while concentrating on the crowd of slaves. But this tale, of course, does not put the crowd in a favorable light.

The rise of the little man in modern literature is not a particularly complicated story on the whole, and it needs no extensive analysis. It should be kept in mind, however, that the underdog's assuming a leading role in culture represents an abnormal situation. Naturally, we all like to believe that our age is normal and that the world of the previous centuries ought to have been like ours. But there is no question here of right and wrong. Nor, it should be reiterated, does the abnormal automatically exclude beauty or culture or sophistication. One must simply get used to the idea that modern man's attitudes are deviations from the classical norm as rule and standard. He distrusts rules and standards because they remind him of authority. In an egalitarian society the restricting rules are taken away so that everyone has infinite opportunities. This social arrangement of open-ended pursuit is something which we treasure as a historic development of liberty. And we may. But only if, with the minimum of thoughtful responsibility, we will recognize that whatever we are doing and achieving is, regardless of any intrinsic merits, the result of an abnormal drift away from a unifying hierarchy of values.

Naturally, we prefer our social state to that of the average man of the Middle Ages. We recognize his constricted existence and the second-class citizenship he had to endure under the unfair allotment of prerogatives to those of "higher" birth. But while the medieval underdog was practically without rights, he had one advantage over us: he knew his limitations, and this feeling of restriction gave him security, a sense of embeddedness in the social stucture. We may not like such a security and reject it, but we must at least recognize what the roots of our own restless insecurity are. Rightly or wrongly, in classical society organized, unifying security was the norm. This norm being absent in the egalitarian order, the rootless drift of political blocks and crowd formations tends toward a superimposed security of totalitarian regimes—a trend fully analyzed as early as Plato's and Aristotle's age.

The open-ended pursuit in literature began with the Romanticist's search for the infinite, that which never reaches completion. Friedrich Schlegel said of Romantic poetry that it is in constant evolution. "It belongs to its essential character that it can only evolve eternally and never be finished." The infinite, however, was not simply a nebulous dream about blue skies. It translated into specific goals, such as the infinite opportunity to use poetic language without limiting rules, to write novels without plot, sentences without syntax or punctuation, to paint and sculpt without the ancient regime of modeling, shading, glazing, or perspective, to write musical compositions without the restricting rules of tonality and its harmonic system. The radical manifestos of the avant-garde schools in the early twentieth century represented the total leveling of the hierarchic standards of culture. What happens in the arts is merely a reflection of the collective mentality, which has translated the Romanticist search for the infinite into the pursuit of a utopian realm of infinite opportunity, where no rules exist to restrain us.

Another favorite theme in modern literature is that of sexual deprivation. Two different issues are at stake here, each of which should be treated separately. There is the exposition of sexuality as such—normal, natural, and universal—and there is the penchant for using themes of perversion in writing. The topic of sexual relationship, happily narrated, is as old as literature itself. But the photographically detailed description of the generative act was taboo in classical literature. There were probably many vaguely associated reasons for this restriction. It is clear, however, that for the classical mind there existed a holy of holies of privacy—the sole domain of the authentic self. For us, in contrast, the intimacy of the sexual experience is shattered. Our exhibitionist disposition is determined to give to the public what should be the individual's. The professional prying and spying, which the art of journalism has become, and the bugging and wiretapping devices that defy the protection of our walls reflect the same disregard of the inalienable rights of privacy. The dissolution of privacy is part of the proletarian world, in which equalitarianism has come to mean the abandoning of all intervening agencies in human communication, as if everyone has the same right to all information.

It is thus that modern fiction, too, has adopted the radicalism of total information by exposing the intimate to technical observation. The days in which the works of D. H. Lawrence and Henry Miller threatened to cause scandal are past. Our age has accepted the psychological range of libidinous excitement as proper material for public narrative, without stigmatizing it as pornographic. Our tolerance is characteristic of a world that dislikes the stratification of rights as well as of values. But by transmuting the private into the public, this generosity becomes the liberty of the abnormal. Sexual passion loses its healthy nature the moment it is exhibited for entertainment, literary or otherwise. For proper understanding it must be added that we are not dealing here with the traditional erotica that appeared lustily as folk art, student lyric, troubadour song, *fabliaux,* the eighteenth century pornographic novel, or the esoteric side show of such distinguished authors as Hugo (*Le Roman de Violette*) and de Musset (*Gamiani, or Two Nights of Excesses*). Nor should we be concerned with the playful amatory verse such as that of cummings' *may i feel said he,* which no one could possibly classify with the unhealthy. The public displays of sexuality here represent exceptions. They are selected from a vast historical and international literature because they mark the unusual. But when the exception becomes a trend and almost threatens to develop into an obsession, we are witnessing a cultural change.

So much for the public display of natural passion. The real deviate, of course, is the pervert, who represents a new type of Wanderer in the twentieth century. Perverted love is virtually unknown in the range of great classical literature. There is a touch of it in Petronius' *Satyricon,* and one may find veiled hints of homosexuality here and there in lyrical poetry from Sappho to Shakespeare. On the whole, however, the classical mind ignored the deviate as something that would destroy the symmetry of natural thinking and feeling. The pervert, above all, did not fit in with the sense of the heroic. It is therefore not surprising that the disturbed, neurotic, asymmetric temper of the twentieth century allows the deviate to be exposed to the public eye. Zola, by no means skittish about facing physiological realities, still balked at describing homosexuality. Since the time of such authors as Gide, Sartre, Genet, and Faulkner making the acts and thoughts of the various types of deviates into popular and readable narrative, the trend has proliferated, and the market is flooded with novels and plays offering this newly gained commodity.

Once one has rejected the modules of the heroic, there is obviously no legitimate reason to exclude the pervert from the roster of viable literary characters. The deviate, as a stranger in the established society, can easily be identified and associated with the social underdog. He can also be exploited as the destroyer of the established hierarchy. Some of the more sophisticated Negro authors in the United States elaborate the complexes of sadism and mashochism to attack the white man's social order. The relationship between libidinous aberration and destructivity lies in deep obscure regions of psychology, too deep to be disentangled for sufficient enlightenment. But it is curious to note that one of the earliest novels to describe frankly and analyze without any pornographic implications a sick, sultry, libidinous world, Schlegel's *Lucinde* of 1799, announced itself as a sort of wrecker's tool. "For me and this book no purpose is more purposeful than that I from the outset destroy that which we call order," the author wrote on one of the introductory pages. Considering the shapeless from of this piece of narrative, one must conclude that the work, at least in this respect, succeeds.

Lucinde is not a great work of beauty, but it adumbrates the twentieth century excursions into the subterranean realm of perversion. Marcel Proust's *Remembrance of Things Past* is its unexcelled masterpiece, not merely because of the unabashed exposition of homosexuality, but also because of the scrupulously detailed lingering on the non-happening of a sick world. Proust's visions were those of the sickbed, and his books were written from the frustrations of illness. The author's personal life showed a faithful devotion to his ailments, and the letters to his mother give a meticulous account of his daily regime of pills and other pharmaceuticals against his asthmatic suffering. This is the contemporary mind at work, preoccupied with the intricacies and gimmicks of medical science. Medicine has become a universal concern, and its humanitarian scope, resulting in the best research, hygiene, hospital care, training and insurance schemes, is impressive. But the question is whether this intensifying concentration on disease may not in itself be symptomatic. Our modern world is obsessed by cures and curing. Popular magazines endear themselves to their readers with luridly illustrated articles on the body and its malfunctions, and the drug industry booms on man's narcissistic devotion to his own physiology. Thus while we should hail the tremendous advances of medical science, we cannot possibly ignore the disturbing question of whether the fascination with illness does not inevitably breed illness.

A world absorbed in physical malfunctions and their cures has its representatives in literature, the greatest of these being Thomas Mann. With the marvelously controlled *Buddenbrooks,* he began a lifelong analysis of decay. The novel, subtitled "decline of a family," culminates in the death of the last scion of the Buddenbrooks. But instead of describing Hanno's personal suffering with typhoid in the traditional manner, Thomas Mann devoted an entire chapter to a detailed and clinically studied account of the disease. The author was particularly preoccupied with the process of dying, and one of his most enthralling efforts in this respect is the novella *Death in Venice.* Lingering patients of tuberculosis and sanatorium atmosphere are depicted in *Tristan* and *The Magic Mountain.*

The latter is a study in social isolation, and the symbolic overtones hint at a link between this community of wasting lives and wasted time and twentieth-century civilization. The link is even more explicit in *Doctor Faustus,*

which, according to Mann's own explanation, is actually
a Nietzsche-novel. It is indeed a story of the German genius going insane. But Adrian Leverkuehn is also a modern composer, possessed by a demoniacal inclination toward destruction. Ultimately he leaves the impression of
the modern artist frustrated in his cultural mission, chan-
neling his great potentiality and vitality into exploits of
utter negativism. Whereas Goethe's Faust, for all his persistent failures, at all times conveys the awareness of an
integrated whole world, Mann's Faustus has gone astray
because of the very nature of his diseased conception.

Too obvious inferences should not be made from the
general preoccupation with disease. Detractors of everything that modern society stands for are eager to condemn
our age as thoroughly sick. This, however, is totally unwarranted. A society such as ours, buoyant with zest and
vitality, still ready for adventurous economic and technological enterprises, is obviously not moribund. But we do
owe ourselves an explanation for our morbid concern
with the mechanics of disease and the cultural symptoms
of a self-conscious decline complex. It would appear that,
if the factor of sickness is unavoidable, it should not be
considered the fatal sickness that announces the last
phase of life, but one which, though of a limiting and crip-
pling nature, leaves the vital organs intact. Metaphysically, our condition may be rheumatic, but it should not
be rashly diagnosed as cancerous. The confusion begins
with the attachment of too much emotional and deroga-
tory value to the condition of disease. Goethe, staunchly
extolling the state of health all his life by labeling the
Romanticist technique as "sickness," pointed merely to a
certain trend of aberration and a historic deviation from
the classical sense of totality. If this is sickness, then
many of his own works are themselves not free from this
phenomenon. Modern literature, indeed, has with increasing emphasis veered into areas of cultural isolation.
Its wandering quality makes the element of aberration
into a search for the accidental, for the parts, away from
the whole, in fact, away from the wholesome. For what

in its psychological content is sickness but a loss of the sense of cohesion and of the whole?

Aliens all?

The loss of the security of space and time, analyzed in a literary context in an earlier section, reveals itself in various other ways. One may, for example, suggest that the appearance of a physical theory of relativity in its broadest implications betrays a loss of faith in the autonomous character of the categories of time and space as Descartes, Newton, and Kant conceived of them. Whether or not Einstein's hypothesis will survive under the growing onslaughts of doubt by physicists, it remains a cultural expression of the mentality of the early twentieth century. The philosophy of existence, especially in Jaspers' conception of "being in suspense" (*in der Schwebe*), conveys the same relativity of man's floating spiritual situation. The estrangement from time and space, which used to be the fixing agencies of man's cosmology, in this philosophy acquires an added dimension which will be dealt with elsewhere. But existentialist awareness extends beyond the boundaries of pure philosophical thinking. It is a universal awareness permeating various fields of culture. In literature it is strongly present in poetry and prose since the Romanticists, usually without the authors being conscious of the presence of formal existentialist thought. That this should be so can hardly be a surprise considering that the man who initiated existentialist philosophy was Schelling, a thinker often labeled as a Romanticist and no doubt one closely associated with the Romantic movement.

Caution in applying the term existentialism would, however, not be amiss. The word in recent times has acquired, on the one hand, a superficial and misleading glamour, and on the other, an equally unjustified odor of absurdity. It would further also be more satisfactory to speak about the issue of existentialism as a universal awareness (stronger in some minds than in others) than about existentialists. Fichte, for instance, was not an existentialist, as some have argued, though with the subjectivity of "the I which posits the non-I" he may vaguely intimate later existentialist thought. To say that Coleridge "had already formulated the terms of an existentialist philosophy" before Kierkegaard, as Herbert Read does, is similarly exaggerated. Yet it is true that the "Rime of the Ancient Mariner" is a tale charged with primeval *Angst*. The albatross, wantonly killed by the mariner, represents a mysterious supernatural force, which haunts the seaman with Kierkegaardian despair until angelic spirits of light redeem the curse.

Friedrich Hölderlin, a German contemporary of Coleridge, has been used by the modern philosopher Heidegger to throw new light on existentialist thought. He has written a number of analytical essays that set out to present this poet as one of the foremost revealers of Being. Going through these detailed exegeses of certain of Hölderlin's poems, one is inclined to wonder if more has not been read into the verse lines than is poetically there. Nevertheless, Hölderlin was the poet, searching for the Being, who seems to have adopted the role of messenger between the gods and men. But the gods are in eclipse. Hölderlin, far ahead of his age, expressed the modernity which in twentieth-century literature was time and again to be depicted as human and social abandonment. Thus in "Bread and Wine" the lament:

> But my friend! We have come too late. Gods indeed
>   are living
> But over our heads, above, in another world.
>
>   . . . .
> Better to sleep than thus to be without companions,
> Thus to wait, and what to do meanwhile and say
> And why be a poet in a barren age, I do not know.

Hölderlin's quest for the Being was a transcendental commitment to the "holy," a mystical occupation, characteristically the work of a poet. With Hölderlin, however, the elusive result, this "lacking of holy name," never caused a note of despair. Yet this is a typical by-product of the penetration into essence. The fundamental awareness of the existential results in an inevitable posing of questions, which are to be answered by silence alone. It is superbly illustrated by Heine's "Questioning," a poem depicting a youth standing, confused and disturbed, on the seashore. The questions he poses to the stars are those related to the basic problem of being in this world: "Tell me, what does man signify? Where does he come from? What is his destination? Who lives above us on golden planets?" Such confrontation with the riddles of the absolute can only result in a mocking silence:

> The billows whisper their perennial murmurs,
> The breezes blow, the clouds pass by,
> The stars, cold and indifferent, glitter.
> And a fool waits for the answer

The fool is the man of failure, destined to search for transcendence in spite of the eternal veto of his efforts to identify himself with absolute knowledge. Romantically, this is the identification with the infinite, as Schleiermacher demonstrated in Romantic theology. The Italian poet Leopardi, in his "Nocturnal Song of an Asian Nomad," presented the yearning of the individual, limited and defeated in his reaching for metaphysical certainty. Whereas Heine's poem deals with a young man at the North Sea shore, Leopardi's relates the story of a shepherd in the Asian steppes. But the questions are the same. Addressing the moon, symbol of the impenetrable "holy," the shepherd asks what this earthly life, this suffering, dying, fading away means:

> What use is this infinite air, and this deep
> Infinite sky? What does this immense
> Solitude mean? And what am I?

With the sense of the eternal revolving and the mystery of universal destiny unrevealed, Leopardi's frustration is as hopeless as Heine's "To me life is evil."

For the born the day of birth is fatal.

Leopardi's version is a rare brand of gloomy fatalism, by no means to be taken as typical of existential probing. More often than not, it presses a determined pursuit for a lost identity and a lost origin. In *Peter Schlemihl's Wondrous Story* by Adalbert von Chamisso, the title character is engaged in regaining his shadow, which he had bartered away for wealth. The symbol of the shadow gives rise to many speculations, and the author, though infuriated by the various explanations of contemporaries, did little to replace them with a solid one of his own. Whatever the wider significance of the shadow, it points clearly to man's authentic being. The source of light being universal, the shadows it casts are the marks of individual projection. The man without shadow is he who has lost his identity, and Peter Schlemihl has lost it in his desire for property. This, in fact, is the reverse of the consciousness of being. The quest turns into a flight from essentials, the "falling away" from essentials in Heidegger's terms, which reveals itself in many ways, but predominantly as a flight into exclusively materialistic indulgence.

In Goethe's Faust existential awareness appears in its most universal form. What is vaguely termed Faustian is an attitude belonging preeminently to the restless disaffiliated modern mind, which, committed to a transcending form of life, defeats its own purposes and through lust, greed, and power goes continually astray. Faust desires the total essence and abundance of life, and to obtain it he makes a pact with Mephistopheles, the spirit of utter negativity. Faust's journeying is a search for Being, but it becomes a flight into crime and failures. Abandoning his original security, he wants to "live," and when his first deed throws Gretchen into misery, he cries out in a Leopardian mood: "Oh, had I never been born!" After this experience, life to Faust means his marriage to Helena, the mystical union with Greek and ancient culture—another flight into failure and catastrophe. Faust is determined to win, but he ends up the constant loser. His lust for life and power, guided by Mephistophelean opportunism, is never able to find rest and security. But he has one quality that ultimately releases him from the clutches of Mephistopheles: awareness. Under the aegis of his companion, Faust's pursuit is a flight into Nothingness, "the eternally-empty," but to the consternation of Mephistopheles, he is redeemed. He is redeemed because he grasps the essence of freedom without ever having attained it. Thus the dying Faust confirms:

> This is the final word of wisdom:
> He only earns freedom as well as life,
> Who must reconquer them in daily strife.

The sense of the existential is fundamentally that sense of freedom which transcends opportunity of power and possession. Faust is its archetype. The Faustian theme from now on runs powerfully, though in numerous variations, through much of modern literature. In Ibsen's *Brand* the transcendence is physically staged by the mountain-scape, which encloses Brand and ultimately destroys him. In Kierkegaardian self-denial he seeks identification with the absolute norm of love, which results in the destruction of the simple relationships and communications of the life in the village below. In doing so, he represents the tragic of the primeval *hybris* of man compulsively trying to unify himself with his ideal, a venture inexorably leading to defeat. Brand's case is thus fundamentally different from that of Solness, for instance, the architect in Ibsen's *Master Builder,* whose pride is concentrated on his tangible achievements, that is, the result of his opportunities. The existential quest as described in Brand's story, rather in contrast, annihilates achievement while reaching for the intangible essence.

Although intangible and elusive, the absolute still becomes real in its decisive confrontation with the human experience. Melville's albino whale does, in the end, realize itself. It is then that what in the human consciousness is the absolute object of conquest turns into absolute

Nothingness. *Moby Dick* is, after *Faust,* the most pene-
tratingly existential manifestation of modern literature.
Whereas Goethe separated the forces for which Faust
and the Devil stand, Melville seems to combine the Faustian and the Mephistophelean in the figure of Captain
Ahab. Yet, this is not wholly true, for the most profoundly existential awareness is shown by Ishmael, and it
is he who, for that reason, remains as the only survivor
after the ordeal with the destructive whale. Moby Dick
belongs to the same mythological species as the Leviathan, Behemoth, Dragon, and in a sense the Mariner's albatross. He also suggests Rilke's "terrible" Angel. The
sailors of the "Pequod" pursue him with a religious passion,
and the whiteness of the whale, as Melville makes clear,
indicates that it is a configuration of the divine. Significantly, it also represents "the heartless voids and immen-
sities of the universe, and thus stabs us from behind with
the thought of annihilation."

The consciousness of the existential appears in many
forms and in many guises, and it is neither necessary, nor
advisable, to give an exhaustive account of its literary
scope. Historically speaking, it is important to note that
existentialism as a philosophy and a concern grows in
parallel development with materialistic tendencies. The
materialist pursuit aims at the greatest number of opportunities for the greatest number of people. Opportunity is
nothing but the freedom to have and to accumulate property as well as pleasures. Existentialist freedom is the
freedom of being what one is.

Ivan's story about the Grand Inquisitor in *The Brothers Karamazov* indirectly reveals Dostoevski's thought on
freedom by making the figure of Jesus the prisoner of the
Inquisitor. Jesus here represents absolute freedom, which
clashes with the authoritarian conception of the old car-
dinal. The Grand Inquisitor, in a long exposition in
which the word freedom recurs with deliberate frequency, boasts of his success in organizing the world into
complete submission. The people have bartered their liberty for a feeling of happiness. "They have brought their

freedom to us and laid it humbly at our feet." For people have a fear of freedom—"nothing has ever been more insupportable for a man and for human society than freedom."

Dostoevski here constructed a scene that rewardingly allowed him to vent his anger about the organized church, the Roman Catholic church in particular. The episode, however, presents more than a picture of sixteenth-century church practices. It obviously relates to the modern era by focusing on an ideology foreign to sixteenth-century Catholicism. The chief point of Dostoevski's story lies in the fact that the people have exchanged their freedom for bread. "Make us your slaves, but feed us!" they have cried to the Inquisitor. There, the author clearly included another of his favorite themes, his utter contempt for organized socialism. Thus Ivan's "poem" serves two purposes at once.

This is not the place, of course, to analyze Dostoevski's emotional biases. What is important, however, is his contrasting of two conceptions of freedom, the absolute freedom represented by Jesus and his consistent silence throughout, and the freedom from want and fear represented by organized socialism. Without either agreeing or disagreeing with Dostoevski's obvious preference, we can simply state that both conceptions have their historical justification. They are factually with us as historical developments. The existential quest is an ambition to penetrate beyond the security of material sufficiency and to replace the short-term freedom of opportunity with the long-term freedom of self-discovery. As we all know, these conflicting philosophies of freedom appear in an increasingly antagonistic manner and split the modern consciousness into, on the one hand, a desire for material security and comfort and, on the other, a desire to escape from conformity into a flight of self-discovery and self-assertion. These two ambitions of freedom are totally incompatible; one seeks to establish peace of mind, the other wants the adventure of mind.

The existential adventure is described in Rilke's *Note-*

books of Malte Laurids Brigge, which deal with a man in search of himself, a man who knows the hardships involved in this enterprise. It is an educational experience in that it teaches the discipline of fear. To discover oneself is to face *Angst.* Brigge, as a boy, is "still bad at being afraid." But since then he has learned to be afraid with "real" fear. These "notes" represent the psychological logbook of a mind journeying into the authenticity of the self, an exploration inevitably involving existential anxiety. This story has a striking counterpart in Hermann Hesse's *Demian,* in which the chief character, the boy Sinclair, goes through frightening experiences on the long way to himself. Sinclair, like Brigge, has to pass through an educational process of finding himself, and this encounter can only occur when he unifies himself with his authentic leader, the *daimon* in Socratic sense, here called *Demian.* Hesse's message goes beyond the particular story of the boy. Man, according to the author, must learn to find the way to authenticity, in spite of the many shocks and fears that are an integral part of the effort. For "nothing in the world is more repulsive to man than to follow the way that leads to himself."

There is a haunting element of absurdity in man's existential search, and to many in this pragmatic age it seems hardly worth the trouble. The reckless "leap" into transcendence, as formulated for the first time by Kierkegaard, demonstrates the sacrifice of intellectual and material security for the sake of a freedom that seems, to say the least, rather nebulous and abstract. Camus in *The Myth of Sisyphus* calls the existential leap a philosophy of suicide. But it should be kept in mind that existential freedom, far from being a worthwhile commodity that can be advertised and promoted as something to be acquired, is primarily an innate potential within the human consciousness, one that requires total realization. The tragic quality in this, as if the gods had imposed a curse upon men, is stressed in Camus' allusion to the myth of Sisyphus, the man forever doomed to roll a stone up the slope of a hill without succeeding in reaching the top.

The acceptance of his plight and Sisyphus' fidelity, which negates the whims of the gods, in itself is life, and Camus concludes rather stoically, "one must conceive Sisyphus as being happy." Clearly this is not the adventurous variety of existential awareness as revealed in Faust or Brand.

The eclipse of the gods, who already in Hölderlin's view seemed to ignore the futile labor of man "in a barren time," is dramatically illustrated in Camus' play *The Misunderstanding*. Based on an anecdote told in his own novel *The Stranger*, this situation presents a woman who, after having murdered a lodger in her hotel, finds out that the victim is her son. When, in despair, she kneels down and frantically begins to pray, her cry of "Heavenly Father!" is answered by an old servant who has not uttered one word throughout the play. Significantly, he ends the drama when to her desperate plea for help he replies simply: No. The mocking irony here is akin to that which meets Heine's youth on the seashore and Leopardi's Asian shepherd. But Camus' irony is without the touch of melancholy since it is born in the climate of crime. His character Caligula, in another play, stoops to unrestrained brutality in order to pursue "the impossible." He has searched for it outside in the world as well as inside in the "secret places of his heart." He has tried to discover it in sexuality but has found only his hatred.

The flight into crime, occurring so frequently in Camus' work, takes the search for Being into the realm of the extraordinary, even the psychotic. But Camus was full of admiration for Kafka who, in contrast, was virtually always concerned with the average man. Whether Joseph K. in *The Trial* or the surveyor in *The Castle*, his characters emerge from the anonymity of daily life, grasping for the sense and mystery of life, without ever being allowed to see even a glimmer of reason. The surveyor tries vainly to make communication with the castle on high. The effort to transcend the daily environment is shattered on the slopes of the mountain, just as Brand

and Sisyphus are never to reach the top of the mountain. The existentialist failure to communicate with the divine or the self-set ideal in Alain-Fournier's *The Wanderer* is centered in the love for a woman, whom Augustin Meaulnes passionately pursues, yet whom he brings to ruin when he marries her. The failure here is double, for the ideal is made tangible in a woman, and in conquering her he accomplishes the destruction of his ideal.

In Kafka's world, man is caught in the web of a puny but tyrannical system, but there still remains the illusion of an escape route. In Sartre's *No Exit* there is not even a chance of release. Garcin, Inez, and Estelle realize that they are eternally bound together—a hell situation. "Other people" hold the freedom-seeking self imprisoned and under perennial torture. Whereas the figure of Jesus frees himself from the hands of the Inquisitor through a kiss, human love is of no avail as a means to escape the bondage of living in an organized society. There is a great deal of intellectual speculation and analysis in Sartre's literary work; a philosophy often seems to determine the turns of the narrative. This is understandable, inasmuch as it is partly the intellectualization of the modern world that has caused the self-consciousness of the existential predicament. Against the existential hero-types—Faust, Captain Ahab, Brand, the Stranger in Strindberg's *To Damascus*—who adventure into decisive action, can be placed the existential non-hero, such as Joseph K. or the little average man in Camus' *The Stranger*, caught, frustrated, and crushed by the social machinery. Ulrich, in Robert Musil's novel, *The Man Without Qualities*, also belongs to the latter category, though only partly. An intellectual, frustrated and uncertain, like most intellectuals in the modern society of self-conscious analysis, Ulrich is unable to translate his potential into real action, and he substitutes for this a flight into sexuality and eventually a flight into the warfare of 1914. The existential leap thus transforms itself into a negative flight, a going into hiding, as it were, rather than choosing heroic exposure on the rugged mountain roads.

Existential awareness reveals itself in many different literary expressions. This survey can merely touch on the most conspicuous varieties, which in the development of our world give an indication of the historical trends. One of the striking aspects of the modern consciousness is its persistent concern with the process of dying. It appears in a variety of fields. In the theory of history from Hegel to Huizinga, one can find a continuous preoccupation with the possible exhaustion of the Western world and with the decline of its culture. In literature the morbid fascination with disease, previously discussed, may point in the same direction. Existentialism since Kierkegaard has concentrated on a new theme in the history of philosophy, "the sickness unto death." This could hardly have been a viable topic for the technical discourse of philosophers in previous centuries. With man's awareness of himself and of his relationship to his environment changing, the philosophic problems change as well. The sickness unto death is fundamentally, according to Kierkegaard, a realization of despair, an agonizing contradiction—"this sickness in the self, everlasting to die, to die and yet not to die, to die the death. For dying means that it is all over, but dying the death means to live to experience death." Heidegger, in one of his most penetrating chapters, has taken up this theme and treats the philosophical concept of death as an authentic root of existence.

This experience of the intermingling of life and death is poetically expressed in Thornton Wilder's *Our Town*. The simple average life of Grover's Corners is given an existential dimension. In the final act the characters of the play are as dead as those in Sartre's *No Exit* and, though less bitterly and cynically than in the French drama, they experience death, not as a *fait accompli*, but as an eternal awareness inherent in life itself. The existential awareness of death, in *Our Town* for obvious reasons more "staged" than philosophically elaborated, is a recurring theme in Rilke's entire work. To understand how Kierkegaardian was his conception of the experience of death, one must, for example, turn to a passage in the verse play *The White Princess:*

> When someone dies, not that alone is death;
> Death is when someone lives and does not know it.
> Death is when someone cannot die at all.
> Death, being many things, cannot be buried.
> In us is daily death as well as birth.

In his "Requiem for a Friend" Rilke speaks of eating the seeds of death, from which the "own death" germinates, and in "Requiem for the Count of Kalckreuth" the "own death" is described as "having need of us because we live him." For Rilke, the greatness and fulfillment of existential life lay in the willingness to let the experience of dying fertilize that of living:

> murders are
> easily understood. But this, to hold
> death, entire death, even before life so
> tender within us, and not being angry
> is indescribable.

The animalistic sense of death is the fright of finality, but existential awareness is a recognition of death as a potential influence on life. It thus becomes a generative force. In this respect, Gerrit Achterberg, whose work is little known outside his native Holland and whose idiom is almost impossible to translate, is one of the most obsessively existentialist poets. His one overriding theme is the resurrection of the beloved woman (whom he has murdered) through the efficacy of his verse:

> In this morning, without guilt
> held in the patience of the dead,
> I feel myself of verse fulfilled
> that has your secret sense revealed;
> you rise like a flower upward.

This is the mystic unification with someone else's "own death," because, as the poet puts it elsewhere, "we were together the same poem." Naturally it represents a hyper-individual experience, probably not shared by most people. But it signifies the breaking up in literature of the time-honored life-death cliché, which, though scientifically correct, has little existential validity. It can be reduced to the disruption of the pattern of time. Eliot's *Four Quartets* is basically a probing into existential time, shattering the physical cliché of chronology:

> Time present and time past
> Are both perhaps present in time future,
> And time future contained in time past.
> If all time is eternally present
> All time is unredeemable . . .

the author speculates in "Burnt Norton." Eliot, after having explored the existentialism of an external void in "The Waste Land" and an internal void in "The Hollow Men," in *Four Quartets* leaves the poetry of spatial relativity for that of temporal relativity, where man is

> Timeless, and undesiring
> Except in the aspect of time
> Caught in the form of limitation
> Between un-being and being.

The same climate is evoked in Auden's "For the Time Being," a deliberate but nevertheless genuine presentation of existential reality, in which the traditional physical world is dissolved and "the Real is what strikes you as really absurd."

For Rilke, the breaking up of the scientific cliché consisted in meeting "things" as autonomous entities with their own life, not indeed as accidental objects that lie around to be used. One finds this abundantly demonstrated in the famous thing-poems that fill the volumes *The Book of Images* and *New Poems*. Elsewhere the poetical justification for this mystique of the object is given, for instance in *Early Poems,* where Rilke conveyed his apprehension about people's chatter and their ruthless touch, which stiffen and silence things, whereas he wanted to "hear the singing of things." Rilke, however, knew that this identification with the essence of physical objects and phenomena is practically impossible, and here too the existential quest apparently is more rewarding in its effort than in its result. We remain outsiders of the phenomenal world, onlookers, as Rilke put it in the eighth of his *Duinese Elegies,* "turned to the world, and never beyond."

Existentialism could never have become so all-pervasive had it not been for the equally universal sway of scientific materialism. Existentialism and materialism are twin-necessities historically. One comes and grows with the other. We are not referring here to those extreme positions that in partisan manner exclude one or the other. Both have become a conscious ideology, and on this basis communist scholars have shown themselves vituperatively unreasonable about existentialist philosophy. What is under discussion here, however, is not primarily the conscious exposition of delineated existentialist ideas, but rather a general awareness that has gradually permeated our forms of culture over the last two centuries. As such, it emerged and expanded surreptitiously without necessarily being expressed.

It is this basic sensitivity that has made possible the more conscious elaborations of existentialist thought to be found not only in modern philosophy but also in new explorations in theology, psychiatry, historiography, literary criticism, and even some of the exact sciences. The spread of existential consciousness, as we have analyzed it in the field of literature, is conspicuous because literature is immediately concerned with thought. But it would be possible to trace existential experience as well in modern painting, for instance, from van Gogh and Munch through the abstract art of Kandinski and Mondriaan. It exists wherever the mind feels itself captive in

the scientific clichés that man's own materialistic preoccupation has constructed.

Existential consciousness appears wherever political
techniques, under the pressure of a mass society, exploit
poll statistics, slogans, and image-patterns to reach for
the crowd. It is there wherever education falls more and
more into tracks of cliché courses guided by cliché textbooks to produce know-how specialization. This pattern-
izing trend is the cultural expression of conformity, making man into an interchangeable part of the social system, a fate against which his feeling of authenticity rebels. Mechanical pattern has replaced authentic form. Or
as Achterberg interprets it:

> The nameless sense of this abandonment:
> to be among the people like a stone
> is lost amid the pavement of the street,
> o number, dead, in empty sum alone.
>
> Let me be earth again
> with earth over my bones;
> the only form me to contain
> is gone.

Number is the nameless, the crowd, the accidental. Or
it is an expression for what can be identified only by
measures of quantity. In the realm of essence the number
is alien. The existential awareness, revealed in much of
contemporary literature, is the apprehension of being
caught in numbers and accidentals—of being alien to essentials.

But what remains is founded by poets.

Hölderlin

7

The Entertaining Way of Living

The mime

Drama to many is merely a particular department of literature, and as such a prosodic subdivision. Naturally, as a mode of literature, drama must be considered a subdivision. In its completed state, however, in the performance, drama transcends its literary limitations and becomes an autonomous form comprising all other varieties of art. It is for this reason that Hegel, in his lectures on esthetics, assigned to drama the highest place in his system. It represents the totality of artistic vision, encompassing all the musical, poetic, and plastic aspects. Indeed, the actor on the stage brings dramatic poetry to life in his musically conveyed diction, while posture, walk, and gesture supply the plastic expression. No other form of art is able to combine oral as well as visual interpretations. Consequently, no other art can portray human experience, of suffering or joy, with such abundant resources, and with such penetrating immediacy.

Moreover, because of its immediacy and the comprehensiveness of its technique, the art of the drama is preeminently equipped to present the contemporary world in a rounded picture. By implication, the history of drama is the social history of the people who produce that drama. An old Roman saying, which needs little explanation, speaks of the theater as a mirror of society's life and manners. It is hard to imagine an art form that would better convey the thought, as well as taste, customs, fashion, and manners of sixteenth- and seventeenth-century England than Elizabethan drama. Louis Quatorze furniture, the ballets by Lully, the satires of Boileau-Despréaux, the paintings of Nicolas Poussin are all representative of the baroque splendor of the age of Louis XIV, but nothing can evoke the spirit of this age with more abundant authority and immediate touch than the comedies of Molière.

It is for this reason that the changes in the history of drama reflect the changes in the general cultural character and that drama aids in illustrating the trends of cultural history. Modern drama in its manifold facets, often strikingly contradictory, represents in its own spectacular way the scene and scope of contemporary culture. The interpretation of contemporary events is undeniably hazardous at all times, and the totality of the present cultural order, as represented by modern drama, must appear chaotic at our close range. The definite meaning of this chaos can be clearly defined only by later centuries. As contemporaries, we can do no more than describe the changes that are evident and supply tentative interpretations.

It should be clear that, though conceiving the art of drama as an expression of cultural totality, we may, and must, consider certain obvious priorities. Traditionally, the history of drama is a pageant of major and minor plays with occasional reference to production techniques as a sort of condescending bow to the lower realities of the stage. Aristotle, in his hierarchic classification of dramatic elements, listed the performance last, after plot, character, thought, diction, and melody. For, as he elaborated, "the tragic effect is quite possible without public spectacle and actors." In the middle of the nineteenth century Richard Wagner, partly under the influence of the Greek drama, promoted his idea of a comprehensive "music drama" in which poetry and music unite in a mystic marriage. This sounds beautiful enough when written down in the pages of his *Opera and Drama,* but in practice the match turned out to be a rather shady affair. The "poetry" of Wagner's operas is a torrent of bombastic versification, and the dramatic arrangements could not possibly be assessed as anything but a forgivable excuse for some of the most superb music ever written. Adolphe Appia, the first of a line of directors to change the old-fashioned techniques of scenic presentation, pointed out that the relationship between "musical yearning and eye" in Wagner's work was inadequate. What this meant was that a new school of dramatic thinking began to question the old off-stage assumptions. The visual qualities were demanding more attention. This, in the twentieth century, led to a curious revolt against the predominance of the play, a movement "away-from-the-word." A new evaluation of drama as the historical expression of performance in the first place was attempted by the leaders of the stage as well as by scholarly critics. *On the Art of the Theatre,* which Edward Gordon Craig published in 1905, is a manifesto for the avant-garde theater, in which the visual elements dominate. It was directed against the traditionally central position of the playwright. In contrast, Craig advocated the performer as the generator of dramatic movement. There was an ambiguity here, for judging by his own splendid settings, it is obvious that he was actually making a plea for the designer. This, however, is not too important, for it is clear that in stagecraft designer, director, and actor are all on the same side, that is, against the dramatist. In Craig's hands the organized cooperation of sets and lighting never impeded the possibilities of the actor.

The new expressionist theater, which aimed at working from the inside out, took its starting point from the stage. In *The Revolution in the Theatre* Georg Fuchs, one of the enthusiastic leaders of this movement, cried out that "the stage creates literature, not the other way round." The new confidence in the generating importance of the performer brought with it major changes in staging technique. It was also vigorously supported by accredited scholarship. In Germany, especially, a number of theorists began to question, in fact to undermine, the old hypothesis that the classical theater was born in the Greek religious cult. The mime was discovered.

The mime, the traveling dancer, mountebank, juggler —in short, the oldest professional entertainer—indeed existed long before Thespis got the idea of converting a Dionysian form of worship into a dramatic representation in which the actor replaced the priest. The theories about the mime are complicated and, predictably, suffer from the fact that he appeared in obscure historical times. Whether or not the ancient assumption of the birth of drama from religious cult is really upset by the mime theory is questionable, for one could argue that the mime's dance itself, before becoming mere entertainment, was mimed magic, that is, again an expression of primitive cult. The complications do not end here. Even as we learn that the medieval drama was born from the Christmas and Easter rites in the church, we should not forget that there was no real vacuum in drama. For after the collapse of the Roman theater art, the traveling mime survived, and he was still around during the early mystery plays. He may, conceivably, have influenced the formation of the new medieval drama. In fact, the mime, under various masks, never relinquished his power. Time and again in history his influence is evident: in the *commedia dell' arte,* in Shakespeare's clowns, in the Hans Wurst plays, and, more recently, in modern cabaret, pantomime, or improvisation experiments.

The scholarly infighting about the cultural role of the mime can be left aside. It is important to know that the contemporary stress on the performer's theater has an historical foundation. When Arthur Kutscher, one of the most informed of these revolutionary theorists, said that "the core of all theatrical science is the mime" and that "dramatic means nothing but mimic," he confirmed what Gordon Craig had found earlier: "the father of the dramatist is the mime, the dancer." The revolt of the theater man against the cult of the word and the poet of the drama received a scholarly backing.

This revision in theatrical thinking clearly destroyed the fundamental premises of the classical stage, which were grounded in the poet's vision. Whether Aeschylus, Sophocles, Shakespeare, Calderón, Lope de Vega, Racine, Corneille, Schiller, or Goethe, the classical dramatist conceived of the theatrical experience as an autonomous poetic experience, detached from the pedestrian surroundings of daily-life emotions. If this suggests an elitist position, it is because the audience as a crowd was supposed to share the elitist experience collectively. The mime, in contrast, was the people's friend, the popular entertainer. And when in this century the performer banished the poetic vision, it actually meant one way of proletarianizing dramatic art.

The predominance of the actor is no novelty. The Roman stage, whose history is not notable for any towering playwrights, was marked by the cult of the star-performer, especially during the Empire. It was the actor, and probably even more the actress, who dominated the theater. Traditionally, in our Christian civilization the actor has been an outcast. Along with the prostitutes, he belonged to the riffraff. He represented sin and corruption. The Council of Carthage expressly forbade "the children of the Church" to attend dramatic shows. The medieval German lawbook, the *Sachsenspiegel* without further comment declared "show-men and thieves" as outlawed. The seventeenth-century Dutch *predikanten* tolerated their dramatists Vondel, Hooft, and Breero, but in their sermons they fulminated against the actor. They closed the theaters.

Although these were the excesses, traditionally the actor was at best never more than a sort of pariah in society. In the increasingly egalitarian atmosphere of the last two centuries, however, the actor has gradually gained ground. At present he not only has come to be regarded as a regular citizen, he seems more and more to acquire a super-status. The actor in the mass mind has become the symbol of ideal life. While to the classical mind the saint represented the ideal power in overcoming the obstacles of death, the actor, more emphatically the actress, represents to modern man the ideal capacity to overcome the obstacles of life. Hence the idolization of the actor. He is the archetype of what the average man thinks of as the utmost in affluence, license, and comfort. In actuality he is far less central than the star-billing suggests. The crucial importance of the performer in modern stage-fare spreads equally over the activities of actor, designer, and director. The three together conspire against the predominance of the "word" on the stage and together succeed in the triumph of "theatricality."

With the ascent of such powerful designers as Appia and Craig, not to mention the painters who, like Derain, Dali, or Picasso, as outsiders lent their talents to the theater, stage decor began to play an essential part. Originally merely background support, it now became a vital function in the show. The designer's stage again was not without precedent. During the Renaissance the theater in Italy and France attracted a number of craftsmen who, by their unexcelled finesse in creating scenic illusion, established a lasting reputation. But the work of Sebastiano

Serlio, Giacomo Torelli, or of Ferdinando, Francesco, and Guiseppe Bibiena was basically an architect's and painter's conception. It fitted in with the love of splendor at that time in those countries, but was not dramatically functional or interpretive. These designers contributed to the lavish grandeur which the then emerging ballet and opera demanded. In all probability they could not have contributed to Shakespeare's plays in the Globe theater. Significantly, their English counterpart, Inigo Jones, reached maturity just after Shakespeare's death.

The really functional stage decorations, that is, those that, far from constituting an autonomous picture, assume an interpretive role on the stage, are an invention of the modern performer's theater. No one could have explained it better than Alexander Tairov, the expressionist stage leader whose consistent objective was the integration of actor, designer, and director. In his book *The Unshackled Theatre*, he promoted the idea that the scenic vision should be "a synthesis of emotion and form born in the creative imagination of the actor." Professional statements like these point to a cooperation of stagecraft, tighter and more concentrated than ever before in the marshaling of resources.

The renewed interest in the possibilities of design and the specialized training ensuing from it result in a highly professional technique that is no longer merely adapted architecture or adapted painting, but a specific theatrical craft, centered more and more in the technique of scientific lighting. There are two sides to this. One demonstrates spectacularity, an aspect that understandably becomes an easy attraction in a mass society, and that lends a quality, especially to the musicals, reminiscent of the late Roman stage shows. The other appears in the symbolic expressionist decor with steps, staircases, scaffoldings, platforms, slanted sets, and machine constructions —all highly characteristic of the representations of the early decades of this century, but still cropping up here and there, even on the Broadway scene when commercial entrepreneurs want to demonstrate their ability to handle "avant-garde" fare.

The third associate in the scenic presentation, the director, is probably the most powerful of the trinity. At least, his rise was the most meteoric. It is only in the twentieth century that the stage director has reached the limelight, indeed reached stardom. With its almost exclusive reliance on the dramatic verse, the classical production had little need for the *régisseur* in the modern sense. Aeschylus and Sophocles, staging their own dramas, above all functioned as choirmasters, and they were concerned with the correct diction and recitation of the verse lines. In the classical European theater the director was a relatively unimportant man, or he was an older actor who from mere seniority and experience derived the authority to tell his fellow players where and when to stand, move, and exit. There are a number of traditional and obvious rules of blocking, balance, and ensemble work that fundamentally aim at promoting the qualities of the play. In so doing they will then indirectly help to promote the qualities of the actor.

The conventional French theater had no director in the modern sense. It employed a *metteur-en-scène* whose name, deservedly, appeared in small print on the posters. His only task was to arrange the actors in, for example, a Molière comedy in the time-honored tradition of triangular patterns. Here, the dramatic situations were almost solely expressed in the changing facets of speeches and dialogues—a presentation seemingly stagnant to the uninitiated but for the French, brought up in this tradition, conveying the correct artistic understanding. The Comédie Française for the most part still retains this conventional style. The modern director outside France, however, who chooses to revive the Molière drama, ignoring all tradition, will experiment with the new skills of lighting, stage-constructing, costuming, and above all with the variety of inventions, gadgets, and general "stage business" that show his ingenuity. He makes the difference between *mise en scène* and *régie*.

He also makes the difference between what the classical theater treasured most, the play in its untouched poetic force, and what the modern stage sets out to present, the visualized "show." This trend originated with the celebrated Meiningen company, which under the management of the Duke of Saxe-Meiningen operated in the last quarter of the nineteenth century. To be sure, not all the novel features introduced by this company had equal value for the coming stage revolutions. Their pre-occupation with the accurate historical costume, for in-stance, and with the correct historical style of furniture and coiffure, though revealing a welcome cultural con-cern, could scarcely be considered of real dramatic im-portance. But the Duke's determined stress on balance and ensemble play was of great seminal significance at a time when the solo virtuoso, such as Talma, Devrient, Irving, Bernhardt, or Duse, often surrounding themselves with smaller satellites, ignored the harmony of the total representation. Nowadays, despite the giant-size billing of the names of stars, the leading actors, with few excep-tions, are perfectly balanced in the performance, through skilled direction. Their reputation may not last as en-duringly as those of the great classical and romantic vir-tuosos, but they render a greater service to the over-all interpretation. We must be grateful to the Meiningeners for introducing this service. They extended their interest in teamwork to the disciplinary staging of dramatically moved and reacting crowds. This was of importance not only for the managing of later musicals and spectaculars, but also for the production of the classics, which such directors of mass scenes as Max Reinhardt and Leopold Jessner were to undertake.

The Meiningen company eventually embarked on large-scale journeys, demonstrating under the leadership of Ludwig Chronegk the workings of a new theatrical trend: the scenic experiment. In this influence, national and international, lay the historical significance of the Meiningeners. They had an impact on the work of the real-ists, Stanislavsky and Antoine, for instance, and no less on the coming expressionists. In the course of the nineteenth century, experiments were accidental and cautious. Goethe, Immermann, and Laube tried technical innovations in order to obtain better stage results for the play. In more recent times, however, the experiment has the theatricality itself, the immediate effect, whereby the mediacy of stage poetry is weakened. The exciting new directors, with their resounding proclamations and manifestos, have had in common the promotion of the performer as the starting-point for drama. But their theories as well as their theatrical products have demonstrated entirely different and sometimes self-contradictory experiments to reach that goal.

What could be further apart in style and mood than the austerely rising columns and curtains of Gordon Craig's sets and the hectic scaffoldings and contraptions of the Tairov and Meyerhold productions? In Craig's designs, following those of Appia, there was a strong puritanical concentration and repose. Tairov's Kamerny stage and the Meyerhold Theatre aimed at movement and mechanics, in keeping with the futurist adulation of the machine. Especially in the latter theater, the actor, in contrast to the theory, became a puppet, a dehumanized part of the machinery. Though this indeed strikingly revealed the social position of modern man, it was not the kind of picture that the average audience liked to see. Soon after the 1920's this constructivist stage representation died out.

In France, as a reaction against the realistic programs of Antoine's Théâtre Libre, a new symbolist movement arose, centered in the Théâtre des Artes of Paul Fort. It marked the beginning of a line of resourceful theatrical groups and studios, the Vieux Colombier of Jacques Copeau, the Diaghilev Ballet Russe, the Théâtre de l'Atelier of Charles Dullin, to name only a few, which were basically laboratories for new techniques in scenic presentations. In general they modified the new ideas according to the French taste, so that their style was characterized by a light and intimate touch. In Germany and Austria, the accent was more massive. Max Reinhardt, the most skillful of them all, was also the most eclectic. Whether it was the tragedy of Shakespeare, the medieval primitivism of *Everyman,* the rococo playfulness of Goldoni, the bronze sonorousness of Schiller, the stark realism of the modern social play, or the explosive spirit of German expressionism, his ingenuity translated it into a vibrant theatrical "happening." He was, above all, the great modern showman.

The performer's stage, by aiming at the immediate rendering of dramatic experiences, tries to do away with the ancient classical conception of theatrical illusion. The development of the contemporary dance supports this tendency. With the resurrection of the mime, the dancer as the originator of primal dramatic expression received renewed attention. The old classical ballet with its strict regime of technical forms and patterns is the actual representative of a superannuated formal court life. In a state of social equality and cultural leveling it obviously has no place. The expressionist dance-drama, of which Rudolf von Laban, Mary Wigman, and Kurt Jooss were some of the outstanding exponents, followed the same trend as the modern drama. It abolished the stylization of the classical ballet for a free expression of the body, thereby insuring, with the aid of new lighting and staging techniques, instant visual conveyance.

When, after the Second World War, the glittering stars of the 1920's and 1930's had left the stage, the original dazzling fireworks and extravagant display settled down into a solid technical skill. The exciting years of defiance and tumult that accompanied the old avant-garde spirit were long gone. What remained was still unquestionably the performer's theater, but one solidified, streamlined into the administrative efficiency of the producer's house or the official and semi-official national repertory groups. The virtuosity of the old actor-manager, which had flourished throughout the classical and romantic eras, broke down in the twentieth century and was replaced by the virtuosity of the starring showman. More recently this in turn made place for a theater of more equalized competence, the fruit of the increased specialization on the stage as well as of highly efficient drama schools.

The sometimes wildly erratic quality of dramatic preparation is gone. The actor-manager could as late as the final dress rehearsal upset basic characterizations or ensemble formations. The modern production, in contrast, is charted and planned in hour-by-hour schedules to integrate the accumulative labor of set building, costume making, stage managing, lighting problems, and acting. If the Yale Drama School operates more like a school for engineers than for artists, it is also true that the modern performances display a height of proficiency and expertise never before seen on this large a scale.

The advantages of this kind of professionalized theater are obvious. In the structure of a mass society, where mass entertainment is in so urgent a demand, the theater has come under the same economic and managerial pressures as any industry. It operates like a department store; that is, without ideology it seeks to satisfy the ever-widening tastes and demands of a well-informed public. The eclecticism of Max Reinhardt and, in later decades, of Tyrone Guthrie, reveals one of the standard characteristics of our age. Like the supermarket, the theater must be latitudinarian in its offerings. Hence the modern repertory has unreservedly widened its scope in recent years, and all the major varieties of styles and schools have become worthwhile commodities.

The hero

The change from the classical to this modern age was marked by the gradual replacement of a centralized way of thinking, including a sense of proportionate values and hierarchy, by a pluralistic mentality which juxtaposes values, talents, and people in disarming equality. The elitist mind, by instinct seeking symmetric harmony, needed a unifying force, a central authority to secure its position. It showed up in its religion, its philosophy, its art. The proletarian mind, dispersed and fragmented, needs diversity and quantity, and has an instinctive fear of authority. Classical society was firmly focused in cultural centers—Florence, Rome, Paris, London, Amsterdam, Vienna, Berlin—which grew spontaneously from a solid, poised community. Modern society is restless and fugitive and has no natural loyalty to a unifying community.

The classical drama reflects this prevailing sense of unity in the society from which it stems. The unity of drama is not necessarily the rule-book concept that Boileau in his *L'Art Poétique* imposed on his contemporaries. It is above all an inner dynamic bond. Superficially it may seem that Shakespeare's plays are rambling accumulations of fairly disconnected scenes. Close analysis, however, will explain why on the stage his works evoke that sustained tension which denies the seeming lack of cohesion. It is because underneath the external unruliness of the scenic material there is a taut development and distribution of action that can be delineated graphically. If one asks what the source and determinant of this central action is, the answer is the protagonist—that is, he who acts first, the generator of the drama. Whatever the attributes of his character, he moves the plot, his decisions determine the favorable and fatal turns toward the ultimate denouement. He is the leader.

He is a projection of that cultural configuration, the hero. The cultural hero, as everyone knows, played an overwhelming part in the emotional imagination of the classical mind. Much has been written about him, and the psychological roots of the hero-ideal are a matter of much wild speculation. Nor do we really know how and to what extent the hero was related to the rise and consolidation of religion. But he was there. Above all, he was there at the crucial points of life and death. Originally, in the dark history of ancient Greece, he was worshipped as part of the cult of the dead. The hero was he who defied death. But soon enough he became simply the great man of great deeds, defying any obstacle in the way of man's happiness, not excluding the gods.

The roots of the death cult remained, however, and

when Christianity was beginning to determine a new cultural era, the saint was again the death-overcoming, death-defying example of mankind. He lacked, of course, the old exuberance and flamboyance of the Greek hero. Naturally enough, Western civilization sooner or later was to be dissatisfied with its pale, almost masochistically passive paragon. It replaced him with a secularized version of a more aggressively brilliant quality. The true hero of Western culture is the great individual defying anything that puts man in bondage: death, danger, or society's rule and prejudice. The cultural history of Europe, more than of any previous historical unit, is colored by the contribution of the genius. During the Renaissance he was the brilliant all-round performer who seemed to overcome death by an unbridled infinite vitality. In the eighteenth century he became subject to the cult of the genius, because he was able to defy reason, which to some had come to imply bondage. The hero in all times of classical civilization was he who rose above the reality of matter and physical determinations. The hero was the cultural symbol of the transcendence sought for in religious and metaphysical philosophy.

Thomas Carlyle, at the end of the heroic epoch, summed it up in his *On Heroes, Hero-Worship and the Heroic in History*—the cultural role of the hero in the Western mind was the determining factor of history itself. Luther, Cromwell, Frederick II, Goethe, or Bismarck were the engineers of historical change. Although he himself did not think of it as such, Carlyle's book is actually a farewell address to the heroic conception of the classical age. At that time, 1841, a new mentality began to express itself in new archetypes, indicating that the sovereignty of the elite individual was no longer unchallenged. The first novels and plays were appearing in which the chief character could in no way be explained as a projection of the hero. We were entering the age of the non-hero.

The cultural hero was the symbol of the leader, not, however, in the boy-scout sense or by any good-guy morality, and definitely not in the sense of the herd spirit calling for the strong man, eventually the despot. The hero represented the leadership of a mental equilibrium of authority, which operated as much with inward persuasion as with outward force. Cultural authority, far from imposing an external regime on the individual, corresponded dialectically to an inner source of leadership. With the emergence of total social equality, the whole classical relationship of freedom and authority became ineffective. Authority came to be understood exclusively as an extraneous power, incompatible with the basic opportunities of men. It had to be abolished. In a society striving above all for the unrestricted distribution of goods, services, and rights, the prevailing stress had to be on the mechanics of accumulation. Man thus tended to live by the authority of expansion, a devotedly material pursuit. In such a dispensation the consciousness of the hero had no place.

The American way of seeing and solving problems is clearly conditioned by the modernity of acquisition, expansion, and consensus. The modern mind almost compulsively reacts against the hero, the great man, the genius. Consequently, it can hardly be an accident that in American history the genius plays virtually no role. This would go against the national sense of equality. Outstanding figures in our society are those who best represent the average man, who evoke the image of the habits and duties of the common people. The literature and the arts of this country by and large are not the manifestations of a heroic temper. They represent the non-hero. For to the average man transcendence is sheer wickedness. It betrays the security of the scientific basis on which his material strength has gradually and carefully been constructed. The traveling salesman replaces the crusading pilgrim, Leopold Bloom supersedes Ulysses, and the gospel of Carnegie eclipses that of Luke.

The history of the drama during the last two centuries reflects the gradual disappearance of authority in the weakening function of the protagonist. For a proper understanding of this development it is helpful to observe how in the eighteenth century the nature of the traditional protagonist in tragedy changed from an elite to a middle-class position. George Lillo's *The London Merchant* (1731) introduced a new genre, the bourgeois drama, in which common people were put in tragic circumstances heretofore reserved for those of more elevated status. Significantly, it was written entirely in prose. Its historic value is not matched by any dramatic or psychological quality. Nor is Diderot's *Père de famille*, with its enlightened didactic overtones, of stirring theatrical importance. Lessing's *Miss Sarah Sampson* (1755) was probably the first bourgeois tragedy with qualities that go beyond the sniveling and sentimental, but on the whole these early specimens of the new genre are chiefly remarkable for bringing the protagonist down from his Olympian heights to the family circle. This bourgeois tragedy soon found its theoretical apologists. Diderot wrote about it as a dramatization of "domestic troubles," and Lessing in his famous *Hamburgische Dramaturgie* believed that the domestic tragedy was more "moving" than one that dealt with monarchs. Finally, in another piece of theory, Karl Wilhelm Ramler, a poet and director of the Berlin Theater, in 1774 saw in the bourgeois drama a welcome opportunity for the theater to conform to middle-class taste. In all these defenses there was the common theme of the advantage of greater immediacy —as we have seen, a sure sign of proletarianization.

Middle-class taste being merely an introduction to twentieth-century popular taste, the early bourgeois drama was similarly the beginning of a long line of trouble-in-the-family situations, which, in a more vivid and sometimes also more vulgar idiom, are still one of the mainstays of the Broadway stage. The question, however, is: What had happened to the hero? Since the protagonist was no longer to be recruited from the lofty and remote regions of the elite, but must be domesticated and home-grown, so to speak, what could make for a better replacement than the center of the bourgeois family, the father? Diderot's *Père de famille* was the prototype for the successive fathers, who from 1759 roamed the stage, trying to overcome the unreasonable onslaughts on their daughters, wives, fortunes, and social position. The *pater familias*, indeed, was the middle-class hero of the nineteenth century. To be sure, a pedestrian variety after the gallery of exalted super-beings, an eagle with clipped wings, but a hero all the same.

The domestic tragedy, pivoting on the domestic hero, is the most successful product of the commercial theater during the last two centuries. Its representative playwrights, such as Kotzebue, Iffland, Augier, Dumas, Scribe, Pinero, and Henry Arthur Jones—all experts on the well-constructed play—are now forgotten by all but the specialist. All except one. Why does Ibsen survive when others no less competent have disappeared? It may be that Ibsen out-mastered them all in the technical engineering of the well-made drama. Undeniably, his plays in their taut economy are case-book examples for drama classes. Technique, however, is rarely important in accounting for the classic. Ibsen was not merely better than his professional colleagues. He was different. His "father" characters are rarely just domestic, his families seldom remain fixed in daily-life routine. The great characters of his prose works—Solness, Gabriel Borkman, Rubek, or Rosmer—are all embedded in the middle class of Norwegian society. They are remembered in history, not, of course, because of the greater technical proficiency of their creator, but because they rise above the naturalist limitations of commonplace bourgeois experience. They do this through the workings of the intangible creative quality that distinguishes art from the mere professional. Unfathomable as this quality may be, we can recognize the result. The father figure in Ibsen's plays transcends his material surroundings. He again represents the real hero.

Ibsen was the unique playwright of the age who succeeded unconsciously in overcoming the limitations of the domestic drama, while others, who were self-consciously aware of them, failed. Thus authors such as Hauptmann, Heyermans, Strindberg, and later O'Neill and Tennessee Williams, who are at their most convincing when working in naturalist materials, have experimented almost feverishly with dream, fairy-tale, and other extra-realist ingredients without ever achieving that unity of purpose and vision which marks the masterpiece, regardless of technical considerations. This does not make their experimental work less interesting; it simply points to an insecurity of scope never felt with Ibsen. In the United States exception should be made perhaps for Williams' *The Glass Menagerie,* in which the author manages to rise above the topical and the material of stark drama. Above all, exception must be made for Thornton Wilder's *Our Town.* This tragi-comedy excels the regular domestic play by that decisive poetic touch without which there can be no enduring significance. Although thoroughly native in theme and scope, it transcends the daily life of Grover's Corners by that sweep of universality which is the prime condition of the classic.

The domestic realist drama was a product of the rational enlightened spirit of the eighteenth century, and it was not altogether accidental that two of its most prominent thinkers, Lessing and Diderot, also helped sire the bourgeois drama. In the nineteenth and twentieth centuries this genre remained consistently rational. This accounts for the proclivity to construct the well-made play, for a streamlined scene distribution, and for the inclusion of a "thesis" or a social, enlightened message, replacing the old, sentimental stamp of virtue. These realistic dramas, though now antiquated and useless for revival, were in their own day widely successful. However, they represented only one line of cultural development. The nineteenth century, as we have elaborated in an earlier chapter, was one of contrasting historical processes and can only be expected to reflect this in its drama.

Parallel with the growth of the drama rooted in the rationality of the age, there is to be seen the unfolding of theatrical forms corresponding to the equally characteris-

tic irrationality of the century. We do not need to elaborate on the Shakespeare revival. Shakespeare's work, of
course, like all expressions of soaring imagination, had its
origins at least partly in the realm into which reason cannot enter. It is precisely on account of this that neoclassical rationalists such as Voltaire failed to appreciate
what was typically Shakespeare's. Some of the Romanticists went to the other extreme and made a cult of his
work. Soon emulations of Shakespeare began to abound.
Hugo, Kleist, and Grabbe were probably the most outstanding of his admirers. To be fair, not all of them paid
slavish tribute. Some infused their own originality into
the Elizabethan form. But this kind of drama found little
historical development. We must look elsewhere for the
new expressions that were to have repercussions for some
time to come.

The influence of the outlook and philosophy of *Faust*
on later literature is not difficult to explain. The example,
however, that Goethe's work was to set for later dramatic
form is extraordinary in view of the fact that the author
deliberately ignored all basic precepts of dramaturgy. It
is precisely the formlessness of the play and its dual appeal to reason and irrationality that make it the prototype of those drama forms which try to give a more profound dimension to the stage than that provided by the
social and domestic theater. Hence, we have the drama
of the "philosophical journey," not only attempted by the
early Ibsen and the later Strindberg, but also by many of
the German expressionists, through Brecht and Max
Frisch, who were dissatisfied with the rational solutions
of the naturalist play.

Goethe's liberation from classical forms in *Faust* con-
tradicted his anxious adherence to them in such plays as
Iphigenia in Tauris and *Torquato Tasso* and made him,
against his own will, a part of the Romantic movement.
The Romantic climate, with the deliberate polarization of
reason and emotion, was obviously favorable to the nursing of irrational tendencies. What in *Faust* is naturally
and intuitively important—the clashing energy between

the forces of reason and unreason—is in Tieck's dramatic fantasies, *Prinz Zerbino, Puss in Boots,* and *The Topsy-Turvy World,* played up with deliberate programmatic design. Tieck was not a particularly talented playwright, nor was he an important poet. Historically, however, he cannot be ignored, for he was the first to produce the full-fledged specimen of a genre today belatedly labeled the drama of the absurd.

Absurdity in the history of comedy is a constant and almost inescapable element. Tieck, a well-read man, knew this and knowingly made use of devices and tricks that such authors as Aristophanes, Ben Jonson, Holberg, and Gozzi taught him. He further added popular ingredients from Italian *commedia dell' arte* and German Hanswurst shows. But by elevating the factor of the absurd from an unobtrusive means to a demonstrative end and providing it, moreover, with a philosophy of irony (borrowed from his friend Friedrich Schlegel), Tieck created a cultural expression all his own. The extreme of chaotic absurdity was reached in *The Topsy-Turvy World* (1799). It begins with an epilogue and ends with a prologue, and in between all that can be reasonably expected from a regular theater performance is deliberately derailed or reversed. The roles of audience and actor, traditionally so uncompromisingly separated, become muddled; and with the public running onto the stage, wanting to act, and players refusing to perform and descending into the audience, there is a general confusion of identity.

By abolishing the fundamental values of reality and illusion, Tieck presented a problem that Pirandello, a century later, was to elaborate more subtly and also more intellectually. More important, Tieck's arbitrary disruption of stage illusion made Brecht's so-called invention of the alienation effect stale and outdated. The modernity of crashing the "fourth wall" between performer and audience is by no means a characteristic of the twentieth century alone. It began at the time (around 1800) when man in general became estranged from what belongs to him most, his community. The Schlegel-Tieck formula of irony, the exchange of "self-creation and self-destruction," is dramatically no different from Brecht's scenic alienation, and in a sense both go back to the dramatic digression, the *parekbasis* in Aristophanes' comedies. Tieck's assault on the stage-illusion, however, represents more than an interest in new scenic effects. The topsy-turvy world he portrays is the classical world upside-down, in his mind disrupted by the forces of the French Revolution, but also, we must hasten to add, by the forces of Romanticism to which Tieck himself lent so unreserved a hand. Tieck submitted his work to the editor of the *Straussfedern,* but it was rejected as "eccentric." The time apparently was not yet ripe for what later was to be advertised as avant-garde. The cult of the excentric, which was to characterize an age not focused on a central principle, had only begun.

From Tieck onward the theater of the irrational and the absurd developed slowly, with ups and downs, until the later avant-garde groups with more spectacular splash and scandalizing fervor were to make it conspicuous. In Vienna, Johann Nestroy and Ferdinand Raimund, with practical experience of stage-potential, based their plays on local idiom and popular humor. Nestroy was the more robust and superficial in his mixing of the absurd with the fairy-tale farce. Raimund, in works such as *The Peasant as Millionaire* or *The Spendthrift,* proceeded in the Gozzi and Tieck tradition, but with a curious bourgeois slant. In fact, it is as if in his plays the lines of poetic fantasy and bourgeois drama intersect. Their themes are symptomatically concerned with money, a topic also pivotal in the realist drama. The German author Christian Dietrich Grabbe shows the eccentricity of absurd imagination in his *Jest, Satire, Irony and Deeper Significance,* whose illogically weird title corresponds with the illogically weird characters (among them Grabbe himself) brought together in the work.

Other writers, while not experimenting with the quality of absurdity tried to supersede the rational frame of realism. Georg Büchner, for instance, in a sense probing the realist psychology of the modern non-hero in *Woz-zeck*, still succeeded in transcending the social conditions of the plot with a touch of universal significance. His *Leonce and Lena* is a short comedy, reminding one at first glance of Shakespeare's love-plays, but closer investigation reveals a poetic playfulness, which like Musset's elegant style in *Fantasio, No Trifling with Love,* and *What Do Girls Dream Of?* belongs to the modern age. Büchner definitely belongs to the modern age with his film-like, kaleidoscopic treatment of the revolution in *Danton's Death,* in which something of the futurist sense of fragmentation and movement seems to be foreshadowed.

The grotesque quality, which meant so much to the Romanticist mind and which Victor Hugo in his preface to *Cromwell* pointedly analyzed, is abundantly apparent in this irrational type of drama. The grotesque was a tool to break up the smooth clichés of neoclassicism, and it later served to offset the rationality of the well-made play. The "theater of the grotesque" was to be a twentieth-century version of early Romantic attempts. In the theater, as elsewhere in the arts and literature, the avant-garde impulse of our age is, despite wordy proclamations, historically the same as that which made the Romanticist rebel against his predecessors. The nineteenth-century history of drama ends with the production of Alfred Jarry's *Ubu Roi.* Whether or not an early surrealist product, as some critics classify it, the play issued from a psychosis of revolution, which, when the hubbub was over, left only tatters and smithereens. Though the work is in itself an insignificant piece of drama, it unquestionably marked a historical turn. The absurd, which with Tieck began in playful irony, found its ultimate consumation with Jarry. While Tieck still borrowed fairy-tale princes, Apollo, and Scaramouche from the traditional stage, Ubu is the undisputed prototype of the anti-hero, the fat, utterly lazy non-man. He reaches his destiny when, in *Ubu Chained* (1899), he decides to complete his happy emptiness by becoming an imprisoned slave—a caricatural image of the proletarian submission to the machine of tyranny.

The professional

At the opening of the twentieth century there stands the complex and inscrutable Strindberg, whose lasting importance for the history of drama one should not pretend to assess at this time. The romantic touch of exhibited suffering makes his life story more exciting than that of Ibsen, with whom, inescapably, Strindberg is often, though not always justly, compared. Ibsen, with his robust psyche of the master, wrote one strong accomplished work after the other, always in unflinching control of his tremendous resources. Strindberg in contrast, erratically struggling, shows an uncomfortable disparity between vision and execution, and never achieved one whole masterpiece. Under the circumstances, a comparison with Ibsen is just as unreal and unhelpful as comparing, say, Bruckner with Brahms, Satie with Stravinsky, or, in poetry, Blake with Wordsworth.

Strindberg's great attraction for the modern mind lies in his nervous temper and in his schizophrenic psychosis, which makes him a true representative of the twentieth century. The nervousness of his imagination drove him to attempt practically all the genres dramatically possible, the realistic (*The Father, Miss Julie*), the chamber play (*The Pelican, The Ghost Sonata*), monologue (*The Stranger*), mystery drama (*Advent, Easter*), surrealism (*A Dream Play*), philosophic search (*To Damascus, The Great Highway*), historical drama (*Gustav Vasa, Charles XII*), fairy tale (*Swanwhite, The Slippers of Abu Casem*), satire (*The New Kingdom*), and verse drama (*Master Olof*). In his seemingly endless stream of works, he was always the experimenter, also, however, the modern eclectic who, from his pluralistic, decentralized world, reached in all directions for satisfaction.

There is a third attribute that makes Strindberg attractive to us, one that, again, characterizes him as the man of the age. Virtually all his works, not excluding his novels, deal with autobiographical materials. But they do this in a manner that, since Rousseau's *Confessions* set the pattern, represents the modernity of exhibitionist display. Regardless of the type of play, *The Father, Miss Julie, The Dance of Death,* or *The Great Highway* deal with Strindberg's embattled ego, his vicissitudes in society, and his entangled relations with women. This narcissistic obsession evidently has a great appeal for the contemporary mind. As in the modern novel, however, this proclivity can only be regarded as a completely sterile principle on which to base one's output in a mass society. Generally speaking, Strindberg was one of the last recalcitrant hyper-individualists who, lost in the proletarian system of leveling, rebelled against the commonplace. His visionary originality failed to create the real drama of the age precisely because it runs counter to the pragmatic interest for which the new mass order stands.

Strindberg had considerable influence on the German expressionists, who, often feeling the same resentment against their society, and the same violent impulse to break realist rationality, found in him a congenial guide. In the United States it was mostly his naturalism that was emulated. O'Neill learned almost everything from him, even including the erratic Strindbergian impatience with naturalism and the misty Scandinavian symbolism, which seems somewhat out of place in such very American works as, for instance, *Long Day's Journey into Night.* Strindberg, above all, represents the antagonism of the rational. Even his harsh realistic works have an elusiveness that suggests symbolic overtones. Many of his later dramas, such as *A Dream Play* and *The Ghost Sonata,* move in the subconscious unreality, where fragmented and juxtaposed dream materials rule out the conventional conception of dramatic action.

In the nineteenth century realistic and irrational imaginative drama had two clearly contrasting lines of development. In the twentieth century the genres became mixed. The influence of Chekhov and his tender aquarelle textures, which gave the old domestic drama a soft impressionist touch, began to work long after his death. His plays, steeped in melancholy washes, and with their strange, cool impotence, could only be truly appreciated in an age that has fully realized the extent of its unheroic nature. There is no real protagonist in *Uncle Vanya, The Three Sisters, The Seagull,* or *The Cherry Orchard.* There are constellations of characters pining nostalgically, floating aimlessly in non-event. Drift has replaced action. The unresolved, frustrated moods and situations created here receive natural sympathy from our frustrated mid-century world. It is during and after the Second World War that Chekhov's work has reached the peak of acclaim.

The distorted realism emerging here becomes characteristic for the century. Without applying too schematic standards, one may say that the previous century on the whole separated the bourgeois domestic play from other genres. Its realism remained fairly intact. With the exception of his last work, *When We Dead Awaken,* Ibsen, for all his interest in symbolic media, never distorted the reality of his scenes. The same can be said of Hauptmann's *The Weavers,* or of Oscar Wilde's *Lady Windermere's Fan* and *The Ideal Husband.* If these authors decided to write a more poetically conceived drama, they switched knowingly to an entirely different category. Shaw, in contrast, though basically a committed social realist, after early works such as *Mrs. Warren's Profession* or *Candida,* disrupted the rational order of reality by excessive wit, caricature, and pamphleteering. One might, moreover, have expected that the socialist Shaw would adapt his drama to the developing proletarian consciousness. Instead he continued elitist forms of literature. His was essentially a one-man show, an individualist's theater with a fundamental disregard or ignorance of the new society growing up around him. He stood for eighteenth-century enlightenment rather than for twentieth-century mass concentration.

Pirandello, too, distorted the boundaries of reality. No less a realist than Shaw, he was far more modern in his grasp of contemporary sensitivity. In virtually all his plays he questions, almost systematically, the very substance of his own foundations: realism. The central problem in Pirandello revolves around the relativity of appearance and reality. It is not surprising that he presented this at his most dramatically trenchant in *Six Characters in Search of an Author*. The rehearsal depicted in this work offered him a rewarding opportunity to probe the psychological disparity between man and mask. While undermining the autonomous validity of time, reality, and truth (*Right You Are If You Think You Are*) the Italian dramatist touched on something which relativity physics and existentialist philosophy have investigated in other ways. He revealed the discomfort of the twentieth-century mind, willing to pledge allegiance to the "reality" of the daily environment and the physical laws that control it, yet doubtful about its universal validity.

Historically, Pirandello belongs, at least partly, to the *teatro grottesco*, which in the second decade of this century attempted in its own manner to disarrange the stale clichés of realist dramaturgy. In the efforts of Luigi Chiarelli (*The Mask and the Face*) and Luigi Antonelli (*The Island of the Monkeys*) one can recognize old patterns taken, for instance, from the *commedia dell' arte* or Gozzi's eighteenth-century *fiabe* and used as tools to satirize and destroy the rational security of the bourgeois world. The distortion may be farcical or allegorical, but it is always in line with the romantic principle of the grotesque, sometimes heightened to the quality of the absurd.

The questioning of reality acquires an added aspect in Priestley's philosophical scrutiny of real time. Here is an author who by psychological and stylistic instinct was predestined to deal with domestic realities, yet who struggled to disarrange the temporal order in which they were fixed. In *Time and the Conways, I Have Been Here Before,* or *Desert Highway* he interrupts time with the same experimental tactics as the contemporary novelists who resort to the flashback or stream of consciousness. These plays come from the same awareness that is behind Eliot's *Four Quartets* and Auden's *For the Time Being*. As with Henri Lenormand (*Time Is a Dream*) and Thornton Wilder (*The Bridge of San Luis Rey, Our Town, The Skin of Our Teeth*), the time continuum is existentially destroyed.

Such tampering with physical space and physical time inevitably leads to supernatural sequences and dream qualities, which, while explicit and almost programmatic in some of the works by Strindberg and his followers, in Maeterlinck's plays seem to grow naturally from a realistic setting, but one steeped in twilight. From his characters and their ethereal whispering relationships, Maeterlinck tried to release a vaporous substance, which one might call "soul." Not dissimilarly, Leonid Andreev's *To the Stars* or *The Black Maskers* search for man's soul beyond the stark material forms of his life. But in such plays as *Pelléas and Mélisande, The Blind, Interior, The Death of Tintagiles* Maeterlinck showed a far greater poetic force than any other writer who at that time was attempting to convey the magic of the trans-real world. His influence on later playwrights accordingly is very substantial. The "static theater," which his plays represent and which aims at dramatizing the little events and subtle communications not pushed by the force of a central action, have in later decades been followed by numerous dramas of non-happening. In such works, among which Samuel Beckett's *Waiting for Godot* and *Endgame* are the most radical, no plot, no action, no dramatic development seem required. Here the classical drama has emptied itself of its vital characteristics.

During the twentieth century the borrowing of Greek mythological materials has become conspicuously popular with playwrights. It represents one more technique of distorting reality. Goethe, of course, wrote his *Iphigenia,* and Grillparzer his *The Golden Fleece,* a trilogy about Jason and Medea. But these attempted to revive classical heroism and purity of harmony. In recent times Greek legends merely have served as tools to add a poetic dimension to contemporary themes. Thus Jean Anouilh in *Antigone,* written during the Second World War, transforms the ancient story into one of resistance against National Socialist dictatorship. In Giraudoux's *Electra* and Sartre's *The Flies* the Orestes story is modernized through spirited prose, which, however, turns the legendary substance into a rather realistic affair, especially in the latter work. The mixture of myth and realism in Anouilh's *Eurydice,* in contrast, seems to give a modern plot and situation legendary overtones. O'Neill, too, experimented with the Orestes story. *Mourning Becomes Electra* is a trilogy using the narrative concerning the House of Atreus, here the Mannon family, but that is all. Since the poetic energy and the mythic vision of Aeschylus and Sophocles are totally absent, the long dramatization of hatred and crime does not rise above its naturalistic conditions.

T. S. Eliot, in using a modernization of the Greek chorus in addition to the Orestes myth in *The Family Reunion,* succeeded with striking impact in destroying the realistic clichés of domestic life. But here we are entering into another problem, the use of dramatic verse as a new technique to overcome the staleness of realist theater. This problem does not arise in *Murder in the Cathedral,* which is essentially a modern revival of the medieval mystery play. In *The Cocktail Party* and *The Confidential Clerk,* however, Eliot seriously aimed at giving to a middle-class setting with middle-class troubles a poetic dimension of transcendence. Understanding that the poetic diction of *Murder in the Cathedral* would not do here, he worked with verses of a vaguely rhythmic quality, but these verses are in reality rather chopped up, regularized, prose lines. Whatever these plays may mean for the art of the theater, they are important in this context because they point up the unresolved problem of the modern drama and the various mixtures of realistic and poetic, rational and super-rational techniques. Whether in Eliot's version or in that of the poetic prose of Federico Garcia Lorca's *The House of Bernarda Alba* and *Blood Wedding*, the search for the new form, which is at once modern, authentic, and theatrical, has not gone beyond the experimental stage.

Fewer problems are caused by the unabashed attempts to revive old forms of verse drama. Verse never really disappeared during the rise of realism. Not only a-theatrical poets such as Shelley, Byron, Swinburne, de Vigny, Yeats, or Rilke kept up the tradition (with or without innovations), but even those dramatists firmly grounded in the realist stage conception—Ibsen, Strindberg, Schnitzler (*Paracelsus, The Veil of Beatrice*), Maxwell Anderson (*Elizabeth the Queen, Winterset*)—returned to it. The German expressionists also tried it, sometimes alternating verse with prose within one drama.

In England, especially since Stephen Phillips in the first decade of the century rose meteorically to success with *Paolo and Francesca*, there emerged the hope that scenic verse might still save the theater from prosaic dullness. The resulting efforts were fundamentally motivated by the same sense of revolt that typifies the avantgarde of expressionist, futurist, or dadaist persuasion, except that they appeared without uproarious claims, fanfares, and proclamations. Many of these poet-playwrights worked in the shadow of Eliot, and most of them, like him, conveyed some religious message. Having escaped this influence, Christopher Fry seems the most talented of those working in verse, not excluding Eliot, with his skillful handling of fast, witty, as well as tenderly dramatic situations. Above all, he painfully demonstrates that for all the deserved success of *The Lady's Not for Burning, Venus Observed,* or *A Phoenix Too Frequent,* no amount of talent can give poetic drama a legitimate and lasting place in the theater of a mass society. Some twenty years after his greatest efforts, the verse drama is a dead proposition. The Shakespeares belong to the Elizabethans.

The poet W. H. Auden collaborated with Christopher

Isherwood in the 1930's to write *The Dog Beneath the Skin* and *The Ascent of F.6,* works rendered in a fluent yet speakable verse diction. However, they differ from Eliot's school in the incorporation of social and political themes and by the fragmentary quality that brings them within the orbit of expressionist drama. Expressionism in the theater actually means more than the narrowly confined German experiments of the 1920's and 30's. It represented a revolt against the nineteenth-century rationalism of scientific and naturalistic formulations, as violent as the Romanticist attack on eighteenth-century formalism. Expressionism was as much a historical follow-up of Romanticism as the Russian Revolution was of the French Revolution. The expressionist revolt was diffused and appeared under various labels in various manifestos. Like Romanticism, it has a central historical significance, despite its often contradictory manifestations.

It would therefore in no way be wrong to recognize the expressionist quality, for instance, in Jarry's Ubu dramas. They laid the foundation for everything that in the next century was to manifest itself as avant-garde, which culturally meant the annihilation of all limiting forms and traditional values. Guillaume Apollinaire called his *Les Mamelles de Tirésias* a "surrealist drama," a label hard to challenge. But this incredible piece of theater about a man and a woman changing sex on the stage clearly belongs to the same category as, let us say, Oskar Kokoschka's *Job* (incidentally written in the same year, 1917), which presents a man whose head first falls off but then is put back again. Yet the latter play is officially classed among the expressionist products.

This type of expressionist drama appeared around 1910 (Reinhard Sorge's *The Beggar* of 1911 and Ernst Barlach's *The Dead Day* of 1912 were already genuine representatives) and petered out toward 1940, although Brecht and his followers continued it during and after the Second World War with spasmodic success. It had its roots not only in the experiments in absurdity from Tieck to Jarry, but also in the Faust-type drama, and in the dream and mystery plays of Strindberg, which have already been mentioned as sources. To this must be added the stylistic innovations of Maeterlinck and the heavily contoured works of Frank Wedekind. Wedekind's activity came just before the outburst of expressionism and partly coincided with the works of Strindberg, with whom he is often compared. Working with the nervous energy of a true genius and, like Strindberg, without the sure control of a great master, Wedekind produced a series of stirring plays, which intimate later trends. His preoccupation with sexual problems and the teenage psyche in virtually all his works, but most notably in *Spring's Awakening,* gave his subject matter an unmistakably modern flavor. His dramatic treatment, moreover, with its blunt jagged lines of development and not too subtle characterizations, adumbrated the two-dimensional quality of much of the following twentieth-century drama.

This quality can indeed be quite effective, as Georg Kaiser was to show in works such as *Gas, The Coral, From Morn to Midnight,* in which the characters stand for movements and masses rather than for individuals. In this manner the expressionist genre gave one of the few indications that drama was responding to the new mass consciousness, other than through topic or superimposed message. The two-dimensionality made the characters allegorical agents, which in itself was not new. But inasmuch as they were agents for social consensus, they introduced something uniquely contemporary. One can find this quality in Brecht's works, in Toller's *Man and the Masses* and *The Machine-Wreckers,* in Fritz von Unruh's *One Race* and *The Son.* The fact that these plays may not all deserve a permanent success does not detract from the historical importance of their transformation of the individuality of man, by abstraction, into ideas and mass patterns—a change paralleled in the work of the abstract painters of the time.

This abstraction served splendidly to destroy the realist picture of human life that the bourgeois theater evoked. To the expressionist this picture was an illusion that had to be torn to pieces. The vehemence with which this was done gives the abstracting technique an air of caricature, as it does with some of the painters of the period, the groups of the *Brücke,* the fauves, the cubists. Thus came about a new version of absurdity, which is neither satire nor the playful perversion of Tieck or Jarry, but serious distortion for the message's sake. This absurdity functions in Kaiser's *Alcibiades Saved,* in which a ludicrous event such as a cactus thorn entering Socrates' foot is made to account for his greatness. It is to be found in Walter Hasenclever's drama *Humanity,* which presents a dead body as the hero.

The element of absurdity and deliberate disproportion also operated effectively in expressionist work outside Germany, in *The Magnificent Cuckold* by the Belgian Fernand Crommelynck, *The Executioner* by the Swede Pär Lagerkvist, *R.U.R.,* the brave new world of robots by the Czech authors Josef and Karel Čapek, in the works of American playwrights such as John Howard Lawson (*Processional*) or Elmer Rice (*The Adding Machine*), in those of French authors such as Jean Cocteau (*Orphée* and *The Infernal Machine*) and Roger Vitrac (*Mysteries of Love*). To these should be added the futurist experiments by Filippo Tommaso Marinetti (*Simultaneity* and *Prisoners*) and Vladimir Mayakovsky (*The Bedbug*), both poets remarkably clever with theatrical effects but inadequate in providing real dramatic action.

In spite of Bertolt Brecht's rejection of the extravagances and absurdities of some of the expressionists, he nevertheless belonged to them; in fact, he represents in the most striking fashion their strength as well as their weakness. The destructive Mephistophelean strand (especially in *Baal*), the two-dimensional characterization, the crude outlines of plot, the blunt exposition of social themes, the fragmented scenes, the allegorical use of personages, are all unmistakable features of the expressionist stage conception. He added to this a didactic insistence, which brings us back to the medieval scene. In fact, his witty Heinean lyric, as earlier indicated, is fundamentally related to the medieval ballad, and his self-styled epic theater is very much akin to the flat, juxtaposed scene sequence of the Middle Ages. Brecht, with great flair for striking stage effects, frequently made clever use of these elements to aid his didactic purpose. The consistently intervening cerebration was his besetting weakness. Though a communist, he was rejected by the communist leaders as an old-fashioned bourgeois. Never attractive to the wide populace, he was really adopted only by intellectuals in the West, who rightly appreciate the inventiveness with which he enriched the theater of ideas, but who are not always aware of the fact that his rather portentous theories are merely a justification for old stage tricks. No more than the other expressionists does he represent the mass consciousness of our time, except that, like most of his contemporaries, he deliberately concentrates on its archetype, the non-hero. Mother Courage is actually a coward. In *Galileo* the pivotal message is "Happy is the land that needs no hero."

After the Second World War the theater in most countries rebounded with extraordinary zest. For those intimately familiar with the international stage, the judgment so consistently repeated season after season that theater art is "dead" can mean nothing but ignorance. An art that has with so much vitality enlarged its range, expanded its audience, and shown its inventiveness in new enterprises and theatrical centers is, of course, by no means dead. Never has the dramatic art been served with more professional expertise or managerial experience than at this time. Not only have the commercial houses, besides making profits, ventured into a variety of new fields, the repertory theater also has found new terrains and audiences, while in numerous countries national companies, aided by understanding governments, have been established to ensure high-quality productions. To this may be added the ever-expanding dramatic programs on the college level as well as in university drama schools. This is productive and constructive and testifies to the broad involvement of the populace in the theater arts.

Once we have duly acknowledged this, however, we cannot fairly overlook the fact that unfortunately one element is badly lacking. The complaint of the absence of great original drama, commensurate with our outstanding skills of stage craft, is hard to counter. There have been penetrating, exciting, and highly competent plays produced since the war, but the great representative work of the era is absent. The problems of peasants and industrial workers have been treated in drama but, significantly, with the same old technique as the realistic middle-class plays.

We can speak only about what is apparent at present, of course. It may be that later centuries will discover a unifying proletarian style in our century. To us, however, the scene is one of a chaos of techniques and methods borrowed from predecessors and usually freely mixed together in untrammeled eclecticism. Whether commercial Broadway or subsidized repertory, the total aspect is no different; one can watch them all—Elizabethan tragedy, the stark realism of Odets, O'Neill, Miller, and Tennessee Williams, the bawdy Restoration wits, the Scandinavian moods of Ibsen and Strindberg, ornate musical comedy, German expressionism, social realism, high-pressured farce, or boulevard play, in addition to the visiting presentations of Schiller, Racine, or Sophocles. Furthermore, there is the inevitable introduction of the "new" drama, which may be any concoction of ingredients taken from the entire gamut of avant-garde shows operating between 1880 and 1940.

Ours is a consumer's theater. Functioning like a department store, it must offer a wide variety of commodities, attractively wrapped and expertly handled for a mass audience that wants to be entertained in a diversified manner. It is here that the performer's stage finds its historical justification. The modern dramatist, in order to be successful, must make it clear to himself that he is important only inasmuch as he serves the immediate needs of the performing functionaries, the actors, designers, directors. There is nothing dishonorable in this. More than ever it gives him the opportunity of being the preeminent professional, the specialist who can concentrate on one of the specific varieties of the consumer's theater.

It would be incorrect to present the change from a dramatist's to a performer's stage in a stark white and black. As in all historical processes one phase followed the other through transitions of mutual overlapping and blending. Nor should one picture the contemporary playwright as a lackey of the showman. He has the same wide range of choices and liberties as the professional of any other field and, precisely because he is an adapter of previous techniques rather than an originator, his professional options are many. During the last quarter of a century he has indeed proved that he can coordinate himself with the performer and transform the wildly rebellious avant-garde experiments into a salable production in the respectable domain of the consumer's market.

The playwright in the performer's theater is primarily concerned with the "exciting." This has come to mean a variety of attractions, such as the "savage" treatment or the display of sexual perversion. Scenically it can involve a number of stage tricks learned from the director or a situation calling for the full potential of stage and lighting equipment to enliven the performance. The playwright in the performer's theater aims at maximum visualization, that is, immediacy. If he desires at all to know how he differs from his classical counterpart, he should study the works of Molière. Molière, a performer himself, and a great one, can quietly allow two characters to spin out a long scene without moving them endlessly from one corner of the stage to another and without the interference of the tricks of "stage-business." Dramatic action here is apparently an inward suspense, a quality usually conveyed through the medium of poetry. Thus, by the standards of today's playwriting, the technique of *Tartuffe* is pretty unexciting stuff, unless an inventive director is given the chance to dress it up. Today the sense of the dramatic is replaced by visualization, action by excitement. The playwright in the performer's theater must take care that something external happens at all times. Visual happening is fundamental to the entertainment of a mass society. The modern dramatist has no other choice. It inevitably rules out the mediacy of the poetic and its musical conveyance, which have traditionally been the mark of the sublime drama. The modern dramatist is by necessity a prose writer.

The priority of the performer over the playwright and the related domination of visual happening over dramatic action suggest a limitation we dislike and emotionally tend to reject. For we are forever reminded that the history of dramatic art is the account of superb playwriting in the first place and only incidentally that of theatricality. It is, above all, a story that mirrors the dramatist's stage: Attic tragedy, Elizabethan play, Restoration comedy, the French baroque, or the Weimer court drama. We do not care to remember the names of those dramatists serving the performer's stage, Roman tragedy, the Italian Renaissance theater, the Jesuit stage, or the Meiningen company. The unfortunate inference then would be that today a playwright, absorbed in the effects of theatricality, is lost for the future no matter how hard he tries. This may or may not be so. But it should not worry us. The main point on which to concentrate is the patent need of our mass society for professional entertainment. The dramatist has never been more professional, has never been more expertly equipped for the difficult art of show business than at the present.

All dramatic art is founded on entertainment. Without it, it cannot exist. But while in the dramatist's theater entertainment indirectly leads to dramatic involvement, in the performer's theater entertainment becomes the exclusive aim. The difference between the former and the latter is that between mediacy and immediacy in the matter of public involvement. Consequently, tragedy with its characteristic mediacy of cosmic transcendence cannot thrive on the performer's stage. The odds for tragedy in our materialistic order are exceedingly slim for another reason. We have lost, and no longer desire, that quality of heroic failure which marks the great moments of

Greek and European consciousness. Ours is an age of success and status—objectives utterly incompatible with the awareness of the tragic. Failure in our world is puny and has no dimension of grandeur. Besides *Our Town,* which is essentially a tragi-comedy, there exists no twentieth-century drama conveying tragic awareness. Incestuous farmers under the elms of New England, apathetic waterfront bums, sorry incompetent salesmen, luckless crippled teenagers, or frustrated and childless professors' wives are pathetic, but they are hardly bearers of the beauty of the tragic. Theirs is perhaps individual and specific suffering. Tragic suffering is existential and of universal depth.

The greatest opportunity for the modern dramatist lies in the unpretentious antics of popular comedy. It is here that he can best apply his close professional cooperation with the performer and his skills of theatricality. Especially in North America, with its resources of native wit and the available talent for remarkably racy and pithy dialogue, comic entertainment, musical or straight, promises the best fulfillment for both present and future needs.

Part
THREE

Play is freedom, is disinterestedness, and it is only by virtue of disinterested free activity that man has created his cultural values.

Herbert Read

8

The Behavioral Way of Living

New avenues of science

During the very period examined in this study the universities of the Western world embarked on various new programs and disciplines to satisfy their traditional appetite for discovery. There is nothing particularly remarkable about this trend, for the history of higher education presents a continuous expansion of academic fields. What is new, however, is the fascinating spread of the new intellectual interests out of the campus into the open street of popular adaptation. Newspapers, television, and easy books have helped to change what was originally a limited scholarly investigation into a mass concern. This could not have happened, of course, if such new disciplines as psychology, sociology, or anthropology had not possessed an inherent popular appeal, that is, if they had not offered a convenient rationale for the masses to justify their emotional problems.

The blending of popular and professional knowledge, once impossible, now becomes attractive. The men of the French Enlightenment began to popularize earlier professional and technical systems, and the emergence of the institution of the Encyclopedia was indicative of the growing diffusion of knowledge, The self-respecting nineteenth-century scholar often resented this tide. Hegel believed that it lowered the quality of learning to the level of the ignorant, instead of raising the people to the heights of scholarship. With the popular press soon joining the trend, the reserved Burckhardt became alarmed and warned against the newspapers as if they were the underminers of society.

The modern sciences, whatever else they achieve, have helped to bridge the chasm between a professional bastion of scholars, jealously confining their discoveries within an intellectual elite, and a semi-educated populace anxious to make useful applications of other people's findings. Naturally, the result of this egalitarian movement has aroused contradictory voices of approval and condemnation. Since we are scrutinizing the totality of modern cultural manifestations, any partisan bias has no legitimate place here. One should be willing to concede that the new behavorial sciences have contributed greatly to the knowledge of man's precarious relations with his environment, without, however, overlooking some of the negative repercussions haunting our world. The various popular types of psychology have undeniably cleared up foggy regions in man's understanding, but they have also created a new brand of fanatics who have merely replaced the Nicene Creed with the dogmas of a libido cult. Undoubtedly the study of sociology has brought forth pivotal works as magnificent or profound as those in other fields, but it has also dumped upon the market vast quantities of cheap works pandering to sentimental and sensational instincts, thus doing a disservice to the very need of popularization.

Karl Jaspers, whose *Man in the Modern Age,* mentioned earlier, is a classic in Europe and known to every undergraduate interested in the "intellectual situation of the time," has taken a rather strong stand against the modern sciences. Although the book is easily the best we have as an analysis of the contemporary world, this fact should not prevent us from taking a critical look at his condemnation. To be sure, Jaspers detects correctly, I believe, the imminent jeopardy of their negativistic tendencies when he points out that sociology, psychoanalysis, and anthropology "are well-equipped to destroy what seemed to have value for man." He is rightly concerned about the process of leveling, which all of us dislike and fear. Nobody stands to gain when "the most sublime and the meanest are clothed in the same terminology and condemned to go forth into Nothingness." But this evaluation one-sidedly leaves unmentioned those constructive insights contributed by the behavioral studies which have prevented our industrialized existence from falling apart in mechanical fragments. It is correct and even imperative to see the danger of the extremes of "downright hatred and praise which have come to prevail in mass-existence," and which have been brought out "by Marxism in the way the crowd wants community and by psychoanalysis in the way it seeks mere life-gratification." But these aspects are by no means representative for the whole field of the popular sciences. Alongside the unmistakable preference for the satisfaction of violence, they have a definite and wide interest in possible healing techniques for a disturbed society.

For our purpose the question is not primarily how beneficent or how malignant the rise of the various behavioral studies has proved itself to be, but rather what it means in conjunction with the other modern phenomena under examination here. It is worthwhile noting, for instance, that it should have taken so many centuries before Western civilization showed that pronounced interest in the external behavior of man, which is the special concern of modern psychology and sociology. Apparently, after a long history of thinking about the essence, meaning, and destiny of himself, man then gradually, with scarcely a historical marker to indicate when the trend actually started, became more and more inclined to observe himself from the outside as if he were part of a laboratory project. Man became a test-case in the clinical pursuit.

With the predominance of the scientific method in all fields of inquiry, it was only fair that in the nineteenth century man himself, as an object, should receive his due share of scientific observation. It seems simply a matter of logic that after he had learned that he too belongs to the species of animals, his sense of equality should compel him to put himself in the academic zoo, so to speak, where he could watch the human race as if it were something outside his living experience. Clearly we are dealing here with that peculiar modern phenomenon of estrangement, the abstraction of human awareness, which detaches the outward forms of an existence, and evaluates them as extraneous to the self-experience. It is unquestionably scientific to do so, and about its useful merits there should be no quarrel. As a characteristic attitude of the modern mind it should, however, also be registered and understood for what it is.

The separation of man as object from man as consciousness had not gone uncriticized. Philosophers from Schelling and Hegel to Whitehead probed its origin and implications. Goethe, in a conversation with his friend Eckermann one year before his death, chided some French scientists for treating natural structures as if they were compositions of mechanical components, thus ignoring their organic spontaneous quality. Rilke, with a less scientifically precise mind than Goethe's, dressed his critique in a lyrical idiom. In one of his early poems he warned: "Stay away! I would like to hear things sing, but you touch them, and they are stiff and numb. You kill things in this manner." Both Goethe and Rilke searched for the essence of things at all times. The behavioral scientist is interested in specific reactions of determined forces under particular circumstances which can be verified in clinical tests. There are obviously two different games involved here, and two different sets of rules.

The techniques of sociology direct themselves primarily toward the group and the interrelationships within the group. Psychology, in contrast, is chiefly occupied with the study of individual experiences. This, no doubt, is an over-simplification, for group and individual are rarely separated from each other in the mind. The distinctness of the two sciences, however, does point to an increasing rift in the human consciousness, but seeing this will serve our understanding only if we grasp that the underlying estrangement is stressed not merely by separation, but also by the dialectical contradiction of this separation. Mass consciousness is usually dialectically supported by hyper-individualization, and the trend of conformity by the frantic fight against conformity. This is reflected in the parallel rise of sociology and psychology, which culturally belong together as mutually responding endeavors.

The psychological basis that underlies any sound study of sociology poses a problem. For somehow, while examining the behavior of the group, we use methods derived from the study of the individual. When, for instance, Wilhelm Wundt wrote *Elements of Folk Psychology*, the very title of this work indicated a mix-up, which is similarly evident when one applies psychological distinctions, such as "phlegmatic" to all the English, "erotic" to all the French, "esthetic" to all the Italians. When Gustave Le Bon, in *The Crowd*, allotted epithets such as "intolerant" and "authoritarian" to the multitude, he based this on the speculative assumption that the external actions of a group of people are driven by the same motivations one attributes to each of its members. Difficult as it is to analyze individual urges, there are surely no methods of treating the masses scientifically. Such phrases of popular sociology as "the lonely crowd," are mixed metaphors which reveal the fundamental problem of the behavioral sciences, namely, that of having to deal with the mutually contradicting responses of the individual and the group.

Scientific wishdreams

The idea that sociology is a markedly modern branch of scholarship is only partly correct. The study of society goes back to the Greeks. Both Plato and Aristotle dealt with sociological as well as psychological questions. Just before them the Sophists can be said to have initiated the study of sociology by their predominant concern with public actualities rather than personal experience. As pragmatic teachers, they are often drawn into an analogy with the authors of the French Enlightenment, an analogy at least partly plausible in that the Sophists too were, in Prodicus' words, "half philosopher and half politician." Like the eighteenth-century publicists, they did away with metaphysical speculations on the essence of man and nature, and concentrated on human behavior—all true prerequisites for the sociologist.

It is not difficult to find in the unfolding Western society a continuous, though at first rather hesitant, attention to the way in which human beings live together. The names of Augustine, ibn-Khaldun, Althusius, Machiavelli, Bodin, Grotius, Pufendorf, Hobbes, Locke, and Spinoza are only a few among those representing the interest in the stability of the common good.

It was not until the eighteenth century, however, that the study of society acquired more weight when it coincided with a growing mass consciousness. Herder's pivotal idea of the organic cohesion of the People, Adam

Ferguson's essays on civil society, Condorcet's ten stages of humanity's amelioration, or Rousseau's sovereignty of the General Will make particular sense when seen in connection with the emergence of crowd dynamics. These authors, though in no way starting from the same intellectual premises, all indirectly pointed to a new need for examining the social collectivity as a unit in order to safeguard its integrity.

To what extent this concern was related to the developing industrial changes may be seen in the efforts of Saint-Simon, a French nobleman who realized that the cement which had held the classical community together was crumbling away, and that new liaisons had to be found to bind the industrial commonwealth together. Consequently, he suggested that the new leaders should no longer be the priests and monarchs of the past, but a hierarchy of scientists and engineers who understood the new *système industriel.* Henceforth in society, therefore, in Saint-Simon's view the government of *things* would be more significant than the government of people.

This new sociology of the collective reveals two characteristics. It was bravely utopian, and its golden future would be scientifically established. Utopian dreams, of course, have at no time in history been absent from man's unfulfilled existence. But when these *New Atlantises, Cities of the Sun,* and *Erewhons* crop up in literature, they can immediately be recognized as playful fantasies. In the nineteenth century, however, there arose the ironical phenomenon of the utopian wishdream turned scientific. Following Condorcet's projections of a constant process of perfecting, the sociological theories of Saint-Simon, Fourier, or Comte aimed at ideal states through the efficiency of scientific laws. The cruel contradiction between belief and empiricism in their doctrine is embarrassingly illustrated, for instance, by the religious cult resulting from Saint-Simonism and the sacred positivist creed of Auguste Comte.

Over the last hundred years, Comte's reputation as a thinker has gradually been reduced to nil. But he must be mentioned here inasmuch as his ideas elucidate the development of proletarian culture. Besides giving the study of sociology its name, his works show how impossible is the task of dealing with the collective in scientific terms as well as those of social amelioration. Comte was a direct descendant of the French Enlightenment in his rejection of religious and metaphysical postulates, and the belief that because society had now reached the stage in which physical laws were its almost exclusive guides, it would at long last proceed toward unknown realms of bliss. Since this gospel of positive thinking was launched in 1830 with the *Cours de philosophie positive,* its optimistic message has suffered irrevocable defeats in the face of some unpleasant and unaccommodating facts of modern history. While one cannot hold Comte responsible for historical events, the unbridled faith of so professedly scientific a mind must be exposed to critical judgment. Comte's thinking ultimately developed into a religion of humanity, replete with the paraphernalia of a high priest (he himself), a catechism, and a calendar of saints.

It would be unfair indeed to gauge the soundness of utopian sociology by its excesses. The excesses, however, are the more lurid demonstrations of a general trend accelerated by a fanatical temper which belies its own scientific claims. The immanent negation is again illustrated by Mikhail Bakunin. On the one hand, under the influence of Comte, he brandished all the scientific slogans of positivism. He was against metaphysicians, against theologians, and for science as the "last stage and the crowning glory of positive philosophy." In his work on *Federalism, Socialism and Anti-theologism,* he made it clear that in order to attain to the anarchist ideal of equity a rigorous knowledge and observance of the laws of the "social body" is required, and sociology is this discipline. On the other hand, Bakunin's rejection of Marx stemmed from an abhorrence of what he elsewhere called a "small aristocracy of genuine and sham scientists" who in the communist state would despotically regiment the common people.

With our knowledge of the actuality of Marx's socialism, we can easily corroborate Bakunin's judgment. It is plain, however, that by dismissing Marx's system on the ground of its scientific claims, he dismissed virtually all the utopian types of sociology, including his own. One does wonder why in Lenin's and Marx's writings it must constantly be hammered home to the reader that the communist state is not a utopia, as one might think (why?), but a product of scientific laws. It would never occur to the real practicing scientist to announce his empirical findings as "science," because no one could have any doubts. The self-conscious claims of the communist theoreticians suggest an embarrassing self-doubt as well as an anticipation of valid criticism, which was to come anyway.

The early papers by Marx were important contributions to the beginning sociological scholarship. The economic-philosophical manuscripts of 1844 gave a masterful analysis of the inequities which the growing industrialization had forced upon the workers. The problem with which Marx dealt was a totally human problem. Labor under the capitalist system had led to the dehumanizing of the worker. He had become a commodity and the most miserable commodity at that. This presented no novelty, for Schiller, and more pronouncedly Hegel, had already probed the idea of alienated labor, and Marx knew it. Though perhaps limited in originality, these essays were nevertheless penetrating and perfectly persuasive in their incursions into contiguous (socioeconomic) fields which the other authors had not explored.

The validity of Marx's sociological studies, including their virulent protest was undermined, however, when his attention eventually was more and more focused on a political program which could be called neither humanitarian nor scientific. It was thus that the innate element

of violence in his character began to affect his thought
and to translate into the philosophy of action which was
to become a blueprint for later regimented terror.

Since the political ramifications of Marx's sociology do
not concern us here, we can confine ourselves to the
view, expressed in his *Theses on Feuerbach,* that the
world must not merely be interpreted, as is done by philosophers, but that it must be changed. Here again we
meet the utopian assumption that worlds can be changed
by force and scientific manipulations, whereas history has
always been the demonstration of change occurring by
growth, gradual evolution, perhaps in small dialectical
steps (Hegel's *Stufen*), but in any event by maturation.

The unfortunate combination of scientific efficiency
and chiliastic projections, constituted a fundamental disservice to the promise of science. Instead of gratefully
accepting science as an agency for urgent social repair
otherwise perhaps not feasible, it was hallowed as the
new messiah of mankind. Or in less ambitious cases, it
was used to prove the utopian unprovable in order to impose upon the mass-mind the inevitability of the future
realization of emotional experiences, better called mirages. The universal application of this kind of "scientific" method is illustrated by the movement of Jehovah's
Witnesses, a sect far removed from the scholarly pursuit,
yet in its tracts anxiously committed to support expectations of a thousand-year realm of peace by an elaborate
logic of numbers and figures. This method, already questionable in religious communications, runs entirely
against reason when used by scholars.

Obviously, sociology was by no means confined to the
utopian way of thinking. Indeed, it reached its great significance in the hands of scholars who could put the con-
textual data of a given society in the perspective of
continuity. With their extraordinary sense of history,
writers such as Max and Alfred Weber or Ferdinand
Tönnies were able to use detailed research for broadly
organizing themes. This in a sense also holds true for
those sociologists, Herbert Spencer, John Fiske, and Wil-

liam Sumner, to name a few, who used the broad sweep of biological evolution as their binding material, except of course that their premises have become rather outdated.

The dangers of popular appeal, which sociology manifested from the beginning, can only be controlled by a firm discipline. The professional awareness of this problem has caused many students, anxious to elevate sociology to a "real" branch of learning, to dress their writings in an unnecessary cloak of portentousness. The general application of artificial idioms and pseudo-technical jargon, though an understandable excess, is no adequate substitute for scholarly discipline. Sociology, however, owes to Émile Durkheim its real vindication as a science. Although clearly rooted in a Comtean tradition and the belief that sociology was preeminently equipped for the new science of mankind, he was able to prevent himself from falling into the old traps. Instead of tying up sociology with political and religious aspirations, or, on the other hand, creating a pseudo-professional language, Durkheim by precisely delineating the limits and rules of the sociological game gave it its own academic dignity. Through terms such as "social fact," and such distinctions, for instance, as the categories of sacred and profane, normal and pathological, new tools were introduced for handling data more reliably than had been possible before.

That sociology should become a favorite field of research in the United States cannot be surprising, since it is a nation where public spirit has always been one of the most determining factors. Whereas the study of history does not seem very congenial to the average practical American, the immediately useful character of sociology naturally appeals to him, a fact reflected, for instance, in the many historical studies which actually deal with sociological questions. In this country utopianism had on the whole prevailed little. In contrast, in the nineteenth century the problems of man in an evolutionary universe were central, until Lester Ward with his *Dynamic Soci-*

ology began to puncture the inflated claims of laissez-faire, social Darwinism, and the prerogatives of the "fittest." Ward is important for bringing the study of sociology up to date, and for tuning it to the new exigencies of a changing world. Detailed investigation of social factors then supported the trend of socialization, that is, the government of a proletarian order.

At the same time a new brand of sociology developed, which, without heralding fanfares, in its modest way represents perhaps the most truly scientific attitude of all sociological endeavors. Designated "sociography" in some European countries, it has indulged in painstaking fieldwork, which at times may appear rather pedestrian, but which no one could possibly deny is a productive contribution to the understanding of common living. It has become particularly strong in North America where the interest in what may be called egalitarian life is natural. No science, of course, will ever be able to elevate such a community as "Middletown," or Muncie, Indiana, to a *polis* of historic forces, but the power of sociographic description lies precisely in the accuracy with which it can present the daily life of the average man, a service perfectly fitting the needs of a mass structure.

Whatever the type of sociology, a significant amount of weight is put on the effects of mechanization and the correlative problems of labor. The nineteenth and twentieth centuries are the age of the consciousness of labor. As early as 1803, Hegel began to bore into the unexplored regions of labor and the psychology of labor estrangement, an activity soon to culminate in his *Phenomenology of Mind,* which provided the classical foundation for further study in this field. Sociologists, of course, had other references besides Hegel, notably Adam Smith's theories on the division of labor, but almost without exception, even when totally ignorant of the primary source, they were concerned with the problem that Hegel originally formulated.

To the question of whether mechanization was to be regarded as the destroyer or the benefactor of humanity, they have, not surprisingly, given different answers. But the point here is that the machine, as the representative of aggregate work, was accepted as decisive. Even the poets knew it:

Technique is decisive for all,

proclaimed the communist Aragon without, however, elaborating his lyricism. Proudhon, in *System of Economic Contradictions*, saw the machine as the human liberator, because it is "the symbol of our command over nature." His Victorian contemporary Matthew Arnold, however, depicted the faith in the machine as "our besetting danger." In *Culture and Anarchy*, in which he analyzed the dangers on our way to perfection, such disparate entities as population, coal, railroads, wealth, and religious organizations were all designated as having become machines. Even "the worship of the mere freedom to do as one likes is worship of machines." And to the utopian socialists, Ernst Jünger gave the warning that technology would prove to be the usurper of human government.

Behind the dispute about the efficacy of machine power and technique as the "tactics of our whole life" (Spengler) is the always pressing fear of human surrender. When Heidegger, in *An Introduction to Metaphysics*, condemned the frenzy of technology which to him, in this respect, identified the United States with the Soviet Union, his attack was plainly on behalf of a metaphysical anchorage now lost, but was also obliquely directed against the surrender to the machine. Whether or not this surrender will ultimately be complete, as Ernst Jünger foresaw, depends in great measure on the question of who in the decisive stage is to be in command. Scientific knowledge is probably the greatest arsenal of future power. Even such an ardent believer in science as Bertrand Russell fears its potential harm if the political establishment were to seize it on behalf of the masses. In an essay on *Science and Human Life* he affirms that scientific knowledge is one of the great glories of man, but warns that the new powers which the scientists have produced must not be put into "the hands of reckless men," the politicians. For science "from the dawn of history, and probably longer, has been intimately associated with war."

The ego and the beast

Sociology, while concentrating on the social collective, is inclined to consider the process of work, as human communication, all-decisive for the formation of culture. That society in its ultimate and lasting manifestations is merely a product of labor is simply not true. Although organized socialism is by no means the only source of this fallacy, it is unfortunately gravely responsible for this widespread misconception. Besides making them "dull boys," as Herbert Read puts it, the emphasis on the omnipotence of labor has rendered the socialist thinkers often less helpful to the cause of culture than they would have liked to be, and than they surely deserve to be. On the other hand, it must be added that those authors who, like Huizinga, focus their interest exclusively on the play factor easily prove themselves to be colorful and fascinating, without demonstrating, however, the necessity of the dynamics of labor in culture.

Culture is the product of both work and play. Their dialectic mutuality determines that peculiar synthesis without which culture cannot exist. While sociology is chiefly occupied with the factor of labor, the psychology of the last centuries stressed the probing of play. Play, like labor, has become a topic of academic interest only in the modern epoch. It is even more striking that, while irrevocably intertwined as active cultural factors, they become separated when selected for scholarly scrutiny.

The notion of play received its due attention almost coevally with the first critical studies of the element of labor. It is remarkable that Schiller should be the originator of the modern study of play, since he was also the first to give a cultural description of alienation. The immediate link seems scarcely visible. But remembering that both problems occur in his *On the Aesthetic Education of Man,* we may expect them to lie within the same cultural frame of research. The concept of play, as Schiller saw it, has a synthetic quality which, when applied to the welfare of civilization, expresses itself as a harmony of beauty, justice, freedom, and dignity. In Schiller's analysis, the world of the eighteenth century had lost these noble attributes and therefore mankind must be re-educated to the understanding of harmony. Behind this lies the psychology of man's innate contradiction of sensate and intelligent needs, urges which in their combined actuality produce precisely that play which makes man a cultural animal. Man "plays" his life.

Classical society, in Schiller's eyes, was the product of this playfully equipoised man. Consequently, when the play-balance breaks down, that is, when either the sensate or the intellectual forces prevail, society is in trouble. To repeat, Schiller did not make the link, but it is not difficult to see, while reading through the famous fifteenth letter, that the separation of emotional content from restricting forms, inasmuch as it was applied by Schiller to the artistic as well as political aspects of his age, is an expression of alienation. One does not have to agree with Schiller's conclusions to grasp the importance of the play factor for the lasting shapes of a historical civilization. Without it, that human form of communication called labor will only result in a dull, plodding community, whose achievements, useful and successful as they possibly may be, will not be recorded for history.

The psychology of play, as we all know, has a generous variety of aspects, not all equally pertinent to a discussion of historical culture. For instance, Schiller's suggestion that, biologically speaking, play represents a surplus of energy (an idea worked out later by Herbert Spencer in his *Principles of Psychology*), might well go unmentioned if it had not been for the fact that this type of explanation set off a trend for other explanations. Against the theory of surplus vitality, the psychologist Lazarus placed that of the need for relaxation, which to him represented the serious and elevating quality making play so eminently suitable for education. Wilhelm Wundt, in his lectures on the human and animal psyche, stressed the importance of imitation for the preparation for life, especially the imitation of purposeful acts of the will. The greatest observer in this field is Karl Groos, who has probably done the most extensive practical research on play, and who concludes that the play of animals and children is primarily a preparatory exercise to develop muscles as well as ingenuity for adult needs.

Most of these theories are plausible enough; all, however, are highly speculative. Some of them, especially those of the youngest vintage, are perhaps more beautiful than persuasive. For instance, the idea, launched by G. Stanley Hall, that play is a training in order to get rid of rudimentary primordial functions no longer useful to man, is an interesting atavistic explanation, which leaves too much unanswered. Similarly Harvey Carr's purge theory is intriguing enough, inasmuch as it applies Aristotle's dramatic principle to the forms of play, an attempt probably not unjustified, but obviously too limiting to elucidate the rich scope of play. Perhaps one ought to adopt the ecumenical spirit of the psychologist Zondervan, who suggests that all these hypotheses may well have something valid to say about aspects of play, but that only when taken conjointly do they explain the fullness of its meaning.

In any case, this kind of psychology was immediately relevant to the new educational ambitions of an increasingly child-centered world. It was a psychology of specialists and pedagogues, and appeared to be primarily directed toward the needs of a professional group. Like all psychology, of course, it had a natural appeal to the outsider, but it was without any strong attraction for the masses. Besides those already mentioned, there were such outstanding figures as Pestalozzi, Herbart, Froebel, Claparède, and Dewey, who, though deliberately concerned with popular schooling, remained in the realm of selective interests.

This changed with the emergence of psychoanalysis, a branch of psychological learning which apparently has all the prerequisites for popular diffusion. Why is it, one must wonder, that studies so allegedly professional as those of Freud and Jung became part of the mass concern? The comment that modern psychiatry replaces the church with its own religious myths and methods is not at all adequate for a cultural evaluation. Nor is it any less inadequate to explain its mass appeal by presenting its sexual preoccupation as a new phallic cult characterizing a vague, barbaric religiosity. Whatever obvious truths there may be in these suggestions, they do not contribute to a very educated understanding of proletarian culture.

This is clearly not the place to give a comprehensive account of a variety of psychology so much of which has become common knowledge and about which so much has been written in both specialist and popular media. Without room or need to dwell on the particular details of psychoanalysis, the stress must fall on its significance in the historical totality. Both Freud and Jung, with brilliant insights and a powerful scholarly command, have opened new regions of understanding and sometimes of healing comfort which we ought to value deeply for the right reasons. They have also helped to create a world of confusion. While we are expecting enlightened reason to guide the egalitarian society, we are instead witnessing an embarrassing neo-fanaticism and a woolly neo-occultism, fostered by a self-proclaimed psychological science.

We should be grateful to Freud for providing us with new instruments, and a knowledge of unconscious motivations which he exposed by his discovery of the ego and the id, of the mechanisms of repression, fixation, projection, or by the analysis of dreams and daily experiences. But gratitude does not exclude the honorable practice of thoughtful questioning, provided, of course, that the questions raised are germane to Freud's own terms.

Freud's terms are patently the symbols, myths, and illusions produced by abnormal, neurotic causes and considered in relation to society or its culture.

Symbols are indeed of crucial importance for all human communications, and they play a special role when one undertakes a study of the ways in which modern man reveals himself. Symbol, as a vital means of communication, however, must be understood in its universal necessity. It is not a homemade invention whose mechanical structure can be disjointed at will. One must seriously doubt whether Freud ever understood the ruling principles on which symbols come into being and become cultural configurations. Right from the beginning, in his earliest writings, he set the stage for a fatal masquerade of meanings which in time, not necessarily through the author's fault alone, developed into a mass frolic. In *The Interpretation of Dreams* Freud handed us a catalogue of "symbols" and their meanings in such a blunt and apodictic manner that what ought to have been circumspect search became dogmatic formula. Symbol is the opposite of dogma. Symbol rises from the depth of inadequacy, typical for any communication, seeking to give form to a substance for which no words are available because the underlying experience cannot be fathomed. Without this inadequacy, poetry, for instance, could not exist.

Hence the structure of symbols is always the same. It invariably presents a graphic image in conjunction with an elusive content. This is confirmed by the equivalent of the word symbol in most Germanic languages (English being the most obvious exception). *Sinn-bild* in German, *Zinne-beeld* in Dutch, or *Sind-billede* in Danish indicate an abstract sense or meaning (the first part of the word) and a concrete picture (the second part). Precisely because this sense or meaning is fathomless, symbolic interpretations are consistently unhelpful. Symbols would not exist if it were otherwise. Such universal symbols as the serpent or the dragon, for instance, may mean anything from absolute evil to absolute good, and to eliminate their ambiguity is to exterminate their very vitality. Symbols then become dead abstractions, index cards for nonexistent experiences.

The objects which Freud offers us in his reference list of symbols are merely interchanging images which play a game with the underlying meaning. From what has been said about the fundamentals of symbol, the lances, tree trunks, knives, hats, boxes, closets, and other favorite objects of dreams cannot symbolically represent other concrete objects—the male and female genitals, in this case. On the contrary the genitals themselves may symbolize inaccessible realms of meaning. Similarly when Freud traces certain cases of neurosis back to the influence of the father, he reveals above all the typically nineteenth-century bourgeois, Victorian at that, for whom the *pater familias* was the central hero of society. In this naturalistic conception, all is reduced to the realistic father experience without allowance for the symbolic functions of the father himself, that is, as representing beneficial or detrimental forces which cannot be adequately known or sufficiently expressed.

The unsound basis of Freud's symbolic exegesis does not invalidate the many splendid discoveries he made in his detailed clinical labors, but it makes dubious their service outside the boundaries of strictly psychiatric therapy. The streamlining of symbols into columns of mathematical equations, aided further by an "index of symbols" in the sixteenth volume of the *Complete Works* as if it were the solution to a libidinous crossword puzzle, ruins the basic potential of man's understanding. To be sure, it makes profound and hitherto merely intellectual problems available to an eager dime-store mentality, but this plainly obliterates the whole purpose of enlightening the masses.

Furthermore, this faulty conception of symbolism precludes any true evaluation of cultural processes. Culture, of course, as consummate human communication, is nothing but symbols in their historical setting. Freud at least twice ventured into this wonderland, and the resulting works, unfortunately, are not the author's most felicitous products. One ought to allow anyone, not thus specifically trained, excursions into the far fields of history, but this tolerance should not be abused by flouting the fundemental methods by which history asserts its real characteristics. It is saddening to see that a mind, so precise and lucidly analytical when dealing with subtle clinical distinctions, should go astray so easily outside the empirical laboratory. Freud, when investigating the historical consequences of Western civilization, far from meeting the historical problems on their own terms treated them with the premises from another science, psychiatry. Such confusing practices are not uncommon. Medieval monks handled most of their scholarly disciplines with the axioms of theology—a procedure patently conducive to distortion. But in the setting of the age, they at least had an acceptable excuse. What is one to say about Freud?

The notion of culture is of exclusively historical quality. Since culture is never society itself, but the product of society in time, there is inevitably a historical distance between the two concepts. The evaluation of this distance and its impact on that product in the process of time is an historical operation. Freud, by confusing the autonomies of society and culture, committed a linguistic inaccuracy easily pardonable, but also an historical error of self-defeating proportions. In both *Civilization and Its Discontents* and the earlier *The Future of an Illusion,* he specifically assigned culture to the domain of human endeavor—accurately. Then, however, he proceeded to describe it as the sum total of achievements, which have two purposes: the mastering of the forces of nature for purposeful protection, and the arrangement of mutual relations. But, one wonders, is this definition not totally applicable to animals as well as humans?

Birds, beavers, and bees (with apologies for the alliteration) have, as everyone knows, ingenious methods by which to harness the forces and potentialities of nature, and, like other animals, highly developed systems of protective social relations. They clearly live in some form of viable society, yet produce no culture. Why not? For the very reason that animals have no consciousness of history. It is therefore no help, either, when Freud introduces religion, not indeed as an historical factor liable to change as any other manifestations—art, drama, music— but as a hand-picked psychological expression. We must assume, at least until expanded knowledge proves the contrary, that animals do not share in religious experience. But Freud, instead of presenting this factor as a cultural expression, preferred to view it as a legal code for the prevention of murder. Animals, however, have a strict code, too, by which they do not kill certain species (especially their own) and need no religion or any other form of culture to aid in its observance.

The only legitimate basis for religion in a discussion of the cultural future (Freud's position) is its symbolic mission, its function in the workings of historical myth. Freud chose to call this illusion. Illusion may well be the right word. But it must still be grasped within its total context. It cannot be arbitrarily plucked out of the cultural tissue as if it were a foreign growth. Religion is an essential part of the cultural energy of a healthy society, indeed, one of the most vital organs in the civil system. But for Freud, the nineteenth-century naturalist, religion was the old-fashioned bugbear which he regarded with a fanatical bias similar to that shown by some of his opponents in relation to materialism, psychoanalysis, or science in general.

A less obsessed mind ought to be able to maintain a calm view of religion and, far from isolating it from the totality of human consciousness, see it as part of the comprehensive body of modern experiences. All cultural expression, be it art, religion, or legal codes, is the historical account of human communication, and, as such, symbolically grounded. Illusion? Yes, in that sense in which all cultural expression is illusion. One misses the point, however, if one refuses to understand this as a normal phenomenon and, instead, makes a pathological case out of what traditionally is accepted as the supreme, that is, the classical, configuration of historical society.

Illusion etymologically derives from *illusio,* which suggests in-playing, that is, the play experienced within the boundaries of preset rules. This reminder serves us the better since it permits us to pick up the strands of our previous analysis of play. We may now tie these up with our more recent psychological findings to round out our scope. Illusion, culturally, is nothing save that profoundly human exhilaration which goes into the making and enjoying of motets and madrigals, of sonnets and satires, of academies and acropolises, of theatrical tragedies and travesties, of libations and liturgies, of triptychs and trilogies, of temples and taverns, of dissertations and disputations, of mosques and museums, of parthenons and pantheons.

On what else did the thrill of the classical theater rest, to take an example of the most comprehensive cultural experience, if not on that illusion which is the play of a splendid make-believe, and which carries the audience into a world transcending daily life? One should draw instructive conclusions from the fact that the modern drama, calling itself non-drama, deliberately sets out to destroy this classical illusion. Instead of staring in bewilderment at disconnected phenomena, we would show common sense if we considered the collected data from the various available sources and evaluated them jointly. It is with this deeply simple common sense (by no means the exclusive prerogative of great poets) that Rilke, in his *Notebooks of Malte Laurids Brigge,* saw that the end of religion signals the end of drama. If Freud and his followers find it appropriate to gloat over the end of religion in the cultural future, they are innocently celebrating the end of Western civilization as a whole.

Finally, in *The Future of an Illusion* Freud promoted his faith that science will elevate the coming society to new heights, for science is no illusion. He was unequivocally right. Science is no illusion in any respect, culturally or otherwise. It is, however, this deficiency in illusional play that may well make science painfully ineligible for future culture. We simply do not know. But it is not inappropriate at this point, I think, to call in the aid of a man who, unlike Freud, was a penetrating cultural historian, and also had something to say about the efficacy of science.

Flinders Petrie, a specialist in ancient societies, in *The Revolutions of Society* described eight successive phases of civilization, each showing the rise of scientific endeavor occurring just before the period of cultural decline and eventual extinction. He concluded that our own civilization, with its typical high priority of science coming as it does after the flowering of the arts and literature, is also bound for doom. I cannot see why this should necessarily follow. I accept Petrie's forecast of finality no more than I do Freud's speculation of progress. I simply think that we should take seriously the odds which a long history of scientific supremacies offers us, without committing ourselves to premature judgments.

There is certainly nothing unscientific about considering probability ratios, provided reasonable carefulness protects our every step. In view of its scientific claims it is distressing to have to face a tide of careless dogmatism which Freudian thinking has engendered. Freud himself, according to an account by Jung, defended his stern dogmatism as "the bulwark of reason" against the "black flood of occultism." Each of us is free to interpret according to his own standards the reasonableness of this statement.

Jung, of course, brought this up to illuminate what he considered his own undogmatic record. There can be no denying that he at least never suffered from a maniacal pursuit of sexual interpretations alone; he was tolerant enough to allow for multicausal explanations of psychic disorder. But whereas Freud's sharply focused mind sometimes narrowed to the edge of fanaticism, Jung's wandering vision tended to blur into solemn fogginess. Jung and Freud complemented each other. Freud's finest hours were those in which he dealt with the case histories of the developing individual. Jung, in contrast, was at his best when delving into the complexities of the collective unconscious. Whereas Freud at his most brilliant excelled in the clarification of psychological tangles, and at his worst became embarrassingly superficial, Jung was superb in the depiction of endless variables, which at his worst ended in a rather turbid presentation. Their positive contributions gain in value when taken together as complementary studies of modern man's problems. With due respect to other remarkable achievements, notably Adler's valuable power theory and Sartre's existentialist psychoanalysis, Freud and Jung together entirely cover the split-consciousness of individual and collective in their interlocking psycho-cultural relations.

Jung, at the end of his life, produced *The Undiscovered Self*, which in a sense was his crowning achievement. It tackles the most basic problem of modern man, his estranged self, and does it in a style uncommonly precise and free from earlier ambiguities. Because it is concerned with the cultural predicament of the West after the Second World War, the book is helpfully pertinent to our investigation. The author's conclusions as to the particular merits of contemporary achievements must go undiscussed. His social criticism, however, is significant inasmuch as it tries to give a remedy for the alienated state of modern society. He saw clearly the "rupture between faith and knowledge" as a symptom of the mental disorder of our time. To overcome this separation of man from his "instinctual foundation," Jung promoted an extreme individuation, reminiscent of some types of existentialism, with which Jung in general showed a curious affinity. Naturally, this is a psychological remedy; it requires "recognition of the shadow," the dark side of our ego which is not merely a negative substance, but which has potentialities for self-knowledge and for changing the individual's psychic make-up.

This rather gnostic self-studying method may well contain valuable psychological assets. It contributes little, however, to the solution of the crisis which Jung saw in the totality of society. For the split-consciousness, the separation of intellectual and instinctual forces within the individual merely reflects the estrangement which exists between man and contemporary society. It is therefore not very realistic to try to cure a social abnormality by promoting hyper-individuation, any more than is the effort of others to champion massification. The healthy society is clearly that in which individual and community are mutually protective, in cultural play if one wants, in cultural illusion if one insists, but free from self-consciousness. This ideal commonweal has of course never yet existed, but it is a goal worth approximating.

We owe to the behaviorists a real behavioral psychological science. Against the psychoanalytic schools, they can rightly claim to have strictly guarded scientific principles, and not to have raised the slightest suspicion of occultism or other speculative beliefs. Just as there is a painstakingly statistic sociology contented with verifiable data from daily life alone, so with the behaviorist school psychology has acquired a branch of modestly self-limiting scholarship. It confines itself, by rigorous obedience to experimental and empirical methods, to the study of human adjustments, in particular concentrating on the relations of stimulus and response.

By limiting his scope so drastically for the benefit of undisputably tangible results, the behaviorist must forego any interest in such magical realms as those of the unconscious and subconscious. Even the notion of consciousness is to be abandoned as a definite or useful concept. What is left then appears to be a study of external actions and reactions, which do not distinguish themselves as exclusively human. John B. Watson, one of the founders of this movement, confirmed "that you as a psychologist, if you are to remain scientific, must describe the behavior of men in no other terms than those you would use in describing the behavior of the ox you slaughter." At least this was candid. It was also perfectly in keeping with the contemporary tendency of identifying man entirely with the beast.

In this concentration on man as beast modern psychology simply drew the inevitable conclusions from the evolutionary premises of biology, a trend which linked behaviorism curiously with depth-psychology. Eventually this evolved into the cult of the bestial, so gloriously the terrain of twentieth-century society. The classical mind conceived man as a creature just falling short of the angelic ranks, but above the zoological. Somehow this fixed position between cherubim and chimpanzee gave him a feeling of security, but like all men of the middle classes he was fervently determined to move into the aristocracy: the divine was his destination. This attitude changed somewhat in the Renaissance when cultural expressions revealed man's more horizontal interests. The humanist vision was one of cool detachment, of an autonomous belief in human inquiry without help from either celestial or bestial powers. With the beginning of the era of the masses, man abandoned the serene confidence of the humanist and turned to subterranean energies. It was then that Benjamin Constant described the spirit of the times as moving from the divine through the human to the bestial. This development finds its climax (or nadir) with us when we cultivate not only "savage" literature and theater or "underground" movies, but also accept Tillich's theology of depth.

It is an inevitable conclusion to think that our disenchantment with man, which leads us to identify ourselves with the libidinous urges to such an inordinate extent, is a form of cultural isolation projecting itself in endless varieties of art, drama, and literature. The proletarian dispensation, however, has no choice but to fulfill its manifest historical role. It is the role of aliens operating under the thrust of a relentless logic which demonstrates that whatever must be done now, must be achieved by emergency, not with that freedom of play which predicates *home*. To us it is of no help to learn from D. H. Lawrence that "men are free when they are in a living homeland, not when they are straying and breaking away," that "men are free when they belong to a living, organic, believing community." We have no other preference than the lowest, the commonest denominator of the total sum of the masses. If that is to be found in the indulgence of the bestial, no self-righteous morality can deny our age its own supreme moment of truth.

O framed for calmer times and nobler hearts!
O studious poet, eloquent for truth!
Philosopher! Contemning wealth and death,
Yet docile, childlike, full of life and love!
Here, rather than on monumental stone,
This record of thy worth thy friend inscribes,
Thoughtful, with quiet tears upon his cheek.
                                    Samuel Taylor Coleridge

9

The Philosophical Way
of Living

The philosophy of totality

The patent usefulness of sociology and psychology puts
them in the proximity of other modern "academic" studies, such as economics, engineering or business administration—all fraternally incorporated as equal constituents
in the academy. However, the oldest discipline of all—
philosophy—has a hard time maintaining itself as a viable field of scholarship. Philosophy departments have

gradually come to be known as assemblies of rather odd people, bogged down in their ponderings, stuck in their endless ruminations about something the public at large is scarcely able to attach to the reality of life as they know it. Philosophy as it is taught and treasured on the university level clearly seems an inappropriate occupation for this pragmatic, egalitarian world. It may well be, since the greatest classical thinkers have almost invariably been concerned with metaphysical problems, that an age so overridingly focused on scientific gains as ours has little time or use for reflective thought.

However this may be, we must reiterate that our own interest cannot primarily lie with the potential merits and successes of contemporary philosophy, but rather with its place within the historical development. There *are*, after all, philosophers and philosophies, and university presses continue to publish an uninterrupted output of their works. Those whose profession or concern it is to consider them know that modern thinking, besides other things, is marked by a diffusion of aims and a confusion of contradicting voices. The eclecticism of today's society, which lies behind this multifarious thinking, is also evident in the forms of our architecture, theater arts, or educational theories. Among the diversity of philosophical schools there is positivism, vitalism, naturalism, realism, phenomenology, logical empiricism, linguistic analysis, Neo-Kantianism, Neo-Scholasticism, pragmatism, instrumentalism and many others, each school claiming, at least to the specialist, a number of distinct varieties. Sometimes one label is dangerously misleading. Existentialist philosophy, the most capacious of them all, can be subclassed by nationality and religious or metaphysical persuasion, each group explaining the existential quest in such terms as to make their kinship often a dubious proposition.

There are, of course, a number of sound ways by which to make order in this confusion; a specialized history of philosophy can easily deal with this situation through a detailed analysis of the diverse schools aimed at grouping the related ones together. Since this obviously lies outside our scope, we must seek a treatment which serves the preset goal of relating individual aspects to the cultural totality. If we therefore choose to divide the philosophy of the last two centuries into the broad movements of utilitarian, vitalist, and existential thought, there is nothing absolute or binding in this method. It is merely one way of providing tools for a particular objective. Before we do so, however, and discuss the era typified by a breaking up of classical cohesion, we must take a brief look at what immediately preceded it.

Most philosophers are in agreement that in a survey of present-day thought it is necessary to go back to one man, whose strange perplexing genius commands the whole field of philosophical inquiry. In a study of cultural history, Hegel stands at the source of virtually all the contributing currents; his panoramic mind scans the horizon of Western civilization for its distant meanings. His writings, taken as a whole, represent the last word on a completed (*fertig gewordene*) world, which according to him could now be understood in the logical terms of philosophy. Hegel was above all a philosopher, but one with an historic though self-chosen task. Assuming himself to be living in an end-phase, his encyclopedic interpretation was fundamentally and historically a farewell address to classical society.

A greater homage could hardly be paid to Hegel than to admit that for practically all modern thinking, however aggressively anti-Hegelian it sometimes may appear, his writings remain the primary reference source. He has this in common with Aristotle, who was to become *the* philosopher for later generations. It begins to look as if Hegel will play a similar role for future centuries if today's prevailing trend is to last. Like Aristotle, he summed up and classified the achievements of a society grown old, and, like Aristotle, he based his world views on the mechanics of a new, universally valid logic.

It is precisely in these underlying logical assumptions that one can also find the differences not only between

Aristotle and Hegel, but in general between the character of the Greek world and that of Western civilization. Aristotle's syllogistic inference moves from premise to premise, locking both in an imperturbable final conclusion. Its static quality stands out. Later the scholasticist was quick to adopt this triad logic and to infuse it with the truths of his own holy Christian Trinity. The triangle is Western culture's favorite compositional frame. Musical harmony throughout the classical period was centered in the triadic tonality by which the third determines the major or minor moods. The Medieval triptych may be merely accidental. More intrinsic and consistent is the structural triangle supporting the traditional European painting from the Renaissance on. Appearing base down, sometimes paired with an inverted counterpart, the triangle conveys the harmonic security of classical art.

Nowhere was it more solidly entrenched than in Western drama. The Greek plays were firmly constructed and books have been written to show their mathematical symmetry. The inner line of action rises and falls with the emotional awareness of the protagonist, thus presenting graphically an irregular triangle. Seneca, though hardly deserving the title of playwright, in his closet dramas preserved this basic pattern in five acts, thus passing it on to the later European theater. No matter how different the outward appearance of the plays by Calderon, Lope de Vega, Corneille, Racine, Lessing, or Schiller, the graph of their plot development was triangular without exception. It may be added, incidentally, that the traditional staging, the *mise en scène,* of Molière's plays by the Comédie Française arranged the actors in constantly changing triangles. Finally, Shakespeare's dramas may appear to the outsider as rather cavalier and casually rambling stage events. Yet all of his thirty-seven plays were structured on the same triangle, rising through the complications of the first acts to the central crisis of the third, turning in greater or smaller *péripéties,* sudden reverses, to speed down to the catastrophe (or denouement).

This digression serves to confirm how fundamental for Western man was the thinking in triad symmetries behind his historical expressions—a propensity conspicuously absent in the twentieth century. Hegel, when looking back at this fulfilled era to clarify its historical achievements in terms of logic, was inevitably led to a formula giving expression to this classical symmetry. Dialectic inferences thus move along triad patterns no less justifiably than do Aristotle's syllogisms. Whereas Aristotle's logic, however, reflects a static mind and eventually applies poignantly to a rather rigid medieval conception, dialectic as handled by Hegel elucidates that ever unfolding process of history through the category of becoming.

Thus in this view the Western mind is represented as ever striving, never arriving, indeed with that restless quality which Goethe too attributed to modern man. In fact, the obvious affinity between Hegel and Goethe has been demonstrated frequently, and the less apparent but equally close link between the *Phenomenology of Mind* and *Faust* again confirms that Hegel's peculiar way of reasoning was not some personal affectation but the true reflection of the type of Western man in his classical aspirations.

We must pause, I think, to add a few words of caution here. In the first place Oswald Spengler's idea of contrasting Faustic man with Apollonian man can be fascinating and perhaps even helpful. But such historical morphologies sometimes tend to suffer the fate of all typecasting and become dogmatized. Spengler's contention that the Western and Greco-Roman cultures are absolutely autonomous and alien to each other seems to run against the historical facts and against historical trends in general. We must further emphasize that the comparison between Aristotle and Hegel as representatives of the ancient and the Western world view is a rather glaring oversimplification which might be misleading if taken too categorically. A number of qualifying buts and ifs would have to be added if one were to treat them side by side on their strictly philosophical postulates, and their differences then might well outweigh their similarities. The comparison as it is offered here only holds if one seeks to illustrate the relative change from one cultural conception to another.

Lastly, a warning must be flashed to those who think that Hegel's dialectic logic is a one-man invention devised to force a tangle of abstract concepts into a more or less clever scheme. Dialectic originally and organically grew with modern man's developing consciousness. There is nothing artificial about it. It merely reflects the way man looks at himself and especially at himself in connection with his cultural past. Hegel was fundamentally the chief interpreter of modern man and his cultural awareness. He did not fabricate a method of dialectic. It was there when he arrived on the scene, and he used it with extraordinary relevance.

Dialectic with Socrates was an exchange of thoughts to arrive at truthful knowledge, with Plato it was to come to general ideas. With the Sophists, however, it turned into the art of proving pseudo-truths. This characteristic was still preserved in Kant's transcendental dialectic, which he called a "logic of semblance," whose faulty results derived from abstract reasoning without the benefit of experience. This logic of illusion was a "sophistic art" which tried to imitate "the thorough method required by logic, and uses its topic as a mask for its empty pretentions." It was only after Kant that a new concept of metaphysical struggle produced the type of zig-zag deduction based on theses and inescapable antitheses, henceforth understood as dialectic logic.

The University of Jena was the birthplace of modern dialectics. There, about 1795, the trio of Fichte, Schelling, and Schiller—also responsible for the first probings into the problem of human estrangement—though not close friends, became friendly enough to exchange their thoughts. The Kantian philosophy had left an unsolved dichotomy between the thing-world, as such, and the subjective mind, and somehow seemed to invite a bridging agency. Fichte, Schelling, and Schiller, although from a Kantian starting-point, moved in new directions which were to result in Hegel's philosophy. Fichte, by opposing a self-posited "I" with a "non-I" posited by the "I," discovered a mutual exchange (*Wechselwirkung*) which was of a perfect dialectic quality. Schelling, in his early work *About the Self as Principle of Philosophy* (1795), set up a scheme of contradicting theses which resolved into a synthesis. Thus, for instance, Being posited its antithetic Non-Being, which contradiction produced the determination Possibility. Turning to Schiller, throughout his writings, poetry or prose, there was an almost innate need to seek out antinomies which he mediated by a synthetic conciliation. In the twentieth letter of the *Aesthetic Education* he gave what was probably the first classical description of dialectic when he declared the notion of the esthetic to be a "medium mood" resulting from the contradiction of sensate and intelligent forces, which negate and suspend each other, thereby using the term *aufheben* years before Hegel was to make it famous.

Hegel was familiar with these historic preparations. He himself was soon to start his career at Jena. He knew and admired the *Aesthetic Education* and kept in close contact with his former schoolmate Schelling. He adopted the dialectic way of reasoning, but for his own purposes, that is, as an agency for explaining the philosophy of man as essentially an historical process. Far from being a mechanical trick to arrange problems in a threefold abstraction, as it is so often erroneously presented, Hegel's philosophy aims at seeing the organic evolution of man's mind as it moves, step by step, generated by an inherent capacity for struggle. Moreover its characteristic synthesizing nature is eminently fitted to comprehend cultural phenomena in a totality. When we say that Hegel's work represents a philosophy of totality, the statement implies that sense of completeness fed by *organic necessity*, not by a mechanical aggregate of quantity.

The *Encyclopedia of the Philosophical Sciences*, probably not one of Hegel's greatest works, is nevertheless a convenient guidebook to his comprehensive purpose. In the fifteenth paragraph, one can find a perfect confirmation of the relation between dialectic logic and the organic development which it expresses. The dialectic quality, Hegel wrote, "thus constitutes the moving soul of evolution, and it is that principle alone by which immanent cohesion and necessity enter into the contents of knowledge." This goes to show that hasty critics should not persist in labeling Hegel's philosophy an exercise in ingenious but empty abstractions (an unfortunate critical practice started by both Kierkegaard and Marx). If one takes Hegel's work on his own terms, that is, without unwarranted emotional projections, it appears as a revelation of the development of man's conscious life no less astonishing than Darwin's study of the development of man's biological life.

The idea of totality, as central to Hegel's view as to that of Goethe represents a mind firmly aware of being at a turning point in the evolution of Western society. To illustrate this, one might say that Hegel and Goethe, as the last great men of the classical era, halted and surveyed the entire output of the Christian age in its organic cohesion, before the decisive dissolution and fragmentation set in. Philosophy after Hegel was never to be the same again. In its own manner it would contribute to an atomistic social order, which replaced cohesion by the opportunities of multitudes. For proper understanding, however, it must be stressed that the breaking up into philosophical schools did not occur suddenly, but like so many trends that represent historical change, developed slowly and tentatively. The early intimations occurred long before Hegel. The actual weight of the modern trends of philosophy upon society as a whole, however, was felt only when there was Hegel's completed *oeuvre* to measure them against.

This in itself should not reflect negatively on contemporary brands of philosophic thinking. We ought to be able to judge them on their own merits, and at least at times consider them free from their historical relevance.

Karl Löwith, who in *From Hegel to Nietzsche* has given one of the very best accounts of the intellectual background of the nineteenth century, seems, however, a little too rash in suggesting that these new schools represent "products of decomposition." Pointing to Marx's dissertation on Epicurus, he puts the latter in the same historical situation as the former in that both arrived on the scene after a definite end (meaning Aristotle and Hegel) and yet desirous to begin something new. This parallel might easily imply that the philosophies of Epicurus and Marx were similar, which is not so. Moreover, by naming Epicureanism and other late Greek schools of thinking products of decay, their positive contributions inevitably get lost in a broad generalization.

This applies with equal force to the philosophical development after Hegel. To be sure, the new ways of thinking undeniably show elements which remind us of the Sophists, Epicureans, Stoics, and Sceptics, but it would be rash indeed to infer that they therefore must end in the same infecund torpor which marks Roman thinking. It may well happen again. It is premature, however, to speculate about decline at a time when there is enough obvious vitality in society to keep our confidence intact.

The philosophy of practice

Admittedly, lumping together a number of strongly autonomous philosophies, such as utilitarianism, positivism, materialism, pragmatism, and analytical philosophy, is not one of the most profoundly philosophical ways of behavior. It would be out of the question for any responsible specialized treatment. In an historical context, however, individual aspects of culture look different. One particular element of contemporary thinking appears to be a stress on practical viability, an attitude especially favored, though not solely, by Anglo-American philosophers.

Quite clearly, philosophy at all times is supposed to

serve the community in general by its discoveries. In this sense, Socrates, Plato, and Aristotle were as practically minded as their adversaries, the Sophists. The difference lies chiefly in the immediacy of conveyance. Whereas classical thinking, that is, that belonging to a society at the height of its normalcy, aims at serving through the deepest penetration into undiscovered knowledge, post-classical interest, at least primarily, is concerned with the widest diffusion of already existing knowledge to the public. Post-classical philosophical education is therefore practical because it seeks out not the ultimate service to the mind but the immediately useful for society.

Connected with this is the age-old question about the priority of universal or individual reality. This whole debate again emerged first with Greek philosophy and was, inescapably, renewed during the Middle Ages when realists and nominalists split the scholastic unity. Although nominalism was known by that name as early as the eleventh century, it was with William of Occam three centuries later that it became a force in Western history. Nominalism in its simplest formula asserts that man's knowledge is merely a quantity of mental signs. Universal concepts are not real but merely conventions, and our intelligence can only grasp individual objects. This primacy of the specific coincided with the first interest in scientific knowledge, and prepared that renewal in the thinking of the Western mind with which Francis Bacon was so prominently connected.

The common sense behind this reasoning was an attribute characteristic of most English and Scottish philosophers. Occam and Bacon stood at the beginning of a long line of scientific skepticism which ultimately extended to the American forms of empiricism. To illustrate how much this practical empiricism is ingrained in the English mentality one could do no better than to read Macaulay's instructive essay "Lord Bacon," which appeared in the *Edinburgh Review* of July 1837. Especially helpful is the section in which Macaulay compared Bacon with Plato, using the occasion to contrast idealism with scientific reasoning. Commenting on such branches of know-ledge as arithmetic, mathematics, astronomy, and medicine, Macaulay thought that Bacon was always on the right side. For Bacon valued them because of their uses "with reference to that visible and tangible world which Plato so much despised." Whereas Plato looked down on medical skills which prolong life no longer fitted to serve society with mind, Bacon welcomed any practical healing. "To make men perfect was no part of Bacon's plan. His humble aim was to make imperfect men comfortable."

The comparison is revealing inasmuch as it demonstrates how easily even such a brilliant mind as Macaulay's could distort and misinterpret Plato's metaphysical world through the aegis of practicality. The point is that, far from being unfair, he was simply incapable of evaluating life other than in terms of its short-range comfort. The essay was written six years after Hegel's death, at a time when utilitarianism and positivism, long in the making, now began to be effective as they fitted into a society ready for them. The next year John Stuart Mill published his study on Bentham in the *London and Westminster Review*, a critique remarkable not only for its thorough analysis of the older man, but also indirectly influential in the development of the utilitarian movement as a whole.

The concept of utility as the central force for social and political well-being was no novelty as Mill correctly remarked. Bentham's idea of a liberal self-interest promoting the least pain and the most pleasure can be traced back as far as Epicurean doctrine. But Bentham, according to Mill, was not important as a philosopher, but rather as a reformer who introduced a new method, a method of detail. It treats wholes "by separating them into their parts, abstractions by resolving them into things, . . . classes and generalities by distinguishing them into the individuals of which they are made up, and breaking any question into pieces before attempting to solve it." It was patently rooted in the empiricist tradition of Bacon and Locke. It also built further on the criticism of Hume, "the profoundest negative thinker on record," in Mill's words.

With Bentham one can see emerge that quality of modern philosophy which, preferring method above message, works primarily toward precision and clarification. Throughout his essay, Mill pointed to Bentham's peculiar province, the field of practical abuses. "His was an essentially practical mind. It was by practical abuses that his mind was first turned to speculation,"—by the abuses of the English law at that time. It was the precision of language and of conceptional streamlining which made Bentham's work practical. Mill himself continued Bentham's trail, but, a subtler thinker, he made a far more persuasive case for the principle of utility. At the end of his life, in his work *Utilitarianism*, Mill defended this philosophy against those who saw in it a cheap indulgence in pleasure.

Mill was at pains to link the fortunes (or misfortunes) of the ancient Epicureans with his own, and sometimes he let them speak for his own case. Indisputably, Epicurean ethics was as much based on the Greatest Happiness principle as its nineteenth-century counterpart, and the key notion of pleasure as absence of pain was as mistakenly used against the earlier philosophers as the later ones. The problem is only that both philosophies came to the fore in an age inevitably bound to interpret the idea of pleasure as cheap comfort and sensual enjoyment. This no doubt did injustice to the more elevated intentions of their founders, but it was in this manner that at least utilitarianism fulfilled a popular task in an egalitarian society. It was only in this manner that the masses understood the utility of pleasure.

The link represented by J. S. Mill to the American pragmatic schools was emphasized by William James who called Mill "our leader were he alive today." Utilitarian philosophy as a whole prepared the way for what was clearly the most American type of thinking. Pragmatism no more than utilitarianism brought a new volume of content; it merely extended the English philosophy of methodical reforms. Modifying a recent slogan, one could say of pragmatism that "the method is the message." John Dewey, in his efforts to relate scientific data with common-sense data and with ordinary experience, stressed the "supremacy of method" in *The Quest for Certainty*. He rejected objects as finalities and turned rather to data as starting points for investigation. He advocated a change from "knowing as an esthetic enjoyment of the properties of nature" to knowing as a means of control. The modern philosophical science which he represented was interested in the "mechanism of occurrences," in the search for "efficient causes instead of for final causes," and he hoped that this method might go beyond the physical sciences to be applied to social practice as well. Thus he believed it would be possible to overcome what he saw as "the historic separation of knowledge and action, of theory and practice." It was this "centrality of method" which Sidney Hook in an instrumentalist version of pragmatic thinking wanted to make relevant to American education. The close connection in general of pragmatism and new educational programs and procedures can hardly be surprising for a way of thinking so much determined by practical efficiency. Thus Sidney Hook in his *Education for Modern Man* can write that "in the educational system of a democracy, the authority of persons and institutions is the determination of truth." This bold departure from classical thinking as well as education is the historical conclusion of Bentham's critical method of attacking "practical abuses" as part of his liberalism. In this sense Sidney Hook concludes that "method is central in a liberal philosophy as in science because it undercuts the absolutisms that would arrest the flow of new knowledge and new insights. Method should be central in educational activity because it not only evaluates the funded tradition of the past but enhances the capacity to enrich it. This is the meaning of liberalism in education."

Maybe so. But one should not, for all the methodical gains, lose sight of the real proportions of that historical change which is our specific topic of investigation. The shift away from message to method indicates a form of cultural isolation which estranges our objectives irrevocably from the classical foundation on which we still live and work and educate. This may well be imperative for our modern collectivist society, and the most beneficial thing we can do for it. It should not deter us, however, from seeing the cultural contradiction in this attitude, that while ostensibly "enriching" the tradition of Western civilization, we turn against its basic contents and ideals.

Pragmatism and instrumentalism, following the open-minded pursuit of the utility principle, caters to a world of ordinary problems. It becomes, almost inevitably, a daily-life philosophy which the common man can understand and from which he can profit. It is not a "cheap" way of thinking, as some continental critics have labeled it, at least not necessarily so. It is part of a public service rather than a profound penetration into those remote strata of awareness achieved only by the greatest minds. This service, rendered in a proletarian order, makes these philosophies welcomingly opportune, and indicative of the new social needs which twentieth-century civilization has expressed in all its other manifestations.

Although the accent on the Anglo-American preponderance in matters of practical philosophy is justified, it should not misleadingly draw the attention away from the Continental participation in this field. Positivism is in its practical extension scarcely distinguishable from the objectives of English and American contemporary thinking. And again one can go backwards through the history of philosophy in order to show how positivist premises have always been at work. Protagoras, the early Sophist of the fifth century B.C., abandoned theological thinking as useless and made man the measure and center of his inquiry. Closer to home, positivism was officially founded by Auguste Comte, who in turn had taken his lessons from the French Enlightenment, English Empiricism, and Saint-Simon's doctrines. Positivism excluded all transcendental speculation, and aimed at the posited, the given objects. It was also positive in that it wanted to be useful and of direct service to the amelioration of society.

Comte's thought rested on two basic principles. It presented a new classification of sciences, arranged according to a hierarchical system. In this "natural" order, mathematics was fundamental. Then followed astronomy, physics, chemistry, biology and finally, as the greatest of all, sociology. The second *leitmotif* of Comte's writings referred to the parallel development of man and mankind which, going through the stages of religion and metaphysics, finally ends up in the enlightened phase of science. While in the first the priests and soldiers rule, and in the second the philosophers and jurists, in the last phase the scientists and industrialists are sovereign. It is here also that theory and practice unite.

As a practical philosophy, positivism becomes almost equated with sociology, a field investigated elsewhere. In the cultural development of contemporary society it has contributed little to philosophy that utilitarian and pragmatic varieties have not done with greater efficiency, and certainly without falling into that utopianism which obviates the scientific footing of the early positivists. As long as positive thinking is merely sociology, its advantages are definite and real, but beyond that it reveals little depth, and Comte's work thus holds little potential for the future.

The inherent problem of positivist thinking is further illustrated by the case of Karl Marx. Not a profound philosopher in the classical sense, he was at his best when analyzing the sociological relationships of his age. He left the Hegelian camp which he understood only very inadequately, and in Paris adopted the tenets of French positivism as set forth by Comte's *Cours de philosophie positive,* a work published mostly after Hegel's death, from 1830–1842. This type of philosophy appealed to Marx for its obvious scientific empiricism and its utopian claims as well. Marx was in no sense an original thinker; his originality rather lay in the manner in which he applied to political activity the idea of "practical" philosophy of his English and French predecessors. The utilitarians were also politically directed. So were Condorcet and Saint-Simon, both prior to Comte, clearly operating in the early positivist climate. Marx, however, regarded philosophy as activism, in the revolutionary sense, and this was to become the basis of his future fame.

This, belonging as it does to the political province, can be left undiscussed here. But we must pause to accentuate once more the significance of this idea of praxis at this crucial point in history. For Hegel, the acts of history had been fulfilled, and it was now up to the philosopher to depict "gray on gray" what had happened. In other words, theory follows action. It is a little surprising that Marx (the empiricist!) rejected this logically empirical view and contrasted it with his own, namely, that since Western man had so far developed a conceptional philosophy, it was now time he started to activate or rather to actualize his philosophy. In other words, for Marx praxis followed theory. Every one is free to pick his own side in this conflict; we cannot here set ourselves up as judge of a philosophical dispute. Historically speaking, however, there can be no doubt that Hegel has the simple facts on his side. History, as a reflection of developing life, renders account of the simple human acts of the past, until late in the growth and maturation of a society its conscious philosophy begins to play a role. In all historical societies philosophical analysis arises only when the activities are congealed into cultural types and symbols, just as in man's mature life reflection enters when his youthful acts have borne their fruits. The unsound premise of Marx's idea of praxis has entailed a number of wild predictions, most of which have proven to be false in the twentieth century.

A philosophy of practice then, after Hegel, can only be fruitful if it adjusts itself to new demands of a proletarian dispensation. This type of practicality is not going to change man or the world, and is not destined to create ideal states of justice but, as pragmatism has shown, can at best serve with modest aims by adapting itself to the limitations of modern man. This praxis reveals its isolation from the classical scope of action. To be sure, it is an estranged activity coming after dusk, when the owl of Minerva, as Hegel put it, begins its flight, and with all the frustrations of working in the dark. But it is activity all the same, and in its restricted way no less honorable than the more spectacular *res gestae* of the classical world.

In this setting the schools of analytical philosophy may seem a little out of place. For the average layman it is probably difficult to discover the practical uses of the highly technical operations of analytic logic. He may well find this a strictly pedantic endeavor, of only academic significance. It ought to be underlined, however, that all analytic thinkers have in common a preoccupation with clarifying meanings and with precision of formulation, which is of course in line with the streamlined world order where lucidity in general is a requisite for massive communication, educational or otherwise. After all, it was Jeremy Bentham's practical mind that set the tone with its own pursuit of clarification. There was the first tie between analysis and utility.

The second connection lies in the overwhelming stress on method which, as we have noted, is also central to pragmatic thinking. Rudolf Carnap, one of the leading logical empiricists, explained that the chief purpose of his book *Meaning and Necessity* "is to develop a method for the analysis of meaning in language." The linguistic analyst Ludwig Wittgenstein was concerned with the social activity of ordinary language; his contention was that we can only have a grasp of the meaning of language by focusing on its practical use, an attitude again close to the relativity of the pragmatists. Thirdly, analysts such as Carnap, also called logical positivists, originated in the Vienna circle which consisted mainly of ex-scientists. They were less enamored of Auguste Comte's writings than of that positivism which, starting with Hume, denies the validity of any but the most scientifically verifiable phenomena.

For the conveyance of their purposes the analysts employ logical systems, which permit them to pinpoint meanings accurately. Ever since Leibniz, ways have been sought to replace the ambiguities of words by signs of mathematical exactness. The history of symbolic logic, which culminated in the *Principia Mathematica* of Bertrand Russell and Alfred North Whitehead, is one of increasingly refined statements, yet, at the same time, of a proportionately declining awareness of true symbol. Through the frantic search for elucidative processes, the field of problems is inevitably whittled down to those which admit only of scientific proof. Symbol, however, by its very nature allows no pinpointing, for, being metaphysically rooted, it reveals those mythical situations of man which the modern logicians so anxiously avoid.

Analytic logic thus estranges itself deliberately from modern man's fundamental questions, with the excuse that these questions have no scientific basis. Aristotle's logic somehow represents the unity of the thinking and culture of the ancient Greek society. Hegel's logic is culturally applicable to the entire world of Western man; it is historically relevant to the total conscious image of modern thinking and explains the meaning of the most diverse forms of development from biological evolution to American techniques of strike settlement or Wagner's use of harmonic modulations. Analytic logic, mathematic or linguistic, in contrast is a teachers' technique with inbred tendencies, refined and urbane, but isolated from the main currents of human questioning.

The philosophy of life

In complete contrast, the philosophies of life go to the other extreme by relating their problems to the most immediate experience of cosmic life. The concept of life is so vague and unhelpful that no amount of systematic clarification could make it a viable field for logic. This, however, did not worry the vitalist thinker in the least, for he was determinedly set against logical and systematic reasoning. In fact, the whole movement began as a reaction against the age of reason and in defense of the vitality of the mind which it saw threatened by sterile and cerebral abstractions.

There are various roots of vitalism. One can trace them in the field of literature and point to the irrationalism of the *Sturm und Drang,* to the cult of the genius, to later Romanticism and its preoccupation with individualistic experiences. More scientifically one can find them in biological theories from Louis Dumas (1765-1813) to the twentieth-century Hans Driesch—theories which assume a mysterious force, the *vis vitalis,* operating behind the chemical and physical actions in living matter. Driesch, in his *Philosophy of the Organic,* revived Aristotle's idea of innate purposes, the *entelecheia,* a natural factor which makes life autonomous and self-continuing. Even though modern science has come more and more to reject biological vitalism because previous "mysteries" have eventually been explained physically, this does not detract from the historical importance of the fact that during the last two centuries even highly accredited scientists looked for a common factor to account for the fullness and totality of life.

The philosophers of life themselves, as can be expected, were easily disposed to veer away from strict philosophy into the more imaginative fields of literature, art, or history. Unlike the pragmatists, they were not much interested in daily life, but rather in the creativity and spontaneity of life permeating man's total awareness. It is not surprising that behind most philosophical vitalists there loomed the imposing figure of Goethe, a poet without much interest or training in formal thinking. But his was probably the most universal of the great modern minds, and in virtually all his writings he was concerned with man in the total arrangement of the macrocosm.

Goethe, in this respect, learned much from Herder. Herder's role at the height of the eighteenth-century Enlightenment was a fascinating one. His idea of the unity of nature and history in the great organic process moving man toward an ideal Humanity was one of the most noble and most enlightened thoughts of the century. But Herder's humanistic enlightenment went against the prevailing rationality of the age. Jointly with authors such as Hamann, Jacobi, and Hemsterhuis, he stood at the beginning of a new, and what was to become a Romantic, era.

Clearly neither Herder nor Goethe belonged to the Romantic movement proper. But both, against the mechanistic trends of an age which produced such works as La Mettrie's *Man a Machine,* promoted the idea of an organic, spontaneous energy which gives both nature and history their unity. To his friend Eckermann, in February 1829, Goethe made a sharp distinction between the organic—living, becoming, and changing—which is filled with the divine and is the object of reason, and, on the other hand, the dead, mechanical, ossified realm which is merely for the service of our understanding. Throughout Goethe's work, whether it concerns Faust's searching journey, Wilhelm Meister's educational trials, or the morphology of plants, there is a continual awareness of the totality of life experience. In this Goethe is the obvious literary counterpart of Hegel, and with Hegel he stands at the beginning of an epoch in which the question of the whole, total man, and the whole integral reality of his civilization becomes of central significance.

Why is it, we must ask, that the question of life is raised at all? Goethe, being a poet, may be allowed to relish the vagueness of generalities, but why should professional philosophers, trained in close thinking and working with subtle distinctions, want to choose as their field of operation such a nebulous, undefinable, and adventurous realm as that of life? Why should scholars prepared for the exercises of reason decide to embark on the emotionality and unreason that goes with the concept of life? There are probably many personal answers, each depending on the individual thinker, requiring psychological probing to reveal them. Looking at the historical context, however, one could suggest that the preoccupation with life is not unrelated to the developing mechanization and the industrial outlook of the modern world. The philosophies of life emerged when rationalization became a predominant factor in society. It culminated in Nietzsche's outcries, at a time when the marvels of the machine had established their irrevocable grip on the contemporary mind.

Vitalist thinking also became more emphatic, sometimes even strident, with the parallel development of decline-and-fall theories. With Nietzsche, cultural pessimism and optimism were emotionally mixed up. Zarathustra's message was a gospel of paradox. He loved him "who wants to create beyond his reach and thus destroy himself." Man had to be overcome in order to create a world of supermen. This is the pagan counterpart of Pastor Russell's millennium. Zarathustra himself was that "thunderbolt" destroying the current values of civilization. But one should not deduce from this that all philosophies of life are necessarily irrational. They develop historically as defense-posts against the sway of abstraction and the hyperlogic of intellectual systems, of mechanical procedures and fragmentation of life. As such, they represent in the first place a trend of alarm with all the emotional equipment of protest.

Schopenhauer was essentially such a protester. He was one of many figures to come, who tried to undermine with explosive charges the bulwark that Hegel had bequeathed. Exploiting Kantian subjectivism, in the course of the nineteenth century his work was to impress many, not so much by penetrating originality as by a clear one-sided presentation. "The world is my conception." There is nothing, according to Schopenhauer, that can be known, except the image that one's conception makes of the phenomena: object and subject become equated. There is no other approach to the knowledge of the world save through the subject. The inner core of the subject, however, is the will, "the blind irresistible force" of all organic nature. The world of appearance is the object and mirror of this will. In the fourth book of *The World as Will and as Conception*, the will is said to be

willing mere life and for that reason it is "only a pleo-
nasm when we instead of the will use the expression the
will to life."

This will to life was, in the nineteenth century, a vehicle carrying the burden of both optimism and pessimism.
For the blind pursuit of the will, so vehemently affirming
man's inner potential, always falls short of satisfaction.
Hence Schopenhauer's almost Buddhist, quietist conclusion that mortification of the will alone can create happiness was an attitude conspicuously directed against
life. The paradox became even stronger when Nietzsche
replaced the will to life with the will to power, thus formulating a message that destroys as it creates. "Only as
creators are we able to destroy!" said Nietzsche in *The
Joyful Wisdom*. The message of ultimate power is indeed
an affirmation of life in its totality, for which, however, it
pays the price of the disruption and annihilation of the
system of civilized values.

The will as blind instinctive generator reveals another
pessimistic aspect in the system of Eduard von Hartmann. Deliberately combining the rationality of Hegel
with Schopenhauer's volition theories, Hartmann posited
a struggle of the intellect with the will. While to Schopenhauer this presented a situation of pain and misery
to the individual, Hartmann's *Philosophy of the Unconscious* (1869) also stressed the cultural consequences.
The unconscious was the source and unity of all life and
created consciousness which operated as reason. In the
increasingly developing civilization, rationality emancipated itself more and more from the unconscious will. In
Hartmann's words, "consciousness is the possibility of the
liberation of the intellect from the will." Consequently,
the greater this liberation as rational civilized living, the
greater is man's unhappiness through the frustrated will.
Modern psychoanalysis, as everyone knows, has been
playing variations on this theme, sometimes rather wildly
and irresponsibly, but clearly extending the line of cultural pessimism which Schopenhauer and Hartmann had
first projected.

The character of the philosophies of life is thus often ambiguous. It asserts life and not infrequently presents itself with a buoyant exhilarating ring which testifies to a creative task. Yet it is curiously self-conscious, as a minority mentality is bound to be, always on the defensive and thus constantly stressing what it most fears, a mechanization unto death. It is for this reason that virtually all vitalist thinkers (with the exception perhaps of Whitehead, whose philosophy is rather elusive in this respect) presented their ideas in a dualistic framework.

For Goethe, this was expressed in the contrast of the wholesome and the diseased, in the symbol and the formula, for Nietzsche in Dionysus and Christ, for Schopenhauer in will and world, for Hartmann in the unconscious and the conscious, for Ludwig Klages in soul and mind, or in experience and consciousness, for Henri Bergson in intuition and understanding, for Wilhelm Dilthey in history and nature, motif and causality, for Georg Simmel in life and form, for Melchior Palágyi in expression and impression, for Ortega y Gasset in vitality and reason, culture and barbarism. Oswald Spengler, the most uncompromising dualist of all, summed up the vitalist situation in a series of antinomies such as organic and mechanic, experience and thought, becoming and essence, image and concept, destiny and causality, direction and extension, time and space, configuration and law, simile and notion, sign and number, physiognomy and system, tension and measure, cosmos and microcosmos, periodicity and polarity, totem and tabu, race and language, desire and anxiety. In all this there lies in the background the signal awareness of a vitalism obsessed with life in the face of death.

The realization of life individually, the life-experience, is especially central in German vitalism and expressed by the word *erlebnis*. *Erlebnis* is the full participation of the individual in cosmic life. Man lives life in its totality, and as Georg Simmel, in his book on Rembrandt, remarked, "each moment of our life is life in its entirety." Man's realization of his insignificant existence is nevertheless identified with a transcendent life because, as Simmel pointed out in another work, life in its essential process is a "more-life" a "more-than-life." *Erlebnis* to Spengler was a new way to knowledge. Whereas for classical thinking only the outer reality was a possible form of knowledge, for him knowledge reached beyond the causal laws of nature. Thus it grasps for the becoming, and life-experience is what has happened, what is history, (*ist Geschehenes ist Geschichte*).

Epistemology, that is, the study of the limits and scope of knowledge, heretofore practiced in only rational terms, now became a matter of intuitive groping. A movement owing so much impetus to Goethe could hardly be expected to do otherwise. Nor is it surprising that its most successful elucidations have been in the fields of the arts rather than in more formal and metaphysical directions. Schopenhauer's gloomy view of man's potential happiness on earth beamed a flicker of hope only when touching on the dimensions of art. The failures of human will could only be overcome through the imagination of genius which elevates human experience to the realm of the perfect absolute Idea. Thus music becomes "metaphysical consolation."

Nietzsche, trying to live up to Schopenhauer's precepts at least in this respect, liked to present himself above all as an artist. His prose was frequently interspersed with poems—bad poems, to be sure, without the true vibration of poetry, but nevertheless testifying to a need for intuitive communication. "We born to clamber . . . somnambulists in the light of day! We artists!" he exclaims in *The Joyful Wisdom.* "We moon-sick and god-sick. Indefatigable travelers. . . ." Thus, the flight of the imagination for the first time became a guided tour through the complexity of man's mind. Georg Simmel used the work of Rembrandt to clarify his thoughts on the preeminence of life over form as it reveals itself in the contrast of Dutch and Italian painting.

Among the philosophers of life, no one has more profoundly understood the relationship between literature and the sublimation of life-experience than has Dilthey. Whereas Bergson merely illustrated man's freedom in the potential identity of acts and personality with the unity of the artist and his work, Dilthey saw in the poet the greatest realizer of the fullness of life, for "the work of the poet rests at all times on the energy of life-experience." The poet distinguishes himself by "the energetic animation of images," which gives us an esthetic satisfaction of life.

Erlebnis, this immediate electrifying experience in the identity of cosmic and personal life, to most of the vitalist thinkers was realized as a current, a galvanizing stream. This *Lebens-strom* (Klages) designated by Whitehead as process, by Bergson as *durée,* and by Spengler as periodicity, makes us realize our lives as flux, indeed as history. Whereas our intellect, according to Melchior Palágyi in his *Theory of Perception,* is static and "punctual," our perception is a constantly moving occurrence. In other words, in a philosophical discourse on the process of life, as in immediate human experience, the concept of time will usually be central. For the philosopher of life, man's experience as historical becoming cannot be *understood* in the moments of logical fixation, as in Hegel's system, but can only be *lived.* Time then is creative time, Bergson's *durée,* which is "growth, uninterrupted activity of creation and maturation." It is organic and self-preserving, in Whitehead's words, through "enduring patterns."

The idea of time, not as scientific measurement, but as lived time, is participation in what Klages in *The Mind as Adversary of the Soul* termed an uninterrupted "experience-stream." This feeling of time-ness reflects the restlessness of modern man, expressed in other fields. The Faustian idea, pursued in detail by Oswald Spengler in *The Decline of the West,* accounts for modern man's awareness of being an alien vagrant in search for a homecoming which seems permanently elusive. In this view, the Greek world, represented by the work of its greatest thinkers, was static and Apollonian serenity. The philosphers of life therefore prefer to draw support from the

theory of flux expounded by Heraclitus, if they are at all
in need of so ancient a source. The modern experience to
them is a continually evolving happening.

The modern archetype of the Wanderer in literature
usually reveals a more or less educational experience of
how to live as "a stranger in a strange land," and signifies
a nostalgic position rather than a militant one. For vitalist philosophy, however, movement and the stream of
lived experience represent struggle. This struggle can be
self-preserving as Bergson's *élan vital,* but frequently, especially in German thought, it is apparent as fatal destiny. To Klages, the metaphysical battle was "the continuing contest of the intellect against life, with the logical impending end of the destruction of the latter." More
historically worked out, this became for Spengler the
fateful conflict within civilization, ensuing in an equally
predestined fall at the end of this century. In his *Man
and Technics,* written just before Hitler's takeover,
Spengler identified life itself with this struggle, which,
like Nietzsche, he viewed as "a battle originating from
the will to power, terrible, relentless, a battle without
mercy." From this fate there is no escape. We are born
in this age, admonished Spengler, and we must go our
way bravely to the end. This requires loyalty to our
destiny. We must stand, unflinchingly, like the sentinel
dug up from the ashes at Pompeii, who died because
they had forgotten to relieve him. "That is greatness. That
is to have character. This is honest and is the only thing
which cannot be taken away from man."

The experience of life, to repeat, is an experience of
totality, with at times a deliberate accent on the wholesome. From Goethe to Nietzsche and beyond, the notion
of health has been the standard of culture. The exalted
status which Dilthey assigned to the poet finds its justification in the fact that the poet teaches us to enjoy the
world as living experience and "in all this the full, total
healthy human being." The introduction of such a sturdy
notion as health, however, into the fragile distinctions of
literary and philosophical discussions sounds a little sus-

picious. The suspicion is confirmed when, for instance, Goethe equated the classical with the notion of the healthy, and thereby assumed that he himself belonged to the robust. Goethe, although definitely not one of the full-fledged Romanticists (those interested in the idea of the diseased!), was all the same the author of *Faust*, which is, ironically, the most profound and complete Romanticist statement in literature. Schiller, who knew Goethe thoroughly, was the first to ascribe Romanticism to Goethe's work, and when Goethe, late in life, mentioned this fact to Eckermann, he made no attempt to refute it.

Vitalist thought here again presents itself in paradox. Nietzsche, one of the most frail and sick philosophers on record, never tired of preaching health and of detesting the degenerate. Similarly, this most refined and humanistic mind proclaimed the abolition of all civilized values and the fight against compassion. Indeed, this most religiously searching of souls was destined, albeit stunned with guilt, to announce the death of God. The self-contradictory aspect here, spectacular in Nietzsche but true in general for the philosophy of life, is an inherent problem. It is an inevitable concomitance for a movement wanting to live its philosophy.

Professional criticism has been quick to point to these self-willed inadequacies of the philosophies of life. In *The Philosophy of Life* (1922) Heinrich Rickert, the most articulate of their critics, charged the vitalist thinkers with a one-sided concern that tries to build a complex world view from the concept of vitality alone. Hence he believed that the philosophy of life "has functioned anti-philosophically and has been as life-destroying." This critique is, of course, one-sided to the other extreme and ignores the important contributions of some of the vitalists. Yet the innate insoluble problem of their thinking and its self-destroying effect is justly raised.

It would appear that by presenting the broad, boundless problem of life as the sole issue of philosophy, even if pared down to more workable determinations such as

Erlebnis, durée, destiny, or will to power, the instrument of reasoning, traditionally the basic philosophical tool, becomes rather ineffective. Life is to be lived. Philosophizing about life cannot get around the content of unreason that characterizes vitality. The philosophy of life is a courageous attempt to reason about unreason, which can be done, but only at the price of self-contradiction.

In this sense, Nietzsche was probably the most consistent exponent of the movement by professing the inherent inadequacy of vitalism as its trademark. This irrationality, with others appearing merely implicitly, is drummed home with force in Nietzsche's work. He even invented a name for this method, calling it philosophizing with the hammer. The element of violence in Nietzsche's work should neither be ignored nor misunderstood. Jaspers, in one of the outstanding interpretations of Nietzsche, based his study on what he believed was the essential tenet of Nietzsche's philosophy: self-contradiction. It is only by accepting these contradictions in their total context that Nietzsche can be fully understood, and thus his philosophy, in terms of violence, be made clear.

Making life—total healthy life—the issue of philosophy is historically a curious trend prompted, it seems, by fear of the analytic rationalism, which in an increasingly sophisticated civilization threatens to harden the arteries of life. The realization that this process is inevitable has given the reaction of vitalism its one-sided and emotional character. It carries an urbane violence within its methods which with Nietzsche, less urbanely, became the strategy of chaos, an infatuation with fatality, and the practice of what he most feared—barbarism.

The philosophy of existence

Existentialism distinguishes itself from the philosophies of life, among other things, by exploring a concept that allows more exact conceptional maneuvering. The notions of life and existence are popularly related, of course, but technically they make the difference between imaginative suggestion and philosophical probing. Whereas life is blindly seeking its destiny, existence is awareness of absolute being.

There are an infinite number of existence philosophies. They can be classed according to religious, national, and methodical traditions, but this division would not be adequate. Berdyaev and Chestov, both orthodox, Russian, and mystically inclined, came to entirely different conclusions in matters of practical application. Sartre and Camus both write from secular and literary premises, and are strong in linguistic precision, yet they differ immensely in philosophical statement. Heidegger and Jaspers both continue the Kierkegaardian line of thought, but one embraces ontology as the sole method, while the other rejects this entirely. Philosophers of existence, however, have in common the inquiry into the relationship between authentic existence and absolute being. Far from analyzing the detailed subtleties of the various existentialist schools, we should rather concentrate here on the historical relevance in general of thinking about essentials in an age confused by the plurality of accidentals.

Existentialist thinking is the most timely of all modern philosophies; it is the most relevant to the situation of contemporary man. It poses the problem of man's being in this modern time. Hegel's philosophy of totality asks the question about man in the comprehensive achievement of his past. The practical philosophies, positivist or utilitarian, ask how man can make truth useful, whereas the philosophies of life ask how man can still have vital and creative experience in the face of total mechanization. The existentialist question concerns man as an estranged being. Philosophy of existence asks: Why is human existence separated from absolute essence,

Of course, one may contend that this question is useless. One may deny any validity at all to metaphysics and its problems about being. Or one may wonder whether the separation of existence from being is a permanent rather than a modern phenomenon. One must, however, take cognizance of the historical fact that this awareness of human estrangement does emerge in the contemporary mind, and that it has to be accounted for philosophically, historically, and culturally. Existentialism simply deals with that historical factor of alienation that has determined the course of much that has happened in the various fields of contemporary culture. As such, it is pivotal to the understanding of the underlying problems of our arts, literature, drama, education, and religion.

Existentialist philosophy can come in strictly technical expositions, and sometimes clothed in a hypersensitive, almost inbred language. The intricate strands of thought weaving in and out of the discourses of Jaspers and Heidegger not infrequently render the structure of their philosophies obscure. Or existentialism may come in a splendidly written essay form such as that of Kierkegaard, in the crisp but sweepingly apodictic style of Berdyaev, in the lively narrative of Camus, in the poetic mysticism of Buber, in the dramatic dialogues of Sartre or Gabriel Marcel, and in the crammed eclectic brilliance of Sartre's *Being and Nothingness*. It shows a vast array of themes and sub-themes to elucidate the basic issue of the plight of the authentic Self. For our purpose, however, we need only select those motifs immediately pertinent to the problems of the new proletarian society.

Throughout the history of philosophy there have been sources of potential existentialism. Kierkegaard himself pointed to Socrates, others to Augustine and Pascal. One may also suspect that the subjective character of Kant's and Fichte's philosophies played a preparatory function in the development of this modern way of thinking. Existentialist philosophy began its career officially, however, in 1841 when Schelling launched his lecture series on positive philosophy at the University of Berlin. He was then just nominated to the chair which Hegel, at his death ten years earlier, had left empty. Hegel's more radical followers in that decade gave Hegelianism a revolutionary aura, and the Berlin authorities planned to stem the tide by appointing to this illustrious chair of philosophy a man whom they could expect to develop a counter-movement to the then established dialectic reasoning and criticism. An ironical twist of history brought Schelling (in old age) again into the spotlight. Originally Hegel and Schelling were close friends, exchanging letters of cooperative purpose and harmony. Schelling, the extremely precocious thinker, became a national celebrity when still in his early twenties, while Hegel was only an obscure instructor. But eventually Hegel caught up and acquired such a commanding position in the world of philosophy that Schelling faded proportionately out of sight.

Schelling's "positive" thinking should not be confused with its contemporary, positivism; in its metaphysical idealism it represents almost the opposite. It starts out from absolute Being, as did Hegel's logic, but, according to Schelling, the mind concentrating on pure essence thinks "of nothing but the existential." This type of philosophizing is positive because it originates in existentialism, a pure notionless experience for which all reason stops. Proceeding from this existential experience, Schelling's philosophy attempts to search for the sense of essence, thus following the direction opposite to Hegel's dialectic, which must then be called "negative."

This positive philosophy has never been accepted as extremely persuasive by anyone, and except for its historic significance it might well have been forgotten. As a colorful touch, it is worth noting that in Schelling's audience were such young rebels in their own right as Kierkegaard, Engels, and Burckhardt. It is scarcely conceivable that the latter two could have been greatly impressed by Schelling's probing of the "notionless." Of Kierkegaard's reactions there is a definitely negative record. An entry in his journals of 1849 refers to Schelling as "degenerating into a Prussian Excellency," and to his philosophy as "stagnant water." On February 27, 1942, he wrote to his brother, "I am too old to attend lectures and Schelling is too old to give them. His whole

theory of potency reveals the greatest impotence." Kierkegaard, moreover, had no need of anti-Hegelian thrusts
from Schelling. His dissertation published in the same
year shows him veering away from Hegel's center under
the influence of Socrates. *The Concept of Irony*, nevertheless, did not yet show the concern with existentialism
which constitutes the core of all Kierkegaard's later
works, and it is just possible that Schelling, by putting
existence in the central position of his philosophy,
opened up avenues to Kierkegaard which he himself was
unable to follow.

From *Either/Or* onward, existentialist philosophy is an
inquiry into relationships rather than into fixed categories. It is neither a "positive" nor a "negative" philosophy,
for it recognizes the coexistence of alternatives, expressed
in the either/or. The situation of either/or does not, however, relate to a particular act, or to a number of decisive
acts, but primarily to the permanent awareness of choice,
the unending dialectic imperative of choice absolute. In
Either/Or Kierkegaard explains that "the absolute antithesis does not exist for reasoning, but for choice . . .
I can choose myself, absolute, and the fact that I choose
myself, absolute, is my freedom, and while I choose myself, absolute, I posit an absolute difference, the difference between good and evil."

This thinking in existential relationships, culminating
in the ultimate alternative Self and absolute Being, (or
absolute Nothingness with Kierkegaard), in the twentieth century understandably becomes a philosophy of relativity, undermining the classical abutments of thought
no less drastically than the physics of relativity dissolved
the Newtonian cosmology. This was markedly true of
Jaspers' thinking, which presented the existential as a
"floating" experience, constantly moving in "border-situa-
tions." Existence thus can never be fixed and known in
the terms by which one can know nature; it can only be
elucidated.

The relativity of our existential situation puts us constantly in a "critical" moment. The philosophies of exist-

ence deal with the dialectic of crises. In most cases this refers to individual consciousness, since existentialism predicates self and the changing borderlines of its authenticity. But it also definitely implies a being-in-the-world, and it is not difficult to see that a philosophy of crisis easily carries its investigation of critical conditions over to the social predicament at large. From the beginning, therefore, existentialism acted at least partly as social criticism. In defense of the individual it tended to submit the foundations and attitudes of the mass society to severe scrutiny, and it was culturally committed for the protection of creative individuality.

The element of social criticism in existentialist writings was, of course, part of a widely developing trend of *Zeitkritik*, which characterized contemporary culture. Social criticism during the classical epoch, although not unheard of, was rare, and when it occurred it was utilized for limited religious and political purposes. Savonarola, Machiavelli, Hotman, Buchanan, Knox, and Locke, for instance, considered merely a small sector of their contemporary world with limited benefits in mind. In other contexts, the social attack evaporated in the beauty of poetry or light satire as in Dante, Chaucer, and Erasmus. Social criticism, however, rose to its full realization only during the last two centuries.

That this should be true must probably be explained by the parallel development during that period of the cultural isolation which seems to set man apart from his own historical society. The strong, sometimes obsessive, awareness of the past and its offsetting function in determining his own historic position has given contemporary man the background for his critical judgments. It is significant, moreover, that the earliest social critiques in the modern sense, those by Rousseau, Adam Ferguson, Schiller, and Fichte, appeared at the very sensitive time of transition when the new consciousness of cultural estrangement was being developed theoretically.

The most important of these is Schiller's *On the Aesthetic Education of Man*, a work repeatedly referred to in this investigation because of its wide cultural implications. There is nothing existentialist in this critique. Its analysis of the age rests on the contrast between eighteenth-century society and the glory of ancient Greece, a device incidentally not wholly fair or wholly explanatory. It does indicate the nostalgic cult of the Golden Age of the past, to which one is somehow culturally related, and which one seeks to restore in a distant future. Man, according to Schiller, is separated from his original state of harmonious freedom and can only be brought back through esthetic, political, and moral education.

Schiller's social critique was on behalf of the autonomous dignity and freedom of man. Others were launched for the sake of nationalism (Fichte), the lower classes (the French Socialists, Marx, Engels), scholarship (the early Hegel), art (the young Wagner), historical tradition (Burke), or true democracy (Cooper). None of these, however, can by any measure be classified as expressions of the existentialist mentality. More difficult to assess are the critical attitudes of literary figures such as Melville and Thoreau. They reveal in some of their writings undeniable existential questioning and, as transcendentalists, a clear sense of essence to focus that questioning. But their doubts about the age in specific instances are not always easy to fit into the obvious existentialist frame of thinking.

Kierkegaard's *The Present Age* is as momentously urgent now as when it was written in 1846. It deals with the new era which had at that time been developing for almost two centuries, and which Kierkegaard surveyed (partly by anticipation) not historically or politically by either preaching return to past forms or progress to utopian forms of society, but existentially. That is, in his own words, he dealt "with dialectical categories and qualifications." This is a technical way of saying that the self is viewed as absolute possibility in confrontation with the world. The individual as absolute possibility remains the issue today in the conformist tendencies of our egalitarian society. Our age, Kierkegaard believed, is one of reflection, analysis, and abstraction. We have lost the passion of true revolution and the "leap of enthusiasm." The result is a process of abstract leveling, "that self-combustion of the human race." The trend will continue, for no single individual can arrest a movement operating under the thrust of the "association," the group, the masses—it is simply too late.

Existentialist criticism is not primarily out to get the scapegoat. Unlike fascism, anarchism, Marxism, Leninism, and Fabianism, it is little interested in distributing blame and removing from the core of society those who oppose self-set ameliorative dogmas. Existential critique aims primarily at man's situation in the time, and it questions his potentiality to become in time and environment that which he essentially is. For Martin Heidegger, this meant the positing of an ontological problem, that is, our being as such is at stake, and his fundamental question was whether this being is merely a vapor or "the spiritual destiny of the Western World."

Heidegger's critique of today's world in *An Introduction to Metaphysics* is directed against the universal trend of taking things out of their metaphysical sphere and using them instead for "the same dismal technological frenzy, the same excessive organization of the average man," which characterize both the Soviet Union and the United States, and we may now add Europe, China, and soon the rest of the world as well. This spiritual decline, according to Heidegger, had taken on such proportions that modern man even lacked the mental energy to evaluate his own position. After having abandoned the anchorage of being, the question for Heidegger was where this would lead. "When time is merely velocity, instantaneousness and simultaneity, and time as history has vanished from the daily existence of the people; when a boxer is valued as the nation's great man; when mass meetings of the millions are looked upon as a triumph—then, yes, then through all this uproar a question still haunts us like a ghost: What for?—Whither?—And what then?"

The most specific social criticism as well as the most comprehensive from the existentialist standpoint is to be found in Jaspers' *Man in the Modern Age*. Essentially, it asks the question whether man under the modern circumstances can still be free, or, in other words, "whether independent man is still possible in his self-chosen destiny." Although in this work Jaspers can aggressively reject the excesses of contemporary trends and fads, and point critically to the weakness of the press, sociology, anthropology, psychoanalysis, or the new sophisms, he shies away from blaming groups or individuals for the ills of the world. This is in keeping with his existentialist method of clarifying situations rather than typecasting human behavior, as the modern sciences do. Existence philosophy cannot find solutions. "It arouses what it does not itself know; it elucidates and stimulates, but it does not fixate."

The existentialist's attitude toward cultural decline, at least inasmuch as he thinks that such a decline is evident, varies with the individual philosopher. Kierkegaard, as we have noted, saw no way of arresting the process. The individual is lost in the "giddiness of continuous abstraction," and can only save his inner self by "the reality of religion." Camus was resigned to a sort of stoic acceptance of an absurd world based on cross-purposes (*Le Malentendu*) and man's useless labor (*The Myth of Sisyphus*). Nicolas Berdyaev clung to a mystical orthodoxy which made him remark in *The Destiny of Man* that after this aeon moving toward catastrophe there will be another aeon, in which the self-destructive urges "will be replaced by a creative flight into infinity and eternity." Jaspers believes that under the threat of technological holocaust our salvation depends on the outcome of the conflict between individual and collective.

In general, however, existential thinking does not see hope in action. Here one should except Sartre, who believes in a vague doctrine of "engagement," but then of course Sartre is not a purebred existentialist. Otherwise, however, this philosophy is one of elucidation, of transcendence. Existence in its continuous search for an identification with an absolute (being) is bound to founder. Man in his incapacity to know pure Being can only experience pure Nothingness, though this solely in the reality of Anxiety. The sublime moment of Kierkegaardian despair is precisely the realization of failure in the face of absoluteness. Existence philosophy thus may become an analysis of human failure, a philosophy of the modern non-hero, who has lost the securities of victory. Existentialism does not seek victories in the sense of comprehension. It does not attempt to capture, harness, systematize, classify, typecast, control. It merely gropes and probes relationships, and elucidates. Thus, for Jaspers, as man searches for absolute reality beyond nature in the existential experience, there is always an element of falling short, of defeat. This transcendental unity cannot be known rationally, and at best man can live with symbols, the *chiffres*, which he may decipher to make his world somewhat more transparent.

Clearly related to this is the factor of nihilism which, in various forms, has played a dominating role in the cultural history of the last centuries. Negation was already a determining factor in Hegel's logic, and the Romanticists, especially Ludwig Tieck and Friedrich Schlegel, were quick to use the element of negation for a rather effective literary irony. Schelling, at the outset of the history of existentialism, declared that by concentrating on Being we actually think of nothing but the existential. The nihilistic implication is that everything brought forth by thought is "beaten down" by the existential. Heidegger, in his book *On Humanism*, hints at the same when he says that "while the mind thinks about Being it thinks about Nothingness." Sartre, in *Being and Nothingness*, uses the classical terms *an-Sich* and *für-Sich* to explain that subjectivity (*für-Sich*) emerges as negation, and what it negates or "neantizes" is objectivity (*an-Sich*).

These are all variations on Kierkegaard's *leitmotif* of the experience of Nothingness as the necessary requirement for self-realization. The category of Doubt, which in the classical mind set the standard for critical reasoning, in the post-classical world is replaced by Despair, not to be understood as helpless fatalism, but as total existential doubt, exceeding its rational limits. This despair is what Kierkegaard called the "sickness unto death," a dialectical awareness by which man tastes the experience of life and death in the same instant. The nihilism in this realization is absolute, and it implies its creative necessity. This viewpoint, although Kierkegaard had not yet presented it as an existentialist idea, emerged as early as his dissertation in which he sought to replace Romantic irony with Socratic irony, "the infinite absolute negativity."

Existentialism is a philosophy of involvement, but this can only be understood as dialectical involvement. Being and existence belong together, in polar exclusion and attraction. What Heidegger calls the "nihilation" by Being, although he does not explicitly say so, can only occur in the mutual return of negation. When this mutuality stops, the historical trend that Heidegger detects is a falling away from essentials. It issues from an attitude of "going it alone" in the multitudinousness of the world and indulging in the plurality of disconnected things. Thus the cohesion of life and community and thinking falls apart. Existential involvement, however, should not be confused with mere social commitment, for it goes far beyond it. The ethical problem for existentialist thinking centers in the freedom by which man in the act of "doing good" chooses himself. Ethical choice, by choosing the other, chooses itself. In the choice, according to Kierkegaard, "the finite personality becomes infinite."

Berdyaev, following Kierkegaard in this respect, elaborated what he called an "ethics of creativeness," whereby not individualism but rather personalism is crucial. These ethics are "connected with a communal spiritual whole." They begin with the individual and are "prophetically directed toward the future." On the whole, existentialist ethics represent an involvement not propelled by commandments, by a categorical imperative, by stoic virtue, or by utilitarian relief of pain, but by that choice between good and evil which liberates the self. There is definitely no commitment to group action since this would infringe upon man's existential liberty.

It is therefore not surprising that in the cultural conflict between individual and collective the existentialist is "existentially" on the side of the individual. He views the collective as the destroyer of the spontaneous, autonomous, and authentic freedom of the self. All that is creative in man will be annihilated in the relentless process of leveling, which results from the consensus strategy of mass power. It means the processing of human choice and alternatives into common abstractions under the sponsorship of the public, that "leveling master" as Kierkegaard called it. True existentialism cannot present itself as other than the champion of individuation, the freedom of the self to become what it potentially is. "The masses," one reads in his journals, "are the only tyrant and at the source of all corruption."

The existentialist does not always view the conflict of individual and collective in historical perspective, and he rarely suggests a political formula to overcome the danger that he believes is to be seen in the developing proletarianization. He is therefore no blind reactionary, trying to reconstruct bygone times. Only Berdyaev had an unfortunate tendency to recreate an "ennobled" society, based on what he termed an "aristocratic socialism." Existentialism in general, however, is consistently preoccupied with the problem of individual freedom in a world order more and more constricted by the patterns of conformity. As such, it is probably the most pertinent philosophy of the contemporary world.

The evaluation of the collective as the agency of human enslavement is a true characteristic of existentialist thinkers. It is therefore questionable whether Sartre in this respect can really be included among them. His works are of uneven literary and philosophical merit. But with the exception of the unfortunate *Existentialism Is a Humanism*, the publishing of which the author himself has come to regret, his writings represent a sincere as well as arduous endeavor to probe into the problem of modern man. His weakness, however, lies in his almost unrestricted virtuosity. Without apparent strain he mixes fragments of systems from Descartes, Kant, Hegel, Kierkegaard, Marx, Husserl, Heidegger, and Freud into a grand medley which leaves one out of breath until one realizes that the nature of Sartre's work is more one of potpourri than of composition.

In *Critique of Dialectic Reason*, he seriously tries to do the impossible by combining a metaphysics of the individual with a practice of the collective. The title of this work itself hints at a mongrel conception with echoes of Kantian criticism and Hegelian logic. These do not make very compatible bedfellows. Nor does the forcing of individual and collective into one system promise much yield for the future. Regardless, however, of its philosophical soundness, this operation is historically nonsensical. Having noted that Marxism is arrested because it wants to change the world, Sartre aims at "another existentialism" which does not have to go against Marxism, but can develop alongside it. The ultimate result of Sartre's concoction is basically an old-fashioned humanism for which neither Being, God, nor collective is sovereign, but only man "inasmuch as he is action."

Philosophical critics have to analyze the complicated discourse of this work in detail. In historical context, however, it reveals a great lack of realism, in that the sovereignty of man in this computerized world-order is sheer fiction. Sartre's claim that the individual "fighting against his estrangement with corrupted tools in spite of all [is] patiently winning terrain," in view of the historical development, verges on the hilarious. True existentialism harbors no illusions about the efficacy of social, political, and religious "actions" to save the autonomy of the self from a world of leveling values. It offers no practical solutions except the impossible one of returning to the mental state of a primal communion with absolute Being.

Despite their elusive character, existentialist philosophies are of major significance for understanding the cultural changes of the twentieth century. They have put into focus the cultural isolation which modern man as a proletarian type of historical consciousness has revealed in his arts and thought. Existentialist thinking has analyzed this isolation that sets man apart in terms of his estrangement from essentials, from that transcendent security which provided classical man with his harmonious sense of unity.

Existence philosophy has, with as much candor as courage, left the contemporary problem open, clarifying without easy pragmatic solutions and, with a few exceptions, avoiding cheap recipes for what must be merely understood as barbiturates against disturbing truths. It is no philosophy of peace of mind. Far from putting the mind to rest in pseudo illusions, it makes an effort to clear the consciousness of nebulous conditions that prevent it from recognizing the contemporary situation. As such, it has gone far in exposing modern man as an irrevocable alien in his own self-constructed environment. Of course, this exposure has not gone unchallenged by those who, unperturbed by the history of the last two centuries, keep hoping for amelioration by practical policies, communist or otherwise. One cannot possibly anticipate the judgment of history, and must leave undiscussed the justification for these hopes or, for that matter, for the existentialist viewpoint. One can merely note that, regardless of the validity of its specific conclusions, existentialist philosophy has contributed by daring to ask the essential question about man and his society.

This does not by any means imply that the existentialist approach is beyond criticism. On the contrary, it must seriously be questioned for its one-sided concern with individuation alone, and its heroism of a metaphysical self, which does not always seem relevant to the very timeliness of its problems. By rejecting the idea of the collective as entirely unviable, it sets its dialectical basis so narrowly that the opposition of those who concentrate (just as narrowly) on mass consensus is excluded from any useful dialogue. As a result, for instance, there have been some dreadfully unenlightened communications in invectives from the side of otherwise highly accredited Marxist scholars.

In part, at least, the existentialists themselves are to blame for such hyper-emotional reactions. Placing themselves squarely in the contemporary actuality, their statements have still been elusive as to the very matter of practical participation. To label existentialism bourgeois, as the communists like to do, is utterly nonsensical, for existentialism moves above and beyond any social or partisan demarcation lines. Except for Sartre, who likes to play around with political realities, none of the existentialist thinkers relate their problems to political exigency. Heidegger stupidly compromised himself with the National Socialist regime, but his writings show no trace of political involvement one way or the other. The disappointing aspect is not that the existentialist involvement is possibly wrong, but, on the contrary, that its involvement stops short of probing the potential creativeness of the collective. A philosophy of individuation especially, it would appear, ought to test the resources of the mass movement in order to assess the intensity of what it believes to be the annihilation of the originality of the self.

Self and collective, authenticity and mass, individual and consensus belong together dialectically. The disruption of this dialectical relationship poses a threat, hanging unresolved over our age. Existentialism, itself so dialectically grounded, has sometimes obscurely, sometimes eloquently, presented the plight of the individual as a stranger in his own domain with unrelenting consistency, but unfortunately without being able to contribute to the preservation of that dialectical nature of society which is cultural freedom. Desparately defending the freedom of the authentic self, it seems to overlook the fact that this freedom is bound up with possible cultural freedom; that is, that state of unity in which individual and collective are harmoniously interrelated. The content of this freedom, as Jaspers himself remarks in his work on the purpose of history, reveals itself in a life of polarity and in movement and dialectic. It is precisely the loss of the dialectical freedom between individual and collective which accounts for that enslavement of man which existentialist philosophy has fought so bitterly.

*Our religions and moralities have been trimmed to flatter us,
till they are all emasculated and sentimentalized, and only
please and weaken.*

Robert Louis Stevenson

10

The Pious Way of Living

The cultural challenge

The dynamics of culture, that play of historical forces
which gives a society its recorded classical morphology,
by its very nature implies movement, change, and the
flux of becoming. The idea of constant becoming, of
never completing, never attaining the serenity of that
metaphysical rest in which the problems of nature and
history dwindle away, plays havoc with man's innate
conservative disposition. We all resist change—basic
change, that is—which redirects our minds; it takes decades for the collective consciousness of a society to catch

up with the new situations which scientific and other external forces impose upon it. Yet it is also true that we are fascinated by the game of change that is the irrevocable law of life.

This dualism in the human mind can never be solved. It is this dualism, in fact, on which culture thrives. While we dream the eternal we produce the transient. What we call culture, the spontaneous expressions of an autonomous social community in time, is an account of this vain reaching for permanence. It reflects the discrepancy between man's temporality and the absolute. Culture is at the same time the pageantry of human achievements, and the inside-out form of man's awareness of falling short in grasping the infinite. The arts, music, theater, literature, political and educational systems, and philosophy are the records of the most sublime of unfulfilled dreams. Among them religion is the most typically revealing.

Religion, as a confessional expression of belief or as a theological discipline, poses more than enough technical (and tactical) problems when it comes to developing its place in history. But one can at least assume one's biased position, denominational or atheistic, which tolerant readers will appreciate as an "honest" stand. In general, we go along with partisanship better than with historical understanding, and this adds a difficulty to any exposition of religion, in this case Christianity, as a cultural expression. By taking away the emotional intimacy of belief, and presenting religion merely according to its changing manifestations (after all, the only thing a historian can and ought to do), the game of for-or-against is neutralized—to the disappointment of the emotionalists.

Nor can one, in order to avoid hurt feelings, eliminate at least a brief discussion of the religious roots of contemporary civilization. For religion is the most decisive impulse behind the passing modulations of society. It stands at the birth of a society, it guides society through its fullest epoch of maturity. We would indeed gain little if we were to ignore the fact that ours is a Christian culture, fed by Christian myths and symbols. Drama in

Western society emerged from the Christmas and Easter liturgies of the Church. It is not accidental that its art culminated in the ceiling of the Sistine Chapel, in *The Last Supper*, or the *Hundred Guilder Print*, that its music found its richest score in the *Missa Papae Marcelli*, the *St. Matthew Passion*, the *Missa Solemnis*, and the *Messiah*, that its literature reached its deepest fulfillment in the *Divine Comedy*, *Hamlet*, *Paradise Lost*, *Faust*, and *The Brothers Karamazov*. In the systems of Western education, the devout convictions of the Brethren of the Common Life, the Jesuits, Comenius, Milton, Francke, and Pestalozzi have been pivotal. Even in professional philosophy, traditionally so skeptical and rational an occupation, the secular thinking of Kant and Hegel still reflects, in conceptional terms, the essential content of Christian belief.

The myths, the symbols, and the language of revealed, historical Christianity have permeated all the other branches of culture. Christian martyrdom and sainthood have set the pattern for the cultural hero of our civilization. No one needs more proof for the centrality of Christian worship in the dynamics that shaped Western culture. Consequently, one must assume that the historical destiny of this civilization is intimately bound up with the vitality of its religion. The future of Christianity is probably indicative of the destiny of our society as a whole. It is therefore rather inconsistent to gloat with Freud over the disappearance of religion, and to trust, nevertheless, that without it an autonomous culture will still be possible.

This is clearly an illusion. Civilizations tend to emerge and disintegrate with the strength of their religious fervor, and although one may hope that this historical pattern is no absolute guide and that this time our own civilized order will not succumb to senescent fatigue, the odds are slim. All the same, there is no reason to anticipate senility while one still has the vigor to hope; and by the same token, to declare Western religion as moribund or worse is impossible, for this verdict would inescapably carry over to our whole cutural vitality. Euro-American civilization will be dead, indeed, with the demise of historical Christianity. The cultural energy of institutional Christianity, having generated Western society, will leave it withering if its saps run out and fail to nurture its own organism.

There is plenty of evidence that Christian religion as a cultural manifestation is by no means dead. One cannot read the minds of believers. We can never know the real meaning of such expressions as nominal or professed believers, for there are no ways of gauging the disparity between truly inwardly experienced faith and formal external worship. Leaving this experience out of consideration, then, one can only concentrate on Christianity inasmuch as it is apparent as social and cultural expression. It is obvious that, as such, it is still very much with us, and still playing an intrinsic role in the shaping of contemporary life.

However, it is a different Christianity. The cultural division of a classical and a postclassical mentality, prevailing in all the manifestations under discussion here, is no less pronounced in religious matters. Christianity, from a spontaneous commitment of faith, is more and more becoming an administrated group-consciousness. Originally exemplified in the elitist quality of sainthood, either in the Catholic or Protestant sense, it is, in the tide of proletarian globalization, gradually changing into a massively organized association of adherents. Classical Christendom represented a spirit confidently setting the tone and standards for a closely united world order and inclined to lead historical trends. Postclassical Christendom means a self-conscious way of living, concerned with a favorable public image and inclined to follow the secular trends of history.

This historic self-consciousness reveals itself plainly in the preoccupation of many of today's Christians with the problem of culture—a concern characteristically modern in the history of the churches. Jesus, standing at the confluence of Semitic, Hellenistic, Persian, and Roman civilizations, seemed wholly uninvolved with their declining glory. He was, of course, aware of the humiliated state of Jerusalem, whose destruction he sadly foresaw. But his life and teachings were those of an outsider in the contemporary social structure. Similarly, Paul of Tarsus broke away from his cultural environment. By religion a Jew, by education a Greek, and by citizenship a Roman, he was soon to isolate himself entirely from his traditional roots. Although brought up in the Pharisaic subtleties of the celebrated Gamaliel, he challenged Judaic theology with his denunciation of the validity of its laws. Facing the skeptic and stoic "men of Athens" in his address on the Areopagus, Paul startled them with his speculations on the resurrection, while in his defense before the procurator Porcius Festus, he upset Roman common sense to such an extent that Festus uttered his famous reply, "much learning doth make thee mad."

Jesus and Paul both operated outside the historical framework of their society, and ignored their cultural heritage. The early Christians, as long as the churches represented a mere underground movement, likewise had no need to attach themselves to inherited outward forms, and were not consciously engaged in creating institutional cultic expressions. This changed, however, with the first ecumenical council at Nicaea in A.D. 325, when the Church acquired its official status. It became part of the old imperial establishment, and soon it was to create its own new imperial establishment. From A.D. 325 on, Christianity slowly began to express itself in new cultural configurations. From merely an inwardly realized generator of hope, it became an outwardly directed manifestation.

For classical Christianity, the outward and inward realities of belief were united in the institutions of the Church. Its intensive participation in the arts or in scholarship was not a conscious involvement in culture (the word was not even known then in that sense), but an integral part of the ministry of worship. In the Middle Ages and the Renaissance, religious education could therefore also be broadly humanistic. The pedagogics of copying ancient manuscripts in the schools of the Brethren of the Common Life rested on furthering the discipline of the *devotia moderna*. The staging of Terentius or the lavishly baroque theater sets in the Jesuit schools were manifestations of their religious education. Whatever contributions the Church—collectively Catholic or individually denominational—made to the classical styles of Western arts and letters arrived spontaneously.

To be sure, there is no point in ignoring the remarkable exceptions, which indicate that the cultivation of external transitory forms of religion was not an altogether unreflective activity. The Cromwellian revolutionaries and the more radical popular leaders of the Dutch Revolt staged iconoclastic raids, based on the puritanical principle that esthetic beauty was sensuous indulgence, tantamount to sin. Not all Protestants shared Luther's love of music. In Zeeland and elsewhere, musical accompaniment, even the most austere organ, was banned from the place of worship. The more tolerant *predikanten* of Amsterdam might enjoy the literature of Hooft, Vondel, and Cats, but they were vehemently opposed to the arts of the theater.

In general, however, Western society at the height and maturity of its religious consciousness was not very concerned about the consequences of its cultural achievements. It did not yet analyze them, nor the necessity of their existence in relation to Christian belief. The gap between culture and creed, so typical of twentieth-century consciousness, and the accompanying cultural guilt complexes, especially evident in the discussion of liberal as well as fundamentalist Protestants, were absent. Culture in classical society was there innocently, without missionary purposes, unashamed of its often secular and sensual appearances, for it was an inevitable fruit of an unchallenged Christian community. It was only in the nineteenth century when the idea of culture in general changed, and when cultural history received its most powerful exposition, that the Christians began to be concerned about the problem.

Culture—originally merely the culture of the land—in

classical society was gradually thought of, if it was considered at all, as the forming of the young. The word came into frequent use only in the nineteenth century when the notion of culture assumed historical connotations. Although Matthew Arnold in *Culture and Anarchy* firmly held onto the function of culture as the "study of perfection," the historical temper of that century as a whole was far more concerned with culture as the total sum of the best achievements of an historical society, or, as the historican Lamprecht in an essay of 1896 defined it, the "product of man's developing society" (*Vergesellschaftung*). It was in this modern period that the Western mind produced a number of full-fledged cultural histories and an endless assortment of definitions of civilization. The West was, for the first time, culturally involved and disturbed; it was also, significantly, increasingly worried about the conceivable finality of the Euro-American civilized era.

It is hardly surprising that the Christian Church, so profoundly involved in the glory of Western culture, now began to share the general historical sensitivity. In the eighteenth century, Christianity as the powerful authority and guardian of the totality of earthly life lost a considerable amount of its prestige. The erosion of its secure position was, of course, partly caused by outside forces. It would be incorrect, however, to present the story of the weakening Church as the work of the rising voices and actions of atheists, deists, or the publicists of the Enlightenment. As we shall see below, it was chiefly the established religion itself which undermined its position as the guiding agency of mankind. As sickly plants attract obnoxious insects, so the Church, while losing her firm grip on life, was attacked by the spokesmen of powers rivaling for the control of society. Inevitably, reinforcement from within was required, and thus we see in the eighteenth century an upsurge of fringe sects, Lutheran Pietists, Moravian Brethren, and Methodists, trying to put new life in an ossifying established religion.

Friedrich Schleiermacher, partly influenced by Mora

vian revivalism, was, at this time, probably the most effective Protestant theologian since the Reformation. Standing at the center of the early Romantic movement, he addressed himself to his friends as a true apologist of the faith, and in *On Religion* (1799) he presented Christianity in the new light of the Romantic revolution. Schleiermacher thus became the founder of the modernist groups in the Church, rejecting the abstraction of restricting dogmas and appealing above all to the vital experiences of feeling and imagination. Religion, to Schleiermacher, was essentially the unification of man and the Infinite, and it was each individual as the realizer of religion who in "his specific way should represent the total humanity."

It was almost inevitable that Schleiermacher, as a Romanticist, should have to come to grips with the relationship of religion and art. In fact, his has been called an "esthetic" theology inasmuch as it focuses on the creative side of religion. In the second speech of *On Religion*, Schleiermacher, stressing the importance of belief as activity, linked art and religion in the experience of life. "They surely do not react as if alien to each other, because what is greatest in art has had a religious nature." It was therefore quite natural for him to see his task as a cultural mission. To be sure, culture to Schleiermacher, as to Arnold, was a way of perfection—self-perfection (*Bildung*)—which, rather than comprehending the past, was an avenue to the future. "I am a stranger in the mentality and the life of the present generation, a prophetic citizen of the future world, to which I am drawn by a lively imagination and a strong faith," he proclaimed in the third of his *Soliloquies*. To Schleiermacher, culture was thus a perfecting religious agency which enabled the individual to approximate to the eternal absolute in the fullness of the finite world.

One of the remarkable aspects of nineteenth-century religious stirrings was the cultural implication of a religious revolt against the established institution of the Church. It revealed itself in such diverse minds as those of Kierkegaard, Nietzsche, some of the more religiously inclined transcendentalists, and such towering Russian novelists as Tolstoy and Dostoevski. For Kierkegaard, as for Schleiermacher, the principal question was how to revitalize Christian belief. But while Schleiermacher remained within the orbit of the broad confessional German Church (and more so as he aged), Kierkegaard ended his life in the conviction that Christianity as an institution must be overcome in order to make religion possible again.

Christianity's position as the unifying source of the Euro-American cultural order makes it plausible that the revolt against established dogmatism should take similar proportions in North America. Here it lacked the total radicality of Kierkegaard or Nietzsche, probably because the flux of the American society made a dogmatic grip less self-frustrating than on the Continent. Yet here, too, the cultural revolution on behalf of a liberal individual religion had a distinct historical shape. No one had given more thought to the function and changes of culture in American society than Emerson. His ideas on this matter, always latently present, crystallized in a special essay dealing with this topic. Culture to Emerson, no less than to Schleiermacher, was a means of self-education and a way to the highest individuation. "Culture opens the sense of beauty. A man is a beggar who only lives to the useful, and however he may serve as a pin or rivet in the social machine, cannot be said to have arrived at self-possession." In the next essay on "Worship," he proceeded to connect this idea to religious problems, and found that "the whole state of man is a state of culture, and its flowering and completion may be described as Religion, or Worship."

Emerson's inferences, as usual, were inconclusive and his guiding judgments evasive, so that the true connections between American life and the religious consequences of its culture were only vaguely suggested. Theodore Parker, a far more determined and radical fighter, made the issue inescapably clear. Together with Emerson he shattered the Unitarian peace of mind. The urbanity of the "Divinity School Address" of 1838 was not for Parker. Three years later in his sermon on *The Transient and Permanent in Christianity* he gave an almost Savonarola type of bluntness to the whole dispute with the Unitarian Church fathers. In 1848, in an address on "The Political Destination of America and the Signs of the Times," he reviewed the gamut of American culture with unmuted criticism, asserting in general that it was weak, un-American, and above all lacking in "first principles." His conclusion built itself on the premise that these true principles were to be found in the right experience of Christianity. Then, when this lack had been overcome, a new autonomous American culture could be envisaged. "There will be an American art commensurate with our idea and akin to our great continent; not an imitation, but a fresh new growth." Then there would also be a typical American literature, and to crown it all, an authentic American Church "with freedom for the mind, freedom for the heart, freedom for the soul."

American transcendentalism, curiously, had no real historical extension; it founded no school. Although its new themes, coming in the midst of the sweep of industrialization were extremely timely, its hold on the American consciousness was never vigorously established. The transcendentalist leaders conspicuously lacked that prophetic visionary radicalism which marked the performance of Schleiermacher, Kierkegaard, Marx, Nietzsche, Wagner, or even Bakunin, and this may well account for the absence of revolutionary performance in the intellectual and artistic life of the United States. In any case, with the exception of a few rebels such as Mencken, actually a sort of journalized Nietzsche, or Eliot, more at home in England, American interest concentrated more on a reform on behalf of the collective than on individuation.

Consequently, in matters of religion, the appearance of Walter Rauschenbusch and his social gospel signaled the turning away from an individually to a collectively grounded religious manifestation. What was no less at stake in this Christian socialism than in Schleiermacher's Romanticism, was, partly, the preservation of Western culture through the aid of Christendom. Only the means had changed. Instead of individual mysticism, collective justice was to save our civilization.

It must also be remembered that the revolt against established Christendom was not, of course, a mere affair of insiders—clergymen—who aimed at restoring the embattled Church from within. There were numerous individualists on the fringe of traditional belief, who could not belong to the official Christian community, yet sympathetically understood the fundamental mission of Christ. Goethe, religiously hard to pinpoint, in 1828 expressed his warmth for Christianity when he called it a "doctrine friendly towards humanity." But he hastened to qualify that it had been distorted from the beginning. The nostalgia for the purity of the early Christians was even stronger in Tolstoy who, excommunicated in 1901 by the synod of the Orthodox Church, tried to establish the Kingdom of God on earth by a life of practical equality.

Dostoevski never set foot in the Church, but his deepest loyalty was to Christ, whom he extolled. In a letter of March 1854 to Madame Fonvisin, he declared himself a child of the age, "a child of unfaith and skepticism," and thought that he would remain so to the end of his life—a thought dreadfully tormenting to him. Then he added that there was nothing more excellent than Christ, and even if it could be proved that truth excludes Christ, he would still prefer Christ above truth. Nietzsche's Christianity was, of course, a highly questionable and disputed issue. However, in his letters he did indicate that in spite of his vituperations against the historical Church, he thought of Christianity at its noblest as the "best piece of ideal life" of which he had ever heard. In his *The Will to Power* Nietzsche declared that Christ, in his life, denied precisely what today is called Christian.

In the twentieth century the cultural concern of liberal Christianity, both Protestant and Catholic, has more and more come to focus on massive commitment instead of on individuation. In this respect the tendencies are rather toward Rauschenbusch's socializing Christianity than toward Schleiermacher's mystical action. Numerous periodicals of varying format try to promote the idea of a mutual assistance between "Christendom and Culture," in which culture usually appears in a popularized presentation. Contemporary culture, on the other hand, cannot be said to reciprocate this interest and seems quite prepared to go it alone. Whether this is possible is a question which, rightly or wrongly, has been posed by some of the most eminent Christians. T. S. Eliot, for instance, in his search for a definition of culture comes to the conclusion that the fate of our civilization is inexorably tied up with the vitality of Christianity. Emil Brunner, one of the most stimulating modern theologians, in his Gifford lectures at St. Andrews, thinks it is a proven fact that the "progressive decline of Christian influence has caused a progressive decay of civilization."

In all this there is an embarrassing lack of understanding in ignoring the fact that Christianity at its most uncompromisingly pure, that is, before it surrendered to the Imperial order at Nicaea, was unburdened by cultural responsibilities. By connecting the glory of classical civilization with the established Christian Church, Eliot and others for whom he spoke chose to overlook the true and humble vitality of the Church when it was merely (and serenely) an unassuming unworldly flock of believers. This state of primitive serenity can, of course, never again be reconstructed. But it should at least make contemporary Christians think about the justification for putting their hopes so categorically on the conjunction of Church and culture. Christ consistently ignored his traditional as well as contemporary culture. Paul wrote them off as intellectual ballast, and became a tentmaker. If their example cannot be followed, then for the outsider, at least, the whole validity of Christian, as a name and a notion, seems to have become questionable.

Summarizing the preceding, it may be said that the revolt against and within the dogmatic, established

Church, beginning at the end of the eighteenth century, represented a movement of the same nature and capacity as that of the political, industrial, and artistic revolts that were stirring the Western world at that period. It was a revolution against an old regime, as laden with consequences as those of the Romanticists or the sans-culottes. None of these revolutions have yet arrived at their ultimate destination. It is impossible to predict what their final meaning is for the future shape of our civilized existence. After almost two centuries, however, we can see that the old order is thoroughly disrupted. The churches, regardless of the vestiges of conventional Christendom, are loosed from theological bondage. They find themselves at this time with a rather bewildering liberty of options. What they clearly lack is a cultural expression corresponding to a central belief.

In classical Christianity the cultural response, that is, its liturgy, belonged to a central volume of creed. With the demolishing of a decisive doctrinal position, the modern Church, culturally speaking, has no voice. Its style of worship, varying from parish to parish, far from being a spontaneous expression of a universal belief, is merely an updated, redressed variety of an ancient rite, cultivated as echoes of nostalgia rather than as testimonies of faith.

The secular challenge

The moment the triumphant Church emerged from the catacombs and established itself as a political instrument of power, the question of communication arose. The Christians had to negotiate with opposite camps, the Empire, barbarian tribes, rival religions—they learned to bargain in worldly compromise. Historical communication over the centuries rose from simple and primitive expressions to the most confident manifestations of culture. Culture is nothing but the conveyance of human consciousness in time. Christianity, like other major religions, has been vitally instrumental in this historical communication. It is a part of its pride and glory. But it has had to pay a price for it. The history of Christianity reflects the development of an increasing accommodation to the secular image of prestige.

For the early Christians there was hardly a problem. They could with unruffled if not always elated expectation wait for the end of the world and the second coming of Christ. Apparently they did not always accept Paul's admonishment of Romans 12 with exemplary zeal, but on the whole they lived and behaved so as not to "be conformed to this world." The uniqueness of the soul, for them, lay in its spiritual isolation, and conformity was a sinful attachment to transitory goods. It should be pointed out that the use of the word "world" in the King James translation is not altogether precise. The Greek equivalent is *aioon*, epoch, age (the Vulgate has *saeculum*), and clearly the implication is that eternal life should not be confused with the temporal.

The historical Church has continuously confused temporal prestige with the original message of eternal hope, a tendency for which she has suffered severe criticism throughout the centuries. Before we, too, throw our stones of indignation and chastise the unrepentant pursuit of power, prestige, and luxury, we may do well to recognize that this underlying worldliness is a complicated problem, which several minority groups within the Church have at various times in her history sincerely, though vainly, tried to solve. Nevertheless, not even the most sympathetic observer can depict the record of the glorious cultural Church as a fitting illustration of what Christ and the early apostles had in mind. Ironically, the superb splendor of its outward manifestation seems to obviate the simple message that can be understood as the core of the gospels.

During the nineteenth century, when the basic validity of the Christian institutions was in various ways reassessed, the question of secularity became acute and was brought into focus along with the cultural claims of the

Church. In his lectures at Jena Hegel tried to translate the historical truths of Christianity into philosophical formulations. In religion, he declared, the spirit becomes object. God is essence, that is, pure thinking, but this abstraction, through what Christian dogma calls incarnation, becomes in its alienated form real Self. That is, "human being with a common spatial and temporal existence."

The Church itself represents the objective form of the spirit. Hegel called this the positivity of Christianity in its body of myths and sacraments. In his later lectures on religion at the University of Berlin, he set out to reconcile this external religion with what he thought was the religion of Reason. He found that in traditional Christianity the concepts of God and world were separated. Only his Absolute religion could, in the philosophical Idea, unite belief and philosophical reason. Hegel's "reasonable religion" should not be confused with that of Lessing and other members of the Enlightenment. On the contrary, it represented a synthetic unity of religious consciousness and the traditional Church, a remote conception for the eighteenth-century rationalists. It is obvious, however, that Hegel's absolute form of religion was hard to realize and still harder to practice. Hegel was wholly aware of the decline of the "objective," externally established Church, but he was not concerned with practical remedies. This, to him, lay outside the realm of philosophy.

Christianity in the nineteenth century, the age of nihilism, was inevitably caught up in the historical trend of negativity. The element of negation inherent in Hegel's dialectic logic was purely rational, but creative. For it set its antithetical determinations in continual evolution. His radical disciples used negation almost exclusively as criticism. In the hands of Strauss, Bauer, Feuerbach, or Marx it became an increasingly one-sided negativity without the moment of a redeeming synthesis. In matters of religion, it became simply the stripping away of the religious "objectivity" of myths. The most radical of the left-Hegelian nihilists was Max Stirner, who in *The Ego and*

His Own (1845) set the ultranegative postulate: "I have based my case on Nothing." Nothing exists, not even the sanctity of man, as Feuerbach claimed, not any belief or *ism*, except "my ego."

Negation in this sense is the ultimate, though clearly misunderstood, interpretation of rationalism, which would have terrified Hegel had he known it. Kierkegaard, adopting the dialectic method for his own purposes, lifted the category of negation from its rational roots, elevating it to a total existential experience. It is here that the supreme religious awareness meets the Absolute. Man, however, can only experience this religious Absolute as Nothingness. Kierkegaard's absolute experience of Nothingness, unlike Stirner's whose nihilism was an egotistic end, represents a necessary means toward transcendence. In his *Attack Upon Christendom* Kierkegaard at the end of his life presented the Church as an institutional obstacle standing in the way of true religious life. He impugned the clergy for preaching only the comfortable—"precisely the thing in which our age excels." His task, Kierkegaard thought, was to revise the definition of Christianity, for the Church merely acts as a tranquilizing drug, promoting peace of mind rather than, as it should do according to its original ideals, disquieting the worldly spirit in which man so easily indulges. The core of the work was an assault on the established sacerdotal order, which as "perjurers on the New Testament," exhibited a new paganism. Nihilism, as the highest moment of devotion, turned itself practically against the Church inasmuch as she prevented the exercise of this devotion.

It is against this background that one must try to grasp the predicament of the contemporary Church. Throughout its history, especially during the Renaissance centuries, the motifs of paganism were an integral part of the Christian style of presenting itself. It was not primarily the pagan outside world which in the eighteenth century rose as the arch-fiend, but the paganism of the Church itself which threatened her position. Secularity is by no means a modern feature in the development of Christianity. What has changed, however, is the way in which it is presented. The classical Church, while preaching eternity, believed it could afford the transitory goods and power symbols as well. It was not hypocritical about it either. This attitude was an almost unchallenged result of her dual role of representing celestial hope and terrestrial control. When the latter was defied by assaults from within as well as from without, instead of concentrating on the celestial only, Christianity became more and more concerned with its secular assignments.

It was at this critical juncture that the question of secularity was also raised in the United States, though with less revolutionary vehemence. Theodore Parker, in his discourse on *The Transient and Permanent in Christianity*, pointed out that a clear distinction ought to be made between the ever-changing forms and dogmas of Christianity and what is basically unassailable essence. Resting his case on a passage from Luke 21, "heaven and earth shall pass away, but my words shall not pass away," Parker accused the religion of his age of having set too much store by the accidental forms of religious life, which he called the outward robe, at the expense of the "divine life of the soul." The permanent to him was simply the Christian message of Jesus' love, not "what passes for Christianity with popes and catechisms, with sects and churches," for they chiefly promote the transient.

This sermon of 1841 caused a tremendous stir in New England. But though Parker's was not altogether a voice in the wilderness, his intentions, like the whole transcendentalist mission, remained merely a part of America's golden age of literature. They had no practical impact. This cannot be said of Kierkegaard's thoughts. By the acid chemistry of his own notion of irony, however, Kierkegaard's influence, at least religiously, was precisely the reverse of what he would have liked. Virtually forgotten soon after his death, in the twentieth century he was discovered by those whom he fought most bitterly. The theologians adopted him for their own objectives. Kierkegaard would have shuddered. In his campaign against traditional Christendom he never considered his devastating strategy as a blueprint for theological reform. While Nietzsche advocated the overcoming of man for the creation of the superman, Kierkegaard wanted to overcome the Christian Church for the sake of new religious experience. The affiliation with existentialist thinking by Protestant theologians (and some of their Catholic colleagues) must be something like folding bleach into a cake-mix. The efficacy of this drastic recipe for the Church must be left undiscussed. Historically, however, the absorption of the Kierkegaardian revolution into theology was an utterly irrelevant maneuver.

It started with Karl Barth, who exploits the existential "leap" of transcendence to build his own theology of crisis. Stressing the absolute other-ness of God, and his unique freedom of grace, the dialectic of his theology inevitably leads to an equal stress on the depth of man's misery. Man, therefore, the Christian at least, must valiantly face up to the reality of this utter humanity. This holds true, too, for the teaching of Emil Brunner, who somewhat mitigates the stark element of crisis by allowing at least a partial self-help to man in bridging the abyss between himself and God. In both cases, however, the practical consequences of existentialist theology lead to an intensified involvement in the social and cultural dimensions of religious life.

Paul Tillich, following Barth, conceives this involvement as a courage to acknowledge spiritual despair itself in order to transcend the being in this world. So as "to confirm one's own being," one must be committed to the courage of participation, a noble activity enough in this era of collectivity, or for that matter at all times. Historically, however, one can observe it in the determination of the Christian leaders and seminarians to invade the most unrelated areas of cultural enterprise. Having found it unprofitable to meet the unbelievers with a latter-day Repent-ye! in their lectures, education, periodicals, and broadcast, they prefer to talk cool jazz, show business, or dodecaphonic music. Surely there must be enough specialists around to do this for us, and what is so wrong with expecting theologians to stick to their own field of training? The modern clergyman who feels that he must be truly up to date has frequently become a dabbler in the arts and letters in his incredible lust for secularity. Whereas classical Christianity led culture and molded cultural expressions into a Christian manifestation, today's church leaders follow the secular forms of our civilization and explain them in the pulpit.

The accommodation of the contemporary Church to the victorious secular temper of the time is understandably no less important when it comes to matters of science. The gradual scientification of man's thinking that has spread not merely into his industrialized life, but also into his arts and literature, is inevitably bound to ease its way into theology as well. Biblical criticism by the Hegelian left is still an activity of scholars, though not without widespread repercussions. It was only with the popularization of evolutional theories, however, that the entire Christian community became aroused. The agnostic T. H. Huxley in *The Nineteenth Century* of December 1885 might with plain justification write that the objection of science is not to religion, "but to the bad philosophy under which religion herself is often well-nigh crushed." But this was obviously not the whole story. Thus two years later he wrote in a more biting attack that the theological apologists should consider the fact that "in the matter of intellectual veracity science is already a long way ahead of the churches, and that in this particular it is exerting an educational influence on mankind of which the churches have shown themselves utterly incapable."

In the twentieth century, at least the liberal majority of the Christian world recognizes that, since a battle against scientific predominance is futile, it must come to terms with it. It has bravely submitted the supernatural foundations of its creed to revision. Various ingenious ways and systems have been introduced to update the popular image of the Church and to demonstrate that it can still be a viable institution in the industrialized world. They are epitomized by the attempt to de-mythologize the traditional beliefs, a trend led most predominantly by Rudolf Bultmann. It does not bluntly do away with the wonders and myths surrounding the revealed life of Christ, but rather tries to reinterpret them without being committed to an antiquated acceptance of supernatural miracles. Bultmann in his *The New Testament and Mythology* transplants Heidegger's a-religious ontology to a theological body of thought, and searches for the being of God by stripping off the drapes of psychological, traditional, and historical environment. The bare religious experience then lies not in the once completed historic act of Jesus, but in his continuous revelation in man's daily existentialism. It is here that man, though not being able to know God, encounters the God who is willing to proclaim himself as devine will in nature.

Whatever the merits and future of this streamlined theology, it clearly represents another hookup with the modern network of secular institutions. The Church is naturally entitled to its preferences. It is merely a matter of historical knowledge to see that it is gradually becoming another social agency among the many—and this too is her responsibility alone. No one, however, should deny that Christianity in its secular preoccupation has estranged itself from what it originally set out to do and protect. The popular "honest-to-God" movement may well be crushingly correct in its rejection of outdated, unscientific doctrines, but it should recognize that what it thinks is left of Christianity can scarcely be served up in the traditional liturgy to which it still clings. The old rites, based as they are on ancient chant, Prayer Book, Apostolic Creed, and the presense of altars, sacramental formulas, and vestments have no relevance to the contemporary religious content. Therefore, those radicals who have tried to eradicate the last vestiges of the old ceremonies by introducing the rock 'n' roll or jazz Mass may well be on the right track of history, provided of course that the Church remodels its cathedrals into dance halls and retains its priests as disc-jockeys.

Before the argument grows exacerbated, however, it

should be realized that the Church has virtually no choice but to adjust herself to the secular objectives of the age. Fundamentalism may be practiced regionally, in isolation. In the contemporary trends, however, this has proved to be against the historical pressure, and it can maintain itself only by withdrawal into insular enclaves. The mainstreams in modern Christianity are clearly for an acceptance of the historical changes and thus it has put itself in an abnormal, estranged position. In doing so it has inescapably had to come to grips with the problem of the collective and the process of proletarianization, a predicament to be investigated separately. By joining the mass movement, though belatedly, the liberal churches have acquired a higher status in the popular secular rating. But, no less important, they have invaded the originally atheist social democratic camp. Thus they not only push socialism, in Europe at least, to the middle of the road, they themselves have become fashionable in the eyes of the world. Gone are the days when atheists in reverse fanaticism launched their crusades against the believers. Gone are the days when it was progressive to join movements to destroy religion as the opium of the people. With Christianity thoroughly secularized, the twentieth-century churchman and the socialist act like pleasant neighbors in the same suburban tranquility of respectable and undisturbing compromise.

The popular challenge

This social stabilization of Christianity as part of the newly developing mass consciousness is by no means something to be easily taken for granted. It has its own confusing and self-contradictory aspects, which cannot be overlooked while acknowledging the general trend. In the first place, one must recognize that in a particular sense Christianity has from its founding been a popular religion. But again this is not to be understood as meaning that it originated from a low stratum of society. The followers of Jesus in the broadest sense were a motley collection of fishermen, prostitutes, tax collectors, and, like Luke, professionals. Paul was a rigidly trained intellectual, who infused the early belief with a refined Greek mysticism. The proletarian character of the primitive Christians rests exclusively on the universality which made them outsiders in their own society. Primitive Christianity absorbed the outsiders of the Roman-Hellenistic order.

The Church has never in its history renounced this claim of universality, nor indeed have her separate Orthodox, Roman, and Protestant branches individually ever considered themselves as anything but the representatives of a truly catholic belief. There are enough grounds to think them to be correct. But the nature of this universality has changed. Once Christianity acquired the glamor of an accepted institution, it became part of an elite-driven vehicle of social relations and communications. Its popular character in this transformation naturally diminished visibly. The Church eventually all but took over and controlled the entire social and political system. But though unmistakably elitist, the classical Christian world cannot easily be termed a monolithic order. Its historical attraction lies in the self-contradicting forces and conflicts which testify to its organic vitality. It would be a great mistake to overlook the strong undertows which, from time to time, acted against the established regime. The Cluniac movement in the eleventh century was fundamentally a thrust against the feudal machine. The Franciscans signified not merely a denunciation of wealth but a far-reaching emulation of primitive Christendom. Savonarola's sermons at the end of the fifteenth century catered to the masses of Florence, warning them against the corruptive collusion of Medicis and popes.

When Protestantism entered history, for a while it looked as if the aristocratic structure was going to be ruptured. But the Council of Trent reaffirmed for Roman Catholicism the old tight sacerdotal dispensation. In Eng-

land the Anglican Church, severed from one establishment, joined its own regal and feudal order. Not only
here, but also in various Lutheran and Calvinist nations,
"established" churches were founded to prove that the
rising particularism in Europe at that time did little to
make Christianity into a real popular force. Nevertheless,
the total picture was not without its ambiguous signs.
Luther's idea of the priesthood of all believers had a
democratic ring. Though he sided with the nobles against
the rebelling peasants, in *Table Talk*, his most spontaneous and human utterances, he asserted that the Christian
community were like helpless sheep, since they suffered
from princes and prelates. The Church must endure misery on earth so that she might keep in mind that her
members are banished servants, exiles from Paradise.

The popular origin of the Church echoed vaguely in
the German idea of a national "folk Church," the *Volks-
kirche*, elsewhere confirmed, for instance, in the Netherlands where the established orthodox Reformed religion
was traditionally that of the common man, the *kleine luy-
den*. In addition, in the eighteenth and nineteenth centuries there arose the vigorous ground swells of popular
Pietism and Methodism. In England the dissenting sects
during the Industrial Revolution got a strong grip on the
lower classes.

The overall impression of Christianity in the middle of
the nineteenth century, however, must undeniably be
that of an organization ill prepared to meet the first
shock troops of emerging socialist movements. Socialism
successfully tried to monopolize the cause of the collective, and it was not until the end of the century that the
Church realized its own historical stake in the development of a proletarian order. The major Protestant denominations, as well as the Roman Catholic administration,
became convinced that, unable to beat the radical movement on their own terms, they must maneuver to take the
favorable winds out of the socialist sails. Gradually,
forced by accumulating hard realities, Christianity followed the general increasing mass-consciousness and submitted itself to public consensus.

What Kierkegaard would have thought of this development is of course a matter of speculation and not altogether relevant. Yet one cannot help observing the irony
in the teaming up of precisely those two forces he considered the most harmful to man, the established Church
and the masses. He might have assessed this change as
not at all accidental, and as an inescapable conspiracy of
power. Leaving this subjective view aside, it is clear that
the socialization of Christianity did not come about suddenly. The Inner Mission, started in Germany by Wi-
chern and Fliedner, soon spread to most northern nations
to bring relief in the slums of the industrial cities. In the
United States, the "applied Christianity" of Washington
Gladden merely preluded the intellectually reinforced social gospel of Rauschenbusch. The Roman Catholic
Church in 1891 suddenly shifted from her isolated position, and the encyclical *Rerum Novarum* accepted the realities which social legislation and organized labor were
creating. Roman Catholicism from then on, while retaining an outwardly feudalist administration, in practice
came to terms with the materialist demands of the
masses.

Religious social participation appeared in the field of
politics, for example. From the end of the previous century Protestant and Catholic parties alike, in various nations of the European continent, had made efficient use
of the voting power. Under pressure to offset their left-
wing colleagues, Christian politicians were originally inclined toward conservatism. Soon, however, they learned
the rewarding art of opportunism in the coalition system. Political cooperation, of course, was not the only exigency forcing Christian politics into social welfare programs. Just as the Great Depression made a "socialist"
out of the conservative Roosevelt, so in Europe no leading Christian political party could in these days escape
the responsibilities of welfare legislation and governmental control.

Outside the parliamentary and congressional arena, political Christianity also went to work in the field of public
lobbying and demonstrations. Formal statements were

made by councils, synods, and Vatican spokesmen, or denominational and ecumenical groups of clergymen spoke
out on selected topical problems. In this proclivity,
grown mightily during the last decade, the secularity of
the churches now presents itself in the most unblushing
fashion. If students, teachers, and trade unions protest,
march, picket, sit-in, teach-in, why should not priests and
parsons follow their lead? There can be no doubt as to
the gains made by the major denominations in popular
stature. Nor can it be said that their joining the public
consensus has always been without risks. There have
been cases in which private financial support for church
funds was withdrawn as punishment for a too radical social involvement. But the newly earned popularity which
returns to contemporary Christianity some authority in
material matters has been paid for by the loss of spiritual
prestige.

How is one to evaluate the new role of the Church as
an agency for mass consensus? Under the obligation of
fairness it is mandatory that one see the relative inevitability of this trend if Christendom is to justify its continued claim to universality. While one must so understand
this popular commitment, it is nevertheless equally necessary to recognize that the nature of this catholicism has
changed since it was the unmistakable mark of classical
Christianity. In those times the changing configurations
of the Church were spontaneously pushed forward by the
fears and hopes of the believing people. Today's popular
arrangements, not rooted in belief, are administered and
designed from above by a clerical apparatus, which, instead of representing a people's creed, has now become
the caretaker of nationally shared opinions about law,
justice, and other good public causes. Hegel, when he
was only twenty-five, declared in his *Popular Religion and
Christendom* that a true folk religion only appears when
a civilization is young, and that society in its declining
phase gradually turns to agnosticism. Undoubtedly he
was thinking of the signals and symptoms that were discernible in his own time.

Is it more doubtful, however, whether Hegel detected a Pharisaic tendency in his contemporary Church, as Wilhelm Dilthey thinks. In an important work on Hegel's early writings Dilthey believes that in Hegel's *The Life of Jesus* the struggle with the scribes and Pharisees runs parallel to a similar conflict in the eighteenth century. It may be so, but Dilthey's parallel is not really borne out by the text of *The Life of Jesus*. Nevertheless, the speculation is interesting in view of Hegel's total conception of religion. It also brings out a significant aspect of modern Christianity. It is not helpful, of course, to assert bluntly that the modern priest or clergyman represents the Pharisee. This notion, with its overtones of hypocrite, surely would be an unfair description of individuals whom one does not know, and who, at least from all external indications, seem to have sincere intentions about social improvements.

It would be irresponsible, however, not to suggest the possibility of a neo-Pharisaism creeping into a contemporary religious situation, which in some respects at least is curiously similiar to that existing at the time of Christ. If one leaves out the discriminating factor of hypocrisy, historical Pharisaism appears to have been a serious effort to understand the national needs in a complicated period, and to unify the Hebrew people by religious laws. The Pharisees catered to the populace and were, on the whole, progressive. Their foremost aim was to bring religion to the masses. It should not be forgotten that they constituted a wide variety of factions from the radical disciples of Shammi to those of Hillel, the moderate. That Jesus clashed so violently with them was not so much because of the content of their teachings as because of their methods. Moreover, while Christ's message was universal, theirs was blindly nationalistic. Flavius Josephus, himself trained according to the rules of the Pharisees, in his autobiography called them akin to the Greek Stoics; in the seventeenth book of the *Antiquities of the Jews*, however, he referred to them as "a cunning sect." They were easily embroiled in national politics, plotting against

Roman occupation and the collaborating Herod dynasty, while Jesus remained above partisanship and taught that one should render to Caeser what is Caesar's.

It would appear, then, that in general the historical position of Pharisaism reveals above all an interest in mass guidance and in turning the religious experience, as it were, inside out. Pharisaism, in contrast to Christ's personalized act of love, instigated public action with the by-products of social and political involvement. It aimed at the group, at consensus, and in its political predilections it was not above what Josephus, in *The Jewish War*, termed "artfully insinuating itself" into the favor of rulers who furthered its national concern. If one chooses to speak at all of neo-Pharisaism it is primarily in the field of public action and popular consensus that the connections may be sought.

In Hegel's time, the Christian Church can hardly be said to have embarked yet on public activity; its potential Pharisaism can conceivably appear in the ossification of dogmatic forms. When Kierkegaard, in his *Attack upon Christendom*, accused the clergy of his time of being Pharisees and hypocrites, he had in mind the outward organization and rituals of the Church, which he believed to be paganism exercised under the name of Christianity. In the twentieth century, however, the Church's unabashed embrace of the topical secular causes of the day could indeed signal a determined effort to regain the status of a popular religion. In this she may well succeed. Maligned and dismissed as an outdated superstition in the early decades of this century, after the Second World War Christianity has refurbished its universal image, and has once again found universal acceptance as a viable secular power. Even Communist nations, disregarding Marx's anti-dogma, are paying obeisance to synod, Vatican, and World Council. Apart from political considerations, this is historically justified. For Christianity, having bartered its spiritual and metaphysical freedom for a voice in matters political, has historically joined those powers which by their very pragmatic nature are concerned with the collective and its material needs.

It would indeed be improper to deny the Church the right to her historical options. No more should she deny the observer his right to describe objectively the transformation of an *ecclesia militans,* that is, a Church combating the popular trends, into an organization redesigned to accommodate public opinion. The neo-Pharisaism in the activity of the established churches clearly cannot refer to a possible display of hypocrisy by individual members. It would be highly irresponsible to accuse of insincerity the priests, rabbis, and ministers who go out and assemble for public prayers, public declarations, public vigils, and public fasts. A number of motivations may drive them. Their actions, for instance, may issue from unusual frankness. They may also be part of the general exhibitionist behavior which characterizes our century in every respect.

Since one obviously cannot make general statements about the individual reasons for this new conduct of pastoral care, one should leave out the psychology and concentrate on the indisputable external development. This clearly points to a growing emphasis on administrated crowd action for the benefit of obvious and noble causes, at the expense of spontaneously engendered personal action. There is, of course, a distinction between public and individual justice, as Plato, without using these terms, explained in the *Republic.* We should not, however, blame the Church for ignoring Platonic warnings in matters of religion, nor even for the trend which deviates from the course of her founder, who vehemently fought against a religion of public display. The leaders of official Christianity may well have all the correct arguments on their side. They should not, however, ignore the fact that modern Christians have, rightly or wrongly, alienated themselves from their origins.

Finally, the significant progress of the ecumenical movement and its historical ramifications ought not to escape our attention. It developed roughly parallel with the growing equalization of Western society, visible also in other fields. Although obtaining universal significance only in this century, and more particularly after 1945, the negotiations for religious unity began as far back as 1846 when the Evangelical Alliance set a pattern of "dialogue," which through consecutive council meetings established itself definitely at the Stockholm Conference in 1925. So far, it was an exclusively Protestant enterprise. When, after the Second World War, the momentum grew rapidly, however, and the World Council of Churches became a center of public prestige, the Orthodox and Catholic branches joined the movement, and the familiar story of decisive streamlining began, making the eventual total unification, at this point at least, an almost foregone conclusion.

The ecumenical temper is irresistibly modern in that it agrees entirely with the general trend of merging, noticeable also in the fields of corporation policy and labor tactics. It is facilitated by contemporary man's unique genius for the administration and management of huge, complicated offices. Thus, the unifying movement of the churches is successfully adjusting to the phenomenon of what is called massification, the unmistakable concomitant of a developing proletarian world order. Like political unification attempts—Benelux, the Common Market, NATO, the United Nations—the ecumenical community is still faced with the problem of how to reconcile the entailing conformity with the individual pride of its separate members. Here again it reveals its modernity. It is willing and even anxious to share the basic predicament of the ages: the consciousness of the rift between individual self and collective mass.

While acknowledging the courage of contemporary Christianity in becoming involved in this disturbing situation, one cannot, on the other hand, help suspecting that the fraternal understanding among the erstwhile hostile denominations, and their unifying choice to side with the collective, is partly prompted by the state of insecurity in which the churches find themselves. It is an insecurity aggravated proportionately by the gradual disappearance of the original ideals, hopes, and faith from the hearts of the believers. From the outside at least, it looks as if the success of ecumenical unity coincides strikingly with the general awareness of "the death of God," a thought with which the Church is more and more forced to live.

From a position in the middle of a development that has not yet reached its ultimate form, it would be unwise to make guesses about the future shape and importance of established Christianity. It is hardly unwise, however, to take a firm look at the almost unavoidable externalizing tendency which goes hand in hand with the process of Church unity. The official statements of the various World Councils reflect the administrative skill by which the leading clergy is able to concentrate attention on collective purposes so as to avoid the old-fashioned disputes on matters of principle. Method now becomes principle. Organization replaces creed. The "Evanston Report" on the second assembly of the World Council of Churches of 1954 stresses this abundantly in its efforts to blueprint the new planning. Thus when it recommends that Christians should work for the development of political actions by which people can change their government, or that "a Christian community must act as a conscience for the nation," the principle involved is not such things as love, hope, faith, compassion, and self-sacrifice, but the duty of group organization. The regular interchurch meetings begin more and more to act like professional conventions, where the old emotional conflicts of belief are streamlined away by managerial expertise.

This, under the circumstances, may well be the best that can be hoped for, but it cannot escape anyone's attention that the newly gained security is of a different nature from that of classical Christendom. It is a solidly engineered mechanical framework, unnecessary at that time in the past when the Christian world found its security in the autonomous vitality of faith. It represents a formalized bureaucratic order, in its expanding officialdom reminding us of the sacerdotal establishment which during the Roman Empire maintained itself outwardly, while a miserable band of believers shared their bread, tears, and hopes in the catacombs of the Via Appia.

11

The Intellectual Way of Living

Knowledge or know-how

When we speak about education, we usually think of its immediate utility. Education in the present society has become one of the most attractive topics of conversation; practically all of us are involved in it as students, teachers, or parents. A discussion about the function of the school in relation to the goals of individuals and society, however, is something different from evaluating education in a cultural or historical perspective. For the notion of culture carries with it an unintentional purpose, a particular historical quality that gains in importance as time proceeds. If a man has a house built for himself, his family and neighbors will naturally evaluate the finished product by the available standards of utility. They will judge the house to be good if it serves the purpose of the owner and his family. They will also submit it to their taste, and like the house if it agrees with the standard types of ranch and split-level models.

It is clear, however, that all this has nothing to do with historical culture. We admire the Renaissance *palazzi* in Florence or Hendrik de Keyser's houses on the canals of Amsterdam, not for their immediate utility, nor because they agree so strikingly with contemporary taste. They do not. Their architecture over the years of changing history has acquired a sur-value, difficult to define and describe, yet clearly present. This value does not necessarily derive from the objects themselves, in this case the houses, but from the mind of man which has replaced the contemporary utilitarian judgment with a more or less universal cultural evaluation. The same is true, for instance, in drama. Drama is fundamentally and practically nothing but social entertainment. The Greeks at their seasonal festivals were highly entertained by the performances of *Prometheus, The Persians, Antigone, Oedipus the King,* and *Medea.* Very few Americans of the twentieth century would feel comfortable during an adequate presentation of these plays. But no one would dispute their cultural value. By contrast, the popular successes of Augier, Dumas, Iffland, and Kotzebue in the nineteenth century have not survived historical judgment. Obviously, their once very high entertainment value, being exclusively utilitarian, cannot be transformed into a cultural universality.

Similar distinctions can be made when cultural assessments of education are required. The practical efforts in this field are not made with an eye on the future. They are supposed to meet the immediate needs of the community. Some of the most fascinating educational theories in history, however, enjoyed little practical application in their own or any other time. Plato's ideas on instruction, for instance, are continually referred to as important sources; yet they would never have made much sense in a viable school system, nor do they represent an historical picture of the education in ancient Greece. Their importance is expressed in a sur-value which represents the accumulated historical thinking on their validity. No such transcending meanings are attached to Roman educational thought. It was useful, well organized, and highly adaptable to the political expediencies of the age. The aim of education to Quintilian, one of the significant Roman pedagogues, was to produce the good orator, the wise man who mingled in political action as well as in the discussions of the schools. But for all its practicality, the Roman educational system exercised little influence on later generations. Clearly, the useful in matters of schooling does not necessarily carry with it a great universal value.

Thinking about the present situation, we can probably all agree that there is little point in speculating on the historical role of our own educational thought and its importance for the future. Educators and parents alike are simply facing the task of determining the means of providing today's students with the schools best serving the present social needs. This is not a cultural concern. But one can, and I believe should, analyze the fact that significant changes have taken place in our educational thinking, describe these changes within the social environment, and deduce from them general meanings of a cultural nature. The most conspicuous change in the attitude toward education is expressed in the rather unfortunate conflict between progressive and traditional education which developed during the first decades of this century. Unfortunate, for it has led to very acrimonious and sterile disputes about the supposed superiority of each side. This investigation has no need for such partisanship, usually caused by ignorance about the opposite viewpoint. Nor can we involve ourselves in similar debates about the question of whether the European or the American educational system is the better. Such questions are commonly raised without giving thought to the particular aims and needs that give educational philosophy its ultimate shape. Education can only be as good as the objectives of a society allow it to be. If progressive education serves a different set of desirable objectives from those served by the classical European education, then any comparison in terms of inferior and superior becomes nonsensical.

Great confusions have been generated in this connection by an absence of historical sense in those who try to present the progressive movement as an entirely new program. Dewey himself, although wise and careful compared to some of his followers, did not always put his case in the clearest perspective. His appearance on the educational scene was a great event. His work in this field must be honored as a unique stimulus to the furthering of American ideals. Whatever doubts one may have about the intrinsic merits of his philosophical thinking as a whole, no one can question the value of his contribution to solving the practical problems of education in a mechanizing world. Since he understood the change in modern society, he promoted an educational program that could fit the new needs.

Yet, however much we are indebted to Dewey, there is no reason to overlook the errors he made, which are partly responsible for the confusion among the educators following his trail. Although he pointed to the danger of seeing the old and the new educations as an either-or, the terms old and new already suggested a historical split. In his *Experience and Education*, Dewey was careful to tone down the controversial element, and proposed a combination of the best parts of both systems. The fundamental issue according to him "is not of new versus old education nor of progressive against traditional education but a question of what anything whatever must be to be worthy of the name *education*." Unfortunately, however, even this conciliatory attitude stressed a split which cannot historically be substantiated. Progressive education did not represent a sudden new order. It did not appear by revolution. On the contrary, it developed gradually from new experiences which had ripened since the end of the eighteenth century.

Dewey's first mistake was to ignore the fact that progressive education grew naturally out of the traditional mainstream. Francis Parker, whom Dewey himself called the "father" of the new education, basically promoted the ideas of Pestalozzi, Herbart, and Froebel. Child-centered education is no novelty of the twentieth-century United States. Its historical growth began in the days of Rousseau, only to burst into full power when the child indeed became the center of society. The progressive element is inherent in later European educational thought. The idea of "shared experience" has been alive since Pestalozzi's *Leonard and Gertrude.* In the twentieth century, this idea came to be organized as a means of reaching a massive public. This was a useful approach at a time when more and more people demanded their share in learning. It was equally sound, as Dewey saw, to concentrate on experiences from the present, which are alive and stimulating to the student. But he misunderstood European education when he believed that the teaching of the classics, on which the traditional school lays so much stress, necessarily means a lingering in the past. The mistake may well lie in the American conception of classical culture as being a sort of museum piece to be admired on Sunday afternoons—an heirloom in the attic with a film of dust to give it a dignified look. For the European, however, the classic is the real thing, the standard of life. The French schools teach their Descartes and Racine as the standards of logic and clarity, and the test for every Frenchman's thought and language. Traditional education naturally relies on tradition—not, however, to dwell nostalgically in the past, but, indeed, to open up the future.

The classical approach is sound enough when a given society is stable. But when, in this century, practically all

Western nations are shaken in their fundamental beliefs, and when "total" wars, revolutions, and dictatorial regimes disturb or even destroy the very roots of national traditions, the aims of their education are understandably questioned. The whole relationship of past and future then becomes a matter of grave doubt. It is for this reason that Dewey's stress on the experience of the present proved to be relevant. Especially in the United States, where the national stability through the influx of continuous waves of immigrants had never been fully established, and where the independent character of racial and national minorities prevented the forming of a social and intellectual homogeneity, a deliberate adaptation to the most immediate needs was mandatory. Since the immediate needs lie within the student, understanding the child as an autonomous entity now became the basic purpose. What with Pestalozzi was only a means, in the progressive school became practically an end. The clear beginnings of this tendency occurred as early as the middle of the nineteenth century, when men like Édouard Séguin started to draw practical conclusions from the early thought on the child-centered school. To Séguin, not the teacher but the activity of the pupil set the educational process in motion. The psychological function of the child must be cultivated before the actual instruction could start.

The child thus became the initiator of education, precisely because he was the spiritual initiator of progress, as Séguin's follower, Maria Montessori, believed—perhaps even the generator of a whole new civilization. In her school system, the process of learning is merely self-development. The initiative must remain with the student. Progressive education of the European as well as American variety made the experience of the child the subject of teaching, Indeed, the real difference between the old and the new school lay in the fact that the mature adult experience, crystallized in the subject-matter, was replaced by the incomplete child experience as the center of education. This was mainly a matter of emphasis. It did not mean that progressive education was necessarily against the imparting of useful knowledge to the pupil. But when it came to the practical application of the child-centered theory, the progressive school more often than not tended to neglect the basic subject matter to such an extent that the idea of learning became questionable.

The new education arrived at its peak in the nineteen thirties. Then it started losing its power. It collapsed during the Second World War, and in 1955 when its journal *Progressive Education* ceased to appear, the optimistic illusions about a totally new school culture vanished. Why did the idea of progressive education die? It was timely inasmuch as it saw new social needs in a changed world. It adapted itself logically to the inevitable consequences of the child-centered age. Why then could it not maintain itself as a viable form to prepare students for this changed society?

Part of the answer may be given by the experience of the Soviet Union, where for a while progressive schooling was thought to be the answer to the new proletarian problems. Soon, however, it was replaced by the rigid continental methods which had been part and parcel of the bourgeois era. The Soviet government understands that a competitive age requires a competitive form of education. The Western mind, on the whole, is unwilling or unable to see the real conflict of this century. Roosevelt and Churchill at Yalta epitomized not so much naïveté, as is frequently suggested, but the blindness of the West to the fundamental struggle of our age, which indeed did not end with the fall of Hitler. The Soviets, by contrast, know that their revolution has not yet been settled. Consequently, all their efforts aim toward a clearly defined goal. Their education is part of the progress toward that goal. It is marshaled by the same firm discipline that characterizes the bourgeois school. Western society, with its manifold particular aims, offers no central purpose for its education. Its schools certainly are not aware of the one overriding conflict which historically is shaping this century.

What then is this conflict? What else could it be but the clash of the two principles which have split the consciousness of modern man: the individual and the collective? What else could it be but the struggle for supremacy of the conformist and the non-conformist elements in an increasingly computerized world, the separation of the person from his natural community, which is the very topic of this work? The Communist governments have put their entire faith and resources behind the idea of the collective. The West cannot commit itself one way or the other. It follows opportunities. It believes in rugged individualism, yet fears to accept the inherent quality of the elite. It also believes in egalitarianism. Yet it is hesitant to accept the full consequences of mass organization. So we compromise. But compromise, useful instrument though it may be in matters of diplomacy, is a deficient weapon in fights for life or death.

Progressive education, when Dewey started to formulate it in the 1890's, aimed correctly at a system harmonizing with an egalitarian democracy. As such, it was timely. It was partly invalidated, however, when in the twentieth century democracy itself acquired a different aspect. Without seeing this historic change, any evaluation of the cultural import of our age is impossible. Without understanding that the democratic society has changed into a proletarian society, the failure of progressive education cannot be fully grasped. The democratic order, as Dewey conceived it, was a gentle arrangement of cooperative persons and groups, sharing common experiences. Therefore, education in a democratic society must be based on the give and take of relaxed teamwork. The word "relaxed" was indicative for the nature of this social exchange. It was also the keynote for progressive education. But everyone can see that there was little relaxed sharing in the growing proletarian order which was mobilizing the total population in a gigantic industrial machine. This is precisely what seems to have been happening during recent decades. The egalitarian principle is enforced to the extent that human beings are becoming fragments of bureaucratic and managerial clockworks.

The question for what purpose we are mobilizing ourselves is difficult to answer, especially for the West, where the trend seems to grow outside our control, against our wishes, as an inevitable historical movement. Ernst Jünger, in the 1920's, had an answer. Few of us, however, will have the willingness and courage to face its consequences. Jünger, who was the first to conceive the idea of the total mobilization of the worker, presented it as an inexorable historical development, which is not man's achievement, but which achieves itself. It controls us in the age of masses and machines. The masses and the machines thus belong together, and with them total wars. After the wars of knights, kings, and bourgeois, will follow those of the workmen. They will be of a terrible, rational and relentless structure. Although an anti-Fascist himself, his work was seized upon by the Hitler administration, which made it a part of its opportunist gospel. The collapse of the Third Reich, however, did not end the global armament. One may not want to share Jünger's gloomy outlook, but one must at least admit that a remorseless technological and industrial struggle is taking place, which makes any idea of a gentle and relaxed democracy utterly naïve.

The appearance of the first sputnik in space was graphic evidence that an inevitable struggle for industrial supremacy was going on. The sputnik was the ultimate blow to the last scattered vestiges of progressive education. A general awareness spread over the country that "something has to be done." Among the many stepping forward with suggestions was Admiral Hyman G. Rickover, who in his *Education and Freedom* advises us to return to traditional methods of education in order to compete with the Russians. His judgment is valuable inasmuch as he is professionally in the center of the serious business of building a competitive war arsenal. When the problem of constructing a nuclear submarine arises, and the situation shows an uncomfortable lack of trained scientists, the American education is questioned on the basis of competitive quality. The drastic measure of installing the old disciplinary European education, as the Soviet government has done, is obviously not congenial to a nation where the general consensus rules. Accordingly, from the multi-interested and multi-voiced population there emerges an eclectic sort of education, borrowing ideas from disparate historical and geographical settings.

Nothing could be more natural. Nothing could be more in keeping with the general eclecticism of our time. As traced in this investigation, our whole cultural pattern as it is represented by architecture, arts, drama, design, religion, or education is derived from pluralistic preferences and tastes. It is definitely not the result of a central conviction to which the individual expressions are related. Traditional education aims at imparting as much factual knowledge as possible as a means of training the student to become, for instance, a good French citizen. Or a good Christian. Milton, in his letter *Of Education,* believed that the end of learning was to overcome Adam's fall "by regaining to know God aright and out of that knowledge to love him." We may not be able to see why thorough instruction in Greek and Latin literature, as he proposed, is immediately helpful to "know" the Christian God. But it is clear that in Milton's conception of education all understanding of particular problems leads to the understanding of a central idea.

In a pluralistic society such as ours, a multi-purposed life must require a multi-purposed education. It is then that instruction is aimed at particular "skills" in order to serve a particular vocation. In other words, the idea of knowledge as such is replaced by "know-how." Knowledge in classical education was seen as useful to man's reasoning power. Know-how is what is useful for selected practical activities. This is admittedly a rather schematic presentation of the change. In daily practice the two principles have always been intermixed. But the major emphasis on one or the other clearly marks the difference in the total outlook. This historical shift does not necessarily mean a deterioration. It simply indicates the trend of fragmentation which characterizes our time. This is a cultural aspect. What is most remarkable in this trend, however, is that it sharply contradicts the other growing reality, the massification of the world. Just as the desire for individual freedom runs counter to the trend of conformity, so our disconnected, decentralized aims of life run counter to the historical movement of mass organization. The full significance of our proletarian age lies in the gradual mechanization of our life in contrast to the appetites and desires we display. It clearly manifests a counterpoint of idealistic program and concrete results.

The mechanized nature of our modern schooling will be discussed below. At this point, we can merely indicate the irony of modern education that, while we want it to serve a number of practical and personal goals in the relaxed democratic way, it steers us, in fact, more and more toward a dehumanized mass-product. Summing up what we have found so far, we can say that the matter of education in the twentieth century is a highly self-conscious affair. There is much public talk about education. There are a number of official committees investigating the value of the existing school systems and philosophies, as well as personal reports and evaluations. The reason for the unrest lies in the changed inner structure of society. With basic beliefs shattered, man's interest is decentralized and directed toward a manifold variety of activities which together amount to his conception of life. Education naturally adjusts itself to the pluralistic social outlook. It does so under the philosophy of shared social experience. Almost at the same time, however, it finds itself facing a new situation: the looming behemoth of mass industrialization. The cultural consciousness is split. Education in the West on the one hand must serve the decent human requirements of enlightened democracy, while on the other it must prepare children for a gigantic and ruthless mass organization, which is no more human than a Detroit assembly line. It claims to teach how to enjoy the greatest comfort and prosperity, while unintentionally turning out men and technical devices useful above all for devastation and warfare.

The separation of personal and collective goals, of intentional and unintentional results was unknown in classical education. What was good for the individual was good for the community. There was no self-conscious split between the self and the group, between non-conformity and conformity. Such an awareness occurs at the time when man's purposes of life are no longer fulfilled in coordinated efforts. His educational aims accordingly are no longer directed toward "knowledge" as such, the diet so to speak of reason, but to practical "skills and techniques," in order to make him fit more efficiently into the bureaucratic and managerial circuits.

Educational freedom

Classical education is based on a principle valid for all levels of learning. Its clearly defined teacher-pupil relationship, centering in the authority of the adult experience, within its limitations is equally valid for grade and graduate schools. But the child-centered program of progressive education breaks down on the higher levels, where the problems of specialization enter. It is obvious that here the authority of the selected subject matter and the teacher-specialist demands a disciplinary approach quite in contrast to the permissive attitudes of the progressive methods. This break again indicates the dualistic outlook of modern school training: it sees a secondary education meant for "life," and a higher education for a particular profession.

The problem of alienation thus acquires additional aspects when we turn to university education. If we try to find out what happens to the imparting of knowledge to the maturing student, we are inevitably led to the gaining forces of bureaucracy and business management. Thorstein Veblen, as early as the beginning of this century, emphasized the changed conditions under which academic instruction was taking place. *The Higher Learning in America* in its own way offered profound insights into the gradually estranging nature of modern education. Veblen, while experiencing the expansionist tendency of the modern university, deplored the fact that this expansion was guided by the principles of business which go to weaken the pursuit of learning. For the presumption is that learning is a marketable commodity "to be produced in a piece-rate plan, rated, bought and sold by standard units, measured, counted and reduced to staple equivalence by impersonal, mechanical tests." Scholarly instruction then, from the living, flowing experience which originally determined the teacher-student relationship now, according to Veblen, is reduced to a "statistical consistency, with numerical standards and units . . . which acts to deter both students and teachers from a free pursuit of knowledge, as contrasted with the pursuit of academic credits." If knowledge has become a commodity, it follows that it has to be mass-produced and sold according to standard procedures like any other product. Universities, like factories, are run on the basis of business management. "Under such a scheme of standardization, accountancy and control, the school becomes primarily a bureaucratic organization, and the first and unremitting duties of the staff are those of official management and accountancy."

Of course, at that time Veblen had to exaggerate a point which is only too clear fifty years later. We have to reckon with monstrosities such as the "multiversity" where the problems which disturbed Veblen have only multiplied. To illustrate what has happened culturally to the administering of knowledge, we may look at the manner in which the small insignificant University of Jena at the end of the eighteenth century suddenly became one of the major focusing-points of Germany. In a simple master-student community the arrival of figures such as Schiller, Fichte, Schelling, and Hegel provided the university with a historical fame, because it was they who administered the new learning which was to have a historic impact on society. The modern university, by contrast, is a gigantic department store where standardized knowledge is sold by the pound.

A university president who has analyzed the workings of the modern multiversity, as he calls it, describes this as a city compared to the original university which has a quality of a village with its priests. Without regrets and apprehension he calls it a "knowledge industry," permeating government and business. Proudly he relishes the fact that the production, distribution, and consumption of knowledge accounts for about 29 per cent of gross national product. "What the railroads did for the second half of the last century and the automobile for the first half of this century may be done for the second half of this century by the knowledge industry: that is to serve as the focal point for national growth."

There it is. Comment would only weaken the impact of this statement. We are clearly only at the beginning of mass-produced learning which owes its triumphant existence mainly to its symbiosis with big industry. Indeed, new factories and industrial laboratories are preferably constructed in close vicinity to large campuses. The bulk of the defense contracts go to areas such as California, Massachusetts, and New York where there are clusters of universities. In the total mobilization of the world, the leading schools of higher learning apparently play their more than dutiful part.

Not all educators, of course, find this trend such a glorious path to the future. Not even all the scientists are convinced that the scientific organization of universities bodes well for the healthy growth of education. A noted astronomer believes that the current trend toward mass-education is jeopardizing the position of the university as a research center. The most significant resistance, however, comes from the student community. The recent outbreaks of campus unrest throughout the United States, whatever their incidental issues, all point to the basic fear of being absorbed into a dehumanizing robot system. Students are prepared as spare parts of a machine into which they must fit at the end of their college training. For a youth, coming out of the leisurely atmosphere of the high school, where he is allowed to opinionate freely and led to believe that his personal thought on any occurring problem matters, it obviously must come as a bruising shock to learn that he has not been prepared for the real society in which he is to live and to work. He must inevitably feel that he is suddenly reduced to a mere IBM card in which a remorseless machine punches a pattern. His use and value for society is expressed in a combination of holes.

He also finds out that his teachers are not the reputable scholars whose names he sees printed in the school catalogue, but for the most part inexperienced instructors whose knowledge of Western civilization is only one page of textbook ahead of his own. Teaching, indeed, like learning, is regulated and controlled by the assembly-line method. The best professors of the future will not improbably be those who best fit into the "system." This process can hardly be conducive to great original scholarship. On the other hand, it would be foolish to make hasty pre-judgments of a situation which is only beginning to establish itself. While we may feel that the modern knowledge industry is likely to produce consumer goods rather than independent thinkers, it is also true that the present mechanized system can provide far more soundly competent teachers than ever before. Whereas one may speculate that the modern university is not likely to produce new Darwins, Hegels, or Rankes, it is without speculation that one may say that it has never been so intimately involved in the immediate needs of the entire society.

Instead of worrying about implications for the future, it seems more helpful to face the educational problems as they reveal themselves today. These problems do not primarily deal with questions about the quality of modern education, important though they may be for teachers, parents, and students alike. Our investigation is mainly concerned with the cultural functions of the school, that is, its place in the totality of life, and the question of how and why it changes in this total context. Historically, education has always been linked with human freedom, and most liberal movements have made popular instruction part of their program. Rightly so. The acquaintance with facts and phenomena lying outside one's own local experience teaches the mind to question illusions that the child naturally spins around himself in self-protection against outside forces he cannot otherwise meet. Education then, as a process of liberation, is a continual fight against prejudices. Classical education, by administering knowledge acquired in previous times and crystallized in philosophy and literature, aimed at testing the immature and still uncertain student on the great minds of the past. On the other hand, it encouraged the search for new knowledge. The breaking up of the Scholastic rigidity led, among other things, to Copernicus' revision of the traditional cosmology.

The liberation of human reason does not in the first place depend on the accumulation of facts but rather on the handling of a great variety of judgments which are, so to speak, the nourishment of the intelligence. Traditional education, with its great stress on languages, literature, philosophical and theological systems, and, later, geography, exposed the growing mind to an infinite number of foreign and unfamiliar judgments. American education has, in this respect, clearly been at a disadvantage. In the nineteenth century it served a pronounced isolationist society, self-satisfied with its own achievements. It had no need to look abroad, especially to Europe, which it saw as offering a totally inferior way of living. The reaction, however, set in during the 1890's when the isolationist outlook gradually started breaking up. The educated American of the twentieth century is far more inclined to see Europe and the United States as included in the same cultural unity. But this is mainly expressed in his general support for political cooperation. His education has not really caught up. The number of subjects which the average student carries at the high school and college level is very small compared with that of his European or Russian counterpart. His knowledge of the geography, language, literature, and social habits of foreign countries is embarrassingly narrow. Under such circumstances there is obviously little incentive to question many of the natural illusions which block the mind of the young and immature.

The fact that this isolationist type of education so far has not led to great cultural disasters must in all probability be attributed to the national common sense, the American feeling for fair play, and the ingenuity of creating new opportunities which obviate traditional judgments. Yet precisely this strong asset of searching for new opportunities has led to a curious distortion of the idea of liberty. The liberty of education originally related exclusively to the independence of the mind. The question of practical application was only of secondary importance. Most important was the emancipation of the individual from group convictions and dogmas, be it those of the church, his family, his community, his race, or his nation. This trend started in the Renaissance and was popularized during the eighteenth century by the men of the Enlightenment. When the University of Berlin was founded in 1810, a new era of intense scholarship began. The towering achievements in science as well as the humanities were, if not exclusively, at least chiefly the result of the German *Lehrfreiheit,* the academic freedom of the professors, by which they could handle any subject in any way they chose. German education exerted a great influence on the United States in the nineteenth century. If one wonders, however, what has become of academic freedom as far as subject matter is concerned, the result points to sad decline. Universities offer carefully planned curriculums. They are the result not so much of the academic pursuits of individual professors, but rather of the managerial wisdom of the "administration." Students are deliberately led through "basic" courses, their careers routed along standardized paths. Why? Because in this manner they will be better prepared for the equally standardized job qualifications after college.

If a student is "brilliant," that is, if his intelligence and character seem to fit most pliably into the academic pattern, a great prestige corporation will descend on him and absorb him smoothly into its organization machine. It will offer him a big salary and a bigger future. He may do advanced work at corporation expense. Not surprisingly, his every move and step are henceforth controlled by the firm, his course work charted by the management. The more outstanding the student, the less independent. What has become, one may ask, of the educational philosophy that cultivates individual liberty? The intellectual pursuit, after having freed itself from social restrictions and taboos as well as religious dogmas, now becomes more and more entrapped in the managerial organization. The modern student has bartered away his individual freedom for a new dogma: the belief in the organization. Education for him is a mere preparation for the rigid security of the executive circuit.

The administrative constrictions on the *Lehrfreiheit*, helpful though they be for job preparation and specialization in general, must in the long run be inimical to creative scholarship. Scholarship as a cultural expression is clearly distinct from scholarship as an instrument for teaching. The first produces works whose significance reaches far outside the strictly academic boundaries, works that retain their cultural impact long after their immediate educational use has ceased. In the classical academic structure, great decisive books not infrequently emerged from classroom lectures. Hegel's *Philosophy of History* was such a product of the old teacher-student relationship. Today's scholarship is either separated from the classroom or it is only part of the teaching apparatus. The modern standardized curriculum has naturally developed its own cultural product: the institution of the textbook. The textbook is the pivotal point where industry and efficient school management find each other. It is the reliable guide on the road to conquering grades and credits.

Besides textbooks there is, of course, the writing of academic monographs. In a sense this has become the extension of the grades and credits system on the postdoctoral level. Its cultural significance is curtailed by the mechanical pressure, especially on the junior faculty members, of having to publish for the next promotion. The necessity of writing is thus of a bureaucratic nature —only incidentally one of a scholarly order. The aspiring instructor must take care to write the book which will not antagonize his senior colleagues and which will avoid stirring up controversy. The market thus has become flooded with insignificant books dealing with topics that at best deserve no more space than a fair number of pages in a learned journal. This points to the new pedantry which Jacques Barzun analyzes in his *The House of Intellect:* "Pedantry results rather from intellectual activity which lacks any intrinsic interest and cannot serve another's; which does not merely postpone, but disregards meaning, understanding, interpretation. The pedant is really not looking at the object, but going through the motions of technique he has learned." The squeeze on academic freedom as described here is not of spectacular proportions. This is in a way unfortunate. For in the blithe security of the campus rut, the college teacher will easily blind himself to the true infringement on his independence. Just as the organization man likes to believe that the social and financial opportunities given to him by the corporation are his own free choice, so the academic officer may be inclined to confuse his bureaucratic status with scholarly achievement.

The alienating tendency of educational liberty is a creeping process. It does not occur because there is a decline in a genuine concern about freedom. On the contrary, man's estrangement reveals a loss of independence *despite* an anxious awareness that human dignity and decency must be defended as vital elements of any scholastic program. It must also be pointed out that, by and large, faculties and students show themselves more and more active in manifestations and demonstrations for human rights and adequate working and living conditions for the less privileged citizens of the nation. Even if one allows for a certain amount of hypocrisy in the motivations, the increasing unrest on the campuses is, in its

general appearance, signal proof of an active consciousness of liberty. Yet, it may well be that precisely this almost self-conscious preoccupation with the outward
forms of human freedom indicates an underlying feeling
of social entrapment.

Modern university education somehow seems to have
lost contact with essentials. It is mainly concerned with
immediate consumption, and only secondarily with the
longer and slower process of cultivation. As an industry
producing a variety of useful skills, it functions efficiently, and it has—so far at least—responded well to the increasing number of those who want and deserve to be
trained for leading posts in this industrial civilization.
For this reason there is no need to look down on it as inferior to previous systems of higher education. It is simply different. It serves a different purpose. What is important, however, is to keep in mind that the cultural
value of the product of education has changed as well.
The academic product has taken on the nature of a commodity. It is prepared by a standardized formula. It can
be labeled, classified, and priced. The degree, the graduate, the academic monograph have all become marketable values. The college professor finally is a commodity.
The weight, measures, and constituents of his academic
contents are statistically put on standardized application
forms. Only with this "record" tagged onto him can the
bidding, buying, and selling begin. The "Academic Mar-
ketplace" functions like any other shopping center. It has
the efficiency to be expected in an industrial culture.

The end of humanism

With the general situation drawn, we may take a look at
some related problems of modern education in order to
see the changed circumstances in their full dimensions.
We can, for instance, study some of the remedies that
have been advanced for the ills of our schools. The experts find it difficult to agree on what precisely these ills

are. Some will deny the existence of any ill whatever. But this is not our concern. It is interesting to study the reactions of those who believe that the modern school, to some degree at least, ought to be improved. The Commission of Higher Education, for instance, which President Truman appointed in 1946, was alarmed about the state of American education in view of the potentialities of the total population. Its report, published a year later, was a diplomatic effort to step on as few sensitive toes as possible, but it nevertheless managed to give firm recommendations for a broad program to expand the educational facilities for the masses. Reading through the Commission's findings, one is immediately made aware that in spite of the wide range of this effort the chief concentration falls on the quantitative improvement of education. We come across phrasings such as "education is by far the biggest and the most hopeful of the nation's enterprises," and "To this end [democracy] the educational task is partly a matter of numbers . . . we shall have to educate more of our people." The recommendations emphasized the need for expansion, for more Federal support; in short, the whole remedial formula of the Commission was for more money, more classrooms, more teachers—more education.

Similarly, James B. Conant in a report to "interested citizens," which appeared in 1959 as a sedation for the alarm stirred up by the first sputnik, gave the impression that the quantitative method is sufficient to put the American school system in shape. "I am convinced American secondary education can be made satisfactory without any radical changes in the basic pattern." All it needs is more concern on the local level of parents, community and school boards, harder work for the students, more language teaching, more science, more attention to the gifted as well as the deficient pupil.

Since these recommendations of "more and bigger" came from the experiences of highly informed educators, one must assume them to be the correct answers to the problems of education in the modern society. One might, of course, like to know why in these reports there was no discussion of the alternatives given by more radical critics. One would have liked to hear the moderate reformer demonstrate why the United States should not adopt the stricter and more demanding European system, as Admiral Rickover suggested. The noted educator R. M. Hutchins attacked the President's Commission for its emphasis on expansion and its lack of revolutionary vision. "What America needs, what the world needs, is a moral, intellectual, spiritual revolution. Higher education in America fails unless it does what it can to initiate and carry through this revolution. This revolution will not be assisted by the infinite multiplication of trivial courses, of buildings, students, professors, salaries, or of colleges and universities. It will come only when the educators of America are willing to admit that the revolution must come and that they must make their contribution to it." How must one meet such calls for radical overhaul?

Let us begin by admitting that these cries for revolution come from sincere minds thoroughly concerned with the intrinsic purposes of life and intelligence, and totally convinced that today's education is inadequate to fulfill those purposes. Inasmuch as they reveal the consciousness of intellectuals experienced in assessing the discrepancies between philosophies, practices, and results of education, they should be listened to. Their words should be weighed and not omitted from the discussions about the improvement of our education. The question must be raised, however, of whether the idealist's vision of moral and intellectual revolution does not overlook the real temper of our time. In urging drastic revision of the standards for quality, it goes against the present trend toward numbers and massification. This trend is not a human invention or a fad. It is an inevitable historical development which cannot be arrested. Quality is the ideal of an elite. In the proletarian order which we have entered, the ideal is numbers. There is little point in arguing about the question of whether this change is for the better or worse. The importance lies in recognizing the historical process. There is the simple fact that the demand is for an increasing quantity of trained and educated men. The "knowledge industry" is not a deliberate contrivance from above. It has grown naturally from the demands of a mass society. It must meet the standardized needs of the consumer, like the assembly-line technique of Detroit. One would be foolish to complain sentimentally about such things as the "loss of identity." The whole tendency of the Industrial Revolution since its beginning at the end of the eighteenth century is, culturally speaking, one of leveling. With industrialization and computerization ever expanding, the leveling of values and identities is bound to take on inhuman proportions. If one wants to make mass education work, it is helpful not to have illusions about the possibility of stopping the equalizing forces of our culture. Education on all levels will be wise to meet the challenge of numbers and masses and realize the exigencies of our hardware society.

Whereas modern education must serve the mechanizing world, and do so forcefully and convincingly, it will defeat its own purpose if it fosters any illusions about cultural glamor. It is only natural that the compromising human mind seeks to serve the master of nuclear and electronic technology as well as the master of classical knowledge. But a technocratic order hardly brooks compromise with poetic ambiguities. It does not mean that the schools ought to give up the teaching of the humanities. They simply must be taught as luxury subjects, and in such manner that they help the student to understand that, attractive though they may be, they have no bearing on practical modern society. This is a harsh stand which many educators will find rather intolerable. But if one sees the extent to which "scientific" principles have intruded into the philosophies of art, music, literature, or history, how the precision of technical skills has become the predominant characteristic of modern scholarship, and how exactness and scientification tend to be the major concern of modern analytic philosophy, one gets some indication of how the humanities have come to accommodate themselves to the scientific mind. Only by so doing can they make sense in a scholastic program.

The increased interest in quantity and the growth of mass-power and of total industrialization go hand in hand. Why they should coincide may be difficult to explain satisfactorily, but the historical change cannot be denied. No education can serve the community ideals of a past era. It will not do to transplant an attractive concept of education from the nineteenth century and urge each other to cultivate it. The cohesion of the future community can only survive if a gigantic mass supply fulfills the massive needs. If our education is to serve these needs it has to play the game of numbers and quantity. Inasmuch as this implies an increased dehumanized use and management of intelligence, we must naturally dislike the new educational purpose. But until the expanding mechanization of the world is arrested, education has no recourse save to prepare minds on the conveyer belt.

Although the process of mechanization is related to the predominance of the element of quantity, it appears as a separate aspect in matters of education. Unsurprisingly, not the faculty but the students have reacted violently against the streamlining of the educational apparatus. For undergraduates, naturally, have not yet completed their training for the technocratic rut. Thus during the riots at Berkeley, California, in 1965, students complained about being treated as mere cogs in a ruthless education factory. In contrast, according to a report in *The New York Times* of April 23, 1965, college registrars and admission officers at a convention in Chicago defended the computer as "the best friend a burdened campus administration ever had." The computer will clearly stay in the university. It is likely to increase its sway over more and more school administrations.

The machine is not only taking over the bureaucratic system of the school, it is gradually mastering the art of teaching as well. Classroom tools are probably as old as education itself. But the sophisticated machine, replacing

the personality of the teacher, so to speak, is a new phenomenon of the industrial age. The fantasy of Swift could
produce one, of course, long before the actual thing was
invented. In the *Voyage to Laputa*, Swift described how
Gulliver visited the Academy of this land, and in the department of "speculative learning" attended a demonstration of a teaching machine to improve "speculative
knowledge by practical and mechanical operations." By
this elaborate contraption, handled by forty students,
"the most ignorant person, at a reasonable charge and
with a little bodily labor, might write books in philosophy, poetry, politics, law, mathematics and theology,
without the least assistance from genius or study." Swift
was in no way satirizing the possible deficiences of his
contemporary education, nor should we use his playful
imagination to ridicule our own. But the pride of the
Laputa professor in his contribution to the mechanization
of learning disturbingly resembles the joyful confidence
of many a present-day educator in the increasing prevalence of mechanical tools in the schools. High schools not
infrequently treasure their mechanical equipment as a
status symbol of "good" instruction, perhaps without having an essential use for it. Often the projectors, slide-
machines, and electronic apparatus function as a shield
for inadequate teaching. Professional evaluators are inclined to doubt the quality of a school if it cannot
present a list of teaching machines. The increasing scientification of modern instruction could be no better epitomized than by the triumphant ascent of the language
lab.

There is clearly no more reason to be proud of mechanical equipment than there is need to be ashamed of it. It
is only natural that in a technological age the simple
school aids of yesterday should become elaborate devices, and that the demand for mass education should
produce new means to reach the new audiences. Educational television, for instance, can under certain circumstances efficiently fulfill new needs. The point here is not
so much to evaluate the inevitable influence of mechani-

cal education as a disaster or a savior, nor even to take a stand between the two extremes. The importance, it seems, lies primarily in recognizing the unmistakable fact that with the mechanization of our social existence the schools are bound to act accordingly. If we, however, do not want to dismiss the new educational techniques when they are clearly serving new compelling situations, neither have we reason to hide from ourselves the fact that in the natural teacher-pupil relationship they have estranged an essential human factor.

The concern about this tendency is by no means new. Pestalozzi, even before the Industrial Revolution had hit the continent of Europe, deplored the mechanical routine of the factories which he found harmful for the development of men. In his book *Popular Education and Industry,* his concern led to plans for an industrial education which might prevent the dehumanizing effects of machine labor, Pestalozzi was naturally unable to foresee the true nature and potential of the new technological order. His brave attempt to reconcile the "two cultures" for the sake of basic human values now looks naïve when we contemplate the ever-widening split between machine and humanity, between quantity and quality, between collective and individual. It would be infinitely more naïve, however, for us to cultivate the illusion that this chasm does not exist, and that indeed we should not rather direct our teaching toward this very reality.

Another frequently uttered apprehension revolves around the often seemingly futile nature of modern scholarship. Although we are all distrustful of comparisons, in particular when they relate our time to what seems to us unattractive historical periods, we keep reminding ourselves of our Alexandrian habits. We like to ignore the vast differences between that age and ours, and single out the curious similarities. Indeed, Alexandria's streets form a practical gridiron pattern. The Ptolemaic culture was one of museums and libraries rather than one of spontaneous arts and letters. It invented professional scholarship. Its striking representatives were grammarians and commentators. It also happens that at that very time when poetry, art, and philosophy were badly lacking, mathematics and science soared to unknown levels of achievement. E. M. Forster, in *Alexandria,* believes that the third century B.C., from the viewpoint of science, was "the greatest period that civilization has ever known—greater even than the nineteenth century A.D." To this he adds, rather gratuitously, "it did not bring happiness or wisdom: science never does."

Comparing civilizations is, of course, not an altogether fruitless pastime, but since the hazards of misleading conclusions in this method are so obvious, it seems that an analysis of the contemporary scene will be far more instructive if it can be made by using the standards of the present urgencies and exigencies. There is no denying that the traditional scholarship as a cultural fruit of education today tends more and more to be reduced to a mere instrument of teaching. No doubt, ours is a period of footnote doctors, concerned with techniques rather than discoveries. We all prefer puny truths to adventurous visions, and like Callimachus, the pedant-librarian under Ptolemy III, we think that "a big book is a big nuisance." But we must understand that our pedantry, if pedantry it be, is not merely a petty attitude, but a necessary requirement for the precision and detail without which our highly professionalized society would not function properly. Granted that profoundly original scholarship is badly impeded by our stress on technicalities, it is clear that the smooth-flowing system can respond more readily to the demand for a great number of competent professional instructors. This is not the place to ask whether one is worth the sacrifice of the other. The historical change must be observed. The difference in the eventual cultural product must be acknowledged.

Connected with the complaint about our supposedly Alexandrian futilities is another: we are behaving like new Sophists. Again one is in the dangerous field of comparative history, which is mined with explosive emotional contents. Through Plato's insistence, the Sophists have acquired a black mark which no attempt at reevaluation seems able to erase. Obviously, if we take the term Sophist with its usual by-meanings of specious and captious reasoning, we may freely dismiss the charge that we are practicing their art. But if we see the Sophist teachers as a part of the Greek Enlightenment and follow Dilthey's judgment—that, although they positively represented the idea of progress, they still expedited the fall of Greek society—we may well have a point of reasonable contact. Not, indeed, that we ought to jump to conclusions and promote the idea that we too are therefore hastening our decline—we know nothing about this. Nor, inversely, should we blindly assume that our advanced educational techniques must necessarily produce greatness, happiness, and glory.

The Sophist was chiefly the type of professional who, for a fee, wanted to impart practical know-how to young people in a complex society. As such, his best representatives were just as useful as today's college teachers. There is nothing wrong with professionalism at a time when all skills and professions are unionized and protected from possible unreliable workmanship. We may as well realize that the age of the genius-amateur of the caliber of Leonardo da Vinci or Goethe has irrevocably gone. Nor can we hope to cultivate the versatility of Leibniz, Hegel, or Wundt. A far more equalized and streamlined teaching apparatus is obviously needed in our highly controlled scientific age. The diminished chances for the extremes in quality must be counted as gains and losses.

The cultivation of the "professional" is an inevitable development, and in a sense a necessary one, in an increasingly complex world. The *cult* of the professional may be just as inevitable an extension, but as a symptom it should not escape our attention. What it symptomizes we may never be able to agree upon, but that does not mean that we should take it less seriously. The cult of the professional has changed the athlete from a man who seeks to balance mind and muscle to a performer of stunts, a slugger, a beater of statistics. While the academic mind is easily persuaded to assess the cultural change in the stadium, the alienation of his own pursuit from the original aims of scholarship would be no less striking to him if he dared to face it. Not that he is out to set records. Not that his work can in any outward sense be related to the sports page. But just as the experience of the total fullness of sports has been replaced by the concentration on specific feats, so the present-day scholar, far from being able to learn (or to teach) from the full experience of knowledge, isolates himself in the smallest details of problems.

Thus the legitimate claim of specialization has changed. Essentially, specialization is a very old function in academic and non-academic professions. It is a token of advanced knowledge; it implies that a man *because* of his thorough all-round training is able to study a separate area. Thus we can assume that a heart specialist relates the special data of his examination to the whole human body. To continue the metaphor, the modern specialist scholar is more like a dentist who completes his repair jobs with little more knowledge of the body than has the patient himself. This does not make the dentist or the scholar less reliable in our eyes. Their specialization is merely of a limited order. It clearly belongs to the category of skills and techniques; indeed, the modern graduate schools have become vocational training centers. The college professor mentioning his "field" more often than not implies his inadequacy in the full range of his own discipline. When a historian explains that he is a specialist in eighteenth-century French institutional history, it may mean that he cannot take responsibility for answering questions, say, about Joseph II, William Pitt, Marivaux, or Lessing. Specialization thus serves more and more as an apology. Instead of a claim to knowledge, it has become an excuse for ignorance.

The nineteenth century was, among other things, an age of education; of *Bildung*, as Burckhardt said, using a term which includes a wider range of cultivation and sophistication that the word "education." For Burckhardt, however, the wide expansion of *Bildung* was a tragic event in the Western world. In 1844, he believed that growing corruption, infecting with "inward lies" even those who had a fundamental integrity, must be attributed to popular education. Why this should be so, he did not explain. But he cursed the trend of universal education as a "fad," building daily a structure of commonplace ideas, which in reality are only illusions of knowledge. Knowledge held by a conformist group is hardly creative, since it does not spring from a personal, original search. It results in a tedious monotony of commonplace truths.

Burckhardt, of course, spoke from an aristocratic, academic height which must be totally unrealistic in the twentieth century, when entirely new requirements of massive and technocratic expansion have become essential. An entirely new type of education has to serve a world in which expansion has changed from an accidental product into the ideal goal. The question of whether Burckhardt's ideal learning is better than ours is immaterial here. Karl Löwith, who saw the nineteenth century in the widest context, described the change as one from a humanist to a political instruction. This is somewhat confusing, inasmuch as the political nature of the various nations differs widely in degree and kind. Better is Löwith's alternative "realistic" education, which conveys its pragmatic usefulness. The humanist conception of schooling, in spite of what seems to contradict this in Burckhardt's words, was of a popular scope. It was rooted in the ideal of humanity as Herder taught it at the end of the eighteenth century. It was probably the noblest cultural idea envisaged by man, since it aimed at the highest achievement of human freedom, which was to ignore all borderlines of nations and classes. Ideally it was the climax of the humanist tradition which had given Western civilization its historical status and stature. Around 1810, when Wilhelm von Humboldt established a new educational system which was to affect the learning of most of the continent of Europe, including Russia, and the United

States as well, he did so by formalizing the ideal of mental freedom. As set forth by Herder and expressed, for instance, in Schiller's "aesthetic" education, this resulted in the cluster of nineteenth-century geniuses from Hegel to Nietzsche. In appealing to the highest possible achievement it obviously showed a definite elite quality, which modern man, rightly or wrongly, equates with undemocratic attitudes. On the other hand, it was also the most democratic type of education, in a sense, since its underlying principle of the *Volksgeist*, the generating popular creative imagination of the people, was a factor operating beyond any consciousness of class prerogatives. By ironical coincidence this humanist ideal of freedom flourished in nineteenth-century Germany precisely at a time when an astounding lack of political liberty was apparent there. It reminds us that, in the complicated counterpoint structure of history, conflicting lines of development must be recognized—lines that defy making sweeping one-sided judgments.

Be this as it may, the humanist ideal collapsed shortly after it bore its fullest fruits. In the first place, the nationalism growing wild in most countries late in the nineteenth century destroyed the real cultural potential of the *Volksgeist*, which converted the idea of people from a historical creative force into a political limitation. To what extent state-controlled national isolationism can lead to cultural suffocation, we know from the dictatorial orders in Fascist Italy and Germany, as well as Communist Russia.

The humanist ideal of education aimed at the highest mental achievement through the cultivation of the individual. The common interest cannot be better served than by setting up an ideal standard which only the nursing of individual potentialities can approximate. By contrast, the proletarian society wants the largest possible common achievement. Instead of the highest personal brilliance, it aims at the largest distribution of average useful knowledge. This does not necessarily have to imply the vulgarization which the nineteenth-century bourgeois mind feared and predicted. Nor is there any reason to ridicule the often unrestrained eagerness of the lower classes in their pursuit of learning, as Flaubert does in his last novel. The title characters of *Bouvard et Pécuchet*, little pedestrian office clerks, are let loose in the world of philosophy, archeology, chemistry, and history where they romp like hogs in a rose garden. Though they are common enough types in the modern "house of intellect," it would be a gross distortion to see them as the true representatives of expanded education as we know it. The proletarian style of instruction has already produced several waves of solidly trained generations. Admittedly, the lines are not yet clear-cut. There is, though in rapidly decreasing measure, a good deal of overlapping. The old elitist strands somehow persist in the fabric. Two aspects seem to stand out simply and clearly: while the expansion and popularization has, in its solid results, vindicated itself beyond all ridicule, it has estranged itself from the classical humanist freedom of mind. It is an administrative institution, routing the student along predetermined tracks which lead to secure positions.

It must be reiterated with some stress that the distinction between the proletarian and humanist era ought not to be taken dogmatically. History moves gingerly and almost unnoticeably, until, sometime after the starting point of a trend, minds come to put it into intellectual relief. The starting point often occurs in obscurity, anyhow. On the other side, millions of fairly intelligent people do not take notice of an historical development during the first two or three centuries of its progress. It would be folly to analyze the proletarian type of education other than in cautious and tentative terms, always keeping in mind that many are unwilling to accept that anything has basically changed since the Founding Fathers or the French Revolution.

It is in this perspective that an evaluation of the present educational purposes and achievements cannot be given in distinct approving or disapproving terms. Much will be won if superannuated aspirations and illusions about restoring past glories can be shed. The pressing requirements of schooling are no longer related to the original principle of training the individual for an ideal in the infinite. Education in the modern sense is detached from its classical roots. It has numerous limited goals which can, with fair effort, successfully be fulfilled. It is a type of education that from time to time seems to be hanging in the air, philosophically speaking. But once its new characteristics are acknowledged, and its limitations accepted, we can better understand the efficient service which today's gigantic educational apparatus renders in the industrial order.

In other words, the fact that education, as a viable system, is divorced from the human ideal which the Western world has traditionally set up is a serious historical factor not to be glossed over and ignored. But exactly a firm awareness that this factor does exist will aid the mind of twentieth-century man in facing and using the new opportunities, no matter how limited and mechanical he may recognize them to be. Nietzsche, following Burckhardt's track, viewed the expansionist trend of the contemporary education with dismay and horror. The popularziation of schooling, he believed, inevitably implies a disastrous leveling and shallowness which ultimately must lead to "barbarism." We, who have seen the egalitarian process at work in education for more than a century, may have to agree about the leveling aspect, but reject the conclusion that popularization and barbarism are of necessity causally related. On the contrary, the managerial "system," which has everywhere become the established practice to realize massive education, is with all its glaring deficiencies probably the only way in which to harness the conflicting drives in this pluralistic age, and to prevent it from disintegrating into real barbarism.

Statesmen are not produced by schools . . . they represent the ethics of a people.

Jaspers

Liberty, like equality, is a word more used than understood.
James Fenimore Cooper

What is the value of political freedom, but as a means to moral freedom?

Thoreau

12

The Political Way of Living

The law of equality

When in Melville's tale "Benito Cereno" the captain of the American sealer climbs aboard the Spanish slave ship, the stage is set for a series of frightening mystifications. These Melville relates with so much narrative effect that one hardly needs an added bonus of "meaning." The symbolism, as is characteristic of symbolism, appears in any case to be elusive. Most literary critics have been prudent enough not to commit themselves too wholeheartedly. A few of the less careful, however, have insisted that the story represents an encounter of the new, innocent American mind with the corrupted state of the old world.

Such a rather chauvinistic interpretation seems the more unwarranted since it conveniently ignores Melville's own complete lack of patriotic ardor. It would be better, it seems, to leave Melville's story alone; it can easily stand on its own narrative merits without the added benefit of professional exegesis.

Yet "Benito Cereno," it must be admitted, does raise an historical, political question. Although it is highly unlikely that the author deliberately meant to infuse a political motif, nevertheless there is no denying that the story essentially deals with revolt and the problem of authority. This problem in the nineteenth century cut across the boundaries of Old and New Worlds. Melville's thematic emphasis on the motto "follow your leader" indicates that the attention should be focused on the aspect of leadership. The rebellion of the slaves against the Spanish captain and his crew has created a situation from which emerges the haunting question: Who is the ruler? Is it the captain hopelessly abandoned to the will of the mutineers? Or is it the crowd of mutineering slaves who, incapable of navigating, must force Benito Cereno and his officers to stay ostensibly in command?

The problem of authority became acutely alive in matters of public government during the last two centuries. It is abundantly discussed by political scientists and political historians, and one may assume that through the treatment of daily and weekly newspapers the ins and outs of popular government have become common knowledge. From our cultural point of view, which is seeing the product of a historical society, the problems of authority are predominantly set by the struggle between man and individual, between individual and group, authenticity and conformity. The exaggerated stress on the struggle of classes leaves much unaccounted for in very stratified nations such as England, the Netherlands, or Denmark, to name a few. In the development of socialization there, violent class struggle has played a negligible role. In these countries, the gradual advance of social protection and control in contrast to the scene in, for example, Italy, Germany, or Russia, has made the notion of struggle inadequate. Especially when one turns to the United States, where one of the most interesting developments of socialization is taking place (and possibly the most decisive one in modern history), the dogma of class struggle is to a great extent, though not altogether, irrelevant.

Clearly the struggle between individual and group is not a spectacular revolt, replete with barricades and bloodshed. It is centered in awareness and expresses itself indirectly in the terms of intellectual history. It betrays itself in the products of nineteenth- and twentieth-century culture. That is our topic, those are our sources. The struggle of the classes *is* relatively important. But it explains only a limited part of the cultural problem, it merely covers political ramifications. The separation and subsequent antagonism of individuality and socialization, on the contrary, is comprehensive.

The first awareness of the political threat of the group appeared during the revolutions at the end of the eighteenth century. Schiller, who designed his "Aesthetic State" in 1795 as a direct result of the impact of the French Revolution, was disturbed about the lawless masses. In the fifth letter of his *Aesthetic Education* he viewed the populace as a force "rushing with uncontrolled fury towards their animalistic satisfaction." These rather inflated feelings were a reaction against the activities of the street crowds, first in 1789 at Versailles and Paris, and three years later in connection with the death of Louis XVI.

Schiller here represents the fear of mob rule. But what is mob rule? It is not a scientifically definable system of government. In history, it has no place among the various forms of state organization. It surely does not deserve such a scientific designation as ochlocracy. Mob rule at its most concrete shows itself as a revolutionary operation always of a transitory nature. As an expression it exists mainly to denote aversion, and the nineteenth-century man of the ivory tower, Flaubert for instance, became easily worked up about the threat of mob rule. But it has no real claim to legitimacy. In history it has chiefly functioned as a threat—which counts. Plato's republic could hardly have been conceived without the fear of the masses. Nor could Schiller's *Aesthetic Education,* for that matter.

What is far more important is the real incorporation of the masses into legitimate governmental power. This touches on the problem of how to safeguard liberty without developing a state of violence. It is an old problem. Plato wrestled with it. For us it has again become historically acute, and it is indeed necessary to see the issue in historical perspective if one wants to avoid the wild sloganeering with terms such as liberty or democracy, so uncomfortably fashionable these days. The fear of the masses, inasmuch as it is not merely a reactionary shield, but a sincere concern about the future of a reasonably founded society, springs from the repugnance for violence as a means of obtaining liberties. This concern is not primarily related to the class struggle. In most cases it represents an awareness of total humanity, and is brought forth by the clash between individual and group.

Historically, the need for democratic equity in Western society arose first during the Renaissance when man's mind awakened and independently began to probe the confines of authority. Although the first intimations were stirring in the late Middle Ages, it was especially the Reformation as a form of Renaissance thinking which was responsible for the early theories of democracy. Not that Luther or Calvin, in attitude or practice, were themselves important standard bearers for new liberal thoughts on government. But such novel conceptions as the priesthood of all believers, for instance, clearly indicated the basis of equality on which from then on social institutions were more and more going to be built.

Equality for the early Protestants was a bond which held the people together against the destructive forces of despotic government. John Knox, in his first and second *Blast of the Trumpet Against the Monstrous Regiment of Women,* challenged the bloody absolutism of Mary Tudor in asserting the sovereignty of the people. His postscript to the *First Blast* of 1558 makes it abundantly clear what, according to him, the rights of the people include: "But if either rashely they have promoted any manifest wicked personne, or yet ignorantly have chosen suche a one, as after declareth himself unworthie of regiment above the people of God . . . most iustely may the same men depose and punishe him . . ."

In France the Huguenots brought forth similar pronouncements. They reacted to the massacre of St. Bartholomew with vehement theories of civil disobedience, thereby reversing Calvin's instructions. The tracts of Beza and the *Franco-Gallia* by François Hotman translated the freedom of Christian man into formulas of resistance against monarchical tyranny. As such, they had a profound influence on later developments. As early as 1581, concrete action resulted in the abjuration of Philip II in the Netherlands, still a mildly rebellious act compared to the later regicides in England and France.

The democratic quality of these early statements was, of course, only of relative value. On the whole they must be seen as merely preparatory steps. Yet the conceptions of a people's compact and of the sovereignty of the people were clearly present. In George Buchanan's *De Jure Regni Apud Scotos* (1579), the emphasis was less on a particular form of government than on the desired equity of administration. Here the political considerations were already beginning to detach themselves from religious feelings. It is especially in Althusius' work, however, that one can find a methodically arranged political theory. In fact, the *Politica Methodice Digesta* of this German Calvinist represents the first basic treatise on modern political science. Published in 1604, it confirms how the idea of authority vested in the popular community had at that time entrenched itself. In the wording of the third edition the author contends that the people have the power to establish the right of national sovereignty. "This right of the nation, or right of sovereignty, does not belong to individual members, but to all members joined together and to the whole associated complex of the state."

The initial theories on national sovereignty and popular rights were of seminal importance for the maturing of a parliamentary system in seventeenth-century England. Locke's *Second Treatise on Government* was the manifesto of the Glorious Revolution. Historically, it climaxed the developing consciousness of individual rights as natural and inalienable attributes. Natural liberty, to Locke, was to be free from any superior power and to have no other authority than the law of nature. In society the liberty of man "is to be under no other legislative power but that established by consent in the commonwealth." Freedom of man under the government meant to be able to appeal to a standing rule, common to everyone.

Individual liberty, so vigorously championed in Locke's exposition, was a logical result of natural law, the axiomatic substructure of his entire theory. Locke never questioned his fundamental beliefs. Cartesian doubt never troubled his mind. Natural law to him was self-evident. Reason "is plain on our side that men are naturally free." That settled the question for him. But does it?

The strength of Locke's manner of discourse was its charming superficiality. He had little grasp of philosophical intricacies and less sense of historical continuity. With blithe confidence he skimmed over disturbing problems to land on his favorite vantage points. His confidence rested on a firm belief in common sense. And common sense he had in abundance. It was the cause of his great influence on the political re-thinking of the eighteenth century, when his thought dominated the French Enlightenment, and shaped the American type of democracy.

A more profound and reflective mind could not conceivably have brought forth this highly useful and acute instrument for political action. Plato's *Republic*, with its uncompromising penetration into stirring metaphysical and human problems, has no politically viable applicability. Common sense prevented Locke from getting caught in the shades and transitions of speculative thought. His was a guideline to practical solutions. He had the temper of a physician, interested more in the ills of society and their cure than in the nature of society itself.

Naturally, society plays an important part in the *Treatises on Government,* as is indicated by the frequent use of such terms as consensus, commonwealth, the people. But at no time does Locke seem to feel the need to analyze the relationship between the individual and the consensus. When the question arises as to who is to judge whether a prince or a legislative body acts against the will of the nation, the answer is simply "the people shall be judge." But who are the people? To Locke society is merely the totality of individuals, and individual judgment carries over to the collective. Locke never envisioned the possibility that individual judgment might lose its character when amalgamated into the consensus. Or that the individuality of the individual might change when conformed to common judgment.

In this, Locke's philosophy is fundamentally contrasted to Plato's examination of political society. Inasmuch as Locke and Plato existed in entirely different ages and social circumstances, it verges on the nonsensical to compare the two. Yet it is also true that the work of both was a response to what they understood to be tyranny. The Republic is meant to be a commonwealth organized on the principle of justice. It is precisely by appealing to the concept of justice that Plato tries to establish the ground for the individual on which he does not have to lose his authenticity, while still serving within a coherent community. One does not have to accept Plato's solutions to see the importance of the attempt. Justice to him is the cement that will bind humanity if there is an understanding of that basic ingredient which all human beings have in common: authenticity.

How can this human understanding be practiced? Plato's answer: by seeing justice not as a vaguely ethical attitude of "giving each man his due," but by realizing the precise contents of justice. To Plato man is just when he does not take other people's belongings. Justice means not to interfere, but rather to concentrate on one's own assigned task. This clearly is anathema to our modern conception of maximum intrusion into our neighbor's privacy. But it should be noted that Plato stresses a safeguard against tyrannny overlooked by Locke, namely the freedom of abstaining, the liberty of constraint. By using the notion of *people* as a judge, the autonomy of individual judgment tends to become undermined and the vital individual resilience to slacken under the monolithic bulk of what Plato calls "that large and powerful animal," the masses.

At one point, however, Locke approximates Plato's view. In his exposition of the requirements for an equitable commonwealth, Locke stresses the conception of property. Like Plato, he considers human belongings to be of a physical as well as a mental order. A century later the bourgeois of the French Revolution was to give the notion of property, as a central constitutional right, an exclusively materialistic value. But for Locke it still represented a wide range of attributes, such as "lives, liberties and estates." God has given the world to men in common. "He gave it to the use of the industrious and rational —and labor was to be his title to it."

Again the relationship between the common good and individual right was not explored. The concept of labor, so vital and central in the exchange of individual and collective, was not at all recognized as a crucial problem. This had to wait until the arrival of Hegel in history. By replacing Plato's key notion of justice with that of equality, Locke rid himself elegantly of a good number of harassing problems for the benefit of a clear-cut purpose, which in the coming centuries was to be realized with varying degrees of success.

Equality is a clean scientific device for the arrangement of a fairly democratic society, in which power is more or less evenly distributed. But this concept bluntly dismisses, even prejudices, the Platonian justice. Equality is not concerned about the "just act" of noninterference, of not infringing on the other man's belongings. This interference with other people's business (*allotria* in Plato's terms) undermines human dignity. *Allotria* is what is alien. Thus, injustice is alienating a part of the other person's authenticity. The twentieth-century trend of conformity in Plato's eyes would have meant the development of unbearable injustice.

It is not important whether one ought to reject or accept this conception of justice. What is important here is to recognize that with the introduction of equality the encroachment on personal authenticity began. The notion of equality is a wise invention to keep healthy and coherent a society in which boundless individualism threatens to frustrate and exploit a large number of members in less favorable positions. As such, it has been a forceful rectifier and adjuster during the expansion of Western civilization in the last three or four centuries. But equality demands a price. Although proclaimed in order to protect individual rights, it does so at the cost of the autonomy of individuality.

John Locke was not aware of this price. In general, the mind of his time was not self-conscious about pragmatic solutions that bear the imprint of scientific reasoning. Half a century later, Rousseau was the first to have at least an inkling that the problem of equality was the problem of the separation of the individual and society. Not that Rousseau was yet able to grasp the essence of social and cultural estrangement. But by intuition he was the first to be conscious of a split between man and his social community. Political theorists have frequently remarked on his contradictory statements regarding individual freedom. Rousseau, indeed, could not clarify the relationship between personal liberty and the general will, because he did not see clearly the social structure of alienation.

He knew the notion from the works of Grotius and Samuel von Pufendorf, who used it as a legal term, as did the Romans. In his essay *Discourse on the Origin of Inequality Among Men* Rousseau takes issue with Pufendorf on the question of whether man can dispose of his own liberty. He denies Pufendorf's contention that man can alienate his freedom just as he can material goods. For freedom is a natural gift. It cannot be sold off. Consequently, man cannot give himself into slavery, as Grotius maintained. Nor can an entire nation alienate its freedom and make itself thus subject to a king. On the contrary, man should render his individuality to the general will of the community. In the *Social Contract* this problem constitutes the core of Rousseau's political theory. In fact, Rousseau himself, in the fourth section of the first book, points to this when he remarks that the clauses of the social compact can be reduced to one single requirement: the total alienation of each member to the entire community.

The ambiguities which have troubled critics and commentators, when considering Rousseau's work, essentially stem from his rather dim notion of alienation. When he uses the term, it seems to appear as a decisive argument. Indeed, his definition is concise enough. Alienation is "giving and selling." But the sharp legalistic basis turns out to be entirely inadequate when it comes to the broadly ramified problem of the surrender of individuality to society. In Rousseau's time it was apparently still impossible to see that alienation is not merely a formal and legal transaction, but an inner experience, a psychological transference, which becomes real only in the consciousness of the mind. It is for this reason that Rousseau's transference of the individual to the collective fails to make any satisfactory sense.

The crisis of authority

Rousseau lived before the impact of both the French and the Industrial Revolutions, and thus his notion about the separation of individual and society was not off-set or brought into focus by these developments. It was only at the end of the eighteenth century that the consciousness of estrangement began to play a role. It was then that the coinciding revolutions gave food for reflection on the nature of man, inasmuch as he is both object and subject in physical space, both active and passive in historical time. This typical self-consciousness was to find its classical expression in the work of Hegel. But before him such seminal thinkers as Schelling, Fichte, and Schiller, in their intermediate position between Kant and Hegel, prepared the groundwork.

Fichte and Schelling in this context are not particularly pertinent since their metaphysical thinking has little bearing on political theory. Schelling stayed aloof from any political involvement altogether. Fichte, to be sure, became an activist when he identified himself with the national restoration of Germany. But his nationalism did not represent an important contribution to political thought. Yet both these men should be mentioned here, since they were the first to provide a philosophical footing for the concept of estrangement.

Fichte in his *Wissenschaftslehre* (1794) was the first to use the term in its modern sense. By splitting up the world of human experience into the self and the non-self, man somehow has to come to grips with the communication of the two polar opposites. The polarity, the exchange action between the self and the objective world is sustained by a continuous surrender of a part of the self's authenticity to the objects surrounding it, that is, it becomes objectified. The self thus expresses itself in the objects, and this expression, which Fichte for the first time called *Entäusserung*, is precisely the alienation of the self.

Schelling, a year later, although not using the word "alienation," was even more succinct while analyzing the idea. Writing about *The Self as Principle of Philosophy* he distinguishes the pure, absolutely free self which, while communicating with the world, becomes objectified. The term "objectified" is to be taken as limited by conditions. What we encounter here is a typically Germanic ambiguity (or a play of words if one prefers). For Schelling's expression *be-dingt* means conditioned, but also hints at a restriction through the concreteness of things. The inference then is that in the communication with the world outside him, man alienates a part of his subjective freedom, and objectifies a part of his authentic being into the concrete surrounding community.

More important for us, however, is Schiller. For his concern with the same problem stemmed from immediate historical developments, such as the Industrial Revolution and the political upheavals at that time in France. Independently of the speculations by Schelling and Fichte, he introduced the idea of estrangement (without however using this term) in its direct relationship to historic events. In Schiller's *Aesthetic Education,* the notion of alienation is anchored in concrete actuality.

The work as a whole is an attempt at reconciling the contradictory forces in society which threaten to tear up the cohesion of human and cultural life. The gist of Schiller's concern appears in the sixth letter in which one of the most haunting of modern problems was for the first time put forth in unequivocal terms. The chasm then developing in society can be variously described. It may be said to be the split between the state and religion, or between law and ethics, to mention a few of Schiller's basic opposites. Regarding man's own experience, however, the modern character of society lies in its change from a vital, organic, and, as Schiller believed, harmonious nature to a mechanistic arrangement which he compared with an "ingenious clock work." As a result, man has become a dead fragment, a mechanical cog, never realizing the totality of life. Under such circumstances "gratification is separated from labor, means from ends, effort from reward."

Commentators have seen in this passage the earliest preparation for the *Communist Manifesto* of 1848. This is overlooking the significant point, however, that Schiller's social critique excludes any foundation for the communist class struggle. He did not lay the blame for the alleged threat to humanity at the door of a particular class, or social group, be it the capitalists, the bureaucrats, or the workers. His concern, since it was chiefly a concern with alienation, lay in the separation of the individual from the collective.

It follows that Schiller inevitably had to come to grips with the idea of the masses. His attitude was that the masses stood for violence, that indeed the cause of the French Revolution was lost when the crowd began to play an important role. The function of the crowd in this revolutionary phase brought to light "impotence and lack of dignity," as he wrote to one of his benefactors. The moment was favorable for a real restoration, but instead "an entire century is thrown back into barbarism and slavery."

This assessment of the result of the French Revolution is obviously debatable, to say the very least. What concerns us here, however, is Schiller's view that the role of the masses is usurping action. In the fifth letter of the *Aesthetic Education* he blamed the masses for storming the civil institutions in lawless agitation to fulfill base satisfactions. This critique is the more important since it came from a revolutionary mind. Schiller was not a conservative like Edmund Burke, who, while reflecting on the same revolution, saw in the crowd merely a band of ruffians and assassins, and who wanted to return to the times of chivalry. Schiller, in fact, was made an honorary citizen of France by the National Assembly. And though the revolutionary regime may well have misjudged Schiller, the fact remains that he was squarely on the side of those who, at Versailles in 1789, shaped the historic new constitution. He was on the side of the popular revolt against Spanish despotism when he described the Dutch struggle for independence. His life as expressed in his writings was a continuous battle against oppression and tyranny. As Goethe reminded us, Schiller's entire work stands under the symbol of freedom.

Schiller's solution to the crisis of authority in those days was not an important one. His imagination being far stronger than his logic, his insight was deeper than his demonstration was convincing. As a powerful playwright, he lived with dramatic contrasts which do not bear transference to philosophical discourse except by the strain of transforming political realities into abstractions. Thus the "aesthetic state," to which he set out to educate mankind, was a chimera. Schiller's thought, all the same, represents a momentous contribution in intellectual history. For he was the first to put down a dialectic of alienation immediately relevant to the time. It was Hegel who greatly benefitted from it. He knew the *Aesthetic Education* and believed it to be a masterpiece. A far more penetrating mind than Schiller, he saw more clearly the exclusive requirements of philosophy and was thus able to avoid the pitfalls of designing future ideal states.

Before we turn to him, however, it is imperative to understand the nature of the age which was to produce a philosophy such as Hegel's. Schiller's fear of mob action and ochlocracy was in itself no novelty in history. In all ages, restricted and oppressed groups have tried to seize power to the horror of the establishment. No examples are needed. At the end of the eighteenth century, however, a universal group consciousness developed with the inevitable concomitant of self-consciousness. The polarity between the self and the group became one of the major determinants in intellectual history.

The function of the crowd in history has drawn the attention of recent historians. They have provided valuable material for demonstrating that the masses are not merely blind and ruthless rabble, but can be described as fairly distinct forces of history at specific times. Much as one ought to welcome these analyses of detailed economic and political factors, they cannot explain the total cultural significance of the crowd. They are unsatisfactory because they ignore the fact that the crowd as historical energy is nothing except in the polar relationship with the consciousness of the individual. The increasing historical role of the masses in recent times must be seen in the light of the self-conscious situation of modern man, in which he finds himself never fully sure of his function as an individual or of his function in the group.

In the age in which a Schiller and a Goethe grew up, this self-conscious split between the individual and the collective marked the beginning of a decisive trend which was to dominate modern culture. The new awareness that individual and society are opposing forces—a conception entirely foreign to the classical mentality—raised the question of authority. Just as the American captain in "Benito Cereno" is puzzled about the authority handling the Spanish slave ship, so the puzzling problem of governmental authority became acute at the end of the eighteenth century. As in Melville's story, the question is: Who is the leader, who the follower? Is it the individual with his autonomous judgment, or the community with its consensus of the general will?

This is slightly different from the problem of sovereignty, which up to this time had been under discussion ever since Jean Bodin introduced it in the sixteenth century. For political usage the term "sovereignty," either that of the monarch or that of the people, is very convenient inasmuch as something uniquely characteristic of the nation-state is indicated. But for this very reason it is less convenient when society is viewed in a wider scope than its mere political development. The term "authority" is more enlightening, since it is not confined to the narrow alternative ruler and subject. Authority is semantically rooted in authorship, that is, origin. It points to the prime source of ideas and processes. And whereas sovereignty belongs to subject, authority suggests totality. Authority is the mainspring of a group of theories and ideas which pay allegiance of its originality. The allegiance of children to their father is not required, as they themselves may think at times, because of the father's dominant position of power, but simply because they are the issue. The father is their author.

Similarly, Plato was the authority of the Neo-Platonic school or the Florentine Academy, Aristotle that of Scho-

lasticism. The Bible is the authority of a large and ramified body of Christian theology. The crisis of authority,
beginning at the end of the eighteenth century, was
about origin and allegiance. The emerging confusion re-
volved around the question of whether the individual is
the originator of power to be imparted to the community,
or whether it is the collective which delegates power to
the individual.

To many of us this may well be a moot question. In
any event, the answer is less important than the fact that
this psychological and cultural crisis began and continued with increasing disturbance. It is its political aspect
which concerns us here. But politics are part of a universal cultural structure and cannot be evaluated historically
without understanding the totality into which they fit.
The historical crisis of authoritative power is obviously
most spectacular in matters of government. It cannot,
however, be severed from the basic social disturbance
which permeates all the constituent fields of culture.

Philosophical authority as reason was being questioned
as early as the late Middle Ages. The growing skepticism
during the next centuries was a gradual development until, with Kant, a Copernican revolution started to undermine the whole historical prestige of human knowledge.
Kant's subjectivism laid the groundwork for the development of Schelling's proto-existentialism, and Kierkegaard's
total despair in which the authentic self finds its real
authority.

At the same time the scholastic dogmas of theology
were rejected by Kant as a "magic lantern of intellectual
ghosts." Hegel's heroic effort, in the *Philosophy of Religion,* to try to reconcile reasonable and emotional belief
resulted practically in a series of radical Hegelians who,
with the modern tool of Biblical criticism, stripped the
traditional Scriptures of much, if not all, their authority.
This spiritual crisis extended no less to the domain of education, where the standard objective guidelines of the
surrounding adults, be it parents or teachers, were now
made relative in such writings as *Emile* and the *Gertrude*

books. The subjectivity of the child gained prestige. Rousseau and Pestalozzi were the actual founders of the modern child-centered education. Again, the psychological reaction against the change from hand to machine tools in the Industrial Revolution represented, though in a more complicated way, the shaking of man's inner foundations. The shock came with the realization that the origin of man's labor was no longer his autonomous authorship, but that this was transferred to the mechanical collective, the machine. This disturbing awareness is still prevalent among us in the age of computerization. The crisis of authority in its artistic dimension was clearly represented by the advent of the Romantic revolution.

Romanticism, fearful of the dictatorship of artistic rules and hollow "poetic diction," sought a new authority in the spontaneous subjectivity of the individual. Sponsored by this authority, the desperate search for *original* expression became the primary demand in modern art and literature.

It is in this social and cultural complex that the political problems about authority receive their legitimate meaning. In this context the struggle of classes, or that of racial and national minorities, for instance, are only secondary themes. They are side branches of one main intellectual realization: that the fate of Western civilization hinges on the outcome of the battle between individual and collective.

The freedom to have and the freedom to be

Facing the breakup of the classical foundation of the Western mind, Hegel saw it as his self-appointed task to analyze in a gigantic encyclopedic effort the entire sweep of the classical achievement. Noting the crisis of authority, he set out to reconcile the opposing forces, indeed to recognize for the first time the opposing forces of individual and community in philosophical concepts. Thus he placed himself deliberately at the historic end of the classical era. Besides his other unique achievements, he was the only person, with the exception perhaps of Goethe, able to see clearly without sentimentality or regrets that Western society had grown old. One hundred fifty years later, this view, though more and more accepted, is still open to challenge. The argument does not concern us. But it is imperative to know that the conception itself is the key to the understanding of Hegel's complete *oeuvre*.

By the same token, it is therefore necessary to keep in mind that Hegel's thought on law and statecraft did not represent a blueprint for the best or most desirable state, but a conceptional form of the development of the classical state. He was merely interested in the historical state as it had matured up to his own time. Any attempt to present his *Philosophy of Law* as a handbook of political science is erroneous. When a well-known political scientist writes that in Hegel's work there is "a conservative and in general an anti-liberal theory of the state," he completely misjudges Hegel's purpose and position. The *Philosophy of Law* never prescribes, it merely describes. It tries to show the logical pattern in the historical development of the human community. It does not set out to show how the state ought to be.

The confusion is the more puzzling since Hegel himself was so explicitly clear about his intentions. He ended the preface to the *Philosophy of Law* with one of the most moving passages of his entire work, stressing that the philosopher always arrives too late in history to teach what society ought to be like. Philosophy, because it represents the idea and the thought of the world, emerges when the history of a society is actually completed. In other words, the task of philosophy, as far as Hegel was concerned, is to rebuild the historical world in conceptional form, thereby trying to understand what has happened, not indeed according to individual events which would merely be history, but according to the essence of the past world. "When philosophy paints it grey on grey, then a form of life has become old, and this grey picture cannot rejuvenate it, only understand it. The owl of Minerva begins its flight only when dusk is falling."

For Hegel the state was "the actuality of the moral idea." From the above passage one can conclude that this actuality, in Hegel's view, has been completed. The historical development of man's consciousness of moral freedom is finished. With the facts in, the philosopher now can begin to translate the historical events of man's actions into logical terms, in order to understand the essential meaning of man's political community. Further, there is a chronological order of maturation in history which shows that the political realities shape themselves spontaneously before they can be analyzed by the political philosopher. In contrast to much erroneous judging, Hegel was here an empirical thinker, inasmuch as he based his conclusions on past but concrete actuality. He compared his own position with that of Plato and Aristotle, whose theories were abstracted from the experiences of Greek democracy.

Hegel thus aimed at showing how one can recognize the historical state as an expression of totality, as the "ethical universe." Implicit in this is the reconciliation of those forces which threaten to split the totality-of-the-state idea. Consequently, Hegel's philosophy of rights and laws represents a synthetic form of the freedom of the individual and the freedom of the community, inasmuch as they reciprocally sustain each other. Without this mutuality, freedom makes little sense. Unrestricted collective or individual liberty both create tyranny. To Hegel, individual liberty as such was whimsical and dangerous. It was rooted in uncontrolled subjectivism which was as objectionable as dogmatic objectivism.

Hegel's *Philosophy of Law* is in a sense a refutation of Kant's theories which make the knowledge of truth relative and subjective. According to some of Hegel's commentators, he saw such subjectivism realized in political forms in the violence of the French Revolution or in the student's riots on the Wartburg in 1817. The inference does not seem to be flawless. Nevertheless, philosophical

subjectivism and boundless personal liberty are historically related, and Hegel, like Goethe in a literary context, saw in this trend a threat to the cohesion of a
healthy mentality and a healthy state.

The separation of subject and object, or of individual
and collective freedom, can also be formulated as the
separation of political and moral freedom. Schiller anticipated Hegel in his alarm about the emerging predominance of political rights, which without the benefit of
moral character rob man of his innate human dignity.
The trend was by no means solely a European affair.
Schiller was, indeed, the first to discover the historical
alienation of freedom. But the actual symptoms of the
phenomenon were no less marked in the United States.
Over half a century later, Thoreau studied it in his own
trenchant though poetic manner. His analysis of the
American society applied to the entire modern scene in
which morals and politics had ceased to be related entities. In the posthumously published essay, *Life without
Principle,* he wondered whether the modern institutions
were like chestnut burs, which contain only abortive nuts
and merely prick the fingers. "America is said to be the
arena on which the battle of freedom is to be fought; but
surely it cannot be freedom in a merely political sense
that is meant. Even if we grant that the American has
freed himself from a political tyrant, he is still the slave
of an economical and moral tyrant. . . . What is it to be
born free and not to live free? What is the value of any
political freedom, but as a means to moral freedom? Is it
a freedom to be slaves, or a freedom to be free, of which
we boast? We are a nation of politicians, concerned
about the outmost defenses only of freedom." One can
hardly conceive of a more poignant description of alienated freedom.

Hegel, standing as he thought at the end of the completed realization of freedom, described the state as an
"ethical whole, the actualization of freedom." It is no
exaggeration to say that real freedom for him predicated
totality. Freedom can only be actual and congruous with

reason if the individual can realize his freedom entirely in the community and thus best serve this community. This was Schiller's idea. But whereas he believed this to be a future ideal to which mankind must be trained, Hegel with far more pragmatic firmness had no illusions about future utopias. The totality of freedom as it was expressed in the actuality of the state had been completed. This does not mean, therefore, that the individual nation-states Hegel had in mind were perfect examples of statecraft. On the contrary, he was emphatic about the fact that nations are no works of art. But like the invalid and the cripple, nations can represent an essential wholeness of actual freedom.

This totality of freedom, the core of Hegel's social doctrine, stands at the polar opposite of totalitarianism. The authority of absolute freedom lies in the harmony between the service of the individual and that of society. The authority of totalitarianism, on the other hand, is the despotism of the collective will at the cost of individual authenticity. Hegel's great epitaph for the classical order implied the falling apart of the classical consciousness of balance. Henceforth there was to be a strategy of individuality and a strategy of collectivism, with the inevitable outcome of the complete defeat of individual expression.

After Hegel, two different camps are clearly discernible: one championing the collective, the other the autonomy of the individual. The former comprises all the varieties of socialism, with straightforward and exclusively political aims. The latter is most articulately represented by the existentialist movement, which, as a general philosophy, deals with most fields of culture, but least of all with political theory. In this chapter, then, the confrontation of socialism and existentialism makes for a rather awkward polarization of uneven entities. Yet, separated and together, they clearly elucidate the problem of social authority and the cultural meaning of equalization.

The concept of equality is not one of the most profound products of the human mind. But it is one of the most pragmatically helpful for a perplexingly expanding society which, without the instrument of equality, would break up in egoistic and cruel excesses. One will never grasp the realities of modern cultural history, however, if one blinds oneself to the fact that the much-needed egalitarian process must inevitably lead to a totalitarian society.

Equality, even before Hegel began his career, had made itself known as a tool for the creation of a massified society. In an introductory chapter, we have pointed to the significance of the *Manifesto of the Equals*, written in 1796 as an expression of Babeuf's communist ideas. In this context it may once more be presented as one of the most powerful manifestations which the whole collectivist trend had produced. The authors of the manifesto assumed that the principle of equality was uncontested. Yet seven years after the revolution which was to bring liberty, they still saw tyrants around, withholding basic rights from a large majority of the nation. Equality can only be total, or else some form of tyranny prevails. Thus the Babouvists proclaimed that the French Revolution was merely a prelude to another upheaval, "far greater, far more solemn, which will be the last." Since the earth is no one's, the manifesto claimed the common good or the community of goods. Private property in land was to be abolished. The fruits of the earth are everybody's.

This communist proclamation in its crude and unspecified rendering is actually the outline for everything that can possibly be done for the leveling of society to a standardized mass. "Let there be no difference now between human beings but in age and sex! Since all have the same needs and the same faculties, let there be for all one education and one standard of life!" There can be no doubt that on this point the Babouvists' vision of the future society was even more clear and uncompromising than that of the *Communist Manifesto*. That document merely states in succinct wording the special requirements for the socialist state. It sets forth that the free development of each member is "the condition for the free development of all." And speaking of education, it merely desires free education for every child in public schools. Half a century earlier the *Manifesto of the Equals*, however, already gave a glimpse of the conformist and standardized life, which in our own age more and more dominates the individual.

The *Manifesto of the Equals* is clearly a document of a band of revolutionaries prematurely bursting into a bourgeois world still counting newly won gains. An idea was ripe, but the masses were not yet prepared. Culturally speaking, it was in one respect more significant than the aspirations of Marx and Engels. The efficacy of its extreme radicalism, to be sure, was even doubted by some of the Babeuf followers themselves. Yet regardless of the doubts within the group, we can read the ultimate cultural nihilism in the clause declaring that total equality must be acquired at any cost, even at the sacrifice of culture. "All the arts may perish, if need be, to provide us with real equality." Whatever else it may mean to each of us, it surely expresses the awareness of the predicament of modern culture.

Collectivism as it has developed during the last two centuries may be divided into various brands of socialism. Most practically, a dual distinction can be made by recognizing humanitarian and doctrinaire branches of the movement. The former inclines toward immediate practical experimentations, and aims at partial results within gradual progress. The latter, more scientifically directed, indulges in broad based analyses of statistics, long-term planning, and rather abstract reasoning. Both are basically, at least at the start, utopian, but the humanitarian socialist believes the ideal realization to be nearer than does his more dogmatic counterpart. It would be a mistake to take these two trends as mutually exclusive. Dogma and experiment intermingle in both.

Saint-Simon, for instance, unmistakably belonging to the warmhearted brand of socialists, nevertheless tried to base his reforms on a faith in science, and thus exerted a definite influence on early positivism. Saint-Simonism as a school of social thought, however, was clearly experimental. It wanted newly proclaimed liberties, such as the abolition of hereditary rights, women's suffrage, and community of goods, immediately established. And if society as a whole was not yet ready for the community of goods, Saint-Simon's followers would set up enclaves of practical socialism on a small scale. This socialism, however, turned out to be far from perfect since the principle of equality was only half-heartedly maintained. Instead the Saint-Simonists of Ménilmontant organized themselves according to a hierarchy of merits, expressed in a sacerdotal system quite incongruous with the egalitarian spirit.

Practical socialism was equally sincere in the experiments of Charles Fourier. The social and economic units, the "phalanges," which he conceived as cells for the future state, were a cooperative of consumption combined with a cooperative of production. Not dissimilar was Robert Owen's reform movement, exemplified by the foundation in 1825 of New Harmony in Indiana. To this may be added the American attempts of the New England Brook Farm and of Red Bank in New Jersey. All these experiments pointed in one direction: the foundation of a new collectivist society by gradual development of small-scale units. They were all ill-fated. It was not so much that bad management or particular financial inadequacies of the individual experiments eventually caused the whole trend to disappear. The failure of this kind of socialism lay essentially in the misunderstanding of the historical character of collectivism as such. Collectivism can only be understood as a movement of the masses, which to succeed demands the relentless drive and dynamics of a machine.

Equally idealistic was the emerging nineteenth-century trend of Christian socialism. It found its expression in the Inner Mission movement, in the tracts of Charles Kingsley, as well as in the later social gospel of Walter Rauschenbusch. Basing itself on the simplicity of the early Christians, the idea of brotherly love replaced that of the class struggle. Again, the attractive humanitarian element in this socialism seems self-defeating. The failure of this movement to become a positive social force is explained by the reality of massification, which is of a mechanical order, and quite alien to brotherhood. Humanitarianism and collectivist necessity are incompatible.

Marx knew it. From the beginning, his conception of collectivism was radical and totalitarian. This does not mean that the starting point of his social theory was not rooted in inequities and mistreatment of the impoverished masses. In his economic-political manuscripts of 1844, Marx gave a masterful analysis of the lot of the workers inasmuch as they were estranged from the product of their labor. In the capitalist system the worker had become a commodity, indeed the lowest kind of commodity. Thus "the brutal becomes human and the human becomes brutal." But beyond this humanitarian starting-point, Marx's thinking became ruthlessly mechanical. Hence his intolerance of the humanitarian socialists. Engels, a wiser and less autocratic man, though rejecting the attempts of Fourier and Owen, at least treated them with sympathetic understanding.

Marx, however, insisted on science. It was abhorrent to him that the Utopian Socialist thought of the proletariat only as the most suffering class, with the implication that society as a whole suffers too, and is similarly in need of help. Not so, Marx responded. The scientific law of history indicates that the industrial laborers are the inevitable demolishing force destined to prepare the future which will meet the conditions set forth in the *Communist Manifesto*.

With hindsight it is easy to point to the failure of Marx's predictions about the role and result of the class struggle, and to the ironic twist that in the modern Communist nations the industrial proletariat has played practically no role in the political takeover. Nor should one make too much play with the fact that in those highly industrialized countries where, according to Marxist speculations about inexorable necessity, the proletarian revolution was first to be expected (England, Germany), Communism is the least evident force. It is above all important to understand that the fiascos of Marx's predictions were not accidental, but inherent in his inadequate grasp of history.

The dogmatism of his political thought is usually said to be derived from Hegel's logical thinking. But it is a misunderstood Hegel who looms behind the structure of Marx's doctrine. The crucial misinterpretation is strikingly clear in Marx's criticism of the *Philosophy of Law*. Regardless of many valuable individual comments, the reasoning as a whole is vitiated by the fact that Marx treated Hegel's work as if it were the exposition of an ideal state, the realization of which was a desirable task. On the contrary, Hegel made it emphatically clear that his concern was a state already actually realized in the past. His was a state which, having completed its actuality, could now be described as it essentially was in philosophical form. Marx's judgment that Hegel based his state on religion was correct, because this was indeed how Hegel knew the historical development of Western civilization, and no one, not even Marx, would dispute it. But it was decisively not the state of an ideal future in which Marx himself was so persistently interested.

There is probably much in Hegel's political theories that invites disagreement, but this can be brought forth without the distortion of his basic purpose. Marx was unable to see that Hegel's interest lay in the actuality which, having been completed, could now be *understood* in conceptional terms, not re-enacted. The empiricism of this method is so obvious that only those who deliberately blind themselves to Hegel's intentions will ignore or deny it.

Marx, however, did not blind himself to the historic place occupied by Hegel, one which makes him immediately comparable to Aristotle. Whether or not Marx was aware of this parallel while writing his dissertation on the materialist philosophy of Democritus and Epicurus does not change the fact that the analogy was stressed.

The almost too-pat conclusion of various commentators that, just as classical Greek philosophy after Aristotle broke up into materialist and relativist schools, so after Hegel classical Western thought was bound to disintegrate into similar groups needs many qualifications. It is certainly at least debatable, I believe, to maintain that the Epicurean and Stoic doctrines which were to become the foundation of Roman thinking, represented the elements of decomposition of Greek philosophy. This view, held by one of the best known specialists of nineteenth-century thought, Karl Löwith, then implies that similarly the fragmented groups of modern philosophy are mere products of disintegration—a suggestion hard to substantiate.

Nevertheless, the all-encompassing Hegelian system did break up into a variety of schools somehow related, now by extension, now by contradiction, to the master. As for Marx and Engels, their collectivism is professedly materialistic. Their concern is not society, even less humanity in the manner of Herder's eighteenth-century idealism, but specifically a concern with a section of society, the industrial proletariat. Whereas to Hegel, man as he communicates by language and labor with the objects outside himself loses a part of his identity in the process of alienation, to Marx and Engels only the workman in the capitalist system is estranged. He will be restored to his full human dignity (the *Aneignung*, as it is called) when the proletariat seizes the production machine and collectively rules society.

How unhumanitarian Marx's conception was about this restoration becomes clear from his contention that Jewry and Judaism must be excluded from the ideal proletarian state. The Jews in Marx's thinking were irrevocably identified with usury. Jewry reached its peak in the perfection of bourgeois society. It was the Jews who had turned alienated man into a saleable commodity. Thus, according to Marx, in order to emancipate the world it had to be emancipated "from usury and money, that is, from practical, actual Judaism." Clearly this represents a kind of reasoning as racist and anti-Semitic as anything we have experienced from the Nazi regime.

More than a century after Marxist speculation on the restoration of alienated man was launched, the historical events have proved that the opposite must happen. In the most socialized states, communist by profession, collectivism has conspicuously only further estranged the workman from his human authenticity. Nowhere in the world is the modern enslavement to the production machine and to the bureaucratic conveyer belt of statism felt more depressingly than in the Marxist order. And, indeed, the Soviet administration, according to correspondents, is worried about the increasing awareness and discussion of the presence of social alienation within its own society. There can be no doubt that the developing massification, also in non-communist countries, represents a historical process of increasing estrangement. Socialization itself is this process of estrangement.

Between the varieties of hard-boiled scientific socialism and soft-hearted humanitarian socialism there are a number of so-called revisionist groupings. In the highly developed European countries they have, as a whole, served well by militantly, though mostly judiciously, pressing for reforms within legitimate legislative boundaries. Over the full century of their activity they have succeeded in obtaining for the workers higher wages than they ever could have dreamed of, and fringe benefits which a hundred years ago would have appeared as fairy-tale conditions. In the various countries these social democratic parties have, after the Second World War, lost their initial militancy and zest. They have arrived. They have assumed the air of successful institutions with a somewhat bourgeois appearance.

Besides the successful development of organized socialism, there were other remarkable attempts aimed at the founding of a collectivist society. Georges Sorel, criticizing the abstract intellectualism of Marx and Engels, followed the pragmatic method of James, which he interpreted politically as the persistent effort of strikes. In his *Reflections on Violence,* he was convinced that whatever was to remain of active socialism would be "an epic of strikes." Thus, to Sorel, violence was a vital part of the proletarian struggle. And so it was to the anarchist.

Anarchism, as a doctrine of revolution, clashed with the theory of Marx and Engels inasmuch as the latter operated in a predominantly doctrinaire manner. Bakunin, the remarkable Russian leader of anarchism, in his *Statism and Anarchism* attacked Marxism as a Germanic abstract theory, not rooted in a popular party. The fallacious premise of this theory, according to Bakunin, lay in its acceptance of abstract reasoning prior to social practice. This criticism, amusingly the same as Marx's criticism of Hegel, was founded in the anarchist's fear of "learned socialists" who make a "small aristocracy of genuine or sham scientists." This inevitably must mean a new kind of dictatorship in which the common people would be "regimented into one common herd." Thus, Marxism with its inherent statism represents a scientifically founded ideology of tyranny. Anarchism, in contrast, advocates the abolition of the state by the destruction of all forms of government. Proudhon, the French anarchist, put the alternative squarely before the world. In *The Social Revolution,* he convincingly developed the thesis that the ultimate choice of modern man lay between the social freedom of anarchy and the tyranny of Caesarism. The idea of anarchism, which in our age seems to be a little too fantastic to be viable, must be understood as one of the desperate efforts to avoid the mechanical and inhuman consequences of scientific socialism with its built-in dictatorship.

As opposed to the advocates of collectivism, there stood the men fighting to retain the supremacy of individual autonomy. The nineteenth century was the age of Kierkegaard, Nietzsche, Burckhardt, Thoreau, Whitman, Emerson, Flaubert, and Melville, as well as the Romanticists. It was the age in which the concentrated, creative, and spontaneous individualism that emerged with the free expansionist times of the Renaissance took its last stand. It is then that we witness the desperate agony of the man in the ivory tower, while the flood tide of the masses pounded at his door.

From his island in Copenhagen, Kierkegaard viewed the masses as the generators of evil, of all corruption. Time and again in his Journals, he fulminated against them as the undermining force of humanity. He appealed to the "ancients" (probably meaning Socrates and Plato), who understood this, and he thought that life indeed was turning again to the ancient condition of continued disorder. To Kierkegaard, the crowd was the leveling agency destroying personality and culture, and elsewhere he used the term "public" as a designation for total negativism. The whole age was becoming a committee. The public was the expression of that equality which represented the "negative unity of the negative reciprocity of all individuals." The public indeed was everything as well as nothing. Although it was the most dangerous force, it was the most insignificant. This sort of denunciation of the crowd was later echoed by Nietzsche when describing socialism as the tyranny of "the most insignificant and ignorant."

The existentialist search for a metaphysical encounter with an absolute Being raises to its supreme urgency the question of the isolated individual in a technological world of things. In a social order which encourages property, acquisition, and accumulation of material goods, it clings to the forgotten rights of *being* something when the crowds are scrambling for *having* something. Existentialism is the last-ditch fight of man to become what he potentially is. As such, as a philosophy of a lost fight, it is the most timely expression of all modern thinking.

Nietzsche, no less than Kierkegaard, appeared as the epitome of cultural despair. In *Human, All Too Human* he quoted Voltaire's phrase which predicted that "when the populace mixes in with reasoning, everything is lost." Nietzsche had already accepted this loss. Nothing could stand in the way of the masses, when they have decided on the most agreeable way of living and put up "with the fatal results of their narrow-mindedness." But a few individuals ought to be allowed to stay aloof from the politics of the crowd. Great culture needs two classes to succeed, the caste of the workers and that of the man of leisure. When the two intermingle, culture will vanish and only a "wide sea of vague wishes" remain.

Nietzsche and Kierkegaard were no reactionaries desiring to go back to irrevocable times. They accepted the trend of proletarianization as inevitable and merely chose to stay free from the melee. To them may be added Jakob Burckhardt, who as a historian knew the indefeasible forces of historical processes. Without judging them to be good or evil, he bent before the inevitable and retired as a hermit to his study at Basel.

Withdrawal from society was no less conspicuous in the United States at that time. Most of the transcendentalists were inclined to distrust the trend of collectivism. But their fear of the masses resulted in no bitter denunciations. None of them was as vituperative as Kierkegaard and Nietzsche. In fact, none of them had as yet the unwavering insight of Kierkegaard, Nietzsche, and Burckhardt that the historical decision was already made, and that the crowd must prevail. The transcendentalist mind had only a vague doubt about the times and the future. Thoreau avoided the crowd in the serene hermitage of Walden, while Emerson tried to keep the "diagonal" line between the realities of solitude and society. Whitman, in *Democratic Vistas,* expressed substantial doubt about the future of American democracy, but until the end of his life he clung to the belief that the principle of individuality, the soul, might still win. It never occurred to him that the American democracy eulogized in his poetry, though only for its partial material success, was precisely the arch-antagonist of the self, and was, indeed, the true expression of collectivism.

Only Melville at times was more outspoken about the threat of the masses. In his poem "Clarel" the somber figure of Ungar forcasts the eventual doom of the American way of life. The "dark ages of democracy" are nearing, when "myriads playing pygmy parts" will be debased into total equality. But this was as explicitly gloomy as an author of the American Golden Age could be. On the whole the American champion of the individual at that time was not yet convinced that the battle was lost.

The stark antagonism between self and society in the nineteenth century was characteristic of an age marked by opposing trends and universal dualism. Immediately related to our problem is the dual trend of conspicuous optimism and conspicuous pessimism. Earlier we have analyzed the seeming contradiction. It should be repeated here that the extremes are mutually tied together. By what? By the realization that the very upward trend in human achievement which gives substance to confidence and optimism is precisely the same trend which causes despair and pessimism. In other words, the opposites are simply a matter of interpretation. In the nineteenth century, what boomed were the productions of material achievement, machines, buildings, crops. The pessimism expressed in works of art, literature, and philosophy merely reflected the deep-seated doubt that expanding production and triumphant sweep of quantity boded well for the human future.

It is not our task here to side either with the optimists or the pessimists. It is only historically useful to see that the split existed and why it developed. The typical distrust of industrial triumphs rested in the human fear of being abandoned to only mechanics and quantity. The battle, whose outcome Kierkegaard, Nietzsche, and Burckhardt believed had been decided, was of course that between the single and the many. But ultimately it was the historical contest between the authority of spontaneous conception and that of administrative plan. Clearly the administration of social planning has no jurisdiction or claim beyond the limits of numbers and objects. The world as it gradually turns into units of gigantic, computerized circuits is obviously more and more exclusively geared to digits, statistics, ratios, measurements, and equations. In such a society human needs are bound to be abstracted into algebraic formulas, only expressions of quantity.

Human freedom, in classical times a reflection of human totality, has now become split into an awareness of individual and of group. The freedom of the self is estranged from social freedom. The freedom to be one's authentic being is separated from the liberty of having communal and equal rights. No one could deny that the two ought to be integrated, yet the history of the last hundred years shows hat the freedom to have rights, to have opportunities, to have an equal share in commodities and material goods, to have comfort, Cadillacs, fur coats, or background sounds in stereo is smothering the origin of all human dignity: the freedom to be what one is. Thus man has become an image of man himself, a huge billboard advertising his inflated status on the main circuits of material and political advantages.

The freedom of the masses

The twentieth century in a sense is the confirmation of its predecessor. One ought not, of course, to take this too narrowly as if our age has no characteristic traits and attributes of its own. The contrary is true. But it is also true that the twentieth century seems to fulfill the inherent promises of the nineteenth. Similarly it fulfills the predictions of Kierkegaard, Nietzsche, and Burckhardt regarding the total leveling and conformity of human society. We need not all attach the same emotional value to a standardized life. In fact, at this point there are probably just as many who enjoy themselves with great faith in this technocratic existence as there are who appear haunted by the dread of its consequences. We are not, however, concerned here with imponderables such as faith and dread.

This age most demonstratively confirms the previous

century in the consciousness of the separation between collective and individual authority. The chasm has become so irreversibly wide that the actual problem itself has almost lost its significance. Whereas in the nineteenth century only a few men of genius analyzed it and drew their radical conclusions, those intellectuals of our time who care to recognize the chasm at all are willing to adjust to the fact and take a compromised stand. Only twentieth-century existentialist thought, at least that of the uncompromising variety of Jaspers and Heidegger, dares to sound the last clarion calls of the beleaguered self.

Heidegger, when questioning what he believed to be the crucial problem of modern philosophy, suggested in 1953 that the idea of absolute Being is either as meaningless as a vapor, or else the spiritual destiny of the Western world. In his view the forgetting and falling away from the Being, which can only be realized in an existential search, was caused by the "cheerless technological frenzy," which characterizes the United States as well as the Soviet Union. Jaspers, always connecting the most subtle metaphysical conceptions with not-so-subtle actualities of contemporary history, gives the modern alternative a frightening perspective. In a lecture about the future of mankind, he declared that under the auspices of the collective the world would destroy itself, while the leadership of the individual, in contrast, would save its cohesion.

Luckily, this cultural survey does not deal with speculation on the chances for an approaching Armageddon, replete with fire and brimstone. In view of the organic cohesion of classical Western society, one is inclined to think that it is the integration of the individual and the collective which matters, and that neither alone will be able to play the part of a savior. In any event, it is imperative to realize that it is impossible for the autonomous individual to serve the technology of assembly-line systems. We are, rightly or wrongly, in the age when the authority of the self has become authoritarian, when the totality of human experience is transmuted into a totalitarian order. It is our assignment here to face without regrets or illusions the actuality of the world as it is historically necessary, indeed, as it is historically developing into a universal proletarian regime.

Some governmental systems and methods that have been employed attempt to anticipate the historical process. For that reason we must first consider the efforts of such figures as Stalin, Hitler, and Mussolini. They tried to force a totalitarian order upon society at a time when man was not yet historically prepared for an unrestrained mechanization of his existence. History rejects extraneous force. It obviously recognizes its own violence of wars and revolution, but they only succeed if the mind behind these enterprises is ripe for the deed.

In the first chapter we introduced the proletariat as the historical alien, a notion that cannot be stressed enough. The word "proletarianization" is vague and misleading. Not infrequently, it is used without proper understanding of the historical function of the proletariat. Originally and essentially, proletariat is simply the common people. As the word derives from the Latin *proles,* that is, progeny, we may assume that the proletarians are those who have no property except children. The proletariat is sharply distinguished from elite, the elect or the chosen few, who are the insiders. The proletarians thus are the outsiders, although clearly and legitimately a part, the majority in fact, of the community.

Those who insist on the importance of class struggle change the meaning of proletariat into the mass of industrial workers in the mechanizing world. Since, however, this class struggle has turned out to be an abstract notion rather than a substantial historical force, it is far more useful to adhere to the original, essential meaning of the word. Thus, proletariat is, above all, the majority of the populace who exist at the periphery of society, and consequently participate little or not at all in the process of culture. They are the outsiders, regardless of their economic position. Jews, for instance, in the classical society belonged to the historical proletariat. Their proletarian satus was determined entirely by the fact that they had no share in the inside functions of their society. A similar position was allotted to other minorities. Although exceptions abound, the Catholics on the whole had only a negligible share in the arts and letters of seventeenth-century Holland. No one has to elaborate on the proletarian nature of the American Negroes, in spite of the fact that their numbers include millionaires who have nothing to do with hand labor.

The idea of proletariat, then, in a cultural sense focuses on the alien nature of a large portion of the population, usually the majority comprising frustrated minority groups as well as agricultural and factory laborers, who exist at the periphery of a culturally active society. The proletarians clearly belong to the community, yet are not in and inside it. They are the large mass of fringe dwellers, merely subsisting, and not participating in the cultural growth of a particular society. They are not in the first place determined by class struggle; in fact, they cover a wide range of social castes. Their most conspicuous quality is mere mass, and mass is their strength. As such, their only common foe is the individual, who in classical times constituted the core of the creative apparatus of their society. To be sure, they cannot be separated from the bulk of the cultural community. They are part of the "people"; in fact, unconsciously they are the spokesmen for the masses. But it is as individuals that they give shape to the historical culture.

With the development of mass needs and mass politics in the nineteenth century, the question of the survival of a strong cultural expression was inevitably raised. The great champions of the individual naturally were convinced that the preponderance of the masses with the proportionate elimination of the individual would ultimately be fatal to the vitality of social life, and subsequently kill any cultural manifestation. But even in the collectivists' camp of the early *Manifesto of the Equals*, as we have noted, there was already doubt whether a totally egalitarian state might not extinguish the arts and letters.

It is in this light and placed in this perspective that one must consider the unfolding of totalitarian systems so characteristic of the twentieth century. Much has been written, and much will be, on the particular aspects of the various brands of fascism and communism. Each has its own history and its marked, detailed development which can be studied separately. Nor do we have to describe here the political instruments of these various totalitarian orders and their efficiency in order to explain the relationship between proletarianization and cultural expression. The strength (and danger) of cultural history lies in its synthetic quality, which directs it toward the totality of the social energy as this expresses itself in more or less permanent manifestations. In this survey, therefore, the focusing point is the *common* motivation of the developing modern world rather than its particular separated aspects. And consequently the question here is more what totalitarianism as a modern phenomenon means in its functional potentialities than in its segmented actualities.

Though, at first glance, it may seem hazardous to lump together such disparate political systems as fascism and communism, in this context they must primarily be understood as culturally related. Fascism, Nazism, and doctrinaire Marxism represent the first, though as yet inconclusive, triumphs of unsparing collectivism. They are the most radical configurations of that purportedly democratic dream of the General Will. In their political and economic regimes, different though they may be in a technical sense, the ascendancy of the crowd is complete. Revolutionary as their seizure of power may make them appear, they are nevertheless the logical, historical, and advanced offspring of the liberal doctrine of equality.

I hasten to stress that this in no way implies that liberalism morally prepared the way for twentieth-century despotism. Historical processes do not develop in so simplified a manner. These may, with hindsight at least, seem to have a logical justification; their social, political and moral values change with the times and circumstances. If we insist (as has been done) on selecting such seminal figures as Darwin, Nietzsche, Rousseau, Herder, or Luther as progenitors of twentieth-century state-systems, then this can only be done, if at all, by detaching any ethical judgment from the historical continuity. In fact, such figures as Rousseau and Luther can easily be declared ancestors equally of autocratic and democratic procedures. This is not contradictory as long as one lifts the historical line out of the emotional context.

When this is understood and accepted, there is no harm in presenting the autocratic mass systems of our age as the natural progeny of eighteenth-century Enlightenment. Understandably, it is appalling to our liberal minds to have to accept that a movement with a professedly liberal claim and a story of successful emancipating activity behind it, now, under a new set of circumstances, ends up in despotic totalitarianism. Only superficially, however, is history a story of comfort. More often than not, in its essential shape it turns out to be a disturbing force that rends the drapery of illusions and wish-dreams with which we anxiously decorate our insecure existence. Communist and fascist collectivism, of course, entirely lacks the humanitarian views of eighteenth-century egalitarianism. It simply applies the principle of equality in the most radical and mechanical manner to the state machine.

In the eyes of the radical and dogmatic socialists, liberalism fails because its programs of equity and equality are merely half-hearted attempts, compromising with an establishment run by elitist bourgeois. In 1905, Leon Trotsky, observing in *The Events in St. Petersburg* the course of the Russian Revolution of that year, made clear the historical misinterpretation by the liberal politicians. Liberalism, he said, is not interested in revolution and it ignores the masses. The Communists' fight for a revolution, he believed, must be a relentless struggle for influence over the masses.

One does not have to agree with Trotsky's own historical view to acknowledge that the liberal movement had little grasp of the actual undercurrent which had been shaping the political realities of the last two centuries. No complete realization of the ideals of liberty and equality can be achieved with hesitant measures. Successful as the revisionist and humanitarian socialists may have been in obtaining rightful advantages in material needs for the workers, they will not establish a truly egalitarian state until they aim at total equality. And equality, by its very nature, is always potentially total.

The methods which the nineteenth- and twentieth-century liberals and socialists employed lay within the apparatus of the bourgeois order. This basically is parliamentary negotiation. Negotiation, according to its Latin root, means carrying on business. It is an act of merchants. In fact, negotiation is a trader's way of reasoning. As such, it was a successful device in the service of equity within the bourgeois world. With the shift toward a new order—the proletarian dispensation—the whole reasonable disposition of parliamentary procedure was put in doubt. It is self-evident that for the communist doctrine of class struggle the bourgeois negotiating technique had lost its validity. It had to be replaced by violence. On the contrary, to the liberal accepting the new challenge of the masses, his successful trader's technique simply had to be expanded, applied wholesale, so to speak, to a still larger commitment.

Taking a look at the Fascist movements in Italy and Germany, one finds that, revolutionary as these upheavals may appear, in another sense they grew almost organically out of the political situations which precede their emergence. In the first place it is to be remembered that both Mussolini and Hitler were founders of typically socialist movements. Their characters and careers were as dissimilar as their parties, but they had, when all the but's and if's are said, the same remarkable intuitive grasp of mass needs and mass satisfactions. Significantly, Mussolini came from the ranks of the Italian Socialist

Party, Hitler started his political activities in the German Workers' Party. Subsequently, they continued one of the most effective methods of political maneuvering of modern parliamentarianism, but amplified it to gigantic dimensions in order to cover the wholesale market.

What was this method? It developed in the liberal tradition of the Third Republic in France, for instance, as *opportunisme*, deliberately and skillfully applied by the father of French parliamentary maneuvering, Gambetta. He was greatly admired for it by later socialists, including Jaurès, himself an incorrigible compromiser when, in 1905, it came to uniting the Socialist movement in France. Gambetta defended himself against the charge of opportunism, which for a politician seems as futile as it is unnecessary. It would, at this time, certainly be naïve to believe that political results can be gained without prostituting social ideals at crucial points. But Gambetta stood at the beginning of the parliamentary game in France when voters had not yet become cynical. Nor should it be said that parliamentary opportunism was unique in France at the time. On the contrary, it appeared as the common aspect of all political procedures.

In Italy, where it was inaugurated by Agostino Depretis as *trasformismo*, it grew to a particular administrative skill in the hands of Giolitti, whose supreme opportunism acquired the name of *Giolittismo*. The Spanish equivalent is called *caciquismo*, a system of bossism cultivated with particular skill by Sagasta and Canovas del Castillo. The fifty years of liberalism after the Italian emancipation were unmistakably marked by the administration of undercover deals, puny chicaneries, and petty lies for the benefit of progress. Benedetto Croce, in *A History of Italy*, acknowledged this procedure as the weakness of a declining parliamentary system, not only in Italy but anywhere in the democratic Western nations. Opportunism, indeed, as a political principle, beneficial and useful as it was in regard to immediate pragmatic ends, also suggested the shifty temper addicted to the little lie. The Fascists, in their attempt to grab the wholesale market, systematically cultivated the big lie. The big lie is the amplification of bourgeois opportunism. Neither Italian nor German Fascism rested on any firm principle. They knew no philosophies, doctrines, or beliefs except the blatant slogans that excited the crowd. Their fundamental policy was coldly pragmatic. To them, success had its own justification. Anything that enhanced and glorified the state organization was justice.

The big lie becomes expedient when the nation, instead of being served by an intermediate organ such as a representative parliament, brings its executive into direct contact with the people. Mussolini, in an effort to dissociate himself from Marxism, originally declared no interest in the masses. In a speech at Udine, just before the historic March on Rome, he scoffed at the crowd, that "new divinity," as being against reason. In the same address, however, he hinted at less reasonable methods when, dealing with the possibility of violence, he divided this revolutionary device into a violence that would liberate and a violence that would enslave. "There is a violence which is moral and a violence which is stupid and immoral." With hindsight, we are now able to interpret this distinction. A month after the takeover, preparing for his dictatorship in the Senate, Mussolini in his speech of November 27, 1922, declared that his announced program for the proletariat was prompted by the reality of facts. There could be no national unity, he noted, when twenty or thirty million workers were condemned to a miserable existence. Here, at the end of the democratic parliamentary procedure in Italy, Mussolini sounded like an old-fashioned socialist, which he essentially was. But the masses were soon to be conquered by more totalitarian means than Senate addresses.

Hitler, with more cynical candor, explicitly denounced the crowd, as well as sought its favor. In *Mein Kampf*, he repeatedly describes how the great leader manipulates the masses, which alone have the power to realize great ideas. "No sacrifice is too great to win the masses." In order to win them, one must show force and will power.

The crowd wants the victory of the stronger and the annihilation of the weaker. In order to unite the masses, the big lie must be invented and endlessly repeated. Hitler's toolbox of power was small but effective. Hysteria, fanaticism, and feigned madness were all deliberate instruments to impress the crowd, and, indeed, he was at his most characteristic when addressing the masses. In the confidential conversations with generals in his headquarters, Hitler explained proudly how he used Marxist methods of propaganda to win the crowd. Whoever has any doubts about the kinship between Communist and Nazi totalitarianism ought to study Hitler's own account of his mass manipulations. He especially singled out the triumphant winning over of the Socialist and Communist metalworkers in Nuremberg to the cause of the Nazi party.

Hitler, confronted with the masses, demonstrated the radical extent of the proletarian revolution. Hitler, indeed, was the epitome of the proletarian. The historical movement of proletarianization as a total leveling of values, aspirations, and classes was successfully achieved for a short moment. Hitler was the complete "leveling champion" in the sense in which Kierkegaard applied the term to the crowd, namely, the monster of utter negativity. The official policy of standardization in the Third Reich, the so-called *Gleichschaltung*, realized the ultimate potential of the principle of equality. The word, usually translated too scientifically as "coordination," is more vividly the brutal and mechanical flattening of all individual distinction, the final act of dehumanization, which reduces man's existence to a sterile fragment in the state machine.

The freedom of opportunity

The totalitarianism of Stalin, Hitler, and Mussolini abused the nature of history, which is one of gentle maturation underneath the rough and seemingly whimsical course of events. Their work was thus doomed to defeat, and in order to sustain their efforts they had to employ policies of violence and savage purges. They failed. But the development of proletarianization nevertheless goes on. Western civilization is slowly transforming itself, by gradual and wiser means, into a totally standardized manner of living. It is in this piecemeal process that the Anglo-American temper excels, and to which it can naturally apply its inborn talent for negotiating.

The warm reception in the United States of Mussolini's early program and policies pointed to a remarkable kinship of social pragmatism. Conservatives as well as liberals in the United States watched Mussolini's experiments in the 1920's with understanding sympathy, until the innate violence of regimentation was revealed. The conservatives wondered if Fascism was perhaps the definite answer to the Russian Revolution, while the liberals saw in corporate socialism a chance for combatting the prevalence of the capitalist tycoon. Beyond this there also lay the suggestion that Machiavellian politics, so self-consciously practiced here, acquired a new glamor in Fascist Italy. No nation has concerned itself so traditionally with *The Prince* as the United States. In no nation is this work a more persistent text for college classes.

Machiavelli's outspoken contempt for the masses and his advice on how to exploit them set perfect guidelines for modern totalitarianism. In the eighteenth chapter of *The Prince,* he promotes the ruler who knows the art of mystifying the minds of men, and who is a master at breaking his word. "A wise leader cannot and ought not keep his word if this is to be disadvantageous for him." For such a man it is absolutely necessary to be able to disguise, pretend, and dissemble. It is helpful to him to appear human and religious, provided that when the opposite is more advantageous he is prepared to shift his position. This is the pocket catechism of a creed to which Mussolini and Hitler served as consummate high priests. They actualized the supreme triumph of their Florentine master. They possessed in abundance the natural talent to practice histrionic demagoguery on a large scale. In contrast, the American student of politics must learn Machiavellian techniques by systematic training from the college level up.

The American concept of politics is primarily a product of the trader's mind, bargaining about commodities. The focusing point of political life thus becomes the Opportunity. Indeed the political life of the United States is basically the story of legislation as negotiation of the commodities of human liberty. This is its strength. It makes for gradual, solid progress. It is also innately conservative, reflecting the merchant's apprehension of risks. This means that its social and cultural enterprise steadfastly looks for favorable precedents. Thus, the American New Deal arrived fifty years after Bismarck inaugurated social legislation in Germany. On the other hand, precisely because the American apparatus treats needs, liberties, and rights not as ideals (with the implied quality of the unreachable), but rather as concrete items of a shopping list, it has a built-in resistance against too great adventures, shocks, and revolutions. American legislative techniques, like the British parliamentary conception from which they stem, deal with practical objects; they are not concerned with vindicating a theory.

American historians, such as Boorstin and Hofstadter, have convincingly stressed the absence of any unifying philosophy behind our political aims. Social progress here is made under the pressure of concrete urgency and of individuals or groups demonstrating that urgency. The inclusion of the power of the masses started in the crucial decade of the 1890's, when in almost every respect a new American consciousness, if not self-consciousness, awakened. On the political scene, William Jennings Bryan through his election campaign of 1896 funneled the forces of agrarian revolutionists and Populists into the *First Battle*, as he himself called it, of a new reform era. The development which found its peak in the Wilson and Franklin Roosevelt administrations, and its greatest fulfillment in that of Lyndon Johnson, curiously coincides with the increasing American involvement in overseas problems. This may well be accidental. Nevertheless, it is important to note that with the greater military and social commitments abroad the trend of massification grows proportionately.

Massification is not the most precise expression that has recently entered the language. It can vaguely be used for many purposes at a time. But it does indicate the gradual replacement of individual responsibility by group opinion. Judgment, taste, and choice have become mass products. With the widening tasks and operations abroad, foreign countries have been subjected to what they often misleadingly consider an Americanization of life and habits. This Americanization, however, is essentially the universal trend of proletarianization—massification—in which the United States is gradually and historically taking the lead.

It is therefore helpful in a synthetic (cultural) account not to separate our domestic and foreign policies too persistently. Both reflect the modern forces in society which push toward huge, standardized, and conformist administrative units, in which the best administrators and engineers will be the new heroes and rulers. In the decades of social reform the gates were opening to the thrust of mass needs, but it was not until Roosevelt's administration that its tremendous impact was felt. It was then that with the new news media an immediate relationship could be established between executive and public opinion. Roosevelt's acute political intuition seized the opportunity, and skillful press conferences and fireside chats before a radio audience were the beginning of a new political era in which the masses entered the White House, so to speak.

Roosevelt has been accused of being a "Hitler"—a charge unfounded on every count. He had neither the spontaneous genius nor the demoniacal destructiveness of the Führer. But he did see that the small-scale opportunism of the nineteenth-century liberals was over, and that the game henceforth was going to be played in large

dimensions. The term "opportunist" has a rather deroga-
tory ring, but it does not necessarily have to be felt that
way if one considers it, regardless of the needed political
machinations, in relation to the creating of opportunities
for a large community. In that sense, Roosevelt belongs
to the great opportunists of the twentieth century, one
who gave the American nation a new sense of scope at
home and abroad.

The public, which Kierkegaard in the early nineteenth
century viewed as the demon of negativity and leveling,
is now setting the standards not only of taste, radio, and
television programs, literature, and education, but also of
political action. What in the Roosevelt-Truman era was
forcefully but rather crudely outlined, reaches its grand
consummation under the consensus policies of Lyndon
Johnson. In between there was a decade of stalemate.

In 1945, the United States reached the peak of its
power and had within its grasp the mastery of the globe.
It could, at will, occupy the exhausted world with tanks,
dollars, economic agencies, and surplus crops. It did not.
Why such a concentration of power, without a single nation to resist its preeminence, ignored the challenge of
filling the vacuums and establishing a military and economic *pax americana* over the world cannot be answered
here. The fact is that, instead, weak and war-stricken nations rebuilt themselves and consolidated into dubious
power blocs. The artificial decisions to allow American
forces to arrive at Berlin coevally with the Russian army
and, at Yalta, to distribute even spoils to uneven partners
proved disastrous and resulted in an artificial East-West
antagonism.

Thus, the world for decades to come must live in the
mounting pressures of global polarization. It must concentrate on power stalemates around arbitrary divisions in
Berlin, Germany, Jordan, Laos, Vietnam, and Korea, to
name only a few places that have created a senseless im-
passe in a world otherwise ready for constructive action.
Senseless, because the polarization rests on essentially
artificial grounds. The Soviet Union and the United
States are in the same historical pursuit. Both are agen-

cies for the realization of the complete egalitarian state, both are engaged in a gigantic endeavor to proletarianize social and cultural institutions. To be sure, their methods differ. One seeks to reach the ultimate goal by violent revolution, the other by gradual political negotiations. But since the Soviet Union at various points after 1917, and recently with increasing conspicuousness, has slid back into time-honored bourgeois and capitalist techniques, the actual antagonism is slight compared with the volume of the propaganda and war-machinery supporting the alleged difference.

This historical stalemate, in 1945 still so unforeseen, showed its full impact during the Eisenhower-Kennedy decade, when it proved itself in domestic as well as foreign policy. It would be premature, indeed, to try at this time to evaluate the work of these two Presidents as a whole. This must obviously be left to future historians, more able to see facts and trends in true perspective. Nevertheless, for the purpose of our inquiry, we may suggest, as a tentative appraisal, how the general line of the years between 1953 and 1963 looks in the cultural setting. In spite of the differences in character and style, Eisenhower and Kennedy had a good deal in common, and it is this common factor of non-achievement which concerns us here.

Eisenhower's reluctance toward activity was an almost deliberate attitude, stemming from an outdated conception of the President as a detached referee in a laissez-faire society. He achieved exactly what he set out to do: satisfy the people in their quest for peace and prosperity. He gave them both. They rewarded him with consistent popularity. In this sense he was unquestionably successful. In his memoirs *Mandate for Change* he can proudly claim: "They were prosperous years. In spite of one mild and one sharp recession the income and productivity of the nation advanced markedly; steady progress toward fiscal responsibility was made, the divisions over internal security were ended; existing wars were stopped, threatening ones halted before they started."

In view of the pressing social needs, however, and of

the historical international forces demanding recognition, it looks at this point as if Eisenhower failed his time badly. The deadlock in civil rights, the need for social legislation in order to adjust the embarrassing inequities within an egalitarian nation were systematically ignored. The stalemated clash between East and West was confirmed rather than loosened by an unfortunate though skillfully executed policy of "brinkmanship." Since the Eisenhower administration made a deliberate point of achieving as little as possible, it must be admitted that in this sense its aims and fulfillments were remarkably congruous.

Practically the opposite is true of its successor. It seems at this time rather harsh to submit to objective scrutiny the attractive, hard-trying, well-intentioned Kennedy, shot out of office by a lunatic's rifle. But then historical judgment is rarely swayed by sympathy votes, and less often by mass hysteria. Louis XVI may have been well-intentioned and Alexander the Great a true moral pest, but history deals with positive results as reference material for the future. As for Kennedy, seldom has there been a President whose formulated intentions were in such painful contrast to their realization.

At least one can say that the Kennedy administration understood the urgency of constructive programs at home and abroad. Its incapacity to actualize them was only the more striking. The domestic legislation showed the miserably meager record. Although heavily committed to civil rights action, it did not make a move until, after two and a half years of promises, the Negro marches forced it to act. It then went overboard with a legislation that it had to modify when the popularity polls sank under the pressure of a white "backlash."

In foreign affairs the helplessness is even more conspicuous. It is unfortunate indeed that the Bay of Pigs disaster took place right at the beginning of Kennedy's tenure, for it set the tone for the next three years. The parallel Suez calamity in England could be repaired by jettisoning Anthony Eden on a vote of confidence. The

American nation being uncomfortably without such an institution, its prestige must be restored in external ways. There are the effective offices of public relations and mass media. We boost morale by advertising an attractive wife, lovely children, brilliant presidential advisers —in short, the wrapping of a non-existent product. Between 1960 and 1963, such ominously provocative events occurred as the appearance of the Berlin Wall, the establishment of the Communist bulwark in Cuba, charged with lethal power, and the breakdown of the military and political cohesion in South Vietnam. The misinterpretation and disguise of these events have served as useful devices for the public relations industry, but they can scarcely affect the odds of future historical judgment.

The Eisenhower-Kennedy years mark a standstill in the preparation of the egalitarian proletarian world. It is with Lyndon Johnson that the productive line of the Wilson, Roosevelt, Truman determination is taken up again, and indeed accentuated with new mastery. Whereas the Kennedy term had a divisive character, playing off business against labor, the South against the North, conservatives against liberals, Johnson's touch unites the country. He is one of the least likable of presidents, but he is the President of all, that is, of the consensus. He is the master equalizer. He is the grand administrator of the masses. It would be even more preposterous to try to assign a place in history to Johnson, still at this time working on his reputation as President, than it is to do so to his immediate predecessors. But so far, through actions as powerful as they are skillful, this President has made it abundantly clear that the impotent stalemate of the preceeding years is unlocked. The historical movement, for whatever it is worth, is proceeding again.

In the Johnson administration the politics of domestic and foreign affairs, both executed by tough negotiated bargaining, are rooted in the same uniting principle of a massive "great society." With Johnson, the governmental aid and development planning can only be conceived in huge designs, and the overseas military and economic programs seem merely an administrative extension of those at home. Never in time of peace has an American President attracted to his office so much centralizing power within the legal limits. He uses his position to equalize public opinion, to weaken dissent, and to mobilize the national sense of purpose.

The almost hostile reaction of artists, college professors, and others belonging to the intelligentsia is a significant confirmation of President Johnson's aims and stature. In the great amalgamated society controlled by the proletarian consensus, intellectuals and artists are inevitably to be leveled. No one at this point could be more painfully awakened than the artist to the technocratic triumph over spontaneous experience. No one in a conformist consensus society could be more frustrated than today's college professor. Whereas in the nineteenth century the scholar was still an autonomous thinker who, like the artist, aimed at original discovery and presentation, today's college teacher has all but lost his claim of independent thinking to a one-track know-how called specialization, to a *unisono* faculty opinion (liberal or not so liberal, depending on the campus), and to a publishing routine based on promotion chances. Naturally he rebels. Having bartered away his scholarly authenticity and not being able to rebel against the deans, he relieves his frustration by attacking the epitome of leveling power. Lyndon Johnson is against neither artist nor intellectual—he simply ignores them. This is perfectly in keeping with the prevalence of a self-standardizing society in which artist and scholar are only minor cogs, and the basic production forces must be streamlined into the national machine. Under President Johnson's regime, the military, economic, and social branches have become one consolidated organization in which virtually all members of the commonwealth are mobilized. Directed toward what?

Answering this question is as impossible as it is to explain toward which goal the Roman principate was directed. Each successive day President Johnson seems to look more like Emperor Augustus, who, while retaining the legal procedures and gestures of the old senatorial tradition, singlehandedly unified a confused and wavering empire into a reasonable, totalitarian apparatus. Compared to the Fascist and Communist experiments, the American way of negotiated progress is slow but durable. Its carefully administered process of proletarianization seems to avoid the shocks and furies of the upheavals on the European continent. To be sure, the recent history of the United States is not without scattered outbursts of unreason, wildcat strikes, Ku Klux Klan, McCarthyism, Negro riots, campus unrest. But these symptoms of unbalance remain within the Anglo-American tradition of gradually unfolding trends. It is for this reason that the American conception, backed by a massive administrative machinery, is the obvious guide in the growing, inevitable leveling and standardization of the world. This is an encouraging thought, for the American system for all its flaws is still the most secure instrument to develop a totalitarian society, without the accompanying fears and atrocities which mark the Fascist and Communist attempts.

The historical trend of socialization, now under way for almost two hundred years, necessarily forecloses the retainment of any democratic ideal. Gradually—perhaps not so gradually—as the crowd begins to set standards, the principle of democracy is steadily undermined. Democracy and proletarianization are incompatible. They rest on antagonistic principles. In order to acquire a true understanding of the twentieth century, one has to shed the illusions of still living in a democratic dispensation. The contrary is true.

The strength of democracy rests on the ability of the individual to make up his mind, to choose, to judge. It emerges with the faith that man's dignity distinguishes him from sheep, and that, far from being a follower, he can make reasoned decisions. The reason and *raison d'être* of democracy is precisely this human dignity, the confidence in man's independent judgment. Consensus is the opposite. The crowd has no judgment. It has opinions. Even if one chooses to disagree with Gustav Le Bon's *The Crowd,* which identifies the crowd with violence, the reason the masses at least are easily driven to and conveniently used for violence by demagogues is their innate need for opinionating. Nothing is simpler than to transform public opinion into weapons of violence. The qualities of leading and following then become interfused. The question of who rules becomes problematic. Is it the excited thrust of the black slaves on board the Spanish ship, or the helpless figurehead of Captain Benito Cereno, forced by the unskilled crowd to stay at his post?

When individual judgment and individual responsibility vanish, a democratic form of government is bound to slide toward block formations, group opportunism, and eventually toward totalitarianism. We have long since left the era of democracy. In this age of conformity and consensus, it would be dangerous to pretend to be still living by the democratic awareness of option and choice. If we want to benefit from the proletarian order, we must be resolved to face the basic facts of mass taste, mass standards, and mass culture, and thus encourage the free development of the American skill for mass administration. In any case, ever since Madison's Federalist Papers and Hamilton's efforts for a "strong" comprehensive government, the American political genius has been essentially far more republican than democratic. The participating democracy of some of the smaller European nations is, with the obvious exception of the early New England communities, impossible over here. Despite the insistence of ardent high school teachers, the political aims of the United States have always tended toward the most massive, most global, most comprehensive, rather than toward the individual or the distinctive. And without these no democracy can exist.

Naturally this new and still developing era demands a price. Proletarian equality is total and wholesale. It requires the abandoning of certain wishdreams which strive to prolong the external attributes of a past epoch. Originally, equality meant that each person be equal under one law. Gradually it came to be understood as a social arrangement whereby all enjoy the same opportunities. In the proletarian world this ultimately must mean complete standardization. The assembly line becomes the spine of society. Schools and universities are production machines of useful commodities, all uniformly polished in conformist treatment. Art, literature, and drama—all are carefully geared to the large market. Total equality, the only legitimate form of equality, demands total sacrifice of individual distinction.

The suspicion of the *Manifesto of the Equals* in 1796 was probably justified. If one sees the necessity and inevitability of the realization of an egalitarian world, the arts are likely to perish. While the totalitarian machines of Communism and Fascism killed the arts abruptly, we are engineering the same result more painlessly and slowly by patient negotiation. It will not serve to harbor any sentimental illusions in this respect. The freedom of equality is the freedom of the collective to divide the material goods and opportunities evenly, regardless of birth, creed, or innate talent. But culture, namely the culture which is remembered in history, is founded in another freedom. This is the freedom of the individual and the collective to enjoy mutual intercourse, and to serve each other in a fairly successful arrangement of harmony. With the historical alienation of the self from the group, of authenticity from public opinion, cultural freedom (which is comprehensive) is bartered for an economic freedom (which is partial).

In the classical era man's freedom was universal because individual and society were not yet self-consciously split. The individual experienced his true free potential within the community, and individualism, far from being against the group, was understood to be the expression of the social community. In the proletarian age the individual is sent into exile. Hence, the liberty of the modern era cannot be comprehensive. Culture has lost its spokesman, society its center. The proletariat is the periphery. It can only live and think and believe in terms of external adjustment. To use the expression of Thoreau, we are concerned "with the outmost defenses only of freedom," which is political liberty. But Thoreau erred when he believed that one can stem the historical tide. The individualism that he championed a hundred years ago was already then a passing factor in the experience of liberty. Today the predominance of the proletarian order, with its innate need to engulf the individual, is an established though not yet entirely consummated fact.

It would be foolish, indeed, to be either exalted or regretful about this new order. No one can ever be given a better task than to serve his own time. We cannot be loyal to the past by living in illusions and wishdreams. Socialization is not an ideal but a necessity. Modern man must serve this necessity or else the expanding complexity of the twentieth-century world will fall apart in self-destroying chaos. Our freedom may be limited, but it can be enjoyed if the limitation is realized. While proletarian man may have lost the flourish, élan, and glamor of the classical age, he is likely to gain in solidity and solidarity.

Part
FOUR

Henceforth, whate'er is wanting to yourselves
In others ye shall promptly find;—and all,
Enriched by mutual and reflected wealth,
Shall with one heart honour their common kind.

Thus was I reconverted to the world;
Society became my glittering bride.

William Wordsworth

13

The Social Way of Living

The egalitarian spirit

The nineteenth century was the era of the last defiant individuals who sent out messages of prophetic warning. Their cautioning against the predominance of the masses has become understood and absorbed in the general consciousness of the twentieth century. We all have now been made alert to the danger signals of mass-communication, mass-culture, and the like; in short, what previously was the premonition of the leading minds of genius, at present is common domain for anyone who has the minimum courage to reflect. This does not mean that we rush to the same conclusions and condemn group-tyranny, mass-conformity, and mob pressure *unisono*. Sometimes we do, sometimes we do not. Most frequently we try to persuade ourselves that our individual creativity is not smothered in conformity, that we can still make our own world, our own life, that we are not really cogs in the machine, that our independence and personal autonomy, though slightly limited, are essentially intact.

These are obviously emotional reactions with which one cannot deal in a logical, historical discourse. It would appear, however, that they represent a clear change in our mentality, that our minds are busy with the idea of the masses; indeed, that we are extremely self-conscious about them. Before we analyze the specific aspects in our society which reveal the detailed effect of this change in mentality, we must make ourselves fully aware not only that the historic turn did take place, but also of its extent, its inevitability, and its future implications. Most of us have either slowly or spontaneously come to accept the principle of equality as a wise and beneficial arrangement for modern life and probably for society in general. This inquiry is based on the premise that equal justice and equal opportunity for all is not only fair, but also expedient in the peculiar make-up of our industrialized and streamlined world. Moreover, equality is not an invention of determined liberals, but part of a gradually developing historical process. Equality is not only here to stay, it is likely to expand its sway over us. It is the only sound way in which to meet the remorseless exigencies of this technocratic age.

But while this is true, and inevitably so, we ought not to blind ourselves to the price we pay. If the price is right and the sacrifice worth the gain, we should not pretend that the commodity is a heaven-sent gift. If surgery keeps us alive, we can be grateful without denying that the amputation has left us an invalid. Whatever our situation, we owe it to ourselves and those immediately connected with us to understand it thoroughly; that is, to fathom our limitations. A helpful and wholesome discipline could, for instance, lie in an objective study of critical analyses of the egalitarian tendency which, without our approval or disapproval, can train our mind to coexist with uncomfortable ideas. We do not have to agree with an idealist, for instance, who—plague on both your houses—holds that both the American and Soviet egalitarianism are menaces, in order to take cognizance of the existence of a belief in a vague and anarchist commune-life. Therefore, when we see in Herbert Read's *Existentialism, Marxism and Anarchism* that "equality is a denial of brotherhood, of communion, of true communism," and that a democratic state "is a house divided (though equally) against itself" because "nature knows symmetry, but not equality," we may think this conception to be naïve, but only if we have first bothered to question how such expressions of disenchantment can emerge from the historical democratic process.

We should similarly not be afraid to remind ourselves of the disquieting likelihood that by abolishing social prerogatives and extending to all the privileges formerly enjoyed by an elite group, we will undermine the value of such privileges. This is Aldous Huxley's contention in *Music at Night*. "Experiences which, enjoyed by a few, were precious, cease automatically to be precious when enjoyed by many." Here he applies the law of diminishing returns, a notion derived from economics, indicating that in each developing process a maximum is reached, after which a decline sets in and no profit is yielded. In leisure, for instance, "beyond a certain point, more freedom from work produces a diminished return in happiness." Applied to the realm of politics we can observe that the "democratization of political institutions gives returns in the form of increased justice and increased social efficiency." But the top is reached and what previously represented an asset now turns out to be a liability. As an example, Huxley offers the proportional representation in Italy whose values soon after its introduction rapidly ceased to be positive and caused, among other factors, the rise of fascism. Of course, we can argue, rightly I believe that the proof is not valid, since proportional representation in other countries did not lead to decline or disaster. This is all for the good. But the point is that the efficacy of the egalitarian system in running governments, institutions, and business should not be dropped from debate and is still open to understanding criticism.

Whether H. L. Mencken's criticism of the American society can still be called "understanding" is debatable. Some abhor his basic vulgarity, others are still fascinated by his capricious wit. Most likely he will be remembered as a second-rate Nietzsche who transmuted a profound philosophical indignation into a popular journalism. But however we may judge him personally, he represents an attitude and a disillusionment of a vibrant and important generation which has left a permanent mark on the American consciousness. Mencken fought the assumption that the masses have an inalienable right to govern themselves, and, moreover that they are competent to do so. "Democracy may be a self-limiting disease, as civilization itself seems to be." The self-defeating element in a democratic society was evident in the fact that old aristocratic values were being restored under a new mask. "The baron has departed, but in his place stands the grand goblin, the supreme worthy archon, the sovereign grand commander." Above all, instead of the feudal nobility, there was the new democratic élite: the plutocracy. Naturally enough, though its function was the same, its nature was entirely different. For "its most puissant dignitaries of today came out of the mob only yesterday—and from the mob they bring all its peculiar ignobilities."

Whether or not we appreciate this picture of our aspirations, we cannot deny that it reveals a remarkable paradox inherent in the egalitarian system. We think to have risen above the unfairness of class distinction, yet we have divided society into a hierarchy of status levels which are not primarily based on merit but on merely external arrangements. Office holders are sacred. The weakest President is, by the sheer status of the White House, the greatest man in the country. Our values, being practical ones, must be proportioned to monetary assessments. The egalitarian rule is that every one should have the opportunity to buy the highest status.

The paradox, however, by no means lies exclusively in our plutocratic tendencies. Our entire way of living, especially what we are proud to call the American way of life, is by all its obvious appearances a persistent escape from what one could imagine an egalitarian community to represent. Benedetto Croce, writing at a particular time (1911) for a particular country (Italy), in his essay "Aristocracy and Youth" still pointed to the problem that in general marks the ascendance of the egalitarian state. Our time is remarkable, among other things, for the need to live as equals, but with a paradoxical hankering for aristocratic grandeur and refinement, both entirely alien to the fundamental nature of the society we have so successfully patterned after our plebeian designs. Mencken himself embodied this curious conflict in *optima forma*. With him, the ringing rhapsodic syntaxes of a Nietzsche became transformed into racy colloquialisms. His straightforward and coarse attacks were in strident contrast to the aristocratic elevation he found so much lacking and tried so ardently to promote in his age. He was the real representative of modern American consciousness: it has adopted a way of life and betrays its principle. Obviously we cannot peel off the icing and reject the dough. We select our cake and are committed to bulk as well as outer attractions. If mass society is preferable to class society, we ought to stick to it. There is such a thing as loyalty. While we are standing solidly in the common man's world of no-nonsense and pragmatism, our thoughts wander off nostalgically, as it were, toward grandeur, elegance, poetry, sophistication, illusion. Our head in the clouds is estranged from our feet in the clay.

For the insistent and greedy, of course, the question arises why we cannot have both worlds at once. For them it does not help to reply that this is a child's dream and that life is simply not arranged that way. It would suffice if they were only willing to realize that one cannot sow potatoes and reap orchids, that one cannot think like Henry Ford and write like Erasmus, nor should one start off on the Oregon Trail in order to reach Parnassus. This kind of day-dreaming betrays a lack of confidence in the tradition we have so gloriously built up and boisterously proclaimed to be the best. We all do it at times, since we all have been made conscious of the existence of this creeping amorphous substance of the masses.

But if we are unable to satisfy a child's appetite with reasoning, or unwilling to produce quick and quack remedies for our ambiguous practice of equality, we should be thoroughly committed to try to make ourselves known to ourselves as we grope for security in an insecure society. What are we in the cultural perspective of this age? If we say that we represent a proletarian phase in an historical development, we threaten to raise more questions than we can answer. Yet if we can only impress on ourselves what it does *not* mean, we will be better able to orient ourselves in the maelstrom of recent social and intellectual changes. Many of us will not buy the label "proletarian" because it smells, we believe, of a despised breed of drudging scullions which does not really belong to our age any more. A cultural proletariat, however, does not here mean a special class in a social stratification; on the contrary, it means a society as a whole viewed in historical proportions. It does not carry the pejorative overtones of, say, the German word *Prolet;* it is by no means discriminatory nor is a distinction to be included in it. We all belong historically to the proletarian dispensation. It does not mean that we have little or no pecuniary resources, that we have bad manners, baggy clothes, bad breath, or a dirty face; most of us have risen far above the state of these sorry attributes.

One of the sure signs of a cultural proletariat is, indeed, not poverty but the tyranny of money. Although emerged and emancipated from bourgeois exploitation, the proletarian mass society, far from outlawing the influence of money, has made it a sacred idol. It does not see that what makes money the tyrant of society is, to a great extent, its own reverence for it. The proletariat has done away with an historical elite and then created a fake one. It betrays itself when we have an Ivy League president with good looks, immense wealth, and Madison Avenue manners, and admire him as upperclass. It cries out from our debutante parties, it drips from the society section of *The New York Times*. It means to substitute the process of growing with that of buying; to force everything on ourselves that we have not acquired naturally. We have learned that culture is characterized by its education. Then we must have education. And because it must be better than ever, we organize gigantic, slickly lubricated school systems. But do we really want to learn? Ortega's experience was that readers nowadays have no intention of learning from books, but consider themselves qualified to judge them on the basis of a commonplace knowledge already present in their heads. Not only are we reluctant to read in a questioning and intelligent manner, we are, the author believed, equally loath to listen. The average man sees no reason for it, for he wants to judge and to pronounce, and for this he already has all the necessary abilities. Even if we would like to disagree with Ortega and find his opinion too generalized, we cannot possibly deny that the described tendency is vividly evident around us.

The modern compulsion to adulate precisely those aspects of a developed society which are atrophic or rudimentary in our own is reflected in the way in which we regard certain conspicuous families as a kind of social super-class. If we single out such Rockefellers, Harrimans, or Mellons, the purpose is not to point to their positions and attitudes, but rather to indicate our own perverse misconceptions about the notion of elite. It is one thing to admire, behind the glamor of their family fortune, the principle that a little man can with intelligence, endurance, and will power become a big man; it is quite another matter to accept that this type of greatness must automatically include the organic greatness of culture. If we suggest that the Kennedy family epitomizes

our proletarian mentality, it is not because Grandfather
Patrick J. was a saloon-keeper. It is merely because they
assess the power of money as being applicable to cultural
achievements. It is not to deny their talents to see the
spectacularity by which they mask and adorn the gaps
between those talents. If they want something of value,
position, reputation, influence, or popularity, they haggle
and manipulate until they have added it to their property. Again, the harshness of this remark is basically directed to ourselves, for we encourage this as "smart." And
smart it is. But is it great? The smartness we worship is
fundamentally a "getting away with things" successfully,
with a minimum of investment and a maximum of windfall. Thus we have supplanted the organic principle of
growing with grabbing. We confuse success and achievement. We construct and manipulate values from the outside, instead of letting them develop from inner maturity.
We think that culture is erecting an expensive center in
Washington, a huge library here, a grand theater there,
or distributing medals and awards on the White House
lawn.

The question arises whether this external manipulation
of culture through the means and power of wealth must
be seen as exclusively typical for our time. Did there not
exist similar situations in previous ages? There did. The
Renaissance popes, the Medicis, the Borgias, the Bour-
bons, or the burghers of seventeenth-century Holland, all
linked their wealth and power to contemporary culture.
But whereas some similarities are plain, it will serve the
understanding of our own time if we keep in mind one
decisive difference. It is not so much that in general we
are inclined to rate the quality of our own achievements
as inferior to those of the Renaissance and the baroque
age. One can always hope, theoretically, that the walls of
the Museum of Modern Art will one day rival those of
the Sistine Chapel. The proletarian attitude is evident in
our frantic concern to force culture upon ourselves at all
costs. We have excelled previous ages in efficient legislation, in economic organization, and in business adminis-

tration, as well as in technological marvels. So why not construct great cultural feats in the same manner? "Because we have decent political institutions, a mobile and egalitarian society, a high standard of living, and a literate populace, they say we can also be the world's greatest philosophers, the world's most amusing conversationalists, and the world's best artists," writes Daniel J. Boorstin in *America and the Image of Europe*. Lorenzo the Magnificent or Karl August of Saxe-Weimar were highly individual collectors of greatness which they happened to find around them, and as history proceeded it became clear that the glory and the real leadership of their courts rested in Angelo Poliziano, Marsilio Ficino, Pico della Mirandola, Botticelli, and Filippo Lippi, or in Goethe, Schiller, Herder, and Wieland. The aristocratic courts were not self-conscious about "greatness" and did not mention the word. Nor did they proceed from a kind of collective feverish consensus that for heaven's sake we must have culture, and let's have it now and here! A splendid culture cannot be conjured up by decree, proletarian or otherwise. The difference between the classical mentality and ours lies in the disheartening fact that we are incapable of understanding cultural energy as the leading and decisive force of civilizations. Instead, we see it as a decorative concomitant. In our rightly or wrongly half-ashamed attitude toward our materialist environment, we want to cheer up the alleged dullness of our shopping-center conceptions with the colorful expressions of mind, otherwise called arts and letters. Culture then becomes an accessory to our machine world, a bonus for solid citizenry, a feather in the workman's cap. We seem to be continuously grabbing beyond our reach, as if trying to snatch roses out of the sky in order to adorn computers and nuclear installations.

A cultural proletariat reveals itself in other respects. The refined Maecenas of the past could enjoy the works of his favorite protégés privately and individualistically, for no other reasons save personal taste. He had no need to amplify what he understood as greatness and broadcast the merits of his age. In his smug self-satisfaction he saw no urgency to publicize his tastes and make converts to his convictions. In the twentieth century, however, when individual judgment is swamped in public consensus, artistic or literary taste is replaced by common opinion and treated as the fashions of the garment industry. As a result, there must be agencies to knead and sway this common opinion, and their inevitable technique to effectuate this depends on a consistent use of superlatives. "The superlative gives a good conscience to the biographer—by applying a rhetorical gadget, he achieves the transformation of the average into the extraordinary. . . . What on first sight seems to be a rather harmless atmosphere of entertainment and consumption is, on closer examination, revealed as a reign of psychic terror, where the masses have to realize the pettiness and insignificance of their everyday life." This is the judgment of Leo Lowenthal. For some decades now, critics have instructed us week after week about the appearance of great new stars and magnificent new genius, but, after hopefully waiting, one finds that the alleged magnificence has a life span no longer than the saleability of the product and the related patience of the press agents. This is the price one pays for culture by fashion.

There is mordant irony in this procedure. For one would imagine that nothing could be farther away from the sober, egalitarian mind than the tenacious effort to insist on magnificence. We have traditionally considered the independent conceptions of outstanding men to be a threat to the peace of our community. Great men are troublemakers. No society has more successfully feared and excluded rebellious genius, no nation suffered less from it than the American. Yet because modern industrialized man realizes that the splendor of civilizations is carried by their most brilliant representatives, he clamors for excellence, a quality incompatible with his alarm at the extreme. His utterances and demands are flagrantly opposed to the security he has helped to build in collectivity. Genius is rooted in obsessive extremism, whether it be the type of a Luther, Cromwell, Rousseau, Frederick the Great, Dostoevski, or Bismarck, and regardless of its being presented in controlled élan or neurotic boorishness. It bursts forth from a demonic source which knows nothing of the artificial limits that society honors. The exigencies of popular rule, however, force the *demos* to moderation, comfort, ease, efficiency, streamlining of trouble—all agreeable attributes, but hardly conducive to unusual excellence. The moderation of the man of genius will lie in the discipline by which he harnesses his radical drives. His inner authenticity is one of rebellion and abundance. On the contrary, the fury to which the crowd can rise is whipped up externally by agitators.

Finally, proletarian culture is recognizable by the curious absence of any characteristic style of living, thinking, and stating. What would be more natural than that an emancipated mentality, released from the narrow conditions of a feudal and bourgeois context, should find its own binding form of expression? Clearly we have a *way* of living, thinking, and expressing. But this indicates exactly an absence of that guiding principle predicated by style. The egalitarian society is marked by drift. It sails like an amorphous cloud, changing direction and shape by the fortuitous thrusts of wind. It does not move by its own dynamics. Hence the culture of a mass-society is eclectic and under extraneous motivation imitates the ornamental forms and fragments of styles from rejected earlier eras. Its modes of expression, far from originating in an inner urgency of energy, are more or less the accidents of an external process. William Hazlitt already saw the coming replacement of private taste by public taste as a threat to society. Whether or not we esteem his judgment as true, it is a remarkable indicator of historical change. "The diffusion of taste is not the same thing as the improvement of taste; but it is only the former of these objects that is promoted by public institutions and other artificial means. The numbers of candidates for fame and of pretenders of criticism, is then increased beyond all proportion, while the quantity of genius and feeling remains the same; with this difference that the man of genius is lost in the crowd of competitors, who would never have become such but from encouragement and example; and that the opinion of those few persons whom nature intended for judges, is drowned in the noisy suffrages of shallow smatterers of taste." The outwardly directed nature of this tendency is recognized in modern sociology, especially by Émile Durkheim whose whole method is based on the *"phénomènes sociaux,"* which are facts marked by their power of external coercion and, in clear contrast to those of psychology, "must be studied from the outside as exterior objects." Thus, sociology as the study of "the group" predominantly analyzes external influences. Rightly so. It means acknowledging the externalization of an egalitarian and conformist world, with which we are more and more permanently identified.

The absence of inner originality has been turned into an asset in industrial organization. Drive is divorced from leadership. The author of a well-known study of this situation quotes one personnel director as believing that "men of strong personal convictions, willing to make unorthodox decisions, are more frequently given to the characteristics of 'drive' rather than 'leadership'," and adds the opinion of a president about the change in today's hiring: "We used to look primarily for brilliance. . . . Now that much-abused word 'character' has become very important. . . . We want a well-rounded person who can handle well-rounded people." The author's comment: "Ideas come from the group, not from the individual. The well-rounded man is one who does not think up ideas himself but mediates other people's ideas, and so democratically that he never lets his own judgment override the decisions of the group." Leadership thus has come to mean the art of following. Obviously, under these circumstances leadership in taste, style, and culture is likely to suffer from the same tendency of judging by consensus. In the period of bourgeois predominance the attrition and demolition of aristocratic forms could take place without great loss of individuality; indeed, originality of thought and formulation became, if not more important *de facto*, at least more consciously promoted. Consequently we can recognize species of art and literature which are patently bourgeois. Naturalism and realism reveal qualities closely related to middle-class life. But the multifarious trends, isms, and techniques of the twentieth-century arts seem absolutely detached from a fundamental proletarian world view, as indeed the Soviet Union has promulgated them to be. For what, one may ask, have the curved *art nouveau* of Frank Lloyd Wright or the Bauhaus puritanism, the subsequent periods of Picasso or of Mondriaan, existentialism or symbolic logic, the puzzles of serialism or the vibrations of electronic music, the futurism of Marinetti or the imagism of Pound—what have these disparate forms of expression to do with the egalitarian masses? The works that ostensibly deal with the problems of the lower classes, such as those of a Gorki, Käthe Kollwitz, Odets, Menotti, or Heijermans, frequently fall back on conventional, usually naturalistic, styles; or in other cases, such as with Brecht or Genet, they are often conceived too intellectually to appeal to the worker.

Two notes of caution must be added to these remarks. In the first place, an inquiry like this, probing the almost overwhelming complexities of the contemporary environment, is admittedly tentative and should hold out the possibility that later centuries may be able to see a unifying style of brilliance and magnitude in our confused and disconnected utterances. We ourselves can only describe our world as it strikes us in jumble and chaos.

Secondly, so far we have related cultural mass-response to achievements of only the highest artistic and literary caliber. But is there not such a thing as popular culture? Should we not take the broadest view possible and include the roles of folklore, movies, vaudeville, and other lighter arts in our investigation? There is, and we should. The range of culture being wide, there is no reason to set the limits of mass-culture only by the highest forms of civilization, and we will, indeed, give due attention later to the increased role of popular entertainment in modern society. The trouble is, however, that by thinking in the awkward terms of "high" and "low" arts, which is as inevitable as it is discriminating, we have already prejudged the case.

The only important inference to be made from the foregoing analysis should be not that our proletarian outlook precludes the enjoyment of great arts and letters (nothing would be more erroneous), but that this mentality implies a discrepancy between what we set out to do on an egalitarian basis in the political, economic, and social sphere, and our forced aspiration toward sophisticated expressions of civilization. The official Soviet policy, so far at least, has been much more consistent and logical. The American today seems to be standing with one foot in the proletarian camp and the other in the bourgeois camp, which is an untenable position in the long run and one responsible for the neurotic and schizoid culture to which he insists on accommodating himself.

The public spirit

The function of language, being one of the most conspicuous assets of our communication system, makes it an appropriate starting point for a discussion on the changes in expression within modern society. The broadening of popular education, as well as the popularization of higher education which has been taking place during recent decades, also produces a greater self-knowledge, a deeper awareness of our place in the wide context of history. The emergence and ascendance during the last century of new disciplines such as sociology, psychology, and anthropology are already indicative of mankind's increased interest in itself. The danger is not so much in these sciences themselves, which can be and have been treated as responsibly as any other; the nature of the subject matter, however, is easily made fit for mass-consumption.

This can have great merits in some respects, but in others tends to simplify intricate problems beyond recognition. Popular sociology aided by commercial promotion has frequently made millions of intelligent but untrained readers aware of contemporary situations without being able to make them understand the historical background and implications or the relationship of these situations to contiguous ones. To take an important instance, the complex problem of alienation with its widespread ramifications has often been presented in a rather cheap and sentimentalized version, thus creating a popular consciousness of something only half-understood—that is, not understood.

Here we are clearly in the middle of the difficult problem of journalism. Difficult, because the weight of journalism is daily upon us; whether we stand at the receiving or at the distributing end, we are involved in the process of a cheap, fast, and massive traffic of facts ranging from news to knowledge. Our emotional response leads us to eulogize or condemn it according to mood, temper, or circumstances. It is plainly not relevant here to list and balance the credits and debits of the journalistic conveyance of information. A case can be made for the news media in the widest sense as a curse or a blessing. Regardless of its merits and deficiencies, journalism means something to modern man in terms of self-knowledge within the context of his time.

"I call journalism everything which interests me less tomorrow than today," said André Gide. This seems a fair enough judgment, and one which is particularly helpful for our own pursuit. By defining the notion of journalism in this manner, the author by implication set it off at once against the nature of history. Whereas history depends on the importance of the future of an event, journalism is essentially concerned with the event inasmuch as it has an immediate appeal to present usage. This is not to say that we cannot derive historical value from the back issues of newspapers, for instance. We can. But only if we allow for the curious distortion which

journalistic practice gives, and is bound to give, of the
world picture in its immediacy. The daily press is directed
by so many diversified pressures and interests that its
projections more frequently than not put the truth of the
contemporary scene entirely out of proportion. If we take
an average respectable newspaper of 1905, for example, a
year fraught with great potentialities for both future disasters and progress, we see plainly demonstrated the
chasm between the real world and its vital promise and
the make-believe world of journalism. New York's *Sun*, in
the issue of December 31, offers a broad variety of political, social, artistic, and other information, arranged in a
serious format which leaves no doubt about sound editorial responsibility. On the front page, the main headlines
(modest in size) are devoted to a slain ex-Governor of
Idaho, to the new head of the New York police force,
various subway mishaps, and the unlikelihood of a world
war. The leading articles on the editorial page deal with
the Mayor of New York and such significant topics as
"Man's house is his own castle" and "King James' English." (The Americans speak better English than the British.) Most of the columns are filled with local politics
and now long-forgotten very important people, with success stories of a Miss Kelly in a gold camp of Alaska and
Billy Sunday's business talents. There is a feature article
on French castles for sale, another on "record making
freaks," like champion ice-cream eating, and a three-
minute record in a divorce case at Cook County. From
the advertisements we learn about "1905 history-making
in music" (pianola-rolls), the new "frocks of mousseline
and Valencienne," and the latest models of cars: the Win-
ton Model K, the Fiat 20 h.p., and the Royal Tourist,
which we are to believe is an "honest car." If one would
like to know the impact of the ominous political events of
the day on the paper, the answer is, according to one
commentator, that a world war is unlikely and, to another, that the revolution in Russia is crushed. The importance of the Russo-Japanese war is made clear in a
book review, and elsewhere Nicholas II is described as an

"unlucky czar" who, though a liberal at heart, declares the principle of autocracy.

The newspaper as a whole thus may provide us with some interesting details for social history, which gratefully studies the trivia of daily life, but as a picture of the important issues and expectations of the time it appears miserably inadequate. Far from blaming it for this limitation, one should acknowledge that the very nature of journalism, even in its least sensational forms, makes it incapable of seeing major events in true perspective, of assessing the Russian Revolution rightly at its onset, or the Moroccan crisis of 1905 which marked the beginning of Germany's fall from power. It cannot and should not want to evaluate the historic changes which in that year began to take place with Einstein's first lecture on relativity and the founding of the expressionist painters' group *Die Brücke*. It is only natural that it fails to see the meaning of such disparate experiments as those of the Wright brothers and of Strindberg a few years before. When one thumbs through the brittle and faded pages of that year's issues, one is struck by the charm of innocence and ignorance in which the historic image of the time is represented in newspapers.

The idea and function of journalism have been with Western society for a long time. Although Julius Caesar's *Acta diurna* were by no means newspapers in the modern sense, they publicized the occurrences in the Senate and elsewhere for everyone to read or to copy. The *courantes* and *nouvelles* circulating in Renaissance times, and epitomized by the *Fugger-Zeitungen* from 1568 to 1605, to a certain extent already approached modern reporting, although their scope was limited to the exclusive use of private individuals and merchant houses. This, however, was no longer true of the seventeenth-century *gazettes*, of which those of Amsterdam, Utrecht, Leiden, and The Hague were the most influential. They might be either translated or circulated in the original language, but they appeared in thousands of copies throughout Europe.

Important as these early forerunners of newspapers

were, they obviously mean little for the problems of mass media. And although it is not true that journalism originated with the writers of the Young Germany movement, as Egon Friedell thinks, one must indeed look to the beginning of the nineteenth century for the modern characteristics of the news press. It was then that the invention of the steam-driven machine press (1810) and the improvements of the rotary presses (1815) opened up a vast field of popular communication never before envisaged. In 1834, not a single provincial town in England issued a daily paper. In 1855, the total provincial papers for the United Kingdom numbered 560; by 1833, the total was 1576, of which 162 were dailies. Naturally, it was not the technique of the Industrial Revolution that was responsible for the alleged evils for which later generations were to blame the newspapers. The question of guilt is usually futile and irrelevant in history. The point is that the opportunity for mass taste suddenly announced itself, and no sooner did it knock than the doors of the eager agents were flung open.

One of them, Émile de Girardin, founded the Paris newspaper *La Presse* in 1836 at a subscription rate of half the usual amount. The rest of the necessary income was to come from announcements and advertisements. With this novelty the number of subscribers grew rapidly, and competition between the papers became keen. The fight between *La Presse* and its rival *Siècle* for the public taste was particularly evident in the realm of the serial novel. The former contracted Balzac and Eugène Sue, while the latter relied chiefly on Alexandre Dumas. In order to satisfy the overwhelming demand, respectable authors began to employ hack writers to aid them in producing the standardized *feuilletons*, which were now turned out in true factories of literature. "Dumas employs seventy-three collaborators, and amongst them one August Maquet, whom he allows to work quite independently. Literary work now becomes a 'commodity,' " Arnold Hauser explains.

The element of mechanization and standardization in

forms of expression heretofore deemed absolutely spontaneous and individual has become a common aspect of modern living. But in the middle of the nineteenth century it represented a novelty which shocked the more sensitive observers. The responses came from many and varied directions. Marx doubted the freedom of a press conducted by greedy businessmen. Kierkegaard believed that "the lowest depth to which people can sink" was defined by the word "journalist." In the American hemisphere, Thoreau turned vehemently against the newspapers which, in *Life without Principle*, he regarded as alienated from real life as he himself knew it. "I do not know but it is too much to read one newspaper a week. I have tried it recently, and for so long it seems to me that I have not dwelt in my native region." The insight that "news" becomes estranged from reality reminds one of Rilke's war-time letters (March 9, 1918) when he complained about the "sham-happenings" in the papers. "Humanity becomes accustomed continually to accept a world of news in place of realities which no one has time or is minded anymore to let grow large and heavy within them. I never was and cannot any longer become a newspaper reader."

These highly subjective pronouncements of individual genius are of course not intended to prove that nothing respectable can be said of the journalistic trade, but merely to indicate danger symptoms as registered by sensitive minds. Obviously, a case can be made for the beneficial functions of modern journalism. Reporters are now better trained and more solidly prepared for responsible news analysis than ever before. But we are not concerned here with giving merit badges to the quality and skills of the news media. It is important to see how journalism in its historical development has come to report not on reality, but on a make-believe world such as the masses want to experience. It would be misunderstanding the structure of modern history to blame either the newspaper men or the masses for changes which run parallel to similar developments in other areas of contemporary society.

The vulgarization of the press is part of a general process which, for better or for worse, must be understood as natural and inevitable.

To what extent journalism is closely interwoven with the changes in the twentieth-century outlook may best be seen in its tight alliance with the politicians. This was already evident in Thoreau's time: "I cannot take up a newspaper but I find that some wretched government or other, hard pushed and on its last legs, is interceding with me, the reader, to vote for it. . . . The newspapers are the ruling power. . . . If a man neglects to read the *Daily Times*, government will go down on its knees to him, for this is the only treason in these days." This compact, however, was only child's play compared to the interdependence of government and news media under Franklin Roosevelt. He was the first President to employ a special news secretary, and in every respect his administration represented a "new deal for the press." His "fireside chats" and the handling of his press interviews revealed that a President was no longer dealing with the "people" but with "public opinion." Press management by the White House has ever since been quietly accepted, and when protests were made during the administration of President Kennedy, it was only because the act of manipulation looked more glaringly undemocratic with a man lacking Roosevelt's talents. Characteristically, it did not worry the public.

Thus news reporting becomes advertising. When one compares the tone, style, and format of a paper of 1905, such as that described above, with the aggressive appearance of any daily five decades later, the change in mass communication becomes manifest. Even before the turn of the century, Joseph Pulitzer sensed the resources of *sensation* for large business and appealed directly to the populace by blaring headlines, "a screaming patriotism, an enthusiastic if somewhat vague reforming spirit, a marked attention to 'human interest' stories of adventure, love and crime, and a profusion of 'special features,' " according to Carlton J. H. Hayes. But drowning out all this are the superlative slogans of the advertisements. Turning the pages of even the most respectable newspaper today, one can hardly find the news event among the wide spaces reserved for the eulogies of our merchandise. No wonder this has affected the tone and approach of news reporting itself. In order to compete, as it were, the "story" must be advertised too. One dreads to think what in the near future is to climax the full-page headline we are enjoying at the present. It is clear that only certain events lend themselves to this type of amplification; hence the predominance of kidnapped babies, divorced movie stars, hold-up men, and corrupt politicians in the social picture of our life. The political event is advertised by blowing it up to the size of a crisis. There must be a crisis every day. Somewhere in the world an American is bound to be snubbed, or his flag to be insulted. Thus, many of the incidents, which in the nineteenth century might have been ended with the appearance of a gunboat, are now proclaimed to be crises and are almost predestined to become so in fact. With due recognition of other influential factors in our intensified world situation, one can see that the role of the press is related, in part at least, to the inflated image of our life and environment. Intimate social values have ceased to exist. The details of human existence are made public, and once publicized they must be enlarged and made-up like the features of a prostitute.

In this game, the politician thrives. As early as 1867, Walter Bagehot pointed to the distortion created by the English newspapers in overemphasizing the facts of political life. "They give a precedence and a dignity to that world which they do not give to any other. The literary world, the scientific world, the philosophic world, not only are not comparable in dignity to the political world, but in comparison are hardly worlds at all." One wonders what Bagehot would have felt had he seen F.D.R.'s time with the new tendencies which, according to Daniel Boorstin, "could be described as the rise of the Nationally-Advertised President." White House administration came to be accepted by the public as a product assembled and marketed along the same line as is expedient for General Motors. "Like other 'nationally-advertised brands' F.D.R. could not, of course, have been successful if he had not had something to offer. But he might not have been able to sell himself to the American public . . . without the aid of certain revolutionary changes in our system of public communication."

Thus, we live in a world whose values are blown up and distorted by the tools of persistent propaganda. The average man dislikes trouble; so we give him mostly agreeable news. But, as in all other fairy-tales, there must be a villain who is to lose. So we give him the black-bearded Castro. The whole equipment of highly trained correspondents informs us day by day that his government is about to collapse, but we learn nothing about the rapid progress of educational improvements, or the close allegiance of the Cuban youth. And we are surprised, during the days of the Bay of Pigs disaster, that the population does not rise against the villain, as we think it should. The ordinary man gets the feeling that he is elevated from the petty rut of his existence by absorbing his daily dose of great news, not unlike the *soma* pills which the people of Huxley's *Brave New World* swallow against psychological depressions. And while they enjoy their *feelies* for continuous excitement, we have our "tellies." Television, indeed, outstrips all other communication media in the immediacy of its pictorial demonstration. In the rush of our time-saving world, this is important. It is also encouraging to realize that millions of differently oriented viewers in every part of the globe can now simultaneously watch the Olympic Games. The B.B.C., the first organization to explore and establish television programs, was justifiably proud in its prophecy of 1948 that "before long a home without this window on the world will be as unthinkable as today one is which has no radio set." A window, however, can only provide a very limited sector of the total horizon, and a real danger lies in the acceptance of a part for the whole. With its quality of greater immediacy, television clearly intensifies the factor of curse as well as blessing in mass communication. In a sense, the ingenuity of a Girardin and a Pulitzer already made the common man a pawn of greedy industry. With the far more vivid and tantalizing representations of television, resistance can hardly be expected of him any longer. His own greed becomes entirely identified with that of the sponsoring business concerns. If we recognize the advantage which radio brings, for instance, to isolated communities by connecting them instantly with the world and the national culture at large, we can see that television is able to perform this task even more efficiently. But it would be folly to close one's eyes to the inevitable ensuing conformity. It is doubtful, to say the least, whether one must welcome this "national homogeneity," as it has been called, with any measure of enthusiasm.

Similarly it should at least be a matter of minimum concern to wonder what happens to the alertness and judgment of mature minds being persistently bombarded by child's stuff. The spiritual erosion involved in this situation is naturally impossible to express in statistics. It is equally hard, however, to believe that it will not in the long run prove to be a blight on the tissue of a coherent society.

Radio and television services are obvious boons for the modern proclivity for talking. The development of parliamentary procedures in government provides a large scope for argumentation, and the increased opportunity for public life, especially in the United States, opens up unusual possibilities for oral expression. One would like to know, however, why no important oratory seems to develop along with this public spirit. We are being told frequently that our age has returned to the means and goals of the Sophists, but, if so, the trend apparently does not extend to a concern about public speech. The Greek democracy produced a line of orators which through Lysias, Isocrates, and Lycurgus climaxes in Demosthenes. The Romans had Cato, the Gracchi, and Cicero. In

both cases we find an educational system prepared to fulfill the needs. In Athens, H. D. F. Kitto tells us, the art of
persuasion was originally a matter of native wit and practice. Under the Sophists it could be learned, at a price,
while in Rome Cicero taught that the highest task for
man was granted to the orator-politician. Contemporary
education, for all its pragmatic claims, is neither willing
nor equipped to incorporate the art of rhetoric in the curriculum. Consequently, with the exception of Winston
Churchill and Adlai Stevenson, few recent politicians can
be considered to have contributed to the tradition of
great oratory. Most of them are satisfied with pedestrian
clichés or more wisely rely on clever ghostwriting. A
ghost-writer, however, is not essentially a composer of
speeches, but a participant in a joint project of two or
more specialists, including the politician. The delivered
speech is a composite product, and the public takes this
as much for granted, argues Daniel Boorstin, as the fact
"that an advertisement of the Ford Motor Company
should not be written by Henry Ford." Modern oratory,
instead of being based on the art of persuasion by means
of a personal and sophisticated style of language, seems
more and more to be an exercise in compliance with public opinion. In politics as elsewhere the leading principle
is that of marketing. The citizen is a shopper. Significantly, the new science of public opinion started with
advertising managers, and the new profession of public
relations developed after the anti-big-business feelings of
the 1890's and the muckraking activities around the turn
of the century. If one can speak at all of a modern style
of political technique and oratory, it is best described as
a product of the Madison Avenue agencies.

   This is also curiously applicable to the popular preaching of our time. The type of evangelical oratory of which
Billy Graham is the perfect master postulates that the
Christian message is a "hot" commodity which can be
marketed by modern, hard-driving selling techniques. In
ancient days, the voice of God appeared in the poetic
rhythms and metaphors of Isaiah, Jeremiah, Ezekiel, or

Nahum. The modern prophets in business suits have adopted the manners and diction of high-class hucksters.

The moving spirit

While communication as language is a transference of human subjectivity to the outside world, transportation relocates man's entire physical being. Since George Stephenson introduced the marvelous locomotive in 1814, modern society has been characterized by perpetual motion, if not restlessness. Once the opportunity was there, man would exploit all its potentialities to the hilt. It is less obvious why, once he has felt the thrill of mechanical movement, he is forever compulsively pressing toward faster and faster speeds, to the point where velocity becomes an abstract experience in outer space.

The change from horse power to steam and mechanics did not occur without resistance. It took the fervent belief and tenacity of John Stevens of Hoboken to overcome the inertia of legislators and businessmen before even the most primitive railroad system could be started in the eastern regions of the United States. In England, where the original triumph of steam power took place, the official acceptance of the new kind of transport was no less reluctant. The early railroad bills, from 1821 on, only passed with delay and against vigorous opposition. A writer in the *Quarterly Review* of 1825 thought that the powers of the locomotive were grossly exaggerated. "We would as soon expect the people of Woolwich to suffer themselves to be fired off upon one of Congreve's ricochet rockets, as trust themselves to the mercy of such a machine, going at such a rate." The Great Western Bill of 1835 was fought vehemently by both Eton and Oxford and only passed after the institutions succeeded in pushing the proposed line away from their territory.

We will be misleading ourselves if we explain these reactions as entirely caused by conservative thinking. Most of the resistance, no doubt, was just that. But there was another element of human concern involved here which cannot be overlooked. Although less conspicuous, it had greater importance. It was partly related to the ensuing railroad speculations and their periods of hysterical mania that resulted in financial breakdowns. For another part it bore on the intrinsic change involved in turning away from organically generated power to mechanical motion. The element of speed itself was negligible. George Stephenson committed himself to keep it down to fourteen miles an hour. Any horse can do better than that. But one should consider the impact, probably mostly unconscious, of the element of dehumanization implicit in the new steam order. Horse riding can still be humanly experienced. But the energy of locomotives, cars, airplanes, rockets is outside the range of human identification. It is hostile to the experience of organic life and growth. The impact of the train, furthermore was far more disruptive than that of the automobile or the space vehicle was to be. For here, for the first time, was demonstrated an encroachment from the extraneous scientific world upon the intrinsically human experience of motion.

The element of mania in the new railroad society revealed itself in another aspect, more easily understood and more frequently mentioned. It was most spectacularly manifest in the United States where the vast expansion offered an almost unlimited source of windfall for the early developers of the railway system. Between 1860 and 1890, the railway mileage increased from 30,000 to 166,000 miles, while by 1900 it stood at 240,000 miles. The unfortunate by-product, however, as James Bryce was quick to point out, emerged in the compact between the railroad companies and the politicians. "In New York the great New York Central Railroad, in Pennsylvania the Pennsylvania Railroad under its able chiefs, exerted immense influence with the legislature, partly by their wealth, partly by the opportunities of bestowing favors on individuals and localities which they possessed, including the gift of free passes, and possibly influence exercised on the votes of their employees. Sometimes, at least in Pennsylvania and New York, they even threw their weight into the scale of a political party, giving it money as well as votes. But more commonly they have confined themselves to securing their own interests, and obliged, or threatened, and used, the State leaders of both parties alike for that purpose."

Thus the change in the conception of transport was twofold. It demonstrated an element of dehumanizing social communication, and for the first time in history it made transport into a speculative commodity. What originally served exclusively as a means of social intercourse, now became detached from its own purpose and was, at least partly, exploited for extraneous purposes. That this exploitation was by no means generally considered harmful is evident in view of the rise of the motor car as a commodity. On the contrary, few of us will dare to deny greatness to the spectacular surge of the auto industry. Leaving economics aside, we merely point to the new social life created by the automobile in the entailing aspects such as suburbanization, parkways, motels, diners, shopping-centers, and billboards.

The automobile also transformed the exclusive tourism of the nineteenth century into an international passion. Whereas leisure travel, having the aura of the upper-class, was originally performed in a certain measure of style and repose even by those who did not belong to it, popular tourism is marked by rushing and bustling. Above all, popular tourism has become a trade. It is the familiar pattern. Like most other developments of mass communication, modern travel is absorbed by the big industry. Tourism also has become a commodity. In the summer months a pushing mass of people, organized and directed by efficient agencies, crowds together in selected spots. We like to think that it is fair to make the beauty of the world and of Western civilization available for as many as have eyes to see it and stamina to endure the strain. We also believe that the educational value ascribed to travel will now benefit a greater part of the population. This is true enough, but no more so than the other consideration that tourism on this scale and in this manner has inevitably led to a leveling of cultural varieties and distinctions. This prompted Aldous Huxley to say "that the more traveling there is, the more will culture and way of life tend everywhere to be standardized and therefore the less educative will travel become."

Travel has also become a part of the technique of government. It is an effective way of exposing oneself. Microphones, cameras, and crowds are organized at selected places to advertise not so much achievement as the symbolic status of high office. Travel for presidents and prime ministers is a pleasurable way to "reach" the people. It is a specially rewarding device in a time when the search for popularity has been substituted for the art of achievement. The accomplishments of a Sully, a William Pitt, or a Cavour did not need mass exposure. Moreover one must wonder if this new technique of "going direct to the people" will not gradually undermine the very principles of democracy. Some authoritarian rulers have exploited it successfully. Napoleon III probably thought so when he went stumping on his handshaking tours. De Gaulle has learned from him. Even the Pope is now seeking popularity by travel. There was a time when all the roads led to Rome. Now the Pope goes out of the Vatican to meet the world. With the increase in number of Roman Catholics during the last century, the influence of the Papacy on world affairs has diminished proportionately. In order to maintain himself among the mass-hungry statesmen, the Pope understandably has no recourse save to advertise his high and colorful office with all the means of modern communication, including the technique of propaganda travel.

When we add to this voluntary motion the daily commercial travel and the shuttling of millions of commuters, we can see how the revolution in the means of transport has caused all repose to vanish from our social structure. But one can also wonder if, on the contrary, the speedier forms of conveyance do not rather conveniently fulfill latent needs for escaping and trekking. However this may be, the picture we have of our world is one of milling restlessness. Modern man of the last decades is best described as a transient. He has no soil but a suburb to root in. "If by roots we mean the complex of geopraphical and family ties that has historically knitted Americans to local society, these young transients are almost entirely rootless—" thus the observation of W. H. Whyte.

This mobility, which now seems to have reached the point of compulsion all over the Western world, has always been native to the United States. Even de Tocqueville had already observed this "secret restlessness which reveals itself in the actions of the Americans." The American "chooses a profession, then gives it up. He settles in a place which he soon leaves to carry his fickle desires elsewhere. . . . Finally death suddenly appears and overtakes him before he is tired of that futile pursuit after a complete happiness which forever evades him." Theodore Parker, in a speech printed in 1852, confirmed this: "We are the most restless of people. How we crowd into cars and steamboats; a locomotive would well typify our fuming, fizzing spirit. In our large towns life seems to be only a scamper. Not satisfied with bustling about all day, when night comes we cannot sit still, but alone of all nations have added rockers to our chairs."

With the modern means of transportation this mobility factor is now compounded, and its intensity has spread repercussions over most of the European countries as well. And what once was only recognized as personal behavior, now has penetrated the major areas of our national culture. The element of mobility has given contemporary man an evasive attitude toward principle. He knows no loyalty to a guiding idea or a *Weltanschauung*. Fascinated by opportunity, he harbors no loyalty to nature, even less to his soil. Estranged from a natural setting he is not really native anywhere, and leads a transient existence between one opportunity and the next, between one station of status and the next. In short, he has no home. Paradoxically, but revealingly, developers and advertising agencies use the word "home" to describe what in uninflated English is called a house. Clearly the L-shaped, ranch-type or split-level boxes of conformity which they put up lack precisely those features of personality and human warmth that traditionally go with the idea of home. But since this notion is entirely absent in our mind, it can mechanically be put in front of us as a desirable but external attribute.

The restless temper of modern man, since it has ceased to be only accidental behavior and has permeated the national institutions, puts its stamp daily on our cultural expressions. We try this style and that style and change our tastes with the wind. We act by impulse rather than by decision. Twentieth-century society, having come to rely more and more on the "culture consumers," as they have been called, is not at home in any style created by its own loyalty, but tends rather to look for the new "market trends" in arts, literature, and architecture.

The loving spirit

The firmness of a persuasive style that characterizes an important cultural epoch is more or less a reflection of the inner cohesion of the contemporary social structure. When this bond begins to lose strength and social compactness and society gradually acquires a more atomistic nature, the style of the cultural manifestations naturally tends to disintegrate proportionately. When the historical evolution has reached a certain point of saturation, what in daily reality is merely a gradual development in the human consciousness becomes split into a new and an old order, and thus history is divided into eras and periods by means of turning points, crises, and watersheds. By the standards of diminished cohesion, Ferdinand Tönnies, in a remarkable study, distinguishes an epochal quality of community as contrasted to that of society, which more or less indicates the difference between culture and civilization. In this conception, organic life is the essence of

community, whereas mechanical formation covers the
concept of society. The distinction, as useful as it is controversial, in its schematic appearance is illustrative of
the change which has taken place in the historical position of the Western world.

The fundamental social cohesion is best demonstrated
in the bond of the family. In contrast, the hordes are, as
Durkheim put it, "anatomistically juxtaposed." Whatever
binds the family together—love, affection, friendship, but
also envy, resentment—exists naturally. It is an element
of "belonging" which is not advertised as a good cause, or
felt as a psychological need. It is not a thing to do or to
promote. It is simply there as an organic *fluidum,* no less
basic than the blood that unites the body system. This is
clearly the classical conception of the family, and it must
at once be added that our own experience makes us less
sure about the natural cohesion. We probably find it far
safer to speak with sociologists in terms of efficiency and
organization. "By social organization is meant a group of
people who co-operate and co-ordinate their efforts in
order to achieve certain goals. The concept is familiar
when applied to the social agency or to a business enterprise." This description of the notion of family, taken
from a sociological journal, throws important light on the
change in the nature of social union, which, easily indicated in the simple family relationships, has a wide application to the more complicated fabrics of our community life.

It would lead us too far afield to analyze here the reasons for the appearance of disintegrating cohesion; they
are manifold, psychologically involved, and, moreover,
not really germane to this inquiry. We have heard of
"teenage tyranny" and blamed either adults or children
for the "trouble in the family" that makes for lucrative
Broadway scripts but little stability in society. Most of
us, however, have succeeded in adjusting ourselves to the
child-centered age and rather encouraged it by sentimen-
talizing the sacrosanct notion of "youngness." "Youngness" is an alienated concept of youth. Youth ascends by

full indulgence in power, speed, and drive, without reflecting on its own characteristics. Youngness, on the
other hand, is a deliberate and self-conscious display of
only the outward gestures of youth. It is wrinkled moth-
ers trying to dress and look like their daughters. It is men
with flagging libido chasing young girls. It is Presidents
in swimming trunks pictured in newspapers with the
studied air: "See, I'm so young! Don't you see I'm
young?" Youth does not talk about itself in terms of
youth. It merely acts, aggressively, impulsively, reckless-
ly, and therefore usually successfully. Youngness suggests
an old mind's adulation of youth. It has become a *chan-
tage,* as Ortega calls it: "We are in truth living in a time
when this adopts two complementary attitudes, violence
and caricature."

It is important to think about this distinction in these
days when we have glorified youth, while youth itself has
responded with self-pity and cynicism. What is behind
this child-focused obsession? Is it fear? Neurosis? Senes-
cence? The question, inasmuch as it lies in the field of
psychology, is difficult to answer in this historical context. One can only limit oneself to the cultural repercussions which Huizinga has described as *puerilism.* Recognizing that each cultural period is characterized by a certain play element, he points out that puerilism, though
superficially similar to play, is actually different and a
sign of dissolution. Among the most conspicuous symptoms of this tendency, Huizinga mentions vulgar entertainment, a need for sensation, mass-demonstrations and
parades, club formation and a mania for wearing em-
blems and insignia, formal hand gestures and greetings
(fascists), recognition themes, yells, marching, and a
lack of humor. Each of us can probably extend the list
indefinitely. However, where Huizinga drifted astray, I
believe, is in the assertion that the United States is the
nation cultivating puerlism more conspicuously than any
other country. Some of the marked infantile expressions,
mentioned above, are entirely absent in this country and
clearly tied up with organizations like the *Hitler Jugend.*

Similarly, there is little here of that obnoxious combination of puerilism and militarism so common in some European countries.

The craving for gadgets, by no means confined only to this hemisphere but just as conspicuous in European countries or Japan, is a form of puerilism. It has, however, a more important aspect. It is an attitude of cultural alienation and can be diagnosed as an unconscious replacing of authentic joy (or need) with an extraneous one. Just as the useless accessories that clutter the inside and outside of our cars do not make for better driving, so the sophisticated hi-fi and stereo contraptions which executives try out on their guests do not make for a more intense love of music. Gadgetism means enjoying the world as a toy; and who is so self-righteous as to declare this pastime a sin? In the thirties a Huxley could still effectively point to the passion for machines as a "second boyhood" and blame the modern artist for growing down and reverting to the preoccupations of his childhood. Since then, those who are willing to reflect at all have absorbed all they can stand in the manner of *Zeitkritik*. They accept some of it, reject some of it, and for the rest fondle no illusion, one way or the other, about puerilism or gadgetism. It should be added, for due understanding, that some of the contemporary infantile attitudes were by no means absent in previous times. But the question here is not about the puerile behavior of a number of individuals, but about an abnormality becoming normal.

In the United States, the most curious aspect of our cult of the child is that we are in no way concerned about giving it an adequate home. We have already pointed out that the restless disposition of our time makes us, if not physically, at least existentially homeless. Under these circumstances, the child we so idealize is bound to lead a waif's existence. We are not now referring to the broken family situations, nor to the agitated and fidgety turbulence that leads teenagers to divide their time between countless causes in countless places—school, camp, street, movie house, corner drugstore—all being treated without any proportionate rate of importance. We are thinking of the idyll of childhood produced by our nostalgic brain. If we ask the modern sophisticated mother what the ideal home she has in mind is like, it turns out to be not a home at all, but a kind of museum. This is verging on the perverse. At no time in history, as far as we know, have houses been built as display places for the general public. Old ducal palaces, long after the feudal vitality has withered away, have been opened to tourists who gape in awe at the historical splendor. But what could be more preposterous than for the modern house owner or housewife to receive absolute strangers in organized tours of "interesting" homes? What, indeed, could be more absurd than for people, born and bred under the egalitarian dispensation, to imitate the museum climate of feudal castles and fill their dwellings with antique, semi-antique, and pseudo-antique furniture, pictures, vases, sculpture, to show their guests? What could be more divorced, indeed estranged, from vital living than to build one's "home" around a collection of paintings, as is not uncommonly done in showplaces of modern "life"?

One may ask whether it is fair to judge a whole generation by the idiosyncracies of what must be a relatively small minority of people. I believe it is. No less so than to treat an ailment according to its symptoms. One or two spots on the skin, a trace in the blood, can betray the whole body. Individual idiosyncracies can hardly be regarded as symptoms as long as they represent merely isolated, queer cases. However, when a whole generation spontaneously responds by making them a part of its dreams, conversations, magazine reading, and aspirations, the idiosyncracies have to be taken as indicative of an underlying process.

In the setting of this "ideal home," certain contents of domestic warmth have become incompatible with showroom living. It is therefore understandable that the often deficient but always human sounds of family instrument-playing have been replaced by the stereo-slick background hum of mechanical music, and similarly significant that the old-fashioned family friend has given way to the cocktail guest. Is there still friendship left? Undoubtedly so. What else can one call the feeling of union in fraternities, street gangs, businessmen's or fraternity clubs, church dinners, masonic lodges, women's associations, or the "pubs" in Great Britain? This is a pleasant and congenial bond, at other times sustained in coffee houses and *Bier-Hallen.* There are clearly many varieties of friendship. But what has happened to the institution of the family friend, otherwise called bosom friend? He finds his cultural expression in the history of drama with such confidants as Pylades, Horatio, or Posa. With Ibsen, he is equally prominent, often in the guise of the family doctor.

Is it possible that the developing friendship cult made the eighteenth and nineteenth centuries the great period of letter-writing? The link is not unequivocally clear. Swift, Pope, and Shaw, following their tradition, wrote letters more from a desire to indulge in wit than because of an experienced friendship. On the other hand, the important correspondences between Goethe and Schiller, Schiller and Körner, Charles Lamb and Coleridge, Burckhardt and Preen were definitely rooted in profound affection. In the twentieth century it is far harder to find the character of the family friend functioning in the typical modern play. As for correspondence, there is the danger of premature conclusions. Letters of celebrities have a natural tendency to become historically important only posthumously, and it will probably take at least another century before one is able to gauge accurately the impact of friendship in this matter. It would appear likely, however, that the present century, with a definite increase in gang-spirit and a greater stress on the value and importance of such institutions as the "buddy" and the "crony," has seen a more or less proportionate disappearance of the function of the family friend.

While the considerations about friendship cannot be entirely conclusive, the historical change in the attitude toward charity and the way to administer it seems more clearly delineated. Charity and love are both historically integrated in the Jewish and Christian religions. In the New Testament, the identity of God with love (agape) is most explicitly pronounced in the three epistles of John to the early Christian communities; he urged them to emulate the divine example and to perfect their love by casting out fear. Although the word charity derives from the Greek (*charis*–gift, favor), there was yet no separation between the expressions caritas and agape. This came later, and the confusion was broadened in the seventeenth and eighteenth centuries when the word "philanthropy" entered the Christian nomenclature. Indicating the attitude of humanitarian care, love of mankind, or social reform, it was still used as such in the nineteenth century, for instance, by Theodore Parker. Soon, however, as new connotations were added, the basic conception of philanthropy began to change. It was not only the size of the giving, it was also the institutionalizing of charity which provided it with a commercial quality. A student of American philanthropy thinks: "It might be argued that the change in the meaning of the term from benevolence and humanitarianism to organized large-scale giving reflects a shift in our society to a greater emphasis on the role of wealth." The stress, it seems, should be equally divided between the opulence and the organizational character of the modern "good works." Once we have prided ourselves on our generosity, we may as well try to fathom the full extent of its roots. If we neither want to join the muckrakers and the cynics who have debunked spectacular philanthropy and made its intentions suspect, nor indulge in blind glorification of our plutocracy, there is still room enough for a reposed contemplation of our new habits. There are simple facts that stand out. Originally, charity was an inseparable part of agape, as a response to the facts of injustice, want, or distress suffered by others, which happened to be strewn daily in our way. In the expanding early Christian communities, it was soon necessary to organize their social service and put it under the supervision of the *diakonos*.

So it remained throughout the ages, at least essentially, without the idea of charity losing its personal touch. James Bryce, in 1893, still believed that charitable contributions were mainly given by religious people under a religious impulse. Philanthropy, as we know it today, has become so mechanized and streamlined that the generous donor rarely knows the recipient of his gifts. Giving, then, is a transaction, totally dehumanized, operating with the same efficiency techniques as business corporations. Indeed, by official statistics philanthropy seems to have become one of the most impressive industries of the national scene. This reflection does not, of course, exclude the possibility of genuine motivations, but it indicates how simple, individual values have become mobilized into the gigantic computer circuits of our machine world.

The notion of agape has the width and fullness that love suggests, but it does not include eros. Of all human affections the vibrant throb of eros is probably one of the most important for the historical forms of culture. The *Song of Solomon,* Ovid's *Art of Love,* the erotic murals of Pompeii, Villon's *Ballad of Ladies' Love,* Shakespeare's *Measure for Measure,* Titian's *Rape of Europa,* the seventeenth-century minuet, Wagner's *Tristan und Isolde,* Rodin's lovers—all reveal something that is the same and yet dissimilar. Although love may be a perennial affection, it neverthless expresses itself in different manners at different times, and its style betrays something of the epochal temper.

However rich the meanings and varied the styles in which amorous feelings appear in history, there is one fundamental factor that cannot be ignored, which provides eros with its most cultural claim. It is the element of play. The truth is underlined by the etymology of some languages. That element which aims at prolonging the enjoyment of love, and which makes it attractive in the eyes of outsiders, is precisely play. It was on the basis of play, too, that the comedies of Plautus or Molière, pastoral poetry from Theocritus to Milton, and no less the ingenious designs of the classical female costume thrived. It is the *ludique* element by which the pleasure of eros is elevated to the realm of culture; without it man would not bother to watch love, record it, make it a part of the Western inheritance. The endless variations in the inevitable struggle between the sexes—the challenge, flirtations, pretended coyness, advance and withdrawal, the gradual conquering and yielding—are all manifestations of that principle of play which we have considered as one of the basic postulates of the historical culture.

A striking combination of eros and play-expression is evident in the cultural aspect of dance, whether as artistic *divertissement,* or as social entertainment. The *sarabandes* and *gigues* which Louis XIV enjoyed were stylized expressions of courting, and the *menuet* was basically patterned on the magnetic play of the attraction and coyness of a love game.

If our century is typified by the appearance of the Charleston, the Twist, and rock 'n' roll, the question arises: What has happened to the play motive. The disturbance which these dance forms have caused in some elderly minds is probably explainable by the rather realistic exhibition of sexual acts and the emphasis on the savage element in physical passion. Indeed, "savage" is the key word today to success and acceptance in gang life and sports, as well as in painting and writing, in clear relationship to the unveiled appearance of sexuality in social conversation and entertainment. It must be remembered, however, that the ancients knew something about the destructive and cruel aspect of love, too. If it be true that the Greek lyrics eulogized love with wine and song as the property of good life, the wanton Cupid was rarely treated as that lovely rosy urchin that sentimental pictures traditionally show him to be. In the amorous poetry of the Syrian Greek Meleager (first century B.C.), Cupid was depicted as a tyrant with "murderous bow" and he,

the ravisher of hearts
for slaughter raging, hurls fire-breathing darts;

with bitter scorn envenoms every wound,
and laughs at every death he scatters round.

Nowhere, as far as I know, is there in the classical statements of love, however bawdy or lewd the approach, any
tendency to undermine the fundamental balance of play.
Neither the ribaldry of Petronius in the first century nor
the raucous fun of the Goliardic songs in the Middle
Ages made the torment and curse of love more essential
than its bliss and its blessing. The contemporary age,
however, seems particularly unique in its drift away from
the play quality which keeps opposing forces together.
The straightforward presentation of sex, inasmuch as its
chief vehicle is commercialized culture, as Denis de
Rougemont points out, uproots the normal character of
eros. Eros indeed is transmuted into eroticism. Play has
become compulsion. What this means in terms of moral
responsibility, I do not know. I owe it to my subject,
however, to devote at least some thought to the impact
which the new order of sexual relations has on social cohesion.

In the nineteenth century when, for the first time, in
the mind of the more daring thinkers doubts began to
arise about continuous progress and civilization itself, the
bourgeois, at least outwardly, managed to smooth over
conflicting tides in a lighthearted compromise, which in
matters of morals later came to be considered hypocritical. But recognizing the hypocrisy should not exclude an
understanding of its causes. The Victorian balance was a
deliberate arrangement to adjust to the fierce scramble of
social Darwinism and the idea of reason promoted by
various revolutions and an expanding education. If the
effort represents a hypocritical makeshift, it also means a
last-ditch fight to prevent chaos from taking over.

The man most clear-sighted about this predicament
was Eduard von Hartmann. In his *Philosophy of the Unconscious* (1869) he presents the conflict between reason
and will in a typical nineteenth-century light. The maturing of man's reason along with the developing of society
will repress his will, rooted in the unconsciousness, and

inevitably create more and more unhappiness. This pessimistic view of society which Hartmann offered in philosophical, categorical terms, Freud adopted half a century later and refurbished with psychoanalytic trimmings. The twentieth-century problem is that either man follows the enlightened trend of reason with the inexorable result of increased frustration and unhappiness, or he releases the brakes on his will and reverses the historical trend of culture. Since either-or's are uncomfortable for the mind of the average man, a great deal of compromise is offered to him, including non-repressive utopian cultures. These confidently hope that where Victorian compromise fell short, twentieth-century ingenuity may succeed. Against this, two notes of warning seem justified. First, the Victorian balance was, at least as long as it lasted and in the eyes of the middle class, fairly successful. Secondly, if the cultural either-or is, indeed, a dreadful prospect, it seems only human that we support the efforts to find a middle road. But, historically speaking, it would mean a lack of integrity if we blinded ourselves to the inescapable indices which show that the temper of the age tends to move away from reason and toward the fostering of impulses. This reverse direction of Western society in the application of reasonable controls has unsurprisingly led to an increased employment of violence. Politically, the twentieth century scarcely needs more proof, it seems, of what results from the abandonment of balance. Hitler's genius succeeded in making impulse supreme over a gigantic bureaucratic and military machine. He could do so by dropping the concept of reason radically. With the play balance upset, the cultural achievement in the Nazi realm disappeared.

On a more human level, we can understand that yielding to sexual impulses and the encouragement of their public display must similarly lead to a decrease in the cultural stimulant. The emphasis on violence and perversity has not only stripped eros of its playful quality, but also the cultural style of its reasonable control. Stylization itself is a synthesis of reason and sensation, and as such must be understood as one of the chief tools of culture. Sexuality presented raw may reveal honesty and, under certain circumstances, may possibly be more purely moral than when appearing in hypocritical wrappings. The alleviation of social taboos may also theoretically promise greater happiness, even though at present the increasing number of neurotic minds seems to belie the alleged advantages of our sexually emmancipated society. When, however, sex shows itself as eroticism and as indulgence in violence, it may be recognized as a clear sign that love has joined the reverse tide of unreason in civilization.

It is self-evident that with sexual emancipation the role of the woman in modern civilization gradually takes on a new dimension. Whether it would be more accurate to speak, as a friend of mine suggests, of the "demancipation of man" is open to debate. The mutual relationship between the sexes has obviously changed to such an extent that an entirely new pattern of living seems to facelift the social physiognomy.

One of the most remarkable concomitants of the new freedom is the exhibitionist trend in social communications. Femininity in classical times seems expressed, undoubtedly to a considerable measure, in the art of dressing rather than undressing; and at least the element of *timing*, so much more natural to the female atmosphere of thinking than to that of the male, made every woman's existence, normally speaking, appear as a variation of the Dance of the Seven Veils. With most of the veils gone, the classical technique of Salome's game has followed the pedestrianization noted in the development from minuet to Twist. The esthetic problem involved in the public display of feminine attractions and distractions, being a matter of subjective taste, can be left aside as irrelevant to this investigation. Nor can one rightly accuse the modern woman in general of a decline in morals. It is simply a matter of communications. If today's man accepts the increased aggressiveness of the female species, the amount of mutual adult happiness is not reduced. And while the more poetic minds among us may still be shocked at the image of predatory birds which girls marketing for a man evoke on the coeducational campus, most of us are pragmatic enough to see that in this security-conscious age the risks of marital adventure are somewhat reduced when we leave the initiative to the woman—especially since most of them are sufficiently equipped with the helpful skill of making it appear that the ultimate leadership is all the man's.

It is obvious that one cannot single out the contemporary woman to demonstrate the whole trend of exhibitionism. She is part of a universal pattern on which our entire public-relations system rests. Long articles, trembling with indignant protest, have been directed against the increasing intrusion on human privacy. In particular, the ruthless practices of the streamlined news media have been blamed. True enough, the modern reporter has abandoned any restraint in exposing what at earlier times may have been thought to be human weaknesses. But are they not merely seizing the opportunities which the contemporary uninhibited way of life provide? Gardens without fences and the general open-mindedness of our outlook, as well as the open-door mentality of our suburban disposition, develop with the egalitarian character of modern times and constitute its major charm. On the same basis we like our politicians, along with movie stars, to be exposed inside and outside, and the President's every move, sneeze, and sniffle must be recorded for history. The charm here is less evident. Some may hail this practice as a participation in government, others probably will understand it as a sign of trivial mentality. The fact remains that the decline of privacy is not caused by inconsiderate characters in certain trades, but is a consequence of the general need for leveling, for equalizing values and attributes. Social exhibitionism is part and parcel of a desire to conform and be like the others, in contrast to man's classical consciousness of individuality which treasured an authentic holy of holies, inaccessible to the public mind.

The exposed attitude is clearly incompatible with the traditional feminine role, and inevitably woman's function in society has to change considerably with the new conditions. Whereas previously her efficiency was not allowed to go further than the mediating capacity natural to women, she now frequently takes a commanding position. Nowhere have conditions been more favorable for pushing women into that leading place than in the United States. From the beginning, the "new" world has meant for her a greater share in the control of central institutions such as religion and education. In politics, James Bryce noted the influence of women in the legislative lobbies at Washington, while in the cultural fields they dictate the standards of literature and art. The predominance of women as a whole has by no means diminished since the pioneer days; on the contrary, we seem to have truly arrived at that state which Lester Ward calls the "gynecocracy."

One would expect that in the eyes of those who believe in normalcy such an historical development would represent a signal of impending doom. Most men, however, content with the affluence and comfort of this woman-directed society—which, moreover, they helped to create—are in no mood to resent the tarnished luster of their masculinity. Only when it comes to the fierce prophets of *Zeitkritik* is there heard a clear warning protest. Brooks Adams believes that "the woman, as the cement of society, the head of the family and the center of cohesion, has, for all intents and purposes, ceased to exist. She has become a wandering isolated unit, rather a dispersive than a collective force." In *Law of Civilization and Decay*, comparing the end-phase of the Roman Empire with his own age, he sees an ominous symptom in the role of women in modern society. Noting that in the third century a Julia Domna, a Julia Mamaea, or a Soaemias sat in the Senate or conducted the administration, he remarks that "when wealth became force, the female might be as strong as the male; therefore she was emancipated . . . . She controlled her own property, and as she had power, she exercised political privileges." It seems rather unwarranted to predict the future of a civilization from the vicissitudes of another one in the past. On the other hand, it would be equally hazardous to deny the possibility that what is an abnormal state by historical standards will, in spite of its pragmatic success, one day turn out to have carried with it a fatal weakness. There are, after all, symptoms that flatter patients with a ruddy and blooming appearance. Thus, if we do not want to commit ourselves to speculations one way or the other, we must confine ourselves to a frank description of realities and understand how they have changed from their configuration in the past.

It is not to challenge the sociologists that one calls our society a mother-directed way of living. But is it fair to typify it for that reason as a matriarchal system? Pounding a type-stamped image on thousands of people living together in the same period seems a rather dogmatic and arbitrary act, which historians prefer to avoid. Working with changes in historical contexts and continuities, they can hardly be expected to welcome rigorous patterns that are useless for handling historical dynamics. Yet no one has ever abstained entirely from using paradigmatic types, and as long as they are merely supplementary illustrations, their use should not be harmful. In a sense, one can expect that in a social order that grants the mother a preponderant share in education, religion, and theater and other cultural fields, certain outwardly matriarchal characteristics are clearly discernible. Taking one's starting point from isolated particular problems rather than from a fundamental, theoretical idea—a method typical for the Anglo-American way of thinking and one preeminently used during the last century—can without strain be classified as a feminine approach. Similarly so, the care for details at the expense of unity, the cultivation of a number of practical truths rather than one dogmatic truth, and the whole modern pluralistic outlook may well be related to the female preference for small utilitarian advances rather than big ideological dreams. Along these lines there is, at least as far as the cultural pattern is concerned, a definite matriarchal predominance.

On the other hand, from a sociological viewpoint one can come to the opposite conclusion and demonstrate that the shift from community to society represents a change from female to male characteristics. Tönnies in his *Spirit of the Modern Age* distinguishes the feminine element in agriculture from the masculine in craft and trade, and thus tries to typify the difference in the prevailing features of Middle Ages and modern times. In its generalization, the schematic view raises all sorts of historical questions, but if one accepts typification at all, this representation can be admitted as sound. The conclusion probably must be that our age shows a remarkable conflict between the feminine nature of the cultural and institutional structure and the masculine quality of the industrial and commercial domination. If this is true, could it be that in this very split a part of the present alienation of culture from the economic and organizational foundations is explained? An accurate answer is hard to give. There are at the present so many confusing factors at play, which only in later decades can be evaluated in proper perspective, that the safest suggestion now seems to be to limit oneself to the most transparent aspect of the problem. This is an existing state of abnormality to which we have adjusted willingly and comfortably, and which we have taught ourselves to treat in our minds as normal.

> Then there is . . . a sort of high-life-
> below-stairs business. Indeed, consider'd
> with any sense of propriety, or any sense
> at all, the whole of this illy-play'd fash-
> ionable play and display, with their ab-
> sorption of the best part of our wealthier
> citizens' time, money, energies, etc., is
> ridiculously out of place in the United
> States.
>
> Walt Whitman

14

The Gracious Way of Living

The gracious spirit

The desire to live graciously is a normal one for a developing society which, one may suppose, by simple social and esthetic needs discovers the importance of polished communications to smooth conflicting human preferences and prejudices. Our age, however, is marked by self-conscious talk about gracious living. What is clearly a natural need at first, gradually becomes an externalized formula, promoted and defined by the advertising houses and their subsidiary agencies, the popular magazines. The self-consciousness of the gracious attitude started in the eighteenth century, and it was again Schiller who gave it the first classical expression. In his essay "On Graciousness and Dignity," published in the *Neue Thalia* of June 1793, he distinguished the element of *Anmut,* a combination of charm and courteousness, from *Würde,* which, as dignity, relates more to the integrity of the character. Graciousness is the expression of beauty in man as a *person;* it is shown in human behavior and conveys freedom of the body. Dignity, on the other hand, results fundamentally from suffering and represents freedom of the mind. Both of these attributes are essential, and Schiller deplored the fact that in his age they were not combined in a unity, an ideal state which would make man as complete and harmonious as were the Greeks, epitomized in Niobe and Apollo.

Confining ourselves to graciousness, how does it fit into our industrial world? How does it blend with the egalitarian society? That social charm exists in abundance, no one could deny, watching our successful executives, lawyers, and politicians at work. According to Matthew Arnold, not one of the most generous admirers of the New World, American women radiate more charm than does their species anywhere else in the world. But charm is not necessarily *Anmut,* for its pleasing quality may well be without the inner radiance of individuality. Graciousness reveals itself best when off-set by dignity. But somehow we do not seem to advertise the dignified way of living, so we are handicapped. We are further handicapped since, as Schiller observed, graciousness is the more feminine and dignity the more masculine attitude, and thus we find ourselves again in the mainstream of female preponderance. This is remarkable, because it goes against the very masculine penetration and aggressiveness which has marked pioneer and modern industrial expansion. It is this countertrend that makes the idea of gracious living seem detached from its basic footing.

We may also wonder if it is really compatible with the conception of an egalitarian society. It is probably part and parcel of that trend which sociologists call the *em-*

bourgeoisement of the workers. Although its extent is under debate, there can be no doubt that the modern community, gradually stripping itself completely of bourgeois prejudices, is at the same time eager to imitate manners and tastes of living identified with the maids-and-servants era. This is only natural, and no less normal than that the wealthy burgher of seventeenth-century Holland looked at the example of the princely courts. The Dutch bourgeois, however, created his own manners, environment, and interior style. It is recorded in the genre pieces of Vermeer, de Hoogh, or van Mieris and reflected in the still-life studies of a Willem Kalf. Twentieth-century gracious living, in contrast, is based on an indiscriminate mixture of Louis XVI, Empire, Biedermeier, *art nouveau,* and Sears Roebuck. Why can we not exist in self-created forms and formulas? Why this borrowing from societies whose beliefs we think to have outgrown? Theoretically, there is no reason why a proletarian age should not be able to produce its own stylistic configurations in simple, solid, harmonious lines, agreeing with its common-sense thinking and democratic mentality. The peasants in some of the backward regions of Europe are known for their courteous and dignified behavior, as well as the simple artistic style of their fabrics and furniture. The moment they emigrate and set foot on the land of liberty they become enslaved to the Woolworth style of living. The explanation of this lies obviously in the golden notion of "opportunity." When the masses are faced with the choice between their traditional handicraft and mass production, they will invariably choose the latter. Even the *shouks* in Aleppo and Damascus have taken on the appearance of nickel-and-dime stores, where gaudy plastic vessels have replaced the graceful clay pitchers. Only the naïve tourist will ask for the real thing.

The eclecticism and bewilderment of the common taste naturally reflects an inner uncertainty in the collective consciousness. The nervousness and diffusion which the age displays in its communications are, as most of us understand it, seated in a general anxiety, mostly unexplainable by particular or individual causes. The lack of a central focusing point, the absence of a guiding ideology, and the loss of religious anchorage have opened up for man the whole abundant world: everything is available to all. But instead of enjoying this freedom, he feels like a boy in a candy store, bewildered and disappointed to learn that he cannot have all at once. This is probably the true cause of modern neurosis—not so much repression, but rather the frustration of not being able to satisfy the opportunity. With the large-scale abolishing of taboos, we have not reduced neurosis, but instead encouraged it to universal proportions.

In this unfocused situation the discipline of conformity provides a safe framework for the security-seeking mind. Since it is as helpful and humiliating as a plaster cast for the broken back, youngsters everywhere protest and stage revolts against the device. They have been told by their high school teachers about the great individualism of the American past, they have been urged to express their little inexperienced opinions on every subject in the world, and are led to understand that this is the way democracy goes. When they awaken to the truth of conformism, the shock arrives unheralded, and by the time they enter college they must shift to the leveling reality of the fraternity stamp, the popularity laws of campus life, and the IBM rut of higher education. College, indeed, is the training-ground where any bump of originality protruding out of the standard mold is systematically removed. Then the student has risen to the state of real citizenship and is ready for Levittown and Park Forest. And if one accepts the judgment of those who have studied conformity in detail, the college administrations are highly successful: "The last thing students can be accused of now is dangerous discussion; they are not interested in the kind of big questions that stimulate heresy, and whatever the subject—the corporation, government, religion—students grow restive if the talk tarries on the philosophical," says the author of *The Organization Man*.

He quotes a theologian to confirm the absence of revolutionary spirit: "It is a kind of authoritarianism in reverse. Theological students today, in contrast to their fellows of twenty years ago, want 'to be told.'" So no more Luthers, Knoxes, Calvins, or Bucers.

Conformity as a compensatory trend of an insecure mentality is clearly not restricted only to the educated, or to any other group, for that matter; it is the common way of living. Yet where it has most embarrassingly appeared is in the academic world which prides itself traditionally on its intellectual independence. A faculty career has become a careful exploration of the prevailing parochial opinions in matters of politics, religion, art, and current affairs. Here conformity often lies perversely in the strict adherence to a nonconformist code. Academic freedom? The aspirant junior professor may well run the risk of being read out of the ranks if he fails to join the current intellectual consensus. Probably no one loses his job for insulting his senior colleague outright. But to deny the greatness of the canonized favorite composer, politician, or pundit is tactless. If Mozart, Freud, and Pope are in, then Wagner, Jung, and Shelley are probably out, at least until the next change of fashion. It would be a mistake, however, to regard this procedure as an intellectual brand of despotism, for no one objects to the arrangement, which, whatever else it does to academic integrity, at least promotes a closely knit administrative unit. University professors acquiesce no less in machine routine than do the young organization men or the businessmen of Middletown who are convinced that the *system* is right, and that therefore human thinking ought to make itself fit in.

Gracious living is a way of life modeled on a pre-set image. It does not flow from an ideal which in previous ages was the generator of life; on the contrary, the image we try to live up to so graciously is derived from previous times, for whose philosophy we have only contempt. This contradiction points to the estrangement from the ideal which seeks security in the image. Daniel Boorstin, who has studied this change in the American scene (it is equally evident, however, in Europe!), points to our passion for pseudo-events: "for made news, synthetic heroes, pre-fabricated tourist attractions, homogenized interchangeable forms of art and literature (where there are no 'originals,' but only the shadows we make of other shadows). We believe we can fill our experience with new-fangled content." We do not live life itself but a picture of life, which popular magazines and other taste-making agencies have declared to be standard. Thus our life is an artificial one, a projection of life rather than the thing itself. We exist in a make-believe world, and act a stage life which we advertise as real. The great advantage of image is that it can adopt the quality of trademark and aid our selling compulsions. In *The Image*, Daniel Boorstin writes: "Now the language of images is everywhere. Everywhere it has displaced the language of ideals. If the right 'image' will elect a President or sell an automobile, a religion, a cigarette, or a suit of clothes, why can it not make America herself—or the American Way of Life a saleable commodity all over the earth? In discussing ourselves, our communities, our corporations, our nation, our leaders, ourselves, we talk the language of images. In the minister's study, in the professor's seminar room as well as in advertising offices and on street corners."

An accompanying urge of gracious conformity is the desire for "belonging," itself an artificial tendency, for, naturally speaking, one belongs or not by innate laws prevailing outside the consciousness. To want to belong is a stranger's attitude, the wish of an outsider to be taken up into the circle of others. Hence the invention and establishment of the institution of "joining." In the Middle Ages or Renaissance times, there was no need to join; one was embedded in the original, native soil and the social as well as religious community. In normal periods man is embraced by the existing institutions, whereas in abnormal situations he must reach out and himself embrace what he believes to be congenial. He is an alien in his own environment. With the ideal having become an image, his church is commuted into a club. The country club, the faculty club, the professional or political club, the woman's club, the lodge are all efficiently satisfying the modern eagerness for fitting in, for making oneself a part of a stereotyped image. The congeniality is not based on an inner conviction or belief, but on the consciousness of "status," which again is not a quality itself, but rather a projected picture of quality. Thus, joining is a mechanical substitute for what in other times was taken care of by organic cohesion. It is a need to be institutionalized and promoted with deliberate zeal, or else society will disintegrate. We should therefore not disparage it, but rather welcome it as gratefully as the cement wall which tries to prevent Leonardo's *Last Supper* from falling apart.

The gracious image, since it is superimposed on us by advertising houses, is patently related to our plutocratic gospel by which money becomes almost equated with justice. Gracious social relations are usually determined by expensive life; sophistication is to be bought. Money in our society has, among other things, become a means to acquire, as it were, by a sleight of hand, qualities which originally were not supposed to be marketable, but derived either from talent or long-cultivated inclination. Money as a social function is no new phenomenon in the history of the West. What Spengler called "Faustian money" is a function "the value of which is based on its effect and not on its mere existence." Originally no more than a symbol of aggregated commodity values, it soon became a tool to increase money, until in the democratic political system it was adopted as a power influence as well. To a certain extent money has played its political role throughout the ages, but nowhere does unabashed plutocracy find a more congenial home than in the United States of the nineteenth and twentieth centuries. If it were only a matter of wealthy family dynasties, the practice of political investment could be considered as merely an extension of capitalistic penetration. But since the workers' unions, with equal flair, transfer millions of dollars to their favorite candidates and parties, the role of money as communication seems to have become one of legitimate blackmail. It would appear that money here acquires a paradoxical function in the equalitarian framework. If used by both "rugged" individualist and staunch collectivist to buy Presidents and legislative programs, the idea of equality becomes twisted around many times. In this manner the function of money is externalized and becomes sheer power indulgence. According to Simmel in his *Philosophy of Money*, it places itself before our inner and ultimate objectives, it removes us from our purposes and emerges as the most abstract technique of external life.

It is on those terms that we see money become identified with justice. Once an old-fashioned socialist such as Proudhon could believe that the just society would be that which accepts "the law of poverty," and could sincerely write: "Poverty is good, and we must consider it as the principle of our joy. Reason commands us to conform our life to it through frugality of behavior, moderation in pleasures, diligence in work, and absolute subordination of our appetites to justice." Needless to say that we in the twentieth century reject this with superior pride as naïve. And perhaps it is. But it would by no means do us harm, either, if we sometimes investigated our belief that wealth is happiness and that equal opportunity for all is equated with equal opportunity to amass wealth. But what is the justice in equal opportunity for crime and greed? Dante, looking at his Florence of the late Middle Ages, could remark:

> The upstart people and the sudden profits, Florence,
> have generated in thee pride and excess.

Such misgivings in our time, however, would mean the undermining of our hallowed way of life. We hate to hear insinuations about possible deficiencies in our fundamental social organization, and if something derails, the institution of the scapegoat is there to make us feel comfortable again. The idea of the *System* streamlines all our doubts, hesitations, and questioning. The system is sacrosanct. And Lyndon Johnson, in a television address of March 16, 1964, spoke for all of us when he proclaimed: "I am so proud of our system. . . . And I want to see it preserved . . . because when the final chips are down, it is not going to be the number of people we have, or the number of acres, or the number of resources that win, the thing that is going to make us win is our system of government." One should not ask when the chips are down what has happened to such bothersome qualities as human talent, thought, and creativity. They are the machine wreckers, they spoil the organization men: system is our savior—as indeed it is.

Man's mind, of course, does not take lightheartedly to this abstraction of human sensitivity into robot perfection. We are totally aware of the fact that our full-time commitment to the system inevitably excludes a great deal of personal experience and alienates us from an authentic sense of life. One would suspect that the general neurotic character, which this century has assumed, is, at least to a considerable degree, caused by the disorder of the increasing factor of dehumanization. A gradual awakening to the simple facts and effects of the systematization of our life has been taking place. It is hard to determine exactly when the restiveness started. At any rate, in the 1890's the change in man's consciousness about his destiny was clearly marked, both in Europe and here. Especially in the United States, where the shift in attitude coincided with rather spectacular social, political, and cultural changes, the decade has a fascinating attraction for historians. We have touched on this in a previous chapter. Here the authority of Henry Steele Commager may confirm our suggestions: "The note of confidence which had long characterized the American accent gave way to doubt, self-assurance to bewilderment, and resolution to confusion." It seems paradoxical that this crisis of consciousness should have happened at the time when the unfolding American energy and expansion was at its peak. It may well be explained by the counterpoint of growing material power and cultural shrinkage. "That confusion and doubt rather than certitude and confidence should characterize the thought of a people at the height of their material prosperity and the maturity of their scientific development was surprising, but no more surprising than that the material prosperity should bring so little general contentment and the science solve so few fundamental problems."

One should not overlook the fact that this sensibility had a twin effect. The break in isolationism not only made the American self-conscious about his own society, but also alert to the possible extension of the frontier beyond the national borders. Whereas before he did not bother to prove the advantages of his world and ways of living, now he toyed with the idea of exporting them to others. An author who found himself "facing the twentieth century" believed it a Christian mission to spread the liberties and institutions of the American civilization abroad. Realizing that his nation, heretofore isolated, had suddenly burst its shell and found itself a member of the family of nations, he urged his readers to accept this historic fact with all its opportunities and responsibilities. The "manifest destiny, divinely ordered, is upon us."

Whereas before the American people had seldom wondered about the righteousness of their existence, from then on they started to look around at others, especially Europeans, and discover the limitations of their purposes and the futility of the American Dream. In Boorstin's words: "This declining sense of American uniqueness is the great trauma of the American mind in the last half-century. It has stirred our dissatisfaction with ourselves by shattering our traditional self-image." In this context, the waves of expatriates who tried to settle in England and France, where they usually found themselves even more dissatisfied than at home, is significant. Up to the twenties and thirties, when Gertrude Stein, Fitzgerald, and Hemingway represented the last generation to emigrate, the criticism of American illusions took on an increasing vehemence. It seems partly unjustified, for materialism and intense greed had by then become just as much evident on the European scene, and Robinson Jeffers' protest was essentially directed to Western proletarianization as a whole, when he wrote that

> this America settles in the mould of its vulgarity,
> heavily thickening to empire,
> And protest, only a bubble in the molten mass, pops and
> sighs out, and the mass hardens.

The unfocused nervousness which has come to typify this century can thus partly be understood from the discrepancy between cultural opportunity and actual achievement. The public at large, however, resents these eschatological speculations of the intellectual rebels. To live in cultural cycles and especially to be on the declining curve is not very compatible with practical people, and Jeffers remarked:

> Practical people, I have been told,
> Weary of the sea for his waves go up and down
> . . . .
> And all these tidal gatherings, growth and decay,
> Shining and darkening, are forever
> Renewed; and the whole cycle impenitently
> Revolves, and all the past is future:—
> Make it a difficult world . . . for practical people.

The organization of gracious living is their solution to the vulgarity of the age. They do not accept vulgarity as a symptom, but believe it to be an accident in history which occurs simply because the nineteenth-century forefathers, in their hurry to build industrial bastions, overlooked the decorations. They have a culinary approach to history: if the pudding turns out too plain, the thing can be "jazzed up" with some ingenuity and sauce. This popular view actually is not unreasonable at all, for all one has to do is to buy the desired ingredients, cook the sauce according to the classical recipe, and spread it as a cloak of sophistication over the solid bulk.

If this procedure can improve the exterior face of vulgarity, it apparently does not solve the growing disturbance of the mind. Neurosis is probably not an exclusive feature of our time, although we tend to treat it as such. We simply have no comparable evidence to prove that the Hellenistic age, for instance, which resembled ours in many respects, displayed the same mental symptoms. We do know that the Alexandrian suffered nervous breakdowns and that the great Erasistratus linked them to sexual trouble. It is likely, however, that so far the twentieth century has been unique in the awareness and self-conscious analysis of its neurosis. We have made it a respectable topic for our conversation or literature; the psychoanalyst has become part of our status system, and the barbiturate a symbol of sophistication. Our basic reaction against the internal and external cultural nervousness can be best summed up in the word "dope." We continually seem to treat symptoms instead of underlying ailments. Is it unjustified to think that the excessive quantities of food, alcohol, and nicotine we absorb, which clearly surpass all reasonable need, have something to do with a general attempt to tranquilize our inner disturbances? People at other times, we may presume, have taken refuge in gastronomic abundance in order to kill their anxieties and boredoms, but we have put this proclivity under the aegis of the egalitarian principle and canonized it for the entire society. The dope attitude is so generalized that we need not confine our attention to smoking, wining, and dining alone; nor is the increasing consumption of narcotics by both young and old an isolated habit. It belongs in the common pattern of nerve-dulling life which seeks to muffle the uncomfortable facts of reality.

Television, of course, is the great boon for our escapist dream-drifting. If the networks can keep the populace quiet and comfortable with their programs, we should perhaps welcome these soporific emissions as a vital contribution to the popular health. What happens to the collective intelligence and alertness is another matter. Anyone who has been in that magic land of electronics and Madison Avenue psychology, the TV studio, knows the golden rule which urges that the program be pitched at early-teenage taste and understanding. Every adult from the President down who decides to watch the television screen automatically gears his perception five or six notches down to the child's level. This no doubt is an efficient way to relax daily tension. It is also one of the more attractive modes of bringing the human mind under sedation.

Two aspects clearly emerge from our aspirin age: one is the soothing and accommodating of our mind in a climate of peace and acquiescence, while the second is the tendency to be concerned with symptoms rather than causes.

The latter habit is essentially linked to our entire pluralistic outlook, with our concern about things rather than about principle, with the eclecticism of manners and tastes rather than with organic style. Although we must accept this development as an inevitable result of the diffuse character of an over-complex civilization, there is hardly any need to encourage the confusion which it entails. For instance, it seems misleading to concentrate, as the popular sociologists do, on the various symptoms of alienation and discuss certain aspects of abnormality, disturbance, and loneliness in the social structure, then follow by well-meaning suggestions for curing them. This is a layman's approach to headaches. It is an alienated treatment of alienation. Cultural estrangement, like chemical change in the composition of the blood, merely betrays itself in outward behavior, and will not respond favorably to the popular magic of the druggist.

The leisure spirit

So far we have been skirting along the field of "popular culture," being aware of the fact that somewhere we have to come to grips with it, yet reluctant to do so. The reason for the reluctance lies in the fact that so much has been written about popular art and culture in a rather partisan spirit, as if the thing had to be either good or evil. It is obviously neither—at least in the eyes of those who see no reason why culture or mass communication should necessarily be either defended or attacked.

With the rise of the socialist political doctrine, the problem of the "ivory tower" as a social refuge for the artist inevitably came under scrutiny. Two contrasting schools of thought now became more and more pronounced and pushed forward on a collision course. One desperately fought for the "utmost individual expression of the utmost individual emotion," while the other followed the collectivist trend and viewed the people *en masse* as the real source of art and literature. Flaubert, harboring a particularly somber presentiment about the future of culture, believed that no bond existed between the crowd and the artist, and if socialism was to be the prevailing trend, then there was no recourse for him, save to climb into his tower and dwell there along with his dreams. Against this esoteric art for art's sake, the populist movement directed its wrath, as in the example of novelist Henri Poulaille in France. He aimed at an art by the people and for the people. The new technical inventions would aid in widening the scope of popular enjoyment: "Our literature is a thing of the past. It no longer gratifies the need of escape that summons man at every moment. At least it cannot gratify it as well as the modern mechanical discoveries." The battle between the individualists and populists took on a special significance in Holland. Probably because the former, represented by the movement of the "Eightiers," had had such a decisive impact on Dutch literature, the reaction from the socialist side seemed the more pronounced. Some of the latter's representatives, such as Herman Gorter, Frederik van Eeden, and Henriette Roland Holst, had been converted from their earlier highly esthetic viewpoint. Although their championing of the people was genuine and forceful enough in itself, it seemed weakened by the fact that their own creative work remained too delicate and subtle for the masses. Only Adama van Scheltema's lyrics are, in their pure and simple diction, consistent with his theoretical manifesto.

We can hardly be expected to solve the problem of whether or not culture should postulate the notion of elite. In the next century historians will probably be better able to answer the question of whether our classical heritage is to be extended and rejuvenated by popularization and proletarianization, or to die in the technical skill of sheer entertainment and mass production which is serving these two trends. At the moment the most useful approach seems to be the attempt to understand the change which has taken place in the evaluation of culture itself. There are two different aspects to be noted, which not infrequently are confused in the treatment of popular culture. One involves the presentation and diffusion of the highest forms of Western achievement to as large a public as possible; the other is concerned with the generating of new expressions of culture from the twentieth-century mass consciousness.

The distribution of classical culture to the masses is the least problematic of popularization trends. We will never be able to prove that the crowds gazing at the "Nightwatch" or the "Mona Lisa" cannot deeply enjoy art because their taste is not trained; or that the essential beauty of *Fidelio* or the *Goldberg Variations,* which through mechanical means is now available to all, is lost for the common man. Nor can we prove the opposite. The whole argument may well be dispensed with as useless for our purposes. There is neither reason to frown at the flocking of crowds around museums and explain it as a degeneration of art appreciation, nor reason to exhalt it as human progress. The actual cultural value here is nil. Mass participation in the traditional heritage of Western culture can, and should, have educational importance. Under certain circumstances it can carry a social significance which ought to be encouraged for that reason. The common man listening to the harpsichord or admiring Dürer's woodcuts can, indeed, represent progress if they open his mind to unkown facts. But let us not deceive ourselves into thinking that this activity differs in any way, for instance, from his visiting the zoo. Just as he will not become more scientific by watching the seals being fed in Central Park, so he will not become more artistic in the Sistine Chapel. This does not need to worry us in the least as long as we do not foster the illusion that any *cultural* goal will be fulfilled when a crowd files past the giants of yesteryear as if they were great auks and rhinoceroses.

Popular culture, for all we know, may thus not produce cultural enjoyment. We certainly can presume that it provides another kind of enjoyment, entertainment if one wants, which makes the dissemination of arts and music worth the effort. Such diffusion is strongly aided by what has been called the "graphic revolution," especially in modern advertising techniques. They make it possible to organize record numbers of visitors to the Metropolitan Museum when it acquires a new Rembrandt, or a milling mob around traveling exhibitions. Various "never befores" can be established in this manner. Never before did so many tourists come to see a new architectural feat as visited the rebuilt Coventry Cathedral. No better proof of the extraneous premises of some modern architecture could be given than by the considerations of the designer of the Kennedy Memorial Library, which, long before the actual building has begun, are primarily concerned with the traffic problems when the hoped-for and no doubt catered-to visiting crowds are to show up. The link between art and tourist attraction is, as we all know, a clearly established one. But the element of record-breaking which has now become so prominently important in popular displays seems to indicate that with the factor of quantity the whole idea of culture tends to become dubious. Culture will be enjoyed culturally if there is a *cultural* response which manifests itself in congenial results: thought, critical insight, conversation, books, works of art, and so on. Otherwise the enjoyment, though probably just as real and genuine, will be no different in the arts from the reaction to the Hardanger Fjord, Babe Ruth, or the Ugliest Man on Campus. Quantity, in theory at least, does not have to be detrimental to culture if the extraneous elements can be kept out of its discussion. The popularity of reproducing works of art, which by the technical skills of the twentieth century surges to significant proportions, again has obvious pedagogic value. But if brilliant reproductions create only an *image* of culture, a fraudulent element seems to sneak in.

Of far more importance is the question of to what extent popular culture can be understood as a new autonomous or authentic manifestation of modern society; in other words, not as response, but as product. It will be judicious, I submit, to look first at new forms rather than at the continuation of traditional modes of culture. The arts, music, and literature naturally are all greatly involved in the new democratic ways of communication, but their changes as far as the process of estrangement is concerned are intricate and labyrinthine. As proof that the proletarian spirit is by no means negative in relation to cultural change and novelty, there has emerged a wide array of fascinating trends that need not be considered on the basis of their artistic potential in order to be accepted as momentous testimonies of social vitality. The new energy is evident in film art, the American musical, and jazz, while some insist on including the better brands of comic strip. They all have appeared from a genuine need and gone through a limited but remarkable historical development, leaving no doubt as to their cultural justification. To call them "lively" arts seems a trifle absurd, for the inference must then be made that the lively element is something new and that Giotto's frescoes in the Scrovegni Chapel, *The Magic Flute,* and *Twelfth Night* are less lively than "Krazy Kat," *Porgy and Bess,* or *The Gold Rush.* Nor does it seem more helpful to insist on the distinction between "high" and "low" art, since there is obviously no yardstick available to determine decisive altitudes in music or painting. There seems to be nothing wrong with designating them simply as popular arts. This the more so since the term implies at once the nature of the product and that of the public response—the two elements, as we have seen, dialectically essential for culture.

It might as well be stressed from the outset that in a sense these modern popular expressions do continue traditional forms and varieties. As we know, there are clear transitions which link jazz to conventional music, the musical to the opera, the movie to the stage. But having severed their umbilical cords, they soon develop on their own and become increasingly autonomous, a change beneficial for both parental stock and offshoot. The very fact of their popular scope releases us from the task of describing the new arts according to their essential nature. We may thus see at once that the element most responsible for the easier accessibility and wider acceptance of cultural entertainment in general, as well as a closer identification with it, is the principle of *immediacy*.

The touch of immediacy in jazz, for instance, as compared with classical music, is probably experienced in the uninhibited presentation of sexuality. The intrinsic sensuality of tonal and rhythmic qualities that characterizes music has always made it a natural accompaniment to love and was, one may presume, already realized from the beginning when Jubal, according to the fourth chapter of Genesis, became "the father of all such as handle the harp and organ." Most jazz, however, with deliberate efficiency, has discarded the traditional techniques of restraint and mediacy that could go under the name of stylization. It gives us sex in the raw, so to speak: in the primordial shiverings and screams as well as in the plaintive whines and whimpers. Just as the graceful, deft notes of the minuet led the measured and formal movements of the seventeenth-century dancing couple, so the hammering beat from ragtime to rock 'n' roll suggests the bumping and jostling of the modern pair. The actual libidinous excitement is probably experienced equally intensely in both cases. But in the earlier age it was stimulated deviously, in the later directly.

Immediacy in its most graphic bluntness is almost indiscriminately exercised by poster and advertising art, which leads the other fields in the skills of attracting and swaying the masses with unequaled psychological cunning. The technique rests solely on the principle of *image selling*. Advertising men, better than any other agencies, know scientifically how to create the make-believe world needed for the homogenized modern society. According to the above-mentioned study, *The Image*, "they are simply acolytes of the image. And so are we all. They elaborate the image, not only because the image sells, but also because the image is what people want to buy." And since we are concerned here with the minor league in the arts, we may accentuate this by a testimony from the great showman and circus director P. T. Barnum, who in the nineteenth century laid the foundation for modern advertising as well as popular art by falling in "with the world's way." This apparently means to "excite the community with flaming posters, promising almost anything for next to nothing."

The stress on the "image" at the expense of the original implies a greater exploitation of the visual sense than ever before. The eye naturally is far better equipped than the ear to cope with faster and more immediate conveyance of ideas, and moreover it is able to absorb an endlessly more accurate and detailed image than any of the other sensory organs. Within its own realm, as the comic strip has shown, the eye can also make considerable shortcuts in the communication process. Whereas reading requires the intermediate stage of the word-image to evoke a thought-image, the strip cartoon presents its narrative with instantaneous imprint on the mind. Thus, like instant food, instant reading became an absolute necessity in the streamlined society, and the "yellow press" was the first to know it. In 1869, the Hearst concern proudly issued eight pages of polychrome strip stories, and from then on the comic strip was syndicated and established.

The fact that twenty million people daily identify themselves with the image-existence of the comic strip demonstrates how great is the need for the fast evocation of the graphic illusion. It is this hunger for immediacy which has banned poetry from our life. It is easy to see that not only the comic strip but also the whole range of image-selling techniques has contributed heavily to the unlearning of concentrated reading, and that for this reason alone the printed poem is a useless device in our age. But we are thinking more specifically here of the poetic element in general, that mystic *fluidum* in life, which is not picture, not tone, not smell, not texture in itself, but rather a strange amalgamation of all these together, and in its function and direction recognizable as the opposite of immediacy. The modern theater, in spite of various frantic attempts to save it, has all but dropped the poetic conception; understandably so, for nothing better reflects the style and purposes of a society than dramatic art. The bourgeois drama abandoned verse diction. But the greatness of Ibsen can retain the poetic overtones in the mystic vibrations of symbolism. The expressionist and existentialist varieties of more recent years fought attractively against the gray conformity of the later naturalist family plays, but they were drowned out by the machinery of the commercial theater.

Under these conditions, however, the musical thrives. It can overcome the pedestrian dullness of the later naturalist drama without having to fall back on the ambiguities of the poetic. The musical is the honest triumph of the American theater and we ought to honor it without the provisos of "buts" and "ifs." For it is the only modern stage form which, properly classless and equalitarian as it is, has lived up to the popular image of our age: fast, immediate, folksy as well as lavish, simple as well as rich, American yet internationally enjoyable, entirely our own, yet not without historical roots. We must, for the sake of this discourse, point to its cultural estrangement, but this by no means takes anything away from its importance as popular art. Limited it is, no doubt, as is inevitable for a format directing itself to unlimited audiences. But it is authentic and indigenous, inasmuch as it does not look back to European greatness of past centuries or to novelty of past decades. As such, it is essentially far more endearing than the ardent attempts to restore "greatness" to the stage by out-probing Strindberg, out-symbolizing Ibsen, out-smutting Genet, out-stunting Ionesco, or out-mystifying Becket. No one, of course, has to remind us that the musical is also a product of a small but efficient kind of industry, and that it has learned from the advertising man; it knows all about the immediacy of conveyance.

The most remarkable aspect of the musical is its outer resemblance to the Greek drama, as if theater art since Aristophanes has swung full circle to arrive back at its original form. After a circuitous journey in history we again have acquired a popular and national drama which combines topical comment, satire, song, dance, and folk plot, all dished up in splendid trappings and trimmings. One dimension is sadly missing, however: the poetical conception, which our nervous urges cannot afford to incorporate. The Greeks needed intermediate devices, such as verse, mask, or metaphor, to bind together the complexity of their stage fare in a poetic unity. This the musical cannot do. Hence, although we do not know enough to reconstruct reliably the ancient Greek performances, we can still, with a little training and imagination, enjoy the profound grandeur of the Athenian drama from the printed page. The musical cannot be printed for enjoyment. Its reality is entirely exhausted in the professional representation.

While the drama and the epos sprang from the elevated heights of mythological grandeur and developed in the dignified environment of religious ceremony and tribal convention, the motion picture was born, so to speak, in the slums. The film grew up in the fairground and the music hall as a technical curiosity. It was sired in the workshops of Edison, Robert Paul, the Lumières, and Ottomar Anschütz—not on Mount Olympus. The cinematographic principle is much older, and even if we do not want to go back as far as the cave-paintings, as some do, and declare that "the film is as old as mankind," or look on Heron of Alexandria, with his mechanical automat of moving representations, as an early cinematographer, we can recognize that throughout the ages man speculated on the idea of kinetic art and looked for its realization. This did not occur until 1895, when almost simultaneously in Germany, France, the United States, and England the first motion picture performances were given for small and unexcited audiences.

The film, as popular art, belongs to the proletarian era as decisively as the novel is the historical property of the bourgeois period. In a sense it replaced the novel, although its earliest crude appearances rather suggested an adapted and photographed theater art. Despite the fact that technically it cannot be classified as drama, and belongs to the epic modes of expression, socially it must be seen as a substitute for the art of both the theater and the novel. This provides it with a truly authentic basis, somewhat hybrid to be sure, yet with historical significance. As popular entertainment the motion picture had to strip off the cumbersome devices which are essential attributes of the traditional epic and dramatic styles. It had to do away with the function of reading and the word-image. It had to abandon the time-consuming maneuvers with unities, not only of time, place, and action (for the theater itself had already jettisoned these), but also of a structural and metaphysical order in the Aristotelian conception. The great technical advance of the film was its speed, not merely in terms of plot movement, but principally as immediate transmission from product to response.

Naturally it has had to pay for this. Since it had come into existence as a technical invention, it was easily incorporated in the industrial management and geared to the wheels of big commerce. So there was a split in its nature, which over the years has widened rather than healed. In 1939, a sympathetic student of the motion-picture industry, with unperturbed confidence, distinguished "the technique of handling apparatus, in which the American makers of films are almost supreme masters, and the technique of handling ideas which they have just begun to learn." The history of the film as art and entertainment is by now, however, old enough for us to recognize its cultural pattern, which obviously is not meant for the distribution of ideas. The understandable human hope of having it both ways has been wisely revised by most people, and certainly the extravagant expectations which ring from a manifesto issued by the Edison studios in 1896 seem naïve to us today. We no longer believe that the motion picture is "the crown and flower of nineteenth-century magic, the crystallization of Eons of groping enchantments," or even the "earnest of the coming age." We are content, or at least should be, that as mass entertainment it is able to serve its purpose and solve some of the problems of mass leisure with efficiency as well as variety and taste.

A similar gap between artistic aspiration and popular industrialization is evident in the history and achievements of photography. Just as we have to distinguish between the art-film and the film industry, so it is, unfortunately I believe, necessary to separate the art-photo from commercial photography as used in the newspaper trade. Although we all understand that the two terms can overlap and intermix, there nevertheless remains this marked division. Since we are dealing exclusively with the popular aspect, the contradiction does not pose a problem here: we can simply leave the artistic form out of consideration. Needless to say, this is an unsatisfactory situation and one which points to the limitations of popular culture as a whole. One is forever self-consciously concerned with the claim for its "classicity," and so we have the sophisticated cinema clubs and the regular photograph exhibitions in museums of modern art to demonstrate something not at all characteristic for these arts as they are accepted and known by the masses. The cultural function of photography does not in the first place lie in the many artistic and technical experimentations (attractive though this aspect is), but preeminently in the power of its journalistic and reporting scope. Photography, in this sense, stands to painting as the newspaper stands to literature. While we have gained in the freedom of immediacy, we have lost proportionately in its bondage to the commercial machine.

The popular arts in general thus constitute a fascinating social change, which cannot be met with either blind jubilation or blunt vilification. While it is obviously not true that if "we give up jazz we shall be sacrificing nearly all there is of gaiety and liveliness and rhythmic power in our lives," as an enthusiast of the "lively arts" cries out, neither is it historically justified to declare that jazz represents the last feverish agony before the world ends. Popular culture is timely when in many respects the classical forms of art become academic and abstract propositions. It is therefore not unwise to adjust the enthusiasm with the suggestion that "except in a period when the major arts flourish with exceptional vigour, the lively arts are likely to be the most intelligent phenomena of their day."

If we then accept popular culture in its genuine and timely appearance, we cannot of course overlook the typical limitations which it has set for itself: the immediacy of its image-evoking world, the abandonment of any poetic conception, and above all its absorption in the managerial order. This is a harsh paradox for our proletarian minds—to have gained the seemingly limitless freedom of culture spread over all the classes of society while, on the other hand, this very conquest is sponsored and controlled by the machinery of a plutocratic system. Mencken saw it clearly: "The plutocracy in a democratic state, tends inevitably, despite its theoretical infancy, to take the place of the missing aristocracy." All the fields of popular arts, as we have noted, are irrevocably identified with commercial ends. Their outward organization is totally estranged from the inner purpose of what we classically understand as the "artist." Popular culture does not allow the autonomy and independence which are the sure attributes of the "master," and, with due respect to their singular talents, a Walt Disney, a Chaplin, a Gershwin, a Louis Armstrong, or a George Herriman are great wheels in the popular industry.

The limitations of popular culture lie not in the fact that it has not produced an Aeschylus, a Shakespeare, or a Bach, but in its sacrifice of the individual resources of art in order to embrace a collective enterprise. That this enterprise turns out to be one of a commercial nature may or may not be accidental, but it has qualified the best expressions of our egalitarian civilization.

To turn from the popular arts to the cultural impact of sports may seem a rather sudden leap. Yet, different though sports appear to be from the arts in their social objectives, their historical change which is being contemplated here reveals the same pattern as that underlying popular art forms. That this should be so is an inevitable result of the common ground, the realm of leisure, which in our era dominates social relations. It is not unlikely that the popularization of art has brought it closer to the sports arena. Whether this is caused by a decline in the arts, as Jaspers believed, can be left aside. But it seems unassailable that inasmuch as "art in the technical order of the masses has become a function in this existence, it approaches sport as an object of entertainment."

Sports have become a means of communication on a grander scale than ever before. The mutual relationships established by contesting individuals or teams have deep psychological roots which need not be analyzed here; nor need we reiterate what has been said about the *agonal* element of play, which Burckhardt stressed in the development of Greek culture. It is clear, however, that in matters of sport we have learned almost exclusively from the Greeks.

Why it took so many centuries for the Christian era to

discover the uses and excitements of sport is a difficult question which one can only approach with tentative suggestions. The Church of the Middle Ages encouraged little admiration for the body and its cultivation, and some of the later Protestant denominations were even more explicit in their denunciation of corporeal pleasures. Thus it would be attractive to believe that with the withering in the nineteenth century of the established churches and the weakening of their grip on the populace, the enjoyment of games could be promoted. Although it is easy to see that the churches could keep the educators in check as far as ideas on physical education were concerned, it does not follow that by lack of ecclesiastic control the popularity of sport must necessarily burst into existence. The emergence of sport games was more likely an indirect result of the expansion of industrialization. Although again one is hard put for evidence, the fact that the cultivation of physical exercise and industrial revolution coincided, and both developed in England first, may point to the possibility that sport represented a psychological compensation, and thus became a new form of life in the industrialized world.

The ascendance of sport was linked with the demand for the harmony and universality that were part of the ideals of the new bourgeois type of education in the nineteenth century. Friedrich Ludwig Jahn, whose ideas on popular gymnastics coincided with the establishment of the new German educational system, declared in 1816 that his famous *Turn* clubs aimed at "the restoration of the lost harmony in the education of man." The integration of sports in the curriculum of the English boarding schools was based on the same ideal of all-round balance and harmonic poise. The revival of the Olympic games in 1896 was but one more example of how the source of the new spirit lay in the Greek idea of play and *agon*, except, of course, that the religious climate stimulating the Olympic festivals in Greece is totally absent in modern sport. There the cult of the body was part of the national consciousness from the beginning of its civilization; with us it appeared after the classical cultural pattern had been set.

The revival of sports came at the end of the bourgeois epoch and still bore all the marks of the cheerful individualism which characterized the nineteenth century. The fierce competition inherent in sports was one of the more tolerable concomitants of social Darwinism. At a time when nationalistic trends increasingly prevailed in the political arena, sport reflected this rivalry in more and more frequent international contests. Sport, for all its patently binding qualities of fraternity and solidarity, was also essentially an exercise in the exploitation of individuality. How then was mass sport possible? What happened when with the beginning of the new century a proletarian era set in and individualism was gradually crushed by the exigencies of large-scale organization? How would the idea of individual sportive freedom behave in the context of an egalitarian world?

Team sport, of course, presupposes restrictions on individual objectives and initiatives. But no one can maintain that the team structure of soccer, football, or baseball has deprived the particular function of the goalie, the center forward, the quarterback, or the pitcher of its individual luster, and that these sports can in any way be related to mass phenomena. It is therefore entirely without foundation to stress team cohesion "as a collective satisfaction of honor," as a German sports-writer does, in order to link it with mass manifestation. On this rather unreal basis, mass sport (whatever it may be) and team sport can obviously not be identified, not even compared with each other. Nor is it very helpful to bring in the massive demonstrations of gymnastics which have become popular in Germany and the Soviet Union. At best they can be healthy, disciplinary, skillful, even to the point of being esthetically attractive, but no more so than the best infantry drill. Though there is no harm in calling this sport, gymnastics as a massive display is certainly not rooted in the popular (or cultural) conception of contest, and lacks the element of spontaneity. If one can think at all in terms of authentic mass sport, one has to resort to pastimes such as the popular skating one sees represented on the sixteenth- and seventeenth-century pictures of Hendrik Avercamp and others, the crammed sailing on the Dutch *polder-plassen,* or the community swimming off the modern resort beaches.

Otherwise one is compelled to conclude that mass sport is a contradiction in terms. When one stops to realize what games have come to mean for the populace as a whole, it becomes clear that participation in sports in the modern mind is a *watching* proposition. Sport in the collective consciousness of our world has lost its original autonomy and is irretrievably absorbed in the entertainment sphere. We have become spectators, that is, outsiders of the realm of sport, all eyes for the daredevil, the slugger, the record-breaker; the essential Olympic qualities of solidarity and fraternity have lost their meaning. Not illogically we have called in the professional. Born in the perspective of the Industrial Revolution, and under the pressures of technocratic predominance, sport was inevitably bound to adjust itself to the managerial order. So the professional makes it fit for the masses. The Greek stadium, as well as theater, was the triumph of the amateur. He gave the Greek games and dramas an unequaled place in history. This may serve as a warning against our unrestricted adulation of the "professional." If we cannot abandon him now, if we should not try to think him out of our existence, there is still leeway for the restrained wisdom of accepting him as a necessary and a useful organization device rather than as a savior-hero.

Sport as a modern institution has taken its adjusted place in the organization of mass leisure. Its new excitements are strong and sensational. It can easily survive the "shaving" of points, the intrusion of gangsterism, the fixing and rigging of boxing bouts. In this sense it is clearly estranged from the *ludique* nature of culture, it has left the true realm of *play,* and as such, Huizinga believes, sport in the present age has set itself outside the actual cultural process. But although it may have been stripped of its religious relevancy, or may practically have lost the innocent freedom of the village-green game, its new orientation gives it a fitting place in the machine age. Not surprisingly, then, sport has even come to be measured by statistics. While in the nineteenth century it was still almost morally impossible to describe a sportsman's greatness or the proceedings of a game other than in emotion-filled terms, the scientific mechanics of our mind have adopted the new technique of formulating achievements in the numbers of punts, fumbles, and rushing yardage.

The scientific spirit

When, in the year 632 after Ford, the director of Hatcheries and Conditioning in *Brave New World* opens the door of the fertilizing room to a group of new students, he is careful to leave out of the indoctrination any general principles and include as many particulars as possible. Huxley's comment: "For particulars, as everyone knows, make for virtue and happiness; generalities are intellectually necessary evils. Not philosophers, but fretsawyers and stamp collectors compose the backbone of society." We, the unvirtuous ones of A.F. 90 or so, however, are not doing all that badly; for slowly we, too, begin to see the light of atomistic anarchy and learn to view the world as a scattering of disconnected fragments, whose unity is no more real and enduring than the accidental pattern of a kaleidoscope. So we have declared ourselves to be pluralists, concerned only with piecemeal investigation (Russell) and pragmatic truths (James). We can conveniently adopt two freedoms (Isaiah Berlin), four freedoms (Roosevelt), or an infinite number (everyone else). We experience it as the true emancipation of our minds that since the single harmonious system which a Plato, a Newton, or a Hegel conceived cannot be proved, metaphysical unity, in fact, does not exist. Our world is true insofar as it is empirically true. Science in the last two centuries appears to have been our only reliable teacher.

In a way we have become less demonstrative about our newly acquired outlook. Historians no longer have to declare that "history is a science, no less and no more," nor is the novelist desperate to be an "observer and experimentalist," according to Zola's precept. The war cries and manifestos, still needed in the previous era, lost their urgency after the Industrial Revolution quietly changed into the so-called Scientific Revolution. So we are blithely empirical about the shaping of our destiny. We have abandoned any pre-set doctrine to fix us on a metaphysical or religious track, any political theory by which to test our government, any module to crystallize a comprehensive art style. True and free is everything that flatters our appetite. We believe in our "way of living," which is a meandering pursuit of the smells we like.

There are questions, of course. There is, for instance, the problem of the "two cultures," which makes it appear as if the intellectual community of the Western world is being split into two hostile camps. The scientist is no longer able to communicate with the "humanist"; each lives and practices in his own world which in self-sufficient illusion is floating detached from the other. At bottom, Barzun thinks there is partly the disuniting force of modern specialization, referring back to the old division of labor. In addition, the trend is anticipated by the traditional opposition of the deductive and inductive methods in arriving at a valid judgment. The awareness of the need for accurate data for the advancement of learning led Bacon to emphasize the scientific method as the manner of "collecting and concluding upon the reports of the senses." The scientific spirit was here cooperating as harmoniously with philosophy as it was in Leonardo's work with art. No obstructive conflict seemed to have arisen yet. Looking back over the centuries, however, it is easy to see that Bacon marked the beginning of an Anglo-American philosophical approach which swerved away from the continental mainstream. If one

tolerates the generalization for a moment, the development of the former can be recognized by a predominant
concern for the particulars, the world of "things," from
which is to be deduced a number of useful conclusions,
whereas that of the latter remains chiefly one of idealist
concepts, categories, and unifying principles. Around
1800, no outward split between scientific and idealist
world seemed evident in man's consciousness, yet there
was a remarkable, almost deliberate, playing with the
contrast; Goethe was nearly as proud of his *Zur Farben-
lehre* as of his *Faust*. Some of the Romanticists, such as
Wordsworth and Shelley, flirted with the idea of science
or dabbled in laboratories, while Novalis was an accomplished mathematician and Chamisso a professional bot-
anist. It was with the advent of positivist philosophy that
a cry of challenge, if not hostility, was launched from the
scientific side to the idealist community. From then on,
the chasm that was to eventuate in the alleged situation
of two cultures widened continually.

It is significant that the development of this cultural
separation started at the same time as, and ran parallel
with, the process of cultural isolation. It seems unwarranted, however, to present the problem of the intellectuals as if it were the total aspect of cultural estrangement. Nothing could be less true. What we have described as an historical split in the history of academic
thinking was basically a growing process of unbalance.
Whereas originally scientific observation and analysis
was absolutely compatible with the speculative or literary mind (Kant, Goethe), gradually we see science
usurping the entire stage, with the old standbys such as
conceptual vision, religious and metaphysical speculation, and transcendent philosophy being pushed into the
wings. It is only an intellectual manifestation of an underlying fissure involving the entire social structure. It
shows up in the arts, in literature, in philosophy, but no
less so in the standards and ways of living of the populace at large. Whitehead was not speaking only of intellectuals when he remarked that in matters of esthetic

needs the reactions of science have been unfortunate. The material basis of modern society has "directed attention to *things* as opposed to *values*." It is for this reason that contemporary man is frantically in search of more and more gadgets. It is for this reason that he is relying more and more on the guidance of statistics. The whole political acumen of the nation is exhausted in the magic numbers of the popularity poll. Its evaluation of baseball is expressed in the formulas of RBIs, ABs, ERAs, PCTs, and IPs, as if it were a matter of chemistry.

There is no founded reason to cultivate, as Flaubert did, a gnawing doom syndrome about the increasing scientific orientation of our world. Yet his last, unfinished novel *Bouvard et Pécuchet* (1881), besides being a significant piece of literature, is an interesting picture of the popularization of culture with the accent on science. The satire does not aim at ridiculing the two rather naïve title characters who dabble in garden science, chemistry, medicine, politics, only to be led to the most topsy-turvy conclusions, nor does it aim at undermining the authority of science itself. It is an assault on the popular distribution of facts and knowledge without the benefit of cultural maturation and balance. As such, it could be a rather useful hint for those who believe that the existence of a double culture will be repaired by more and better education. Education during the last two centuries has been promoted (if that is the word) as a cure-all for the most disparate ailments. Poverty, Christianity, communism, atheism, fascism, all have been declared eradicable by educational treatment. It does not come as a surprise then when a university professor, writing about the two cultures, suggests that in view of the dangers that threaten our society it is "obligatory for us and the Americans and the whole West to look at our education with fresh eyes." Education can only cure ignorance. But it by no means follows that the removal of ignorance necessarily has to produce peace, health, or tolerance, to name only a few attractions. We have already been enjoying a spectacular expansion of educational service during the last century. It coincides precisely (and embarrassingly) with the separation of the two cultures, a trend which we are supposed to reverse with more education. Where is the logic?

It will bring us a step further if we can see that the divorce of the humanities from science is only one outward aspect, a symptom of a fundamental inner change. And just as disease should be given more attention than its symptomatic pains, so this fundamental change ought to be our primary concern. We have first encouraged our existence to spread into a pluralistic thing-world, and when the multifarious abundance of our culture runs out of hand to the point of disintegration, we want to be rescued by a deus-ex-machina education. This is nothing less than the insatiable urge of addiction. Once education ceases to be a discipline for hardening the tender intelligence, and is applied as a panacea for social disorders, it is estranged from its intrinsic purposes and behaves like a drug.

Ignorance is obviously not the reason that modern man seems to become more and more lost in his limitless abundance of social freedoms. He is simply not equipped for the world which both his greed and his technical skills have built for him. No amount of training will ever make him master of his own technomiraculous house, for the cult of objects has proportionately dehumanized his existence. The very "human" relationships which sociology studies apparently can only be handled adequately if they are observed scientifically as "things." According to Durkheim, it is obligatory to consider social phenomena, as such, divorced from the consciousness of the individual who observes them; they must be studied from the outside as exterior things. In this connection Georg Simmel distinguishes the new culture as a *Kultur der Dingen* which is replacing the *Kultur der Personen*. "The things . . . have been cultivated beyond all proportion, but the culture of individuals has decreased." It is not illogical that this pronouncement should appear in a philosophical discourse about the notion of money, for to Simmel the curious aspect of money is that its quality consists exclusively of its quantity. Inevitably, with the increase of money and the increase in the importance of money, we have come to believe that the plurality of things itself accrues to their quality. The imbalance of our preponderantly scientific understanding has separated us from the things as they are; that is, we are alien in our own environment—nature—and have transformed the phenomena into useful but dead machines.

We should make it clear to ourselves that this process is inevitable, and that any attitude of criticism, as if some faction in the social community were trying to tyrannize the whole, is unrealistic. Yet we need not expedite it, either, by ignoring its nature and extent. Jacques Barzun believes that the chaotic state caused by the scientific usurpation can be remedied if modern man will restore to himself a guiding philosophy—or rather, if he will restore the act of philosophizing. For "until Western man reasserts his right to be, as far as he can, a natural and moral philosopher, he will feel like an exile in his own place." It is indeed *reflection* which can unite us with the inner life and meanings of objects in nature, which the scientific pursuit dismisses, and must dismiss, as unreal. Without the dialectics of reflection we must remain outsiders who observe, collect, possess, but cannot really participate in the natural phenomena.

Though nothing can bring back the hour
Of splendour in the grass, of glory in the flower;
We will grieve not, rather find
Strength in what remains behind.

William Wordsworth

15

The Future Way of Living

Looking back

To such close and involved observers as ourselves, the rich and complex structure of contemporary culture surveyed in the foregoing pages can only appear chaotic. Yet, in summing up the results of this exposition, we ought to be able to arrive at conclusions which, tentative as they must be, serve to provide the picture of our age with a guiding contour.

Contours, of course, are dangerous, because they tend to act as authoritative statements. They should be handled as mere instruments, not as final definitions. The course of history, cultural or otherwise, is gradual, and develops with infinite shades and values. In discussing a specific period, the proletarian era, the first problem, that of locating the period in historical time, already causes trouble. The actual beginnings of Western mass society went unnoticed at the time, but they have become a matter of speculation for the twentieth-century mind, which has gradually become aware of an historical change. This study places these beginnings in the revolutionary times at the end of the eighteenth century, since it was then that awareness of the estrangement of the individual from society began to express itself. This is done, however, in full recognition of the fact that before that time there were early intimations of that awareness. They can be seen in the increasing preoccupation with the notion of equality in the seventeenth century, in the related question of the sovereignty of the people, and in the faint proletarian consciousness which becomes apparent with the rise of bourgeois culture in Switzerland and the Netherlands. In fact, one can go back to the early Reformation to find the first undermining of hierarchic values which twentieth-century man was to complete. In this respect, Luther was the first modern man. Radical Anabaptists, Diggers, and Levelers were the forerunners of the Babouvists of 1796.

In spite of these preludes, the awareness of a collective order became a cultural factor only when, toward 1800, men in most artistic and intellectual fields began to rebel against the forms and formulas of the classical world. There lies the watershed between the stable classical and the restless modern way of life. It divides cultural history into two periods, one of hierarchical values and one of leveled ones, one of elitist judgment and one of mass consensus. The former was confident, more or less harmonious, formal and controlled; the latter is self-conscious, unbalanced, amorphous, and nervous. The division makes it understandable why Goethe thought that Voltaire was the last of an old order, Rousseau the first of a new.

The development of classical culture was controlled by

a small, superb elite. The elite in matters of art, literature, or scholarship, however, rarely meant a minority
privileged by birth. It simply represented the top of the
hierarchical pyramid. The elitist structure of classical society is contrasted to the status structure of modern life.
In spite of the intrigues occurring at papal and royal
courts (in which artists and scholars were not infrequently involved), the achievements of classical society
were not rated by outward success and were not, as they
so often are now, the result of extraneous help, smart
manipulations, or commercial saleability. Regardless of
the many violations of its high principles, classical culture at its best was determined by quality alone.

We, today, obviously also want the best. The search
for quality is innate in human beings. There is no reason
to believe that quality cannot at times prevail in a mass
society. But the odds are narrowed. Our society, constantly calling for adjustment, must be one of compromise. Quantity thrives on compromise. Quality does not.
On the contrary, for all our good intentions, it suffers
whenever collective demands cry out to be fulfilled. If we
want to prepare the next generation for a mass order, we
must prepare the many. Consequently the history of recent popular education is, inevitably, that of a steady
lowering of standards in order to compromise with the
massive demands for schooling. Classical society was
trained by a humanist education. It developed on the
premises of Erasmus, Hutten, More, and Valla. It focused
on the study of the best minds of the past and their best
works. Modern education has this objective, too, but it is
primarily interested in the useful. Utilitarian efficiency
replaces the humanist pursuit of learning.

The self-conscious character of contemporary thinking
in matters of art, education, philosophy, politics, or theology has psychological roots hard to trace. The historical roots, however, are more exposed. When in the
eighteenth century the notion of the collective as a separate cultural force began to preoccupy the human mind,
the reality of mass communication became a factor. The

rise of the popular novel was indicative. Equally important was the introduction of the encyclopedia as an institution of popular education and distribution of knowledge. The French Enlightenment was not very remarkable for its profound and original thinking. Its strength
lay in the popularization of existing knowledge, produced
by the Renaissance.

We see here the beginning of a trend which was to
become characteristic for the modern scene. Although
undoubtedly new pivotal ideas continue to emerge, the
stress in the proletarian era is more and more on the distribution of cultural contents. Our epoch, being one of
economic expansion, is also one of the dissemination of
ideas and art. Whereas classical culture was spontaneous,
modern culture is administrative. Classical culture happened to rise in various nuclei of the Western world; our
cultural centers are superimposed upon the landscape.
They are the work of financiers and developers. Applied
to education, the administrative principle means huge
school "systems," professional educators (as distinct from
teachers), the dominance of standard courses and standard textbooks. Applied to the military, it results in the
replacement of the old hero-type general by the executive team-man as top commander. The administrative
principle has so thoroughly permeated the structure of
our society that even religious faith has abandoned its
original spontaneous quality for organized social activity.
Personal charity has been replaced by institutional philanthropy, the example of the Good Samaritan by that of
the "good guy," who programs his actions deliberately,
supporting causes rather than persons.

The administrative principle is of great service to the
public spirit of our age. We prefer to exist in group formations. Apparently we like every act and move to be
watched and witnessed. Although we complain vaguely
about intrusion of privacy, we invalidate the complaint
by our inordinate desire for public exposure. American
life especially does not allow for hedges—an attractive
aspect, but one indicative of a mentality that will not tol-

erate, either, the hiding places of human thought and opinion. The freedom of privacy is not one of the great marks of the twentieth century. It certainly would be difficult to cultivate at a time when common opinion decides action at the expense of individual judgment. Action at such times is group action, protest is group protest. In the classical era the historical protest was launched by the unique individual: Luther, Giordano Bruno, Swift, Rousseau, Thoreau, Kierkegaard, Nietzsche. Today most intellectual unrest is organized into mass protest.

The difference between classical and modern society is further characterized by a shift away from a central source of authority to a plurality of references. Whereas in former times, Greek philosophy, the Bible, or the Church each supplied all the answers to the whole of life, today man has a wide range of favorite pundits, radio commentators, sports reporters, textbooks, politicians, and other public figures to support his specific opinions. The pluralistic temper is patently useful for scientific pursuits. It is totally incompatible with metaphysical probing. Metaphysics seeks an absolute unity which transcends the disconnected events of daily life. Heidegger, scorning the lack of metaphysical sense in modern thinking, in essence battles with the pluralistic wandering mind. Modern scholarship has benefited from scientific pluralism in that it has become more specific and precise in its analysis. It is thus able to avoid the fuzziness which so often spoiled nineteenth-century expository writing. By the same token, it has suffered from the entailing Alexandrian narrowness with which it treats details, frequently losing sight of the really significant and lacking strong organizing themes.

How does this trend of diffusion affect the arts? In general, art and literature in classical times were firmly controlled by unifying technical devices. Perspective in painting, tonal harmony based on major and minor triads, and dramatic plot-structure were some of the more important means to establish concentrated form. The contemporary arts have abandoned any central, form-controlling agency. Instead, they decentralize their interests. Hence the fragmented patterns in paintings, poems, and novels, all discussed as typical for the twentieth century. The proclivity for juxtaposing disjointed elements such as words, colors, lines, tones, and harmonies, tends to break up unifying context and cohesion. It means the democratizing of technical values; the sense of hierarchy is abandoned. The leveling evident in social relationships is in its own way no less characteristic for modern esthetics. The surrealist, dadaist, or futurist manner of painting deliberately fractures the conventional forms, with the result that the representation appears flat and decorative, without a compositional scale of importance.

Classical culture showed a natural sense of form. In contrast, modern man believes that form infringes on his liberty. Thus he is consistently set on destroying the old forms of communication. He is the sans-culotte. He does away with monarchical court life as well as cumbersome fashion, in the same contemptuous gesture. In the arts he streamlines away all mediating agencies. In doing so, he eliminates the classical mark of culture: style. Style is almost the opposite of function. It is play. But while cultural play is as essential to the elitist mind as games are to the child, the proletarian disposition deems it impractical. If style means courtly manners, they must be abolished in a practical society. If style means the pediments, architraves, clover arches, arabesques, gargoyles, fluted columns, and fan vaults of public buildings, then we must have bare, streamlined architecture in a functional world. If style means an elegant and elaborate ritual to mask the sexual impulse behind the social dance, then it is to be replaced by the raw gestures and movements of unabashed sexuality.

The classical artist, his technique being equivalent to stylization, communicated in represenative tokens, that is, by mediacy. His picture of life was representative inasmuch as it conveyed the essence of life by indirect means. The modern artist, in contrast, aims at the particulars of life. He wants the immediate effect, the quick connection. The mass mind demands that he be clear, direct, functional, entertaining. Our culture has cut off the roots of civilization as manifested in the traditional forms of play. This has happened in a series of operations, which, since Romanticism, have been proclaimed as liberations. But rootlessness and freedom are not synonymous.

It would not be difficult to continue summarizing the previous chapters in this rather schematic manner. There is no need for this. The main lesson to be learned from the comparison between classical and modern society concerns the change from a heroic, visionary, idealistic aspiration to a pragmatic, scientific, no-nonsense pursuit. This should mean a gain in common sense. Unfortunately, modern man does not always live up to his maturity. With the abandonment of the heroic vision, much of the poetic quality of life must disappear for him, but he can benefit from his increased experience. However, instead of relying on the solidity of a hero-less existence, he has created a substitute—the idol.

The idol is a dangerous substitute, a product of an hysterical temper quite hostile to the very common sense which should be the strength of a mass society. The hero is the projection of the super-individual who has conquered the fear of death. He is the symbol of vitality. Of cultic origin, he becomes the guiding star of culture. The hero has a history; he develops with the history of a civilization. The idol, however, is launched as a fashion. He has no roots either in cult or culture. He is the product of press management. Whereas the hero is the exponent of the superb, the idol is the inflated image of the average. We do not adulate Jean Harlow, Rudolph Valentino, Marilyn Monroe, or Brigitte Bardot for their great acting skills; their talents in this respect are insignificant. We do not idolize Elvis Presley, the Beatles, the Rolling Stones, or whatever else they may be called, because they are unparalleled entertainers. Their success stems from our desire to be "in" with a mass-worship sustained by large commercial and publicity concerns. In a different category, we have made a best-seller cult out of Jack Kennedy in spite of his rather inadequate performance as a President. We are the image-makers, the idolators, who, having abandoned the real gods, carve ourselves homemade substitutes which come and go with the change of fashion.

Looking forward

The great men of the nineteenth century—Hegel, Goethe, Kierkegaard, Melville, Thoreau, Nietzsche, Flaubert, Burckhardt, Dostoevski—although pioneers in their own fields, with various degrees of regret expressed their doubt about the vitality and future of Western culture. They were the last representatives of a humanist tradition, originating in the Renaissance. They eyed the rising influence of mass opinion with alarm. Their concern was shared by a number of historians who began to draw parallels with ancient civilizations to demonstrate that, on the principle of recurring cycles in history, our culture is a declining proposition. Whatever the truth in the speculations of Vollgraff, Lasaulx, Danilevskii, Brooks Adams and Henry Adams, Eduard Meyer, Petrie, Toynbee, Sorokin, and Spengler, their impact on the modern consciousness, especially through the prophetic radicality of the last, has been so thorough that in itself it must be accepted as an historical factor.

The historian, of course, should deal exclusively with the past. This investigation, being chiefly an historical survey, cannot be supposed to make prognoses. The future lies beyond our scope. Yet there is no point in being fanatical about this. Burckhardt, though in his writings and lecturing *ex cathedra* committing himself to nothing but the past, in his letters indulged with conspicuous frequency in predictions about the future. Besides working as specialists, historians are also human beings. They have a daily human existence. One does not expect a dancer on his way to the corner drugstore to move in arabesques and pirouettes. No more should one require the historian to deal with the past at all times. As a human being, as a family man, he is constantly involved in the future. One must suppose that even when analyzing the events of history, he is unconsciously guided by a latent thought of the future.

The proletarian era, studied here in its comprehensive cultural aspects, has by all visible signs not yet reached a conclusive form. Under the circumstances, although our approach is historical, it is hard to suppress curiosity about the ultimate destiny of this mass society. If we cannot know the outcome, we can at least for a moment concentrate on the present and trust that the soundest evaluation of our position today will yield the best results for the future of Western civilization.

It is unrealistic to expect that a mass society will produce the same type of culture that issues from an elitist world. The social order ruled by the average man will have an average man's culture. Common sense should teach us the limits as well as the strength of our potential. If we are proud of our egalitarian system, we owe it the loyalty of understanding. If we are proud of having dissolved the hierarchic structure of the classical community, we may enjoy the resulting liberties only if we recognize the dangers inherent in the loose, incoherent, disjointed nature of our own world. If we boast of having jettisoned a chain of burdensome social values, we cannot ignore the fact that this revolution has taken away an inward repose, which we try to replace with the outward security of a status system. If we believe that the leveling of the traditional techniques of art and literature has liberated artistic expression, we must not blind ourselves to the resulting eclecticism marking our own cultural output.

Looking at our present culture with all the limitations of contemporaries, we can, I think, agree about certain obvious characteristics, which it is imperative not to lose sight of if we are to advance safely into the future. Our age, strong in statistics, indices, tables, and graphs, clearly excels in economic and military management. It can hardly be expected to deliver profound metaphysical systems. With the falling apart of the natural cohesion of family and community, it has been driven to protect the underdog and the socially deprived, and hence it is conspicuous in the provision of a vast legislative body of social measures enacted as emergencies arise. But it has no unifying philosophy of society. The churches, strong in numbers and in wealth, have never before been so efficient in organizing their resources for public causes. They are clearly not the bulwarks of faith, however.

This age, highly skilled in translating social problems into abstract codes for administrative processing, has an amazing success in schooling unheard-of numbers of students, who in previous times, through lack of money, will power, and outstanding intellectual capacity, would have had little or no education at all. The twentieth century so far, however, has not been remarkable for its unique scholarly geniuses. This century, brilliant in the technique of planning, will be remembered for the precision and streamlining of technocratic power. It is the era of engineers. Their skill is transforming both townscape and landscape with the technological marvels for which later generations will honor us. If our art is known to them at all, they will probably compare our painters with those of the golden age of the fifteenth, sixteenth, and seventeenth centuries and find them coarse and clumsy. Our poetry they will presumably measure by the standards of Dante, Shakespeare, Milton, and Goethe, and find it insignificant. Nor must we deem it likely that they will remember our playwrights when they think of the superb dramatists who, from Aeschylus to Ibsen, stand out by the unique original power which makes for historical change.

There is nothing dishonorable in this. Only self-deceit is dishonorable. Our strength lies in the solid common sense of practical people who look at the daily occurring problems as so many jobs to be done, and to be done well. Our egalitarian structure has a tremendous power potential, but it lies almost exclusively in the fields of economic, technocratic, and military administration. It is an illusion to think that by applying this talent to the arts, and by organizing art councils, governmental programs and festivals, and increasing awards and scholarships, we can construct great culture. We will not succeed in these fields. History, of course, like life, admits of lucky flukes, and we may hope for them. But it would be wise to realize that the odds are formidably against us. For the sake of self-protecting wisdom we ought to commit our intellectual energy only to our strength and try to fulfill the promises innate in our system.

Many, unfortunately, will find this a depressing message. They are wrong, I believe. There is nothing more uplifting than to honor one's potential. Dabbling is a self-defeating activity. Naturally we all suffer only too easily from delusions. But if solid practical sense, which after all is the most valuable asset of the modern mentality, is not to be applied to our self-examination, then it is difficult to see what else can help us to define in forms of culture what we really are.

The scientific endeavor, which, beginning with Francis Bacon, has marked the modernity of Western civilization, should be an aid in protecting us from enslavement to our illusions. Unfortunately, however, the extraordinary successes of science have often fed utopian dreams. If we are not prepared to follow Flinders Petrie in his doctrine that the flourishing of science comes at the end of a civilization, neither should we speculate that science is the glorious demiurge of a new golden age. Science is of a more modest nature. It simply aims at the useful. It repairs. When our eyes grow dim, science can provide us with lenses. We should be grateful for this service, though it cannot restore our original sight. When our teeth disappear under the wear and tear of our civilized diet, science can fix them. But we should accept our artificial molars with some grace and not pretend that we are better off than before. Science does not rejuvenate.

Science has helped us to adapt ourselves to the new exigencies and demands of the rising mass society. The invention of the telephone has made it possible to expand personal communication beyond its local limitations to a worldwide network. Medicine has decreased infant mortality and the chances for longevity. Printing machines first, then radio and television, have helped organize instantaneous communication with the masses. The scientific and technological revolutions of the last two centuries, with new techniques of growing, packing, preserving, and transporting, have served to feed the spreading multitudes of the modern era. We must not make the error, however, of believing that the replacement of original, organic power by mechanical ingenuity can create bliss. Science does not create at all. It adjusts. It is a companion, not a father. It does not sire historic cultural movements. At best, it mends and fixes and adjusts. And for its own adjusting's sake we should not want to endow it with mystic powers, or we will inflate our existence beyond recognition.

Indeed, the greatest danger threatening the development of our egalitarian potential is intellectual inflation. It goes against everything that our scientific sense of order stands for, yet it is the most glaring propensity we nurse. One look at our newspapers will confirm that what often passes for news is merely magnified gossip and chatter. Journalists are under constant pressure to deliver their "big story." But daily events are rarely big, and historical news does not usually break in large dimensions. Therefore, the great event is first invented and then inflated to headline proportions. The public mind is continually eroded with streams of overwhelming emotional disturbance, in no way commensurate with reality. It would not be so if the mass society rejected this sensational turmoil. Unfortunately, however, the average man, rightly or wrongly thinking himself to be dull, tends to seek "excitement" outside his own reach. Excitement has become the keynote in life. Man must always be entertained. There must always be movement and noise around him, or else life seems nonexistent. Thus he becomes more and more dependent on extraneous forces inflating the reality of his daily existence.

This danger is increased by the expansionist character of our national consciousness. To be sure, it appears most visibly as an economic expansion, but it is directed by a mind reaching for vastness. It has pushed the American nation across from the east to the west coast and now threatens to extend itself beyond the borders of this hemisphere. Economic expansion is only one aspect of this trend of reaching out beyond existing borders. Our whole intellectual energy inclines toward spreading itself thin over vast enterprises. We live in an age of borrowers. We buy stocks on margin, cars and dishwashers by installment. Our economic system is based on borrowing, and the richer we are, the more we borrow. We are systematically behind our resources and always out of breath trying to catch up.

Modern man is continually reaching beyond his means. Our mental endeavors suffer from overextending themselves into foreign territory. The proletarian pursuit, far from building a cultural edifice on its own authentic foundations, borrows from elitist treasures. Understandable though it may be that in expansionist times our cultural thinking is swollen with inflated dreams, it is nevertheless mandatory to suppress this tendency. The greatness of this egalitarian society rests on the solidity of tangible opportunities, which brook no wishdreams. The strength of an elitist culture—its creative imagination—in our version becomes hallucination. It should not be encouraged. Mental inflation will only dissipate the promising potential of the mass order. Politically speaking, this will mean mass hysteria, the sure ferment for Caesars and Hitlers. No one should deny that the warning signs are daily around us.

This investigation is not unlike a self-portrait. It is hazardous, it is painful. It is also a test of integrity. Placing a mirror before a young mother fondling her first child amounts almost to revealing a madonna. To do the same before a widow's face is tactless. But studying wrinkles is not necessarily diagnosing a fatal disease. It is a test of truth. None of us is too well equipped for the task. We are appalled by our wrinkles, bewildered by our psychotic tension. We are emotional about our cultural standing in history. Above all we are partisans. We must be for or against in order to give ourselves a security check. Integrity, however, is not for or against. It is as simple as reporting. If we do not choose to eliminate all comment here, the least we can do is to base it dispassionately on the facts in the mirror—not on the mirages of the image-makers and professional taste-setters.

Our severest handicap is the constant need for glamor. Clearly, no civilization can manifest itself fully without brilliance and abundance. Equally no civilization can survive without the creative growth of inwardness. There is bloom and there is seed. We seem to be swept off our feet in the tide of public glitter. Our ideal is the headline, our creed popularity. No culture can long endure in a persistent state of fever. The real maturity of a mind is tested both by its thoughts and their formulation. There must be settlers as well as pioneers, popes as well as martyrs. For every Joan of Arc there is a *Roi Soleil*. Just as the theater depends on audience as well as on performers, so must society rely on public as well as on genius.

We belong to the public. We watch the proceedings and submit our comments. We are outsiders to the play and foreign to the life that exists on the stage and in the wings. The public has no grasp of the flash of imagination that lights up the mind of the unique performer. The proletarian mind is alien to the classical vision. This limitation does not make it second-rate. It has its own distinguished function. We will be second-rate only if we try to play a role on the elitist stage and think we have a show on our hands. We have not. We are not likely to kindle the fires of imagination. We are not the magicians of the arts. Our legacy will be a common man's culture, one to be remembered for its administrative brilliance. Our descendants will praise it for its solid purpose and technical perfection. It will have its own historical justification—provided we dare to be what we are.

Selected Booklist

This work is based on a substantial number of foreign sources. For the benefit of the general reader, however, the following books in the English language may help with possible further studies. It is clearly a very limited list, but most of the works mentioned have a detailed bibliography in their specific fields. They are not selected because I necessarily agree with their conclusions, but simply because I have found them useful.

1 / The Average Way of Living

Arendt, Hannah. *The Human Condition.* Chicago: University of Chicago Press, 1958.

Arnold, Matthew. *Culture and Anarchy.* New York: Cambridge University Press, 1932.

Burckhardt, Jacob. *Force and Freedom: Reflections on History.* New York: Pantheon, 1964.

Cassirer, Ernst. *An Essay on Man.* New Haven: Yale University Press, 1944.

Daedalus (Spring 1960 issue): "Mass Culture and Mass Media."

Hoffer, Eric. *The True Believer: Thoughts on the Nature of Mass Movements.* New York: Harper, 1951.

Huizinga, Johan. "The Task of Cultural History," *Men and Ideas.* Cleveland: (Meridian) World, 1958.

Huxley, Aldous. *Brave New World.* New York: Harper, 1932.

Jaspers, Karl. *Man in the Modern Age.* 2nd ed. New York: Humanities Press, 1951.

Kierkegaard, Søren. *The Present Age.* New York: (Torchbooks) Harper, 1962.

Le Bon, Gustave. *The Crowd: A Study of the Popular Mind.* New York: Viking Press, 1960.

Löwith, Karl. *From Hegel to Nietzsche: The Revolution in Nineteenth-Century Thought.* New York: Holt, Rinehart & Winston, 1964.

MacDonald, Dwight. "A Theory of Mass Culture," *Diogenes* (1953) no. 3.

Regin, Deric. *Freedom and Dignity.* The Hague: Martinus Nijhoff, 1965.

Riesman, David. *The Lonely Crowd.* New Haven: Yale University Press, 1950.

Rosenberg, Bernard, and D. M. White, eds. *Mass Culture: The Popular Arts in America.* New York: Macmillan, 1957.

Rudé, George E. *The Crowd in History, 1730–1848.* New York: John Wiley, 1964.

Schiller, Friedrich von. *On the Aesthetic Education of Man.* New York: Ungar, 1965.

Toynbee, Arnold J. *Civilization on Trial.* Cleveland: (Meridian) World, 1948.

Van den Haag, Ernest. "Reflections on Mass Culture," *The American Scholar* (Spring 1960).

Williams, Raymond. *Culture and Society, 1870–1950.* New York: (Torchbooks) Harper, 1959.

2 / *The Rebellious Way of Living*

Ashton, Thomas S. *The Industrial Revolution, 1760–1830.* New York: (Galaxy) Oxford University Press, 1964.

Barzun, Jacques. *Classic, Romantic and Modern.* 2nd ed. Boston: (Atlantic Monthly Press) Little, Brown, 1961.

Bowden, Witt, and others. *An Economic History of Europe Since 1750.* New York: American Book Co., 1937.

Bowra, Cecil Maurice. *The Romantic Imagination.* New York: (Galaxy) Oxford University Press, 1961.

Brinton, Crane. *A Decade of Revolution: 1789–1799.* New York: Harper, 1935.

Cooper, James Fenimore. *Home as Found.* New York: Putnam, 1961.

———. *The American Democrat.* New York: Vintage, 1956.

Dugas, Rene. *A History of Mechanics.* New York: Central Book Co., 1955.

Flaubert, Gustave. *Selected Letters.* ed. by Francis Steegmuller. New York: Farrar, Strauss, 1954.

Kierkegaard, Søren. *Journals.* ed. by Alexander Dru. Gloucester, Mass.: Peter Smith, 1959.

Le Bon, Gustave. *The Psychology of Revolution.* New York: Putnam, 1913.

Lefebvre, Georges. *The Coming of the French Revolution.* New York: (Vintage) Random House, 1957.

Lovejoy, Arthur O. *Essays in the History of Ideas.* New York: (Capricorn) Putnam, 1960.

Miller, Perry, ed. *The American Transcendentalists: Their Prose and Poetry.* New York: (Anchor) Doubleday, 1957.

Palmer, Robert R. *The Age of Democratic Revolution: A Political History of Europe and America, 1760–1800.* 2 vols. Princeton, N.J.: Princeton University Press, 1959, 1964.

———. *Twelve Who Ruled.* New York: Atheneum, 1965.

Postgate, Raymond W., ed. *Revolution from 1789–1906.* New York: (Torchbooks) Harper, 1962.

Sieyès, Emmanuel J. *What Is the Third Estate?* New York: Praeger, 1964.

Silz, Walter. *Early American Romanticism.* Cambridge, Mass.: Harvard University Press, 1929.

Toynbee, Arnold. *The Industrial Revolution.* Boston: Beacon Press, 1956.

Venturi, Franco. *Roots of Revolution: A History of the Populist Movements in Nineteenth-Century Russia.* New York: Knopf, 1960.

Woodring, Carl R. *Prose of the Romantic Period.* Boston: (Riverside) Houghton Mifflin, 1961.

3 / The Violent Way of Living

Artz, Frederick B. *Reaction and Revolution: 1815–1832.* New York: Harper, 1935.

Barzun, Jacques. *Darwin, Marx, Wagner: Critique of a Heritage.* rev. 2nd ed. Garden City, N. Y.: (Anchor) Doubleday, 1958.

Binkley, Robert C. *Realism and Nationalism: 1852–1871.* New York: Harper, 1935.

Boorstin, Daniel J. *The Image; or What Happened to the American Dream?* New York: Atheneum, 1962.

Büchner, Ludwig. *Force and Matter.* trans. by J. F. Collingwood. London: Trübner & Co., 1870.

Carnegie, Andrew. *The Gospel of Wealth and Other Timely Essays.* ed. by Edward C. Kirkland. Cambridge, Mass.: Harvard University Press, 1962.

Cochran, Thomas C., and William Miller. *The Age of Enterprise, A Social History of Industrial America.* New York: Harper, 1961.

Craig, Gordon A. *Europe Since 1815.* 2nd ed. New York: Holt, Rinehart & Winston, 1966.

Greene, Theodore M. *Liberalism: Its Theory and Practice.* Austin, Texas: University of Texas Press, 1957.

Hayes, Carlton J. H. *A Generation of Materialism: 1871–1900.* New York: Harper, 1941.

Hobson, J. A. *Imperialism: A Study.* Ann Arbor, Mich.: University of Michigan Press, 1965.

Hughes, H. Stuart. *Consciousness and Society.* New York: Knopf, 1958.

———. *Contemporary Europe: A History.* Englewood Cliffs, N. J.: Prentice-Hall, 1966.

Lange, Friedrich A. *The History of Materialism, and Criticism of Its Present Importance.* 3rd ed. New York: Humanities Press, 1950.

Lipson, E. *Europe in the Nineteenth Century, 1815–1914.* New York: Humanities Press, 1961.

Merz, John T. *A History of European Thought in the Nineteenth Century.* 4 vols. New York: Dover, 1904.

Niebuhr, Reinhold. *The Irony of American History.* New York: Scribner, 1952.

Ortega y Gasset, José. *The Modern Theme.* New York: (Torchbooks) Harper, 1961.

Schumpeter, Joseph A. *Capitalism, Socialism and Democracy.* 3rd ed. New York: Harper, 1950.

Thomson, David. *Democracy in France Since 1870.* 4th ed. New York: Oxford University Press, 1964.

Wagner, Richard. *Art and Politics.* Vol. 4 of *Richard Wagner's Prose Works.* trans. by W. A. Ellis. London: Kegan Paul, 1893–1900.

Woodcock, George. *Anarchism: A History of Libertarian Ideas and Movements.* Cleveland, Ohio: (Meridian) World, 1962.

4 / *The Ornamental Way of Living*

Giedrion, Sigfried. *Space, Time and Architecture: The Growth of a New Tradition.* 4th ed. rev. Cambridge, Mass.: Harvard University Press, 1962.

Goldwater, Robert, and Marco Trevers, eds. *Artists on Art.* New York: Pantheon, 1945.

Hauser, Arnold. *Naturalism to the Film Age.* Vol. 4 of *The Social History of Art.* New York: (Vintage) Random House, 1958.

Lowenthal, Leo. *Literature, Popular Culture and Society.* Palo Alto, Calif.: Pacific Books, 1967.

Morris, William. *The Aims of Art.* London: Office of the Commonweal, 1887.

———. *Useful Work versus Useless Toil.* London: Socialist League, 1886.

Mumford, Lewis. *The Culture of Cities.* New York: Harcourt Brace, 1938.

Myers, Bernard S. *Art and Civilization.* New York: McGraw-Hill, 1957.

Pelles, Geraldine. *Art, Artists and Society: Origins of a Modern Dilemma.* Englewood Cliffs, N. J.: Prentice-Hall, 1964.

Ritchie, Andrew Carnduff. *Masters of British Painting, 1800–1950.* New York: (Museum of Modern Art) Doubleday, 1958.

Rivera, Diego. "The Revolution in Painting," *Creative Art,* IV (1929).

Ruskin, John. *The Political Economy of Art.* New York: John Wiley, 1868.

The Masses, Socialist Monthly of New York (1911–1917).

Tolstoy, Leo. *What Is Art?* tr. by A. Maude. Indianapolis, Ind.: (Liberal Arts) Bobbs-Merrill, 1960.

Van Gogh, Vincent. *The Letters of Vincent van Gogh.* ed. by Mark Roskill. New York: Atheneum, 1963.

Whitman, Walt. *Democratic Vistas.* New York: Liberal Arts Press, 1949.

5 / *The Artistic Way of Living*

Barr, Alfred H., ed. *Fantastic Art, Dada, Surrealism.* New York: Museum of Modern Art, 1947.

Copland, Aaron. *Our New Music.* New York: McGraw-Hill, 1941.

Drexler, Arthur. *Twentieth-Century Engineering.* New York: (Museum of Modern Art) Doubleday, 1964.

Eckermann, Johann P. (*see* Goethe)

Ford, Ford Madox. Foreword to *Imagist Anthology 1930.* New York: Covici, Friede, 1930.

Goethe, Johann W. von. *Conversations with Eckermann.* New York: (Everyman's) Dutton, 1930.

Gropius, Walter. *Scope of Total Architecture.* New York: Collier, 1962.

Haftmann, Werner, and others. *German Art in the Twentieth Century.* ed. by A. Carnduff Ritchie. New York: (Museum of Modern Art) Doubleday, 1958.

Hirschfeld-Mack, L., et al. *The Bauhaus.* Victoria, Australia: Longmans Green, 1963.

Kidder-Smith, G. E. *The New Architecture of Europe.* Cleveland: World, 1961.

Kierkegaard, Søren. *The Concept of Irony.* New York: Harper, 1966.

Le Corbusier. *Toward a New Architecture.* New York: Praeger, 1959.

Lewis, Wyndham. "A Review of Contempory Art," *Blast* (July, 1915) no. 2.

Malraux, André. *The Voices of Silence.* tr. by S. Gilbert. Garden City, N. Y.: Doubleday, 1953.

Mondriaan, Pieter. *Plastic Art and Pure Plastic Art.* New York: Wittenborn, 1945.

Pound, Ezra. "Vortex Manifesto," *Blast* (June, 1914) no. 1.

Read, Herbert. *The Philosophy of Modern Art.* Cleveland: (Meridian) World, 1955.

Rewald, John. *Post-Impressionism from van Gogh to Gauguin.* New York: (Museum of Modern Art) Doubleday, 1958.

Ritchie, Andrew Carnduff. (see Haftmann, W., and others)

Rosenberg, Bernard, and N. Fliegel. *Vanguard Artists.* Chicago: Quadrangle, 1965.

Schumann, Robert. *On Music and Musicians.* New York: McGraw-Hill, 1946.

Stravinsky, Igor. *Poetics of Music, in the Form of Six Lessons.* New York: (Vintage) Random House, 1956.

Sypher, Wylie. *Rococco to Cubism in Art and Literature.* New York: Random House, 1960.

Wölfflin, Heinrich. *Principles of Art History.* 7th ed. New York: Dover, 1929.

Wright, Frank Lloyd. *The Future of Architecture.* New York: (Horizon) American Heritage, 1963.

6 / The Poetic Way of Living

Balakian, Anna. *Surrealism.* New York: Noonday, 1959.

Camus, Albert. *The Myth of Sisyphsus, and Other Essays.* New York: Knopf, 1955.

Commager, Henry Steele. *The American Mind.* New Haven, Conn.: Yale University Press, 1950.

Fairley, Barker. *A Study of Goethe.* New York: Oxford University Press, 1947.

Gautier, Théophile. "A History of Romanticism," *Complete Works.* London: 1900–1902.

Graff, W. L. *Rainer Maria Rilke, Creative Anguish of a Modern Poet.* Princeton, N. J.: Princeton University Press, 1956.

Hazlitt, William. *Table Talk.* New York: (Everyman's) Dutton, 1960.

Heidegger, Martin. "Hölderlin and the Essence of Poetry," *Existence and Being.* Chicago: (Gateway) Henry Ragnery, 1949.

Heller, Erich. *The Disinherited Mind.* New York: Farrar, Straus, 1957.

Lukács, Georg. *Studies in European Realism.* New York: (University Library) Grosset, 1964.

Parrington, Vernon Louis. *Main Currents in American Thought.* 3 vols. New York: Harcourt, Brace, 1927–1930.

Pritchett, Victor S. *The Living Novel and Later Appreciations.* Rev. ed. New York: Random House, 1964.

Read, Herbert. *Coleridge as Critic.* New York: Haskell House, 1964.

Ross, James F. *The Social Criticism of Fenimore Cooper.* Berkeley, Calif.: University of California Press, 1933.

Scarfe, Francis. *Auden and After.* London: G. Routledge, 1942.

Silz, Walter, ed. *German Romantic Lyrics.* Cambridge, Mass.: Harvard, 1934.

Wilson, Edmund. *Axel's Castle.* New York: Scribner, 1931.

Woodring, Carl, ed. *Prose of the Romantic Period.* Boston, Mass.: Houghton Mifflin, 1961.

7 / The Entertaining Way of Living

Andrews, John, and Ossia Trilling, eds. *International Theatre.* London: Sampson Low, 1949.

Appia, Adolphe. *Music and the Art of the Theatre.* Coral Gables, Florida: University of Miami Press, 1962.

Beaton, Cecil. *Ballet.* London: Wingate, 1951.

Bentley, Eric R. *A Century of Hero-worship.* Boston: Beacon Press, 1957.

———. *The Playwright as Thinker.* Cleveland: (Meridian) World, 1955.

Brown, John Mason. *The Modern Theatre in Revolt.* New York: Norton, 1929.

Carlyle, Thomas. *On Heroes, Hero-worship and the Heroic in History.* New York: Oxford University Press, 1965.

Craig, Edward Gordon. *On the Art of the Theatre.* London: Heinemann, 1957.

Fuchs, Georg. *Revolution in the Theatre.* Ithaca, N. Y.: Cornell University Press, 1959.

Krutch, Joseph Wood. *American Drama Since 1918.* Rev. ed. New York: Braziller, 1957.

MacGowen, Kenneth. *Footlights Across America.* New York: Harcourt, Brace, 1929.

Nicoll, Allardyce. *World Drama, from Aeschylus to Anouilh.* New York: Harcourt, Brace, 1949.

Pearson, Hesketh. *The Last Actor-Manager.* London: Methuen, 1950.

Priestley, J. B. *Theatre Outlook.* London: Nicholson Watson, 1947.

Ridgeway, William. *The Dramas and Dramatic Dances of Non-European Races.* Cambridge, Mass.: Harvard University Press, 1925.

Shattuck, Roger. *The Banquet Years.* Garden City, N. Y.: Doubleday, 1961.

Sokel, Walter, ed. *An Anthology of German Expressionist Drama.* Garden City, N. Y.: (Anchor) Doubleday, 1963.

Stanislavski, Constantin. *An Actor Prepares.* New York: Theatre Arts, orig. pub. 1936.

Thouless, Pricilla. *Modern Poetic Drama.* London and New York: Oxford University Press, 1934.

Trewin, John C. *The Theatre Since 1900.* London: Andrew Dakers, 1951.

8 / *The Behavioral Way of Living*

Bakunin, Mikhail Aleksandrovich. *Political Philosophy of Bakunin.* ed. by G. P. Maximoff. New York: Free Press, 1964.

Boring, Edwin G., and others. *History, Psychology, and Science: Selected Papers.* New York: John Wiley, 1963.

Brown, Norman O. *Life Against Death: The Psychoanalytical Meaning of History.* Middletown, Conn.: Wesleyan University Press, 1959.

Freud, Sigmund. *Civilization and Its Discontents.* London: Hogarth, 1930.

Huizinga, Johan. *Homo Ludens: A Study of the Play Elements in Culture.* Boston: Beacon Press, 1955.

Jacobi, Jolande. *Complex Archetype Symbol in the Psychology of C. G. Jung.* New York: Pantheon, 1959.

Jones, Ernest. *The Life and Work of Sigmund Freud.* ed. by Lionel Trilling and Steven Marcus. New York: (Anchor) Doubleday, 1955.

Jung, Carl G. *The Undiscovered Self.* New York: (Mentor) New American Library, 1959.

Manuel, Frank E. *Prophets of Paris.* Cambridge, Mass.: Harvard University Press, 1962.

Maximoff, G. P., ed. (*see* Bakunin)

Munroe, Ruth L. *Schools of Psychoanalytic Thought.* New York: Holt, Rinehart and Winston, 1955.

Newman, James R., ed. *What Is Science?* New York: Simon and Schuster, 1955.

Nisbet, Robert A. *The Sociological Tradition.* New York: Basic Books, 1966.

Petrie, W. M. Flinders. *The Revolution of Civilization.* London and New York: Harper, 1911.

Proudhon, Pierre J. *System of Economic Contradictions.* Boston: B. R. Tucker, 1888.

Read, Herbert. *Existentialism, Marxism, Anarchism.* London. Freedom Press, 1949.

Saveth, Edward N. *American History and the Social Sciences.* New York: Free Press, 1964.

Watson, John B. *Behaviorism.* Chicago, Ill.: (Phoenix) University of Chicago Press, 1958.

9 / *The Philosophical Way of Living*

Blackham, Harold J. *Six Existentialist Thinkers.* New York: (Torchbooks) Harper, 1959.

Carnap, Rudolf. *Meaning and Necessity: A Study in Semantics and Modal Logic.* 2nd ed. Chicago, Ill.: (Phoenix) University of Chicago Press, 1956.

Ferrater Mora, José. *Philosophy Today.* New York: Columbia University Press, 1960.

Dewey, John. *The Quest for Certainty.* New York: (Capricorn) Putnam, 1960.

Hartman, James B., ed. *Philosophy of Recent Times.* 2 vols. New York: McGraw-Hill, 1967.

Heidegger, Martin. *Introduction to Metaphysics.* tr. by Ralph Manheim. New Haven, Conn.: Yale University Press, 1959.

Heinemann, Frederick Henry. *Existentialism and the Modern Predicament.* New York: (Torchbooks) Harper, 1958.

Hook, Sidney. *From Hegel to Marx.* New York: Humanities Press, 1950

———. *Education for Modern Man.* New York: Knopf, 1963.

Jaspers, Karl. *Nietzsche.* tr. by C. F. Wallraff and F. J. Schmitz. Tucson, Ariz.: University of Arizona Press, 1965.

Kaufmann, Walter A. *Nietzsche.* Princeton, N. J.: Princeton University Press, 1950.

————. *Hegel: Reinterpretation, Texts, and Commentary.* New York: Doubleday, 1965.

Lowrie, Walter. *Kierkegaard.* 2 vols. New York: (Torchbooks) Harper, 1962.

Marcuse, Herbert. *Reason and Revolution.* 2nd ed. Boston: Beacon, 1960.

Mill, John Stuart. *Utilitarianism, On Liberty, Essay on Bentham.* ed. by Mary Warnock, Cleveland, Ohio: (Meridian) World, 1962.

Moore, Edward C. *American Pragmatism.* New York: Columbia University Press, 1961.

Mora, José Ferrater (*see* Ferrater Mora, José.)

Spengler, Oswald. *Man and Technics: A Contribution to a Philosophy of Life.* New York: Knopf, 1932.

White, Morton, ed. *The Age of Analysis.* New York: (Mentor) New American Library, 1955.

Whitehead, Alfred North. *Science and the Modern World.* New York: Macmillan, 1926.

10 / *The Pious Way of Living*

Brunner, H. Emil. *Christianity and Civilization.* New York: Scribner, 1948.

Buber, Martin. *The Eclipse of God.* New York: (Torchbooks) Harper, 1957.

Bultmann, Rudolf. *Theology of the New Testament.* New York: Scribner, 1955.

Dawson, Christopher. *Religion and Culture.* New York: Sheed & Ward, 1948.

Eliot, T. S. *Christianity and Culture.* New York: (Harvest) Harcourt, Brace, 1940.

Fogarty, Michael P. *Christian Democracy in Western Europe 1820–1953.* Notre Dame, Ind.: University of Notre Dame Press, 1957.

Goodall, Norman. *The Ecumenical Movement.* 2nd ed. New York: Oxford University Press, 1964.

Kierkegaard, Søren. *Attack Upon Christendom.* tr. by Walter Lowrie. Princeton, N.J.: Princeton University Press, 1944.

Latourette, Kenneth S. *Christianity in a Revolutionary Age.* 5 vols. New York: Harper, 1958–1962.

Parker, Theodore. "The Transient and Permanent in Christianity," *The American Transcendentalists: Their Prose and Poetry,* ed. by Perry Miller. Garden City, N.Y.: (Anchor) Doubleday, 1957.

Rauschenbusch, Walter. *Christianity and the Social Crisis.* ed. by Robert D. Cross. New York: (Torchbooks) Harper.

Robinson, John A. T. *Honest to God.* Philadelphia: Westminster, 1963.

Schleiermacher, Friedrich. *On Religion: Speeches to Its Cultured Despisers.* New York: (Torchbooks) Harper, 1958.

Tillich, Paul. *The Courage to Be.* New Haven, Conn.: Yale University Press, 1952.

Tolstoy, Leo. "What is Religion?," *Novels and Other Works by Tolstoy.* New York: Scribner, 1904.

11 / *The Intellectual Way of Living*

Barzun, Jacques. *The House of Intellect.* New York: (Torchbooks) Harper, 1959.

Cole, Percival R. *A History of Educational Thought.* London: Oxford University Press, 1931.

Conant, James B. *The American High School Today.* New York: McGraw-Hill, 1959.

Cremin, Lawrence A. *The Transformation of the School.* New York: Knopf, 1961.

Daedalus (Winter 1959 issue): "Education in the Age of Science."

Dewey, John. *Experience and Education.* New York: Collier, 1963.

Flaubert, Gustave. *Bouvard et Pécuchet.* New York: Odyssey, 1967.

Hutchins, Robert M. *The Conflict in Education in a Democratic Society.* New York: Harper, 1953.

———. *Freedom, Education and the Fund.* New York: Meridian, 1956.

Kerr, Clark. *The Uses of the University.* Cambridge, Mass: Harvard University Press, 1963.

Montessori, Maria. *The Secret of Childhood.* Notre Dame, Ind.: Fides, 1966.

Rickover, Hyman G. *Education and Freedom.* New York: Dutton, 1959.

Silber, Käte. *Pestalozzi, The Man and His Work.* 2nd ed. New York: Humanities Press, 1965.

Veblen, Thorstein. *The Higher Learning in America.* New York: (American Century) Hill & Wang, 1957.

12 / *The Political Way of Living*

Arendt, Hannah. *The Origins of Totalitarianism.* New York: Harcourt, Brace & World, 1966.

Berdyaev, Nicolas. *The Origin of Russian Communism.* Ann Arbor, Mich.: (Ann Arbor Books) University of Michigan, 1960.

Berlin, Isaiah. *Karl Marx: His Life and Environment.* 3rd ed. New York: (Galaxy) Oxford University Press, 1963.

Boorstin, Daniel J. *The Genius of American Politics.* Chicago, Ill.: University of Chicago Press, 1953.

Brecht, Arnold. *Political Theory: The Foundations of Twentieth-Century Political Thought.* Princeton, N.J.: Princeton University Press, 1959.

Brogan, Denis W. *Politics in America.* New York: Harper, 1954.

Carr, Edward H. *The Twenty Years' Crisis, 1919–39: An Introduction to the Study of International Relations.* 2nd ed. New York: St. Martin's, 1946.

Cole, George D. H. *History of Socialist Thought.* 5 vols. New York: St. Martin's, 1954–60.

Friedrich, Carl J., ed. (*see* Hegel)

Gooch, George P. *English Democratic Ideas in the Seventeenth Century.* New York: (Torchbooks) Harper, 1959.

Hegel, George Wilhelm Friedrich. *Philosophy.* ed. by Carl J. Friedrich. New York: (Modern Library) Random House, 1953.

Hofstadter, Richard. *The Age of Reform: From Bryan to F.D.R.* New York: Knopf, 1955.

Laidler, H. W. *Social-Economic Movements.* New York: Crowell, 1942.

Lipset, Seymour M. *Political Man: The Social Basis of Politics.* New York: (Anchor) Doubleday, 1959.

Meinecke, Friedrich. *The German Catastrophe.* Boston: Beacon, 1963.

Sabine, George H. *A History of Political Theory.* 3rd ed. New York: Holt, Rinehart and Winston, 1961.

Sorel, George. *Reflections on Violence.* New York: Free Press, 1950.

Tawney, Richard H. *Equality.* New York: Barnes & Noble, 1964.

Webb, Sidney and Beatrice. *The History of Trade Unionism.* rev. ed. London: Longmans, Green, 1920.

Wilson, Edmund. *To the Finland Station.* Garden City, N.Y.: (Anchor) Doubleday, 1953.

Woodcock, George. *Anarchism: A History of Libertarian Ideas and Movements.* Cleveland, Ohio: (Meridian) World, 1962.

13 / *The Social Way of Living*

Adams, Brooks. *The Law of Civilization and Decay.* New York: Vintage, 1955.

Adams, Henry. *The Degradation of Democratic Dogma.* Gloucester, Mass.: Peter Smith, 1919.

Boorstin, Daniel J. *America and the Image of Europe.* Cleveland: (Meridian) World, 1961.

Briar, Scott. "The Family as an Organization," *Social Services Review* (1964) no. 3.

Brinton, Crane. *The Shaping of the Modern Mind.* New York: New American Library, 1953.

Bryce, James. *The American Commonwealth.* ed. by Louis M. Hacker. 2 vols. New York: (Capricorn) Putnam, 1959.

Curti, Merle E. "American Philanthropy and the National Character," *American Quarterly*, X (1958) no. 4.

———. *The Growth of American Thought.* 3rd ed. New York: Harper, 1964.

Hauser, Arnold. *The Social History of Art.* 4 vols. New York: (Vintage) Random House, 1958.

Hazlitt, William. *The Round Table, Complete Works.* London: J. M. Dent, 1930–1934.

Hicks, John D. *Republican Ascendancy, 1921–1933.* New York: (Torchbooks) Harper, 1960.

Huxley, Aldous. *Music at Night.* London: Chatto & Windus, 1960.

Lynd, Robert S., and H. Merrell. *Middletown in Transition: A Study in Cultural Conflicts*. New York: (Harvest) Harcourt, Brace, 1963.

Marcuse, Herbert. *Eros and Civilization: A Philosophical Inquiry into Freud*. Rev. ed. Boston, Mass.: Beacon, 1966.

Mencken, Henry L. *A Mencken Chrestomathy*. New York: Knopf, 1949.

Ortega y Gasset, José. *Revolt of the Masses*. New York: Norton, 1932.

Pappenheim, Fritz. *The Alienation of Modern Man*. New York: Monthly Press, 1959.

Pierson, George W. "A Restless Temper. . . ," *American Historical Review* (July 1964).

Riencourt, Amaury de. *The Coming Caesars*. New York: (Capricorn) Putnam, 1957.

Rougemont, Denis de. *Love Declared: Essays on the Myths of Love*. New York: Pantheon, 1963.

Salmon, L. M. *The Newspaper and the Historian*. New York: Oxford University Press, 1923.

Toffler, Alvin. *Culture Consumers: A Study of Art and Affluence in America*. New York: St. Martin's, 1964.

Trail, H. D. *Social England*. New York: Putnam, 1895–1901.

Untermeyer, Louis. *An Uninhibited Treasury of Erotic Poetry*. New York: Dial, 1963.

Whyte, William H., Jr. *The Organization Man*. New York: (Anchor) Doubleday, 1957.

14 / *The Gracious Way of Living*

Barzun, Jacques. *Science, the Glorious Entertainment*. New York: Harper, 1964.

Forster, E. M. *Alexandria: A History and a Guide*. New York: (Anchor) Doubleday, 1961.

Freedman, Morris. "The Dangers of Non-Conformism," *The American Scholar* (Winter 1958/59).

Manvell, Roger. *A Seat at the Cinema*. London: Evans Bros., 1951.

Runciman, Walter G. "Embourgeoisement, Self-rated Class, and Party Preference," *The Sociological Review*, XII (1964) no. 2.

Seldes, Gilbert. *The Seven Lively Arts*. New York: A. S. Barnes, 1962.

Snow, C. P. *The Two Cultures and A Second Look.* New York: Cambridge University Press, 1964.

Thorp, Margaret F. *America at the Movies.* New Haven, Conn.: Yale University Press, 1931.

Index